THE APOSTOLIC FATHERS

THE APOSTOLIC FATHERS

AN INTRODUCTION AND TRANSLATION

William Varner

t&tclark
LONDON • NEW YORK • OXFORD • NEW DELHI • SYDNEY

T&T CLARK
Bloomsbury Publishing Plc
50 Bedford Square, London, WC1B 3DP, UK
1385 Broadway, New York, NY 10018, USA
29 Earlsfort Terrace, Dublin 2, Ireland

BLOOMSBURY, T&T CLARK and the T&T Clark logo are trademarks
of Bloomsbury Publishing Plc

First published in Great Britain 2023

Copyright © William Varner, 2023

William Varner has asserted his right under the Copyright,
Designs and Patents Act, 1988, to be identified as Author of this work.

Cover design: Jade Barnett
Cover image: Roman mosaic depicting the Chi-Rho symbol with alpha and omega.
Museum of History (Barcelona, Spain) © PRISMA ARCHIVO/Alamy

All rights reserved. No part of this publication may be reproduced or transmitted in
any form or by any means, electronic or mechanical, including photocopying,
recording, or any information storage or retrieval system, without prior
permission in writing from the publishers.

Bloomsbury Publishing Plc does not have any control over, or responsibility for,
any third-party websites referred to or in this book. All internet addresses given
in this book were correct at the time of going to press. The author and publisher
regret any inconvenience caused if addresses have changed or sites have ceased
to exist, but can accept no responsibility for any such changes.

A catalogue record for this book is available from the British Library.

Library of Congress Control Number: 2022947936

ISBN:	HB:	978-0-5677-0818-2
	PB:	978-0-5677-0817-5
	ePDF:	978-0-5677-0819-9
	eBook:	978-0-5677-0821-2

Typeset by Integra Software Services Pvt. Ltd.

To find out more about our authors and books visit www.bloomsbury.com
and sign up for our newsletters.

I dedicate The Apostolic Fathers: An Introduction and Translation *to Stanley Porter, President of McMaster Divinity College, whose mastery of early Christian literature has been evident to many. This dedication is also in gratitude to him for being gracious to me in a time of personal need.*

CONTENTS

FOREWORD *Clayton N. Jefford*	viii
PREFACE	x
ABBREVIATIONS	xi
Introduction to the Apostolic Fathers	1
1 The Didache or Teaching of the Apostles	5
2 The Shepherd of Hermas	23
3 The Letter of Clement of Rome to the Corinthians	85
4 Introduction to 2 Clement	117
5 Ignatius	137
6 Polycarp	165
7 The Martyrdom of Polycarp	175
8 Epistle of Barnabas	185
9 Letter to Diognetus	209
10 Fragments of Papias	225
11 The Apostolic Fathers in the Twenty-First Century	235
SCRIPTURE INDEX	237
INDEX OF AUTHORS	242

FOREWORD

The underutilized writings of the Apostolic Fathers offer a wide spectrum of early Christian literature from the late first-through late second-century Mediterranean world. Their breadth of viewpoints embodies authors from Italy to Greece in the West, as well as Asia Minor to Egypt in the East, and preserves letters, homilies, and instructional tracts not otherwise seen in the earliest apostolic tradition. As William Varner hints, these collected works preserve a treasure trove of biblical motifs and theological themes that portray the development of Christianity's oldest struggles and triumphs, while at the same time providing any novice to the early patristic world an abundant occasion to explore within the creative verbiage of the materials so many of the various roots of a faith tradition that swiftly transformed into the broad foundations of later ecclesiastical thought.

The Apostolic Fathers encompass diverse approaches to evolving opinion about the nature of scripture and canon, as well as disparate trajectories related to liturgical ritual and spirituality. A savvy reader will discover many of the materials that patristic authorities surveyed with an eye toward determining what eventually would become Christianity's firmly established canon of literary authority known as its Bible. While the individual works preserved here did not pass that particular test for numerous reasons, their contents preserve much of what ancient believers considered to be essential for how they themselves lived and thought about their own faith. Thus, basic elements of the creedal experience, including the "Apostles' Creed," varied baptismal ritual and contemporary prayers, intriguing parables and teachings (*logia*) "of the Lord," individual perceptions of pneumatology and Christology, identification of ecclesiastical and eschatological consciousness, affinity for assorted theological opinions and resistance to unnamed "opponents" as so regarded by dispersed authors, and delineations of what the early Church considered to be critical paths to salvation are all to be discovered within these pages.

But what is an essential element of concern for those who opt to investigate these materials is a reliable hand to navigate the history of the literature concerned, as well as a vigilant rendering of the texts themselves to offer assurance for those who might wish to incorporate the individual writings into a broader scholarly sphere of knowledge about the evolution of early ecclesiastical tradition. In this regard, students and scholars alike will discover the current volume to be a refreshing alternative to the various introductions for and translations of the Apostolic Fathers that have appeared in recent decades of academic investigation. Of specific value for the casual reader with limited resources at hand is the convenient blend of both approaches—introduction and translation—that offers a comprehensive angle for each work within the collection, together with a fresh reading of the writings themselves. Varner's prose, style, and analytical method are lively in form while giving honest attention to numerous issues about the background of each text that matter most for assessment of these early Christian literary works, their origins, and relevant implications for how they were employed by later Church writers.

FOREWORD

I am delighted to endorse and recommend the materials that Varner has provided within these pages as evidence of careful consideration of an important body of ancient Christian writings that have too often been ignored by both biblical scholarship and students of patristic literature alike. A new flavor of scholarship is to be discovered here by those who give time to the literature and its careful introduction. I invite you to drink deeply and enjoy!

Clayton N. Jefford
Saint Meinrad, Indiana

PREFACE

In some ways I came late to the Apostolic Fathers. Throughout the early days of my theological education, I was only occasionally exposed to these Christian writings that were the first to appear after the New Testament books. Later in my academic career of teaching Greek, I offered some sections of these writings to my students to translate. Soon I fell in love with the simple beauty of the *Didache*, the "Teaching" of the Twelve Apostles, and this love affair led to my writing a commentary on the book. From there I delved into the Clements and Ignatius and Polycarp, second-century writers who opened further a Christian world that I thought I had known fairly well. Then came an invitation to write another commentary, this time on Second Clement. Finally came an invitation to write a chapter on the Fragments of Papias. By then I was hooked. I have read and taught these books from Greek-English editions and also benefited from other "Introductions" to the Apostolic Fathers, especially the modest volume by Simon Tugwell. I even seriously considered issuing a second edition of Tugwell's work with added chapters on Diognetus and Papias. Slowly the idea developed of writing a new volume that introduced each Apostolic Father and also offered a fresh translation of each book that is introduced.

Therefore, added to the introduction to each author is a translation of the book(s) of that Apostolic Father. In this way readers do not have to depend on what I say about a book but can discover both its beauties and its difficulties on their own. I am responsible for the translations of these primary texts, although I mention some of the standard translations in the numerous bibliographies that accompany each chapter. The order of the books is in the probable order in which they were written, although dogmatism about the dates of some works like *Shepherd of Hermas* and *Barnabas* is simply not possible.

This introduction presents an interpretation of these writings, not attempting to provide a full account of the innumerable scholarly debates which they provoked. Some attention, however, is given to the most important academic issues related to each book. This approach can be readily seen, as an example, in the lack of footnotes in the text. When I cite an author, the source will be mentioned in a following parenthesis and the necessary information about that work will be located within a following bibliography. Furthermore, while Greek-English editions of the AF are available, this edition can be helpful to the reader who may not have access to the original language texts. The translation and introduction of each work and the comments on it are still based on my examination of the Greek and Latin originals. I am honored to be able to offer this *Introduction and Translation* to a generation of students and scholars who I hope will appreciate these ancient writings as much as I do. And if these works are new to you, I pray that you will develop the same affection for them that I developed years ago. I would like to thank my wife, Helen, and my student, Teresa Seitz, for their help in preparing the Index.

William Varner
The Master's University

ABBREVIATIONS

BIBLICAL BOOKS

Gen.	Genesis
Exod.	Exodus
Lev.	Leviticus
Num.	Numbers
Deut.	Deuteronomy
Josh.	Joshua
Judg.	Judges
1–2 Sam.	1–2 Samuel
1–2 Chron.	1–2 Chronicles
Neh.	Nehemiah
Esth.	Esther
Ps.	Psalms
Prov.	Proverbs
Eccles.	Ecclesiastes
Song of Sol.	Song of Solomon
Lam.	Lamentations
Isa.	Isaiah
Jer.	Jeremiah
Ezek.	Ezekiel
Dan.	Daniel
Hos.	Hosea
Obad.	Obadiah
Mic.	Micah
Nah.	Nahum
Hab.	Habakkuk
Zeph.	Zephaniah
Hag.	Haggai
Zech.	Zechariah
Mal.	Malachi
Matt.	Matthew
Rom.	Romans
1–2 Cor.	1–2 Corinthians
Gal.	Galatians
Eph.	Ephesians
Phil.	Philippians

Col.	Colossians
1–2 Thess.	1–2 Thessalonians
1–2 Tim.	1–2 Timothy
Philem.	Philemon
Heb.	Hebrews
1–2 Pet.	1–2 Peter
Rev.	Revelation

APOCRYPHAL BOOKS

Bar	Baruch
1–2 Esd	1–2 Esdras
Ep Jer	Epistle of Jeremiah
Jdt	Judith
1–2 Macc	1–2 Maccabees
3–4 Macc	3–4 Maccabees
Pr Man	Prayer of Manasseh
Ps 151	Psalm 151
Sir	Sirach
Tob	Tobit
Wis	Wisdom of Solomon

APOSTOLIC FATHERS

AF	Apostolic Fathers
1 *Clem.*	*1 Clement*
2 *Clem.*	*2 Clement*
Eph.	Ignatius, *to the Ephesians*
Magn.	Ignatius, *to the Magnesians*
Trall.	Ignatius, *to the Trallians*
Ign. Rom.	Ignatius, to the Romans
Phld.	Ignatius, *to the Philadelphians*
Smyrn.	Ignatius, *to the Smyrneans*
Ign. Polyc.	Ignatius, *to Polycarp*
Pol.	*Polycarp to the Philippians*
Did.	*Didache*
Barn.	*Epistle of Barnabas*
Man.	*Shepherd of Hermas, Mandates*
Sim.	*Shepherd of Hermas, Similitudes*
Vis.	*Shepherd of Hermas, Visions*
Mart.	*Martyrdom of Polycarp*
Diogn.	*Epistle to Diognetus*
Pap.	*Fragments of Papias*

OTHER ABBREVIATIONS

AD	*Anno Domini*; Year of the Lord
ALNTS	Ancient Literature for New Testament Studies
BCE	Before the Common Era
BDAG	Greek-English Lexicon of the New Testament, 3rd Edition
CE	Common Era
CGL	Cambridge Greek Lexicon
Contra Cels.	Origen, *Contra Celsum*
EH	Eusebius, *Ecclesiastical History of the Christian Church*
Haer.	Irenaeus, *Against Heresies*
LXX	Septuagint
Strom.	Clement of Alexandria, *Stromata*

Introduction to the Apostolic Fathers

The expression "Apostolic Fathers" refers to a collection of early Christian writings traditionally viewed as being authored by people who knew or were associated with the New Testament (NT) apostles. A modern edition usually includes the following works, although the order varies considerably: *1 Clement, 2 Clement, Ignatius, Polycarp, Didache, Barnabas, Papias, Hermas, Martyrdom of Polycarp, Diognetus,* and *Quadratus*. This introduction describes the history of the collection as a whole with some suggestions about how the study of the Apostolic Fathers (AF) can impact both the study of the New Testament and the history of Christianity as a whole.

The term "Apostolic Fathers" is actually an artificial one, never having been used by others in the history of the church until a collection was made by J.B. Cotelier in 1672. The expression "Apostolical Fathers" can be traced back at least as far as William Wake, who in 1693 published a translation of the above titles, minus *Didache, Diognetus, Papias,* and *Quadratus*. The expression "Apostolic Fathers" was used by Thomas Ittig in his edition of 1699 and by Jean Le Clerc in his edition of Cotelier in 1698.

The discovery by Archbishop James Ussher of what is called the "middle recension" of the letters of Ignatius (1644) is generally accepted as genuine today. Additions to the number of the AF were made by Andreas Gallandi, who included also the *Letter to Diognetus*, the *Fragments of Papias*, and the fragment of *Quadratus* (1765). The truly amazing discovery of the *Didache* by Bryennios (published in 1883) led to the inclusion of that document also among the AF.

The Bryennios manuscript, a 1056 codex discovered in Constantinople and now in the library of the Greek Patriarchate in Jerusalem, included *Barnabas, 1 Clement, 2 Clement,* the *Didache*, and the long recension of the letters of Ignatius. This collection of the books copied in the eleventh century was made when little had been mentioned about the AF and the understanding of second-century Christianity had been shaped mostly by Eusebius' discussion of Ignatius as well as Clement of Rome, Dionysius the Areopagite, and Justin Martyr.

Interest in the AF centered primarily on the Christological significance of Ignatius' description of Jesus. Much less use was made of *Polycarp, 1 Clement, 2 Clement,* and *Hermas,* and occasionally some references were made to the writings of Papias which had not survived. Writers from Irenaeus, Clement of Alexandria, Origen, and Eusebius shed some light on their usage during their times. Eusebius placed *Hermas, Barnabas,* and the *Didache* among the *antilegomena* that comprised the second section of writings "not universally accepted" as scriptural. He mentioned that *1 Clement* was still read in many churches, but that *2 Clement* was not often mentioned by the ancients. He also suggested that *Hermas* was useful for instruction but expressed some caustic doubts about the intelligence of *Papias*.

Attention to these books later called the AF often has been related to their possible canonicity. The presumed association of the authors with the apostles provided them with credentials as valid as some of the NT writings. Irenaeus apparently viewed *1 Clement* and *Shepherd of Hermas* as scripture, although he was not always consistent in this view, and the early Tertullian dealt with the *Shepherd* as scripture. Clement of Alexandria regarded *1 Clement, Hermas, Barnabas*, and the *Didache* as inspired writings, while Origen viewed *Hermas, Barnabas*, and the *Didache* similarly. As was mentioned, Eusebius was less positive about a canonical status of these books and regarded them as spurious. In his famous *Paschal Homily*, Athanasius placed the *Didache* and *Hermas* outside the canon, but still encouraged their reading by the faithful. The fourth-century Codex Sinaiticus included *Barnabas* and *Hermas* at its end, and the fifth-century Codex Alexandrinus contained *1 Clement* and *2 Clement*. A canonical list in the sixth-century Greek-Latin Codex Claromantanus lists among the books of the NT the works of *Barnabas* and *Shepherd of Hermas*.

The opinion that dominated about these writings was their assumed connection with the earlier apostles. In other respects they are quite diverse. While *1 Clement, Ignatius*, and *Polycarp* are genuine letters, *Barnabas* is more like a theological tractate, the *Martyrdom of Polycarp* is obviously a martyrology, and *Diognetus* is an apology. Thus they are letters only in their external form. The other writings approach the nature of a homily (*2 Clement*), a church order (*Didache*), and a sort of allegory/apocalypse (*Hermas*). Papias' "exposition" of the "oracles" of Jesus is known to us only in a series of fragments cited by others, while only a short quotation from the apologist Quadratus has survived.

The specific ministry roles of the reputed authors are also quite diverse. Ignatius, Polycarp, and Clement had some kind of official role in their churches. We are not certain about the specific role of the author of the *Martyrdom of Polycarp*; the individual who wrote to Diognetus is unknown; *Barnabas, 2 Clement*, and the *Didache* are clearly pseudonymous; and *Hermas* was written by a man who clearly distanced himself from any of the official "clergy."

While displaying a common conviction about the nature of the newly emerged Christian faith, some different forms of that early faith are exemplified in these writings. Sometimes, although not always, the worldview of Paul can be detected. *Polycarp* often reflects the contents of the Pastoral Epistles. *1 Clement*'s Christianity is simple and straightforward, while Ignatius reflects attitudes that recall Johannine streams of thought. Clement's approach to church succession and Ignatius' clear advocacy of monepiscopacy at least prepare their readers for a later view of apostolic succession and primacy. Some of the AF display a striking connection to various forms of Judaism, while others attack Jews and Judaism with language that may shock modern readers. The *Didache* is almost an extension of Matthew's gospel and draws on many Jewish ethical materials. *Barnabas* is more negatively disposed to Judaism as a historical and social fact and indicates a serious negative awareness of Jews. *2 Clement* communicates a faith that reflects a late Judaism frame of reference. *Papias*' eschatology reflects themes of apocalyptic thought that were still alive in some circles. *Hermas* often conveys a Jewish "theology" within an apocalyptic worldview. The apologetic approaches of *Diognetus* and *Quadratus*, however, reflect a different and less Jewish-related approach.

Most of the AF emerged relatively early in the history of the church. Apart from *Clement, Didache, Polycarp*, and *Papias*, no significant link with the apostles seems likely, and *Barnabas* and *2 Clement* are certainly pseudonymous. *Diognetus* includes an ambiguous reference to the author as "a disciple of apostles" (11.1), but most consider that to be a general, not a literal reflection. The following Introductions to each of the individual books will show that there is much disagreement on the dating of these works and it is at least possible that some may fall outside the period in question (c. 90–150 CE). Also there are other early Christian documents that fall within this period. There also may be some differences and variations between the specific forms of the Christian faith reflected in the AF.

This diversity within the AF has meant that studies that have focused on this collection as a whole have worked with a sample of early Christian literature sufficiently broad enough to guarantee some interesting results. Of particular interest is what we call the "reception" of the NT writings in the AF. Each treatment of the AF book that follows will pay at least some attention to that issue, especially as it relates to the use of the Synoptic Gospels.

My church and academic experiences have been in an ecclesiastical tradition that does not give much attention to Patristics. I have occasionally teased some of my evangelical friends that they often seem to believe that church history stopped around 96 CE (the traditional date of the *Apocalyse*) and then resumed in 1517 (Luther) or maybe around 1540 (Calvin). This is reflected in a comment made to me about one person's perplexity at why I would write a commentary on a non-canonical book like *2 Clement*. I resisted the temptation to ask if he thought it would be perplexing to him if I wrote a commentary on Luther's or Calvin's works! My own evangelical world has been characterized by a sad neglect of the Apostolic Fathers, despite the fact that these authors wrote in the shadow of the New Testament. Even if these works are not viewed as "inspired" and canonical, they have much to teach us because some of them knew the apostles or at least conferred with those who knew the apostles personally! Allow me to quote at this point the notable scholar Robert Grant in his opening chapter titled "The Historical and Theological Significance of the AF." These words also express my attitude toward these writings.

> They (the AF) are important today because they contain the earliest reflections of Christian life outside the New Testament. They show us what, for better or for worse, the Church was coming to be. They show us the Christian life in process. Whether one views this process as a decline or a development, it did in fact take place, and Christians today, whether rejecting or accepting the ideas of the Apostolic Fathers, are their heirs.
>
> (Grant, 12)

"Further Reading" lists are at the end of each Introduction to the appropriate Apostolic Father.

In addition to those works, helpful general volumes on the Apostolic Fathers are as follows.

FURTHER READING

Barnard, L. W. *Studies in the Apostolic Fathers and Their Background*. New York. Schocken, 1966.

Bird, Michael F. and Scott Harrower, eds. *The Cambridge Companion to the Apostolic Fathers*. Cambridge. Cambridge University Press, 2021.

Brannan, Rick. *The Apostolic Fathers: A New Translation*. Bellingham, WA. Lexham Press, 2017.

Ehrman, Bart D. *The Apostolic Fathers*, 2 vols. Loeb Classical Library, 24–5. Cambridge, MA. Harvard University Press, 2003.
Foster, Paul, ed. *The Apostolic Fathers*, ALNTS, vol. 4. Grand Rapids. Zondervan, 2023.
_____, ed. *The Writings of the Apostolic Fathers*. London and New York. T&T Clark, 2007.
Grant, R. M. *The Apostolic Fathers. A New Translation and Commentary*, vol. 1, *An Introduction*. New York. Nelson, 1964.
Glimm, F. X., J. M. F. Marique, and G. G. Walsh. *The Apostolic Fathers*. Fathers of the Church 1. Washington, DC. Catholic University of America Press, 1947.
Gregory, Andrew and Christopher Tuckett, eds. *The New Testament and the Apostolic Fathers*, vol. 1, *The Reception of the New Testament in the Apostolic Fathers*, vol. 2, *Trajectories through the New Testament and the Apostolic Fathers*. Oxford. Oxford University Press, 2005.
Gurtner, Daniel M., Juan Hernandez Jr., and Paul Foster, eds. *Studies on the Text of the New Testament and Early Christianity: Essays in Honor of Michael W. Holmes*. Leiden. E. J. Brill, 2015.
Hill, Kevin Douglas and Paul Foster, eds. *Christianity in the First and Second Centuries: Essential Readings* (Patristic Essentials). Dallas, TX. Fontes Press, 2022.
Holmes, Michael W. *The Apostolic Fathers: Greek Texts and English Translations*, Third ed. Grand Rapids, MI. Baker Books, 2007.
Jefford, Clayton N. *The Apostolic Fathers: An Essential Guide*. Nashville. Abingdon Press, 2005.
_____. *Reading the Apostolic Fathers: An Introduction*. Peabody. Hendrickson Publishers, 1996.
Moreschini, Claudio and Enrico Norelli. *Early Christian Greek and Latin Literature: A Literary History*, vol. 1. Peabody. Hendrickson Publishers, 2005.
Pratscher, Wilhelm, ed. *The Apostolic Fathers. An Introduction*. Waco, TX. Baylor University Press, 2010.
Quasten, Johannes. *Patrology. Volume One. The Beginnings of Patristic Literature*. Notre Dame, IN. Christian Classics, 1983.
Rothschild, Clare K. "The Apostolic Mothers," in *The Cambridge Companion to the Apostolic Fathers*, ed. Michael Bird and Scott Harrower, 175–85. Cambridge: Cambridge University Press, 2021.
Tugwell, Simon. *The Apostolic Fathers*. Harrisburg, PA. Morehouse, 1990.
Wilhite, Shawn J. and Jacob N. Cerone, eds. *Apostolic Fathers Greek Reader: The Complete Edition*. Wilmore, KY. GlossaHouse, 2019.

CHAPTER ONE

The Didache or Teaching of the Apostles

INTRODUCTION

The telephone call came after we had just finished our evening meal at the Knight's Palace Hotel in the Old City of Jerusalem in May 2005. The message instructed me to come now to the library of the Greek Orthodox Patriarch if I wanted to see the manuscript. I excused myself from my tour group, changed my clothes quickly, and began to scurry through the labyrinthine lanes of the Old City. After entering the Orthodox monastery, I made my way upstairs to the library. Soon the gentle librarian, Bishop Aristarchos, delivered to me what I had waited years to see: a 950-year-old, 200-page parchment codex containing over a dozen individual writings from the early church. My particular interest was in a little work in the middle of the codex, consisting of only ten pages (five leaves) in length. Its name is the *Didache* (the "Teaching," pronounced "didakhay"), short for *The Teaching of the Twelve Apostles*. For the next two hours, sometimes with trembling hands, I poured over this precious document, finding answers to some questions that I had for years. Why was I so excited to see firsthand this parchment "book," containing the only complete copy of this work that is known to exist?

Earlier I began a serious consideration of the Didache when I translated sections of it with my Intermediate Greek class. In subsequent years, the class began to translate the entire document, which is about the length of NT Epistle to the Galatians. I became captivated by its contents and began to read and research widely in an academic area that I soon learned was quite extensive. During a sabbatical in the spring of 2004, I had made the *Didache* one of the main interests of my research. By the time I attended a conference on "The New Testament and the Apostolic Fathers" at Oxford University, I was convinced that I would someday make my own contribution to the field of *Didache* research. I have personally spent hundreds of hours closely examining its contents, attempting to pull out of its chapters its "message." I have also studied intensively the scholarly issues that have been discussed by writers on this document from the 1880s until the current day. In 2007 I published a book, *The Way of the Didache*. This chapter is a condensation of that book.

Of all the "Apostolic Fathers" included in this book, the Didache has probably garnered the most attention in recent decades. And yet, many Christians by and large neglect the study of the *Didache* particularly and the Apostolic Fathers generally. It is this author's contention that the Evangelical commitment to *sola scriptura* and the general Evangelical lack of engagement with the tradition of the Church have contributed to their non-participation in such discussions. Therefore, only when discussions of patristic or apocryphal writings directly impact issues raised in the canonical books do Evangelicals get involved in this area of study. But the *Didache* and other early Church writings constantly discuss many issues related to New and Old Testament studies.

There is a host of important questions that swirl around the study of the *Didache*. (1) When was it discovered and what has been its history in the tradition of the Church? (2) Who was its author and when was it written? (3) What is the theological framework of the *Didache*? (4) What implications for liturgy, sacraments, and ministry does it have since it appears to so many readers to be a "church manual" in its literary genre? (5) What is its eschatological teaching, since the last chapter has often been viewed as an apocalypse? Only these issues will be explored in this chapter, and the reader is invited to study further issues in the various volumes in the bibliography.

A summary of some suggested conclusions about these *Didache* issues will help to provide the reader with a framework for how this writer approaches the document. I hold to a first-century date for its writing, with its provenance probably being Syria. I believe that a strong case can be made for its compositional unity, while acknowledging that it may have utilized a number of Jewish sources and have been edited by its author(s) at least once, although all versions were from the first century. The document exemplifies an early Jewish-Christian frame of reference, while primarily addressing new converts from the Gentile world. The book is intensely practical in its philosophy of the Christian life, and it is also orthodox in the theological framework that underlies its writing. I am also convinced that the Didachist knew and used what was later called the Gospel of Matthew. The basic function of the *Didache* in the early church was as a "catechetical handbook" for those who had recently joined the Christian family from among the Gentiles.

THE DATE OF THE *DIDACHE*

One of the first questions about the *Didache* is: "When was it written?" Occasionally some scholars have proposed a very early date (prior to 70 CE) for the writing of the *Didache*. A safer approach is to follow Lightfoot and a number of other scholars who recognize that we are reading a document that reflects the views of a group of Jewish Christians who lived and ministered in the generation following 70 CE. The strongest arguments for a first-century provenance are: (1) the primitive simplicity of the *Didache*'s teaching about the person and work of Jesus; (2) the absence of any warning about doctrinal aberrations; (3) the continued existence of itinerant apostles and prophets; (4) a simple pattern for the church's leadership (overseers and deacons); and (5) its silence about any persecution experienced by its readers or writer(s). All of these characteristics seem to be uncharacteristic of the church in the second century. Although there are some exceptions, the trend of current scholarship is toward a first-century dating. It should also be acknowledged that a date even earlier than 70 CE is still possible. In my opinion, the dating of the *Didache* is directly related to the relationship of the document to canonical Matthew.

THE REDISCOVERY OF THE *DIDACHE*

When I was privileged to personally examine the *Didache*, I experienced a real sense of euphoria as I perused its millennium-old leaves. Yet, what I felt was probably small compared to the excitement that Philotheos Bryennios must have had when he discovered in 1873 the little work buried in a larger codex. The story has been re-told many times in dozens of works on the *Didache*.

Perhaps it is best to allow Bryennios himself to relate his own story of his discovery. In an article published soon after the publication of Bryennios' volume, an American scholar teaching in Constantinople named Edwin Grosvenor reported in the *Andover Review* an interview that he had with the then Metropolitan of Nicomedia. I quote it in its entirety along with its original unique punctuation and other eccentric characteristics.

AN INTERVIEW WITH BISHOP BRYENNIOS –

THE DISCOVERY OF THE "TEACHING"

Last Thursday Bishop Philotheos or (as he is more commonly known in America by his non-episcopal and family name) Bishop Bryennios gave me a detailed account of his discovery of the *Didache* or *Teaching* manuscript, and of his subsequent connection with it. Since anything that has to do with that manuscript or with its learned discoverer is of interest, I am inclined to write down what he said, and give the reader the benefit of his remarks. As nearly as possible I shall quote his own words: –

"In 1873," said the bishop, "I had been looking over the manuscripts in the Jerusalem Monastery of the Holy Sepulchre at Phanar. I had looked over them many times before, but on this occasion my eye chanced to fall on a small, thick, black volume which had always escaped my notice. Though I was about to go from the library, I said to myself, 'I will give just one glance at that book.' I found first in it the Synopsis of St. Chrysostom, which did not interest me very much. As I listlessly turned over the pages, I came next upon an *Epistle of Barnabas*. 'What have I here?' I cried to myself; 'Is it a treasure I have found?' I carried the book with me to my house, and at once began to study it further. I thought I could not take my eyes away from the *Epistle of Barnabas* long enough to look at the other contents; but nevertheless I did. Directly after the *Epistle of Barnabas* came the first and second *Epistles of Clement* to the Corinthians, perhaps more precious still. 'Marvelous book!' I cried. 'I will edit the *Epistles of Clement* and the *Epistle of Barnabas*, and give them to the world.' But I read on in the manuscript. A short catalogue of the holy books came next, and then immediately after, a little treatise occupying about ten pages, introduced by two inscriptions, one of which was, 'Teaching of the Twelve Apostles,' and the other 'Teaching of the Lord through the Twelve Apostles to the Nations.' The title made no impression upon my mind, I read those ten pages over; neither did they make any impression, and I passed on to the other contents of the manuscript. But one thing stood out distinctly before me. Wherever I was, whatever I was doing, I seemed to see, to think, to feel nothing but the *Epistle of Barnabas* and the two *Epistles of Clement*. Which should I study and edit first? I could not work on them both at once. I was then Bishop of Serres. I was in feeble health. The labors in my diocese occupied almost every moment of my time. At last I went back to Serres, and studied and worked and wrote every moment that I could upon the *Epistles of Clement*. I thought hungrily of the *Epistle of Barnabas*: but my comfort was in feeling that as soon as my present occupation was finished I should devote myself to that. Two years I toiled at my work, and at last it was complete; edited as carefully and as faithfully as it was in my power to do. But the *Epistle of Barnabas* was not yet. For several years I was sick and could only wearily drag myself about. I was promoted to the diocese of Nicomedia, and larger and more responsible cares were overtaxing my feeble strength. In seven years' time, from 1873 to 1880, I barely gave the *Teaching* a thought. When I did think of that manuscript volume, it was only to recall the *Epistles of Clement* which I had edited, and to look forward to like work upon the *Epistle of Barnabas*. During the five years after the publication of my notes on Clement, I was in constant receipt of letters from Germany and from England, urging me to go on with the work which I had promised to do. In a footnote I had promised, with the help of God, as soon as I was able, to give to mankind not only Barnabas, but the twelve *Epistles of Ignatius*, likewise contained in the volume. All these letters from Harnack, from Lightfoot, from Funk (I think also from Hilgenfeld) were upbraiding me for my delay and inciting me to fulfill my promise."

"In 1880 I again chanced to read over the Didache. Something seemed to strike me like lightning. It appeared to me very different from what it did when I saw it before. Surely I had read this once, but then it did not seem the same as it did to me now. I was all of a tremble. This! This! This!" I wish I could give the rising emphasis, the gesture, the fire in Bryennios' eyes as he dwelt on the moment of realization of what he had found. This must be the Didache, the book that so many ancient fathers quote, the book that was lost, that the church mourns over to this day, the foundation of part of the *Apostolic Constitutions*. 'Eureka eureka eureka!' I shouted like Archimedes. From that hour I began to pore over the *Teaching*. Every spare moment was in some way devoted to it, until it appeared from the press in 1883. Then the letters began to flow in again faster and more numerous than they did after I had finished the *Epistles of Clement*; most of them flattering letters, and some of them full of gratitude at what I had done. One man who has a great name over Europe wrote, 'Hail, thou equal of the church fathers!'

"But the translations of some scholars have been so badly made and their comments so erroneous that I have gone to work again on the *Teaching* and am preparing a new volume to refute and correct them. If one wants to understand it and get the spirit of it, he must feel like a Greek. Only in that degree in which one does feel like a Greek can he breathe the soul of the *Teaching*. And now," said the bishop, with a smile half humorous, half sad, "now that they are making me work again on this book concerning which I thought that my labors were all done, when shall I ever get to the *Epistle of Barnabas*? Barnabas must wait!".

Edwin A. Grosvenor
ROBERT COLLEGE, CONSTANTINOPLE, *Sept.* 10, 1884. ("An Interview with Bishop Bryennios—The Discovery of the Teaching." *Andover Review* (Nov. 1884): 515–16.)

Sometimes, however, we are left wondering if we know all the details of this momentous discovery, as is the case with the romantic "story" told by the Taamireh Bedouin about their accidental "discovery" of the seven initial manuscripts that came to be called the "Dead Sea Scrolls."

Writers have noted that at least two scholars in the early part of the nineteenth century catalogued the contents of the monastery library and missed the presence of the *Didache*. My own handling of the manuscript in 2005 and the recognition that it composes only five leaves in the midst of over one hundred leaves helped me to understand how that could possibly happen. In 1887 the manuscript was transferred from Constantinople to the Greek Orthodox Patriarch Monastery Library in Jerusalem, where it remains until today. It is usually referred to as "The Jerusalem Manuscript" or "H" (Hierosolymitanus 54).

The manuscript consists of 240 "pages" on 120 "leaves" (or folios) containing a careful minuscule script on both sides of each folio "leaf." The scribe's own colophon informs us that he was named Leon, adding, in good monastic humility, that he was a "scribe and sinner." He also provides the date when he finished copying the manuscript: the Greek dating is equivalent to Tuesday, June 11, 1056 CE.

Leon's careful transcription of the ancient texts included not only the *Didache*, but also a number of other previously known writings attributed to various patristic authors or to people who knew them. Those works, in the order in which they are found in the Jerusalem manuscript, are as follows: A Synopsis of the Old and New Testaments attributed to Chrysostom; the *Epistle of Barnabas*; the *First Epistle of Clement*; the *Second Epistle of Clement*; a canonical list; the *Didache*; a Letter by Maria of Cassoboloi to Ignatius of Antioch; Twelve letters by Ignatius of Antioch in the longer recension; and a colophon followed by an anonymous treatise on the genealogy of Jesus.

The first line title of each work is also written in red ink, including that of the *Didache*. J. Rendel Harris published in 1887 an exact transcription of the Jerusalem manuscript along with a photographic reproduction of the pages where the *Didache* is located. Unfortunately the black-and-white photographs do not indicate the red color of the ink in the title. Furthermore, Harris cut the photograph of the first and last folio at the place where *Didache* begins and ends. This obscures the fact that the *Didache* and each work in the manuscript begins on the next line after the previous work ends (lectio continua). Also, one cannot clearly discern that at the end of the *Didache* Leon left six additional blank lines, each with the scribal "scoring" for the straight line, but with no text hanging from those lines! The significance of Leon's scribal activity is that he is indicating to the reader that he recognized that this is not the original ending of the *Didache*, but he simply is reproducing what he sees in his exemplar.

THE HISTORY OF THE *DIDACHE*

Bryennios eventually realized that the five leaves of his precious find contained an ancient work that was known to the early church but of which no manuscript had survived. The evidence of the footprints left by the *Didache* is as follows.

Soon after its publication, scholars recognized that the first five chapters of the *Didache* were strikingly similar to three chapters in the well-known writing generally known as the *Epistle of Barnabas*. The earliest scholarly view was that this section of the *Didache* showed dependence on *Barnabas*. This led Bryennios, therefore, to conclude that the *Didache* should be dated from 120–60 CE. Other early scholars either saw the dependence in the other direction or that neither was dependent on the other but that they both went back to a common source. Because of uncertainty about the relationship between the two works, it is best not to confidently assert that *Barnabas* is the first patristic document to refer to the *Didache*—although that is the view of this writer.

Clement of Alexandria is usually mentioned as the first church father to cite the *Didache*, although he does not do it by name. He rather refers to a statement of "scripture" that calls one a thief. "Son, become not a liar, for lying leads to theft." This agrees almost word for word with *Did*. 3.5. However, because Clement does not mention his "scripture" source by name, there have been some who are not positive about his specifically citing the *Didache*.

Origen, the pupil of Clement, although again citing his source only as "divine scripture," in *De Principiis* III.2.7, quotes *Did*. 3.10. "You will accept the experiences that happen to you as good things, knowing that nothing happens apart from God." Also, Origen in Homily VI on the Book of Judges likewise uses the designation of Jesus as the "Vine of David." It is debated whether or not these two early third-century "citations" are undoubtedly from the *Didache*.

From the fourth century, however, there are at least three clear references to the *Didache*. The first is from the church historian, Eusebius (d. 340). In *Ecclesiastical History*, Book III, 25 as he is discussing the books that are acknowledged as scripture, he classifies among the ecclesiastical yet uncanonical and "spurious" books "The so-called Teachings of the Apostles." He uses the plural and omits the number twelve. The description "so-called," which appears also later in Athanasius, qualifies the book's apostolic origin as being only indirect, even as we speak of the "Apostles' Creed." In this same category he places *The Shepherd of Hermas* and the *Epistle of Barnabas*. These books were read in some churches but were not important enough to be classified among the undoubted "homologoumena" nor even among the seven "Antilegoumena" which eventually came to be recognized as part of the New Testament canon.

The second clear reference from the fourth century is from the famous *Festal Letter* of Athanasius (367). In defining what books are canonical, he mentions the "*So-called Teaching* (s) *of the Apostles* along with the *Wisdom of Solomon*, the *Wisdom of Sirach*, *Esther*, *Judith*, *Tobit*, and the *Shepherd of Hermas*." Although these books were not canonical, they were "appointed by the fathers to be read by those who are now coming to us and desiring to be instructed in the doctrine of godliness." This catechetical function of the *Didache* mentioned by Athanasius describes how the book came to be used in the churches, certainly by the fourth century when there was a great influx into the church of converts from paganism.

The third clear reference to the *Didache* in the fourth century comes to us as a result of the discovery in 1945 of a cache of Coptic papyrus codices in Thoura, Egypt. Most of these works are commentaries on various biblical books written by the great head of the Catechetical School of Alexandria, Didymus the Blind. In his commentary on *Psalms* (227.26), Didymus is commenting on the verse, "Because they are speaking peaceably to me" (Ps. 34:20). "For this is what is said in the catechetical book of the *Didache*, 'bring peace to those who quarrel'," a clear reference to *Didache* 4.3. In another commentary on *Ecclesiastes*, he quotes the same verse and refers to the source as "the Teaching of the Apostolic Catechesis." In both these references the *Didache* is tied to an apostolic provenance. However, these references and others in his commentaries that treat the *Shepherd of Hermas* as a catechetical book are consistent with the role that his patron Athanasius had assigned to these books—profitable for catechetical instruction of new converts, at least in Alexandria.

These are the clearest patristic references to the *Didache* through the fourth century. The last reference to the little book by someone who had personal knowledge of it is from the ninth century by the Patriarch of Constantinople, Nicephorus (d. 828). In his *Stichometry*, he refers to a book named the *Teaching of the Apostles* as among the New Testament apocrypha and that it consists of 200 lines. Many authors have noted that in the Jerusalem manuscript the *Didache* consists of 203 lines. This, however, may not be as obvious as it may appear. When we compare the size of the *Didache* in the *Stichometry* with some of the other works that are mentioned, some serious questions are raised. For example, Nicephorus mentions that the combined length of the two Epistles of Clement as 2,000 lines, while in the Jerusalem manuscript they comprise 1,120 lines. Also, the length of *Barnabas* is given as 1,360 lines, which would make the *Didache*'s length as about 14 percent that of Barnabas. In actuality, *Didache* is about 34 percent its length! Obviously, the length of Nicephorus' "stichos" is not the same as that of the Jerusalem manuscript's "line" of text. But there is another fact worth noting. If we remove chapters 7–16 of the *Didache*, the length of chapters 1–6 then is about 14 percent of the length of *Barnabas*. My conclusion is that the length of the *Didache* which he measures is not that of the book that has come down to us. I suggest that by the ninth century, the liturgical latter section of *Didache* 7–16 had become separated from the more ethical first section of *Didache* 1–6 and comprised the work that is referred to in Nicephorus's *Stichometry*.

In the fourth century the *Apostolic Constitutions* incorporated most of the *Didache* into its seventh chapter. Furthermore, the book's liturgical sections probably seemed out of date with the emergence of a multileveled church hierarchy and a more ornate liturgical practice than what is described in chapters 7–15. By the ninth century the book evidently had been stripped down to its earlier ethical section. Some further confirmation of this is found in the Latin *Doctrina Apostolorum*, whose existence came to light in the late nineteenth century. It actually answers closely to the earlier chapters of the *Didache*. A growing number of modern scholars now believe that this Latin version most closely represents the original "two ways" document that is the common source of *Didache* 1–6 and *Barnabas* 18–20. This Medieval Latin document, in my opinion, is an adaptive translation of this abbreviated *Didache* that is referred to in the Stichometry.

We also have ancient translations of the *Didache*, such as the Coptic and Georgian versions. One more "remnant" of the *Didache* exists from ancient times, a tiny leaf from what was a miniature papyrus codex, dated to the fourth century and found among the Oxyrhynchus papyri and published in 1922. The leaf is written on both recto and verso in rather large letters for its size (only five by six centimeters). One side has the words of 1.3c–4a and the other has 2.7b–3.2a. I believe that this tiny fragment may help us to discern how the *Didache* came to be used in Egypt in the fourth century. This miniature codex is actually the smallest example of a Christian codex that has ever been found. The original copy could have easily fit into one's hand! In other words, it was probably part of a literal "handbook." The Greeks referred to such a miniature codex as an *enchiridion*. The word "manual" reflects the same Latinized root.

AN ORIGINATION HYPOTHESIS

The "effective history" of an interpretation can help us to ascertain the originally intended meaning of the passage interpreted. "Effective history" can help interpreters to recognize if their interpretation has also made sense to interpreters who were in the biblical writer's future and who are a part of the modern interpreter's past. While no method is an infallible guide, the effective history of the interpretation of a non-canonical text like *Didache* can also be helpful in our arriving at an "origination hypothesis" for the original *Didache*. In other words, can the effect that the *Didache* had on the Fathers who used it up until the fourth century be helpful in understanding what its original function was intended to be?

Many writers have noticed that the command to baptize in 7.1 adds that the baptism was to take place "after you have said all these things beforehand." In other words "all these things" must refer to the instruction that had already been given in the first six chapters. It seems to be evident, therefore, that the first six chapters are a compendium of pre-baptismal catechetical instruction that was to be taught to recent converts from paganism to prepare them for that decisive act by which they entered the Christian community. If that was indeed the effect that the text had on later generations, it will help to confirm our explanation of why the book originated. Our brief survey of the references to the *Didache* by such writers as Eusebius in Caesarea and Athanasius and Didymus the Blind in Egypt in the fourth century confirms such an origination hypothesis.

Therefore, in light of the patristic references to the *Didache* combined with the evidence of the miniature papyrus codex, I propose that this little book was often placed into the hands of young converts as the first "manual" for their new life. Therefore, I believe that we can safely conclude that the *Didache* was the first Christian Handbook of which we are aware.

AN OVERALL ANALYSIS OF THE *DIDACHE*

The *Didache* itself indicates that it is not simply a pastiche of disjointed elements. The discourse markers that the Didachist employs indicate that his work is divided into two main sections. The first is marked off by the expression "way of life" in 1.2 and the expression "way of death" in 5:1–2. Further markers are the expressions, "This is the teaching" in 1.3a and "this is the way of life" in 4.14b. These expressions serve as an *inclusio* framing the first part of the book. Thus, chapters 1–5 are intended to embody in a self-contained literary unit the teaching that was to be given to a new believer before his or her baptism. This is clear from 7.1, "After you have said all these things beforehand, immerse in the name of the Father and of the Son and of the Holy Spirit in flowing water." "These things" can only refer to the teaching embodied previously in chapters 1–5.

The second main section of the book (chs. 6–16) consists of instructions about how the young believer is to relate to life in the public worship and ministry of the church. The similar expressions "you will be perfect" in 6.2 and "unless you are perfected" in 16.2 again serve as an *inclusio* that frames the second section. Thus, the last chapter is not simply an eschatological appendix but is deliberately crafted to advance the overall plan of the Didachist. Within that frame in the second section, the Didachist employs the discourse marker "and concerning" (*peri de*) a total of five times, each time to introduce a new topic for the catechumen to learn about and in which to participate. These are: (1) Food to eat and to avoid (6.3); (2) Baptism and how it is administered (7.1); (3) the eucharist (9.1) of cup and bread (9.3); and (4) the role of apostles and prophets (11.3). This discourse marker function of *peri de* can be seen also in NT letters to the Corinthians and Thessalonians (see 1 Cor. 7:1, 25; 8:1, 12:1; 16:1, 12; and 1 Thess. 4:9 and 5:1). It is probably too much to conclude Pauline influence, however, since the Didachist does not show knowledge of Paul's writings in any other way. One possible suggestion, however, should be considered. Paul used *peri de* to enumerate his successive answers to the questions that the Corinthians had asked him about in a previous letter (7:1). Could its use by the Didachist also imply that the subjects he addresses were ones that local congregations had asked him about in previous communications? Thus, chapters 6–11ff. could be providing guidance by answering queries that had arisen in the churches within the circle of the Didachist's influence.

Chapter 6.3, therefore, with its mitigated command regarding kosher eating, thus would be separate from chapters 1.1–6.2. It also serves, however, as a bridge to the following material due to its being the first example in the *peri de* schematic. The Didachist desired that this point of guidance about eating food should be included in the teaching to be given to young believers. The material in chapters 7–16, as important as it was to the corporate life of the body, was not part of the individual instruction that was given in chapters 1–6. The final chapter (16) contains an earnest exhortation, therefore, to "seek what is appropriate for your souls" in light of the coming of the Lord. That which is appropriate would primarily be the pre-baptismal instruction of chapters 1–6 but also include the "church" teaching in chapters 7–15 that would cover post-baptismal experiences. See, for example, the exhortation in 9.5, "And let no one eat or drink from your thanksgiving meal except those baptized in the name of the Lord."

THE *DIDACHE* AND CANONICAL SCRIPTURE

Some *Didache* scholars do not affirm that the work clearly utilizes any of the books included in what became the New Testament. If there is one Gospel, however, that may have played a role in the author(s) thinking, it is the *Gospel of Matthew*. The group of precepts in 1.3b–2.1, often referred to as the "evangelic section," come quite close to reproducing expressions in Matthew. Other sentences that appear to be very close to Matthean material are 9.5 (Matt. 7:6); 11.7 (Matt. 12:31); 13.1–2 (Matt. 10:10); and the remarkable similarities to the Matthean form of the *Pater Noster* ("Lord's Prayer") in 8.2 (Matt. 6:9-13). The eschatological section in 16 also appears to echo sections of Matt. 24 and has legitimately been referred to as the "Didache Apocalypse." The word "gospel" utilized in 8.2 and 11.3 could refer to an early form of the Gospel which came to be known as Matthew. The reference to certain precepts that are to be found in "the Gospel" could again be a reference to Matthew, although some Didache writers simply affirm that these are oral *logia* rather than a written source. It appears to this writer that the answer to the Didachist's use of NT Gospel material is totally dependent on the dating of written Gospels like Matthew.

In regard to possible use of the Old Testament, a rather clear citation of Mal. 1:11 and 14 sums up a point made in 14.3. Finally the references in the eucharistic sections to Jesus as the "Servant" (*pais*) seem to recall the LXX of the Isaianic "Servant Songs" and at least echo the Petrine sermons in Acts 3 and 4. The reader is invited to peruse the translation of the *Didache* that follows this introduction. He or she should note the bolded words that are quite similar to some OT and NT written texts. Then he or she can make up their own minds if they are drawn from those canonical texts.

SCHOLARSHIP ON THE *DIDACHE*

Probably no other work in the corpus of the Apostolic Fathers has received more attention by scholars in the last forty years than the *Didache*. The reader is referred to the bibliography following this introduction for some of the most capable authors on the *Didache*. In addition to the major commentary by Niederwimmer, the three most prolific authors have been Draper, Jefford, and Milavec. The last author's works are marked by some views not shared by most writers on the *Didache*. In addition, *Didache* scholarship has been well-served by the major 2019 work by Shawn Wilhite. This author is thoroughly conversant with all previous *Didache* scholarship and has particularly helpful insights into the *Didache*'s "Reception of Sacred Scripture" (30–59) with a thorough exploration of the theology reflected by the Didachist (60–98), especially as that theology impacts the ethical and liturgical parameters of the work.

Wilhite, for example, also provides a comparison of Didachean ethics compared with the Sermon on the Mount in the canonical Gospel of Matthew (e.g., 133–6). He has a brief but keen analysis of the work's eschatological teachings found especially in 16:1–8 (86–8). His insights are appreciated even if he is not convinced by my own suggestion that the original ending of the work may have been intentionally edited to remove a chiliast perspective! His analysis of the possible lost endings of the work also deserves careful consideration (232–5).

VALUE OF THE *DIDACHE*

It should be obvious to the reader that this brief but compact text preserves some fascinating insights into the earliest stages of a "Jewish Messianic Movement" that had begun to admit Gentiles into its community. "Although there is little speculative theology in the *Didache*, this short manual gives us an interesting and quite attractive picture of a rather under-developed Christian community trying to make sense of itself and to deal with the problems it faced" (Tugwell, 17).

FURTHER READING ON THE DIDACHE

Draper, Jonathan A. "The Jesus Tradition in the Didache," in *The Jesus Tradition Outside the Gospels*, ed. D. Wenham, 269–87. Gospel Perspectives, vol. 5. Sheffield. JSOT, 1985.

Draper, Jonathan A. *The Didache in Modern Research*. Leiden. E. J. Brill, 1996.

_____. "The Didache," in *The Writings of the Apostolic Fathers*, ed. Paul Foster, 13–20. London and New York. T&T Clark, 2007.

Jefford, Clayton N. *The Sayings of Jesus in the Teaching of the Twelve Apostles*. Leiden. E. J. Brill, 1989.

_____, ed. *The Didache in Context. Essays on Its Text, History, and Transmission*. Leiden. E. J. Brill, 1995.

_____. "Didache," in *The Cambridge Companion to the Apostolic Fathers*, ed. Michael Bird and Scott Harrower, 248–67. Cambridge. Cambridge University Press, 2021.

Kraft, Robert A. *Barnabas and the Didache*. The Apostolic Fathers, vol. 3. New York. Nelson, 1965.

Milavec, Aaron. *The Didache. Faith, Hope, and Life in the Earliest Christian Communities, 50–70 CE*. New York. Newman Press, 2003.

Niederwimmer, Kurt. *The Didache*. Hermeneia. Minneapolis. Fortress, 1998.

Pardee, Nancy. *The Genre and Development of the Didache*. WUNT 2/339. Tübingen: Mohr Siebeck, 2012.

Scacewater, Todd A. "Economic Ethics in the Didache," in *Written for our Instruction: Essays in Honor of William Varner*, 285–311. Dallas. Fontes Press, 2021.

Varner, William. "The Didache's Use of the Old and New Testaments." *Master's Seminary Journal* 16 (2005). 127–51.

_____. *The Way of the Didache. The First Christian Handbook*. Washington. University Press of America, 2007.

Vokes, F. E. *The Riddle of the Didache. Fact or Fiction, Heresy or Catholicism?* London. SPCK, 1938.

Wilhite, Shawn. *The Didache. An Introductory Commentary*. Eugene, OR. Cascade Books, 2019.

The reader of the translations that follow should be aware of a few matters of style. Pronouns referring to God and Jesus are not normally capitalized. Furthermore, the noun often translated as "bishop" (*episkopos*) is rendered as "overseer," following the meaning of the word throughout its earlier history. The word referring to church leaders often translated as "elders" (*presbuteroi*) is rendered as "presbyters." Finally, a preference for "will" over "shall" is generally followed. Although not the practice throughout all the translations, in the following translation of the *Didache*, possible Scripture quotations are in bold font.

TEACHING (*DIDACHE*) OF THE TWELVE APOSTLES

Teaching of the Lord through the Twelve Apostles to the Gentiles

Chapter One
There are two ways, one of **life** and one of **death**. And there is a great difference between the two ways. 2 On the one hand, then, the way of life is this. **First, you will love the God** who made you; **second, you will love your neighbor as yourself.**[1] The way of life is this. **As many things as you might wish not to happen to you, likewise, do not do to another.**[2] 3 And concerning these matters, the teaching is this. **Speak well of the ones speaking badly of you,**[3] **and pray for your enemies, and fast for the ones persecuting you; for what merit is there if you love the ones loving you? Do not even the Gentiles do the same thing? You, on the other hand, love the ones hating you,**[4] and you will not have an enemy. 4 Abstain from fleshly and bodily desires. If anyone should strike you on the right cheek, turn to him also the other, and you will be **perfect**[5]; if anyone should press you into service for one mile, go with him two; if anyone should take away your cloak, give to him also your tunic; if anyone should take from you what is yours, **do not ask for it back**[6]; for you are not even able to do so. 5 **To everyone asking you for anything, give it and do not ask for it back**[7]; for to all the Father wishes to give from his own free gifts. Blessed is the one giving according to the commandment, for he is blameless. Woe to the one taking; for, on the one hand, if anyone having need takes, he will be blameless. On the other hand, the one not having need will stand trial why he received and for what use; and being in prison, he/she will be examined thoroughly concerning the things he has done, **and he will not come out from there until he pays back the last cent.**[8] 6 But also, concerning this, on the other hand, it has been said. "Let your alms sweat in your hands, until you know to whom you might give it."

Chapter Two
And the second rule of the teaching [is this].
2 **You will not murder,
you will not commit adultery,**[9]
you will not corrupt boys,
you will not have illicit sex,

---

[1] Matt. 22:37-39; Luke 10:27; Deut. 6:5; Lev. 19:18.
[2] Matt. 7:12.
[3] Luke 6:28.
[4] Matt. 5:44-47.
[5] Matt. 5:48.
[6] Luke 6:30.
[7] Luke 6:30.
[8] Matt. 5:26.
[9] Exo. 20:13-17; Matt. 5:33; 19:18.

you will not steal,
you will not practice magic,
you will not make potions,
you will not murder a child by means of abortion,
nor will you kill one that has been born,
you will not desire the things of your neighbor.
3 you will not swear falsely,
you will not bear false witness,[10]
you will not speak evil,
you will not hold grudges.
4 You will not be double-minded nor double-tongued,
    for being double-tongued is a snare of death.
5 Your word will not be false nor empty,
    but will be fulfilled by action.
6 You will not be covetous, nor greedy, nor a hypocrite, nor bad-mannered, nor arrogant. You will not plot an evil plan against your neighbor.
7 You will not hate any person, but some you will reprove, and concerning others you will pray, and some you will love more than your soul.

Chapter Three
My child, flee from every evil and from everything like it. 2 Do not become angry, for anger leads to murder; nor envious, nor contentious, nor hot-headed, for, from all these, murders are begotten. 3 My child, do not become lustful, for lust leads to illicit sex; nor one using foul speech, nor one lifting up the eyes, for from all these adulteries are begotten. 4 My child, do not become a diviner, since this leads to idolatry; nor an enchanter, nor an astrologer, nor a magician, nor wish to see these things, for from all these idolatry is begotten. 5 My child, do not become false, since falsehood leads to theft; nor a lover of money, nor a seeker of glory, for from all these thefts are begotten. 6 My child, do not become a grumbler, since it leads to blasphemy; nor self-pleasing, nor evil-minded, for from all these blasphemies are begotten. 7 But be gentle, since **the gentle will inherit the earth.**[11] 8 Become long-suffering and merciful and harmless and calm and good and trembling through all time at the words that you have heard. 9 You will not exalt yourself, and you will not give boldness to your soul. Your soul will not be joined with lofty people, but with the just and lowly people you will dwell. 10 You will accept the experiences befalling you as good things, knowing that nothing happens apart from God.

Chapter Four
My child, the one speaking to you the word of God you will remember night and day, and you will honor him as the Lord, for where the dominion of the Lord is spoken of, there is the Lord. 2 And you will seek every day the presence of the saints in order that you may rest upon their words. 3 You will not cause division. And you will reconcile those fighting; you will judge justly; you will not take into account social status when it comes time to reprove against failings. 4 You will not be double-minded whether it will be or

---

[10]Exod. 20:16.
[11]Matt. 5:5; Ps. 37:11.

THE DIDACHE OR TEACHING OF THE APOSTLES

not. 5 Do not become, on the one hand, one stretching out your hands for the purpose of taking, on the other hand, pulling them back for the purpose of giving. 6 If you should have something through the work of your hands, you will give a ransom for your sins. 7 You will not hesitate to give, nor will you grumble when you give, for you will know who will be the good paymaster of your reward. 8 You will not turn away the one in need; but, on the other hand, you will share together, all things with your brother, and you will not say that such things are your own. For if you are partners in the immortal things, how much more are you partners in the mortal things. 9 You will not take away your hand from your son or from your daughter, but from youth you will train them in the fear of God. 10 You will not command in your bitterness your male or female slave who are hoping in the same God, lest they should never fear the God who is over both of you, for he does not come to call according to one's social status, but those whom the Spirit has prepared. 11 And you, the slaves, will be subject to your masters as to the image of God in shame and fear. 12 You will hate all hypocrisy, and everything that is not pleasing to the Lord. 13 Never forsake the commandments of the Lord, but you will guard the things that you have received, **neither adding nor taking anything away.**[12] 14 In the congregation you will confess your wrongdoings, and you will not go to your prayer with an evil conscience.

This is the Way of Life!

Chapter Five
The Way of Death, on the other hand, is this. First of all, it is evil and completely accursed, murders, adulteries, lusts, illicit sexual acts, thefts, idolatries, magic arts, sorceries, robberies, false testimonies, hypocrisies, duplicity, deceit, pride, malice, stubbornness, greed, abusive speech, jealousy, boldness, arrogance, boastfulness, 2 persecutors of good people, those hating truth, those loving a lie, those not knowing the reward of righteousness, not adhering to the good nor to righteous judgment, those who are alert not for the good but for the evil, far from gentleness and patience, those loving worthless things, those pursuing retribution, lawless judges of the poor, not working for the oppressed, not knowing the one who made them, murderers of children, destroyers of what God has formed, turning away the one in need, oppressing the afflicted, advocates of the rich, lawless judges of the poor, and totally sinful.
May you be delivered, children, from all these things.

Chapter Six
Look out lest anyone make you wander from this way of teaching, since he is teaching you without God. 2 For if you are able to bear the whole yoke of the Lord, you will be perfect; but if you are not able, that which you are able, do this. 3 And concerning eating, bear that which you are able, from the food sacrificed to idols, very much keep away for it is worship of dead gods.

Chapter Seven
And concerning baptism, baptize this way. Having said all these things beforehand, **immerse in the name of the Father and of the Son and of the Holy Spirit**[13] in living water.

---

[12]Deut. 4:2; 12:32.
[13]Matt. 28:19.

2 But if you should not have living water, immerse in other water; and if you are not able in cold, immerse in warm water; 3 and if you should not have either, pour out water onto the head three times in the name of the Father and the Son and the Holy Spirit. 4 And prior to the baptism, let the one baptizing fast; also the one being baptized; and if any others are able. And order the one being baptized to fast one or two days prior.

Chapter Eight
And **let your fasts not be with the hypocrites,**[14] for they fast on the second and on the fifth days of the week but you should fast during the fourth and the preparation day. 2 Do not pray like the hypocrites but like the Lord commanded in his gospel. Pray this way. **Our Father, who is in heaven, may your name be made holy, may your kingdom come, may your will be done upon earth as in heaven, give us today our daily bread, and forgive us our debt as we also forgive our debtors, and do not lead us into trial but deliver us from the evil one,**[15] because yours is the power and the glory forever. 3 Three times daily pray this way.

Chapter Nine
And concerning the eucharist, give thanks thus. 2 First, concerning the cup. We give you thanks, our Father, for the holy vine of your **servant** David which you revealed to us through your **servant** Jesus. To you is the glory forever. 3 And concerning the broken bread. We give you thanks, our Father, for the life and knowledge which you revealed to us through your **servant** Jesus. To you is the glory forever. 4 Just as this broken bread was scattered over the mountains and gathered together became one, so in this way may your church be gathered together from the ends of the earth into your kingdom. Because yours is the glory and the power through Jesus Christ forever. 5 Let no one eat or drink from your eucharist except those baptized in the name of the Lord, for also the Lord has said concerning this: **"Do not give what is holy to the dogs."**[16]

Chapter Ten
And after being filled by the meal, give thanks in this way.

2 We give you thanks, holy Father,
>for your holy name,
>which you have caused to dwell in our hearts,
>and for the knowledge and faith and immortality
>which you revealed to us through your **servant** Jesus.
>To you is the glory forever.

3 You, almighty Master, created all things
>for the sake of your name,
>both food and drink you have given to people for enjoyment
>in order that they might give thanks;
>to us, on the other hand, you have graciously bestowed
>spiritual food and drink for life forever through your **servant**.

---

[14] Matt. 6:16.
[15] Matt. 6:9-13.
[16] Matt. 7:6.

4 Above all we give you thanks
>   because you are powerful.
>   To you is the glory forever.

5 Remember, Lord, your church,
>   to save her from every evil
>   and to perfect her in your love
>   and to gather her together from the four winds
>   the sanctified into your kingdom
>   which you have prepared for her,
>   because yours is the power and the glory forever.

6 May grace come
>   and may this world pass away!
>   Hosanna to the God of David!
>   If anyone is holy, let him come!
>   If anyone is not, let him repent!
>   **Come Lord!**[17] Amen!

7 And allow the prophets to "give thanks" as much as they wish.

Chapter Eleven
Therefore, whoever teaches you all these things said beforehand, receive him. 2 But if the one teaching has been turned around and should teach another doctrine for the destroying those things said beforehand, do not listen to him, but if it is for the bringing of righteousness and knowledge of the Lord, receive him as the Lord! 3 And concerning apostles and prophets, in accord with the decree of the gospel, act thus. 4 Every apostle coming to you, let him be received as the Lord. 5 But he will not remain more than one day; and if there is a need, also another day; but if ever he should remain three days, he is a false prophet. 6 And when he departs, let the apostle take nothing except bread until he is lodged. And if he asks for money, he is a false prophet. 7 And every prophet speaking in the Spirit you should not put on trial nor judge, **for every sin will be forgiven, but this sin will not be forgiven.**[18] 8 But not everyone speaking in the Spirit is a prophet, but if he is, he should have the habits of the Lord. Therefore, from these habits should be known the false prophet and the true prophet. 9 And every prophet ordering a table in the Spirit will not eat from it, and if he does otherwise, he is a false prophet. 10 And every prophet teaching the truth, if he does not do what he teaches, he is a false prophet. 11 And every prophet who has been put to the test and found true, doing an earthly mystery of the congregation, but not teaching you to do what he himself does, he will not be judged by you; for he has his judgment from God, for also the ancient prophets so acted. 12 But whoever should say in the Spirit, "Give me silver or any other thing," you will not listen to him; but if he should say to give to others in need, let no one judge him.

---

[17] Cf. 1 Cor. 16:22.
[18] Matt. 12:31.

Chapter Twelve

And everyone coming in the name of the Lord, let him be received; and then, having put him to the test, you will know, for you will have understanding of right and left. 2 If the one coming is a traveler, help him as much as you are able. He will not remain among you, except for two or three days, if there should be a necessity. 3 If he wishes to settle down among you, and if he is a craftsman, let him work and let him eat. 4 If he does not have a craft, according to your own understanding, plan beforehand how a Christian will live among you, without being idle. 5 But if he does not wish to act thus, he is a Christ-peddler. Beware of such ones!

Chapter Thirteen

And every genuine prophet wishing to settle down among you is worthy of his food; 2 likewise a genuine teacher is **worthy, just as the laborer, of his food.**[19] 3 So, you will take every first fruits of the produce from the wine vat and threshing floor, of both cattle and sheep, and you will give the first fruits to the prophets; for they themselves are your high priests. 4 But if you should not have a prophet, give it to the poor. 5 If you should make bread, take the first fruits, and give according to the commandment. 6 Similarly, when you open a jar of wine or of oil, take the first fruits, and give it to the prophets. 7 And of silver and of clothing and of every possession, take the first fruits, as it seems good to you and give according to the commandment.

Chapter Fourteen

And on the divinely instituted day of the Lord, when you are gathered together, break bread and give thanks, having beforehand confessed your failings, so that your sacrifice may be pure. 2 If anyone has a conflict with a companion, do not let him come together with you until they have been reconciled, in order that your sacrifice may not be defiled. 3 For this is that which was spoken by the Lord. **"In every place and time, offer to me a pure sacrifice. Because I am a great king,"** says the Lord, **"and my name will be wondrous among the Gentiles."**[20]

Chapter Fifteen

Appoint for yourselves, overseers and deacons worthy of the Lord, gentle men and not money-loving and truthful and tested. For they likewise carry out among you the ministry of the prophets and teachers. 2 Therefore, do not look down upon them, for they themselves are your honored ones along with the prophets and teachers. 3 And reprove one another! Not in anger, but in peace. as you have in the gospel. And to everyone wronging a neighbor, let no one speak to him nor let anyone hear from you about him until he should repent. 4 And **do your prayers and alms and all your actions** thus as you have in the gospel of our Lord.

Chapter Sixteen

Be watchful over your life; do not let your lamps be quenched, and do not let your waists be ungirded. But be prepared, **for you do not know the hour in which our Lord is coming.**[21] 2 And frequently be gathered together, seeking the things appropriate for your

---

[19]Matt. 10:10.
[20]Mal. 1:11, 14.
[21]Matt. 24:42.

souls. For the whole time of your faith will not be of use to you if in the end time you should not have been perfected. 3 For in the last days the false prophets and corrupters will be multiplied, and the sheep will be turned into wolves, and love will be turned into hate. 4 **For, when lawlessness increases, they will hate each other and they will persecute and they will betray each other.**[22] And then will appear the world-deceiver as a son of God, and he will do signs and wonders, and the earth will be delivered into his hands, and he will do unlawful things that never have happened from eternity. 5 Then the human creation will come into the fiery testing, and many will be led into sin and will perish, but the **ones remaining firm in their faith will be saved**[23] by the curse itself. 6 And then the signs of the truth will appear. The first sign will be an opening in heaven, then the sign of a trumpet sound, and the third a resurrection of dead ones, 7 but not of all, as it was said. "The Lord will come and all the holy ones with him."[24] 8 Then the world will see the Lord **coming atop the clouds of heaven** …[25]

---

[22]Matt. 24:10-12.
[23]Matt. 24:10, 13.
[24]Zech. 14:5.
[25]Matt. 24:30.

CHAPTER TWO

The Shepherd of Hermas

Many modern readers of the *Shepherd of Hermas* come away from their first exposure to the book with either or both of the following reactions. (1) "This is a very long book." (2) "This is a very strange book." Despite the possible negative reactions that readers today have to the *Shepherd*, it was actually one of the most popular written works in early Christianity, judging from the manuscript copies that have survived. It was copied and read more widely in the first two centuries of the early church than any other book that did not make it into the New Testament canonical lists in the fourth century. Surprisingly, it may have been copied and read more than some of the books that came to be included in the New Testament! If it is really that long and that strange (at least to modern readers), what explains its popularity? And why was it not eventually included in the NT canon?

EARLY HISTORY OF THE *SHEPHERD* AND ITS TEXT

To sum it up concisely, the *Shepherd* was cited and referred to by early writers in both the Eastern and Western parts of the Roman Empire. These well-known ancient writers include Irenaeus, Clement of Alexandria, Tertullian, Origen, Jerome, and Augustine (just to include the more famous names), and a number of these actually considered it as "scripture." The famous Athanasius of Alexandria in the fourth century did not consider it as canonical but recommended it as being useful to read, along with other books like the *Didache*. The unknown author of the famous Muratorian canon also thought well of it, but not as scripture. More will be said later about that.

Other important placements of the book include the fourth-century Codex Sinaiticus where it appears at the end of the "New Testament" books along with the *Letter of Barnabas*. Another important sixth-century Greek-Latin manuscript known as Codex Claromontanus also contains it alongside *Barnabas* and the *Acts of Paul* and the *Apocalypse of Peter*. While those last large codices appear to be "official" publications, the evidence left by papyrus copies of the *Shepherd* in the sands of Egypt is surprising and quite impressive, compared to the other Christian texts uncovered there. There are at least twenty fragmentary Greek papyri from the third to fifth centuries that are housed in five academic libraries (see the list in Ehrman, II, 170–71). Latin versions survive in a number of codices as well as other translations, many partial, like Ethiopic, Coptic, Sahidic, Persian, Georgian, and Arabic.

Despite this amazing pedigree of the *Shepherd*, no complete Greek copy of the work has survived until modern times. The discovery of the fifteenth-century Codex Athos in the nineteenth century has provided the most complete Greek copy but even that manuscript still lacks a few chapters at its end. The text as found in other versions helps scholars to conclude that the original work probably contained 114 chapters.

DATE OF THE *SHEPHERD*

Most scholars date the *Shepherd* generally in the first half of the second century with most leaning toward the 140–50s. This is due mainly to a statement in the Muratorian Canon that the work was written "recently" while the author's brother, Pius, was the bishop of Rome. This would be between 142 and 154. This judgment obviously is intended to cast doubt on any possible apostolic origin of the work. There are, however, some serious questions that have been raised about the date of this "canon list" that was discovered and published by Lodovico Muratori in 1740. This is not the place to address and settle all the issues raised by this document, but we should address how it relates to the possibility of another date for the *Shepherd*. If the original "Muratorian canon" was composed soon after the pontificate of Pius I, why does Irenaeus cite the *Shepherd* as scripture (*Haer*. IV, 20.2) if it was *not* apostolic? As we will see, the *Shepherd* describes the church as governed by presbyters with no mention of a single "overseer" or "bishop" at its head (*Vis*. 3.5; 13.1). Irenaeus was confident of a succession of bishops/overseers in Rome (*Haer*. III, 3.3) which would not be consistent with the simpler church structure envisioned in the book. Whatever one thinks about other issues related to the Muratorian Canon, its testimony about the *Shepherd* is suspect and probably motivated to disprove its canonicity as non-apostolic.

There are some good reasons for actually placing the book much earlier, possibly as early as *c*. 70 CE. The persecution in Rome referenced in the book could very well be the Neronian persecution after the great fire in 64 CE. Everyone recognizes the rather "underdeveloped" theology of the book which would suggest an earlier rather than a later date. The teachers denying the possibility of post-baptismal repentance probably based their teaching on the *Letter to the Hebrews* in 6:4–6. Furthermore, if our book is dated to the seventh decade or even slightly later, there is nothing to prevent us agreeing with Origen's observation that the author is the "Hermas" mentioned in Rom. 16:14. Also the "Clement" mentioned in *Vis*. 2.4 could very well be the Clement who would send a letter from the Roman church to the church in Corinth. The role of the Clement mentioned in our book would be similar to the role of Clement as "sender" of the letter from Rome to Corinth (Tugwell, 63, who also cites the work of Robinson, *Redating the NT*, 319–22). Even if not all readers are convinced of a first-century date for our book, we should be at least doubtful that its writing must be around a mid-second-century date.

Mediating between these two extremes of dating is the suggestion that the work may have been issued in two stages.

> Hermas gives the impression of living between two periods of persecution. On the one hand the persecutions are over (Vis III 1.9,2.1, 5.2); on the other hand persecutions are expected in the present (Sim I 3; IX 21.1–2, 28.3–5). The present persecution situation might have occurred under Trajan and Hadrian, that is, before 138. In that case, the Book of Visions would have been written at the beginning of the first quarter and *PH* (the rest) around the middle to end of the second quarter of the second century.
> (Hellholm, 238)

GENRE AND SUMMARY OF THE *SHEPHERD OF HERMAS*

Even with its perplexing issues, this work is a valuable and interesting witness to the life and thought of the early Roman Church. It could be described as a manual of personal religion, cast in an imaginative form. It has been compared by some writers with

Bunyan's *Pilgrim's Progress* and even Dante's *Divine Comedy*. It has also been viewed as a work of allegorical fiction, or as a record of an actual dream experience, or possibly as a combination of both. Whatever the genre it breathes a strong moral earnestness and unveils a didactic purpose, since both are equally evident. Another genre type that has been suggested is that of an apocalypse, echoing themes portrayed in the OT apocalyptic chapters of Daniel and in the NT "Apocalypse." Perhaps, however, before we make any conclusion about its genre, we should survey the contents of the *Shepherd*.

The work has three sections: Five Visions; Twelve Mandates or Commandments; and Ten Similitudes or Parables. The divisions of the work are historically referenced by the number (often a Roman numeral) of the Vision/Mandate/Parable followed by an Arabic number for the chapter and verse (*Mand.* X. 1, 3 could also be written as 10. 1, 3). This rather bulky method of citation was relieved by a creative idea of Molly Whittaker (1967), who suggested that the 114 chapters simply be numbered that way with the appropriate verse. Thus the above reference to *Shepherd Mandates* 10, 1, 3 would be simply expressed as *Shepherd* 40.3. Traditionalists have not always accepted her brilliant suggestion (patterned simply on the Biblical method of citations). Many commentators will now even use both methods of citations for each reference in the book, making for an even longer citation! I prefer the shorter method but will use the traditional method in this Introduction but add the Whittaker numbering in the following translation.

Some consider Visions 1–4 as a separate work, but most manuscripts sustain the inclusion of all the chapters. In Vision One Hermas is introduced as looking at his former owner while she was bathing in the Tiber and desiring her. Later in his travels the woman appears to him from heaven and explains to him his guilt. A chair appears and Hermas is kindly rebuked for not properly training his children. A year later in Vision Two the woman appears again and gives him a heavenly scroll which Hermas copies. After fasting he understands the meaning of the text is to practice abstinence and to let it be known that believers can have a second and final chance to repent. In Vision Three six young men are building in the water a tower, explaining that salvation comes from the water of baptism. The stones correspond to different types of believers, including church leaders. Seven girls represent seven virtues. In Vision Four a huge sea monster represents the Tribulation and a girl with white hair the revived church. The Shepherd appears in Vision Five and tells Hermas to write down the coming Mandates and Parables. This obviously important character who lends his description to the title of the book is only introduced clearly after the fifth vision. Earlier the one who plays this part is a woman who represents the church. The "Shepherd" who provides the work its title (it is better to call it *Shepherd* than simply *Hermas*), is Hermas' guardian angel, serving as both mediator and interpreter of the revelations.

In the following Twelve Mandates, practical and personal messages emerge about faith and continence; simplicity and love to one's neighbor; purity and love of truth; relations with adulterous spouses and second marriages; patience and anger; justice and wickedness; fear of God (not the devil); avoiding vices and following good works; praying with perseverance and true and false prophets; and finally the difference is explained between good and evil desires. The way in which the above list is presented does not imply that the way in which these virtues are portrayed is in any way boring or trite, since they are conveyed through vivid characters and images.

The First Parable describes the pilgrim nature of Christians as strangers on earth and members of the true heavenly city. Parable Two, under the figures of an elm tree and a vine, describes the rich and the poor in support of each other each with their possessions and their prayers. Parables Three and Four utilize the figure of dry winter trees to describe the condition of the just and the sinners in the current world. The Fifth Parable presents a faithful slave who has cared for this master's vine in his absence and is set free and made a co-heir with the master's son. The referent is Jesus in whom the Spirit dwells. Some have observed that this "pneumatic" Christology does not always clarify the difference between two Divine persons and may support a more Binitarian theology.

The Sixth Parable illustrates the theme of the two ways by portraying two shepherds, who represent the angel of pleasure and error and the angel of punishment. This theme is continued in the Seventh Parable with the tribulations inflicted on Hermas as a punishment. In Parable Eight there appears a large willow tree that covers both the plains and the mountains, which symbolizes the law of God that is given to the world and is identical to the proclamation of his Son throughout the world. The details of the vision are given a creative and detailed allegorical interpretation as the members of the church. The Ninth Parable is a full repetition of the vision of the tower with many new details and changes (e.g., the stones taken from the water are now not the martyrs but the baptized, *Sim.* 9.16). In Parable Ten, the Son of God appears and exhorts Hermas regarding his future life.

THE MAIN MESSAGE OF THE *SHEPHERD*

As is often the case in a work of literature that is symbolic and/or allegorical, the main point of it all can be easily lost amidst the numerous symbols. Many have discerned that if there is a central point in the *Shepherd*, it is the message of a second repentance offered to Christians after baptism. This overarching idea returns repeatedly throughout the different parts of the work. Here is the Shepherd's response to Hermas' inquiry about this subject. "But this I also say to you," he said. "After that great and holy call, if a man sins after severe temptation by the Devil, he has one repentance. But if he sins and repents repeatedly, it is no benefit for such a man, for only with difficulty will he live." The answer is "Yes, but only once" (*Mandates* 4.3; 31.6)

Perhaps this theme should be understood in the context of persecution, a theme mentioned in the above reference. "The place at the right side is for others who have already pleased God and have suffered for the Name. To sit with them, there remains many things for you to do. But persist in your sincerity, as you are now doing, and you will sit with them. So also will all who do what they have done and who endure what they have endured."

"What have they endured?" I asked. "Listen," she said: "Floggings, imprisonments, great afflictions, crucifixions, wild beasts for the sake of the Name. For this reason, theirs is the right side of holiness, and for anyone who suffers for the Name" (*Vision* 3, 1–2). A huge issue arose later in the second century over what would be called in Latin, the *lapsi*, those who sinned greatly in the face of persecution by denying the Lord. Could this stress on one repentance be in reference to those who sinned greatly in this way? There were those in the church who responded simply to that question with a resounding "No, because they denied the Lord and their baptismal vows and they cannot so easily return." Earlier in the chapter Hermas mentions those teachers who espoused this view. The Shepherd actually is more compassionate and in effect says "Yes, but only once. This is not a game." If persecution is in play, it affects the tenor of this discussion.

The idea that there was no further forgiveness of sins after baptism had been linked not only to a passage like Hebrews 6, but also to the expectation of Christ's imminent return. As this imminent expectation gradually weakened and Christianity spread, it became less and less realistic to maintain this position. The *Shepherd* desires to develop a community that retains a strong moral code, hence the fervent passages on the mutual behavior of Christians and of the danger of various vices and the promotion of various virtues. This should be accomplished, however, without an undue rigorism in one's behavior. The book looks for a way to satisfy these two requirements in one, and only one, repentance that will wipe out sins. Roman Catholic authors have appreciated the *Shepherd* as a prime source for the Church's teaching on penance. "The doctrine of penance in Hermas is already thoroughly permeated with the idea that the Church is an institution necessary for our salvation" (Quasten, 99). The allegory of the tower is intended to make it obvious that the time for repentance is not without a limit. The work ends with a tension between the announcement that work on the tower is being suspended in order to allow for repentance, and the exhortation to hasten the labor because the tower is almost finished (*Sim.* 10.4.4). In *Vis.* 3.8.9 this tension is connected with a simple refusal to say how close is the *eschaton*.

Having surveyed the content and message of the Shepherd, we must return again to the question of its genre, but that task is still not as simple as we may desire. The *Shepherd* as a whole takes the form of an apocalypse inasmuch as a heavenly mediator reveals to a human being a revelation of divine mysteries through the means of particular visions and allegories. Subjects like a heavenly scroll or letter are also typical of apocalypses (cf. Rev. 5:1; 20:11-15), but a parenetic element is also not always omitted. Lacking in the work, however, is any over-arching vision of world history, especially of the eschatological end time events that characterize the struggle between spiritual forces. The *Shepherd* chooses the apocalypse format in an effort to give his message the highest authority by linking it directly to God. Hermas' intention is to propose a decisive change in a prevailing strict view of behavior. He recognizes the authority of the presbyters in the church, but desires that his message take priority over that authority. This accounts for the vivid picture in which Hermas is invited to sit beside the Lady but says, "Let the presbyters sit down first, lady, I said." (*Vis.* 3.1.8). But she makes him sit down at once, though not at her right hand, which is reserved for the confessors and martyrs.

THEOLOGY OF THE *SHEPHERD*

The doctrinal references, if we must insist on them, reveal a creed which is simple and yet has its own special peculiarities. Only a few observations will be made on some of these special features.

Christology

When the Shepherd at first appears, Hermas fails to recognize him as apparently he should have done, to be the being to whom he was "delivered." Only when the visitor changes his form does he recognize him. Perhaps the most striking of these appearances is the conception of the Son of God. In the Fifth Parable, namely of the vineyard, the Son of God is represented as a slave placed in charge of the vineyard, with a promise of freedom if he fulfils his assigned duty. He does so much more than is expected of him that the Divine master of the vineyard decides that he will be made joint heir with his Son, who is represented as the Holy Spirit. This almost Adoptionist conception, which illustrates early Roman speculation on the Person of Christ, finds frequent expression in phrases identifying the Spirit with the Son of God, for example, "For that Spirit is the Son of God" (*Parables* 9. 1). Concerning his view of Jesus, while the Savior is mentioned a number of times, it is striking that the words "Jesus" and "Christ" are never utilized.

Pneumatology

The last practice of identifying the Spirit with the Son of God illustrates what has perplexed many modern readers of the Shepherd. A clearly enunciated theology of the Trinity in later Nicean terms simply cannot be found. In addition to *Parables* 9.1 passage mentioned above, *Parables* 5.6.5–7 seems to teach that there is God the Father, the Holy Spirit whom he identifies with the Son of God, and then the Savior who was elevated to be their companion because of his merits. An emphasis in the passage on the glorious angels who had served the Spirit is a complication that may also point the way ahead.

In the earlier canonical "Apocalypse" (1:4-5) there is a reference to the one who is and was and is to come, who corresponds to the Father, while Jesus Christ is clearly described as the "faithful witness." The reference to "the seven spirits before the throne" is possibly a reference to the Holy Spirit in his seven-fold ministries (cf. Isa. 11:2-3). If this is a fair reading, then perhaps the *Shepherd* combines an angelic Pneumatology with a spirit Christology. Thus the Son of God is the "supreme Spirit" (see Batovici, 299). Admittedly, this does not satisfy every detail in the text, but it may be a possible road ahead in grasping the apparently contradictory way the *Shepherd* describes the Son of God and the Spirit. Perhaps also it is a lesson about how not to expect logical doctrinal consistency in an apocalyptic genre.

Ecclesiology

The "Church" is portrayed in a number of ways, most often by the figure of a woman. These have resonances with the OT picture of Israel as a woman and the NT portrayal of the church as a bride. But even the woman is portrayed in various modes in the earliest "Visions" section. As a "Lady" (1) the Church incorporates various aspects of the OT Wisdom tradition (Prov. 1–9). When portrayed as an "Old Woman" (5, 18–20), her decline is stressed because of the misbehavior of her members. She is a "Virgin" (23) where the purity of the community is being stressed. In *Vis*. 3.9 her role as "mother" addressing her children is presented with her pedagogical role being stressed. The famous symbolism of the Church as a mighty "Tower" is described in *Sim*. 9.13. The Tower is still under construction, with the dynamic process of inspection and improvement being stressed.

It also seems curious that while Baptism is plainly mentioned two or three times (*Vis*. 3, 3; *Mand*. 4. 3; *Sim*. 9. 16), the Lord's Supper or Eucharist does not come under consideration. Fasting is often promoted, and once we find Hermas keeping a "station," as the early fast-days in the early church were sometimes called (*Sim*. 5. 1). In this case he is commanded not to abstain entirely from food, but to take bread and water.

Eschatology

The *Shepherd* also seems to teach in the Ninth Parable that the first apostles and teachers who have already died descended like Christ and preached to the Spirits in prison (9.16). In *Vision* Five there is an apparent reference to a belief in guardian angels. Unlike the apocalypses in the Bible, one searches in vain for any detailed description of a sequence of events in the *eschaton*. There are references to a "great coming tribulation" (*Vis.* 2.2.7; 4.1.1; 2.4–5; 3.6), but this suffering is part of a transformation in preparation for the building of the tower and is part of a movement toward the end. There is no mention of a Parousia that concludes that "tribulation." Finally, his general eschatology is in one respect quite severe and narrow. Not only are unrepentant sinners to be burned, but also the Gentiles, because of their ignorance of God.

THEOLOGY AND LIFE IN THE *SHEPHERD*

This topic may seem contradictory but doctrine and duty in the *Shepherd* are not isolated from one another. While the book indicates few if any traces of Pauline influence, it does seem to reflect the Letter of James, with whose themes the author shows great familiarity. In that echo of James appears the prominent theme of "double-mindedness" or literally "double-soulness." The related verb and adjective occur fifty-five times in *the Shepherd*. This is striking considering that the cognates appear only a total of ten times in other early Christian literature up to this time. The Letter of James is known for the use of this word in 1:7 and 4:6, the adjective appearing first in that book. All the Christian references (also in 1 and 2 Clement) approximate its meaning in the *Shepherd*, which have to do with one's relationship to God. In *Mandate* 9 the struggle of the double-minded is between trust or lack of trust in God. The double-minded person hesitates to ask anything from God because of previous sin but is assured that God does not keep grudges (vv. 2–3), and is encouraged to ask boldly and without hesitation, the opposite of double-mindedness, and therefore to choose faith and abandon doubt. The double-minded person is caught between two spirits, that of courage over against discouragement and doubt. The latter causes disruptions such as dissension (*Sim.* 8.9.4) and an unwillingness to act justly (*Sim.* 8.8.1–3). The problem is a lack of trust in God. The double-minded are drawn to the false prophet in *Mandate* 11 because they both are earthly and empty (see Osiek, *Shepherd of Hermas*, 30–31).

The *Shepherd's* own office is that of a prophet, and his mission is to recall Christians from the danger of a too intimate contact with pagan social influences. He speaks of those who have never investigated the truth, nor enquired about God, but have merely believed and have become embroiled in daily affairs and riches and pagan friendships, and many other affairs of this world (see *Mand.* 10. 1). These people are especially without understanding and corrupt. Hence his standard of Christian duty is quite practical: "faith, fear of the Lord, love, harmony, words of righteousness, truth, patience, ... helping widows, to visit the orphans and the poor, to ransom the servants, of God from their afflictions, to be hospitable, ... to resist no man, to be tranquil, to show yourself more submissive than all men, etc." (from *Mand.* 8). The indwelling of the Spirit of God is a feature of the Christian life, and if intermediate beings like Faith, Continence, Power, Longsuffering (*Sim.* 9. 15) shape the Christian character, these are declared to be "powers of the Son of God" (9. 13). God is the Creator alike of the world and of the Church. "Behold, the God of Hosts, who by his invisible and mighty power and by His great wisdom created the world, and by his glorious purpose clothed His creation with comeliness, and by his strong word fixed the heaven, and founded the earth upon the waters, and by his own wisdom and providence formed his holy Church, which also he blessed" (*Vis.* 1.3, 4).

Various emotions are portrayed quite vividly in the *Shepherd*. One of the most visible is the Greek word *lupe*, rendered regularly by the standard translations as "grief" (Brannan, Ehrman, Holmes). The noun appears around twenty-five times, with the majority of these occurrences in chapters 41 and 42 (*Man.* 10.2.3). The gloss "grief" is problematic because of the association of that English word with the loss of a loved one. That sense of "grief" does not appear to be at all associated with the word in its occurrences. The trait is considered to be evil because it is associated with the repeated charge of "double-mindedness" so often condemned in the book. One then wonders why "grief," which is an understandable experience in humanity, is such a problem to the author. One standard lexicon lists the following as a definition and possible glosses for the word: "*pain of mind or spirit*, sorrow, affliction" (BDAG, 604). A recent lexicon defines the word without any mention of "grief": "annoyance, anguish, pain" (CGL, 882). In 42.1, 4 it is contrasted with the word "cheerfulness" (*hilaros*). This last association occurs also in the NT, namely 2 Cor. 9:7. The other occurrences of *lupe* in 2 Corinthians also do not bear the meaning of "grief" (2:1, 3, 7; 9:7). The contrast between "godly sorrow" and "worldly sorrow" in 2 Cor. 7:10 also provides a possible background for the use of the word in the *Shepherd*. The activity described as *lupe* is removed by repentance and replaced by "cheerfulness" in 41 and 42. Therefore, we have resisted the translation "grief" and adopted "sorrow" for the word in the following translation. One wonders if a psychological approach to this discussion might suggest "anxiety" as the emotion that is being described.

INTERTEXTUALITY IN THE *SHEPHERD*

The task of identifying so-called "scriptural" sources of this work can be a bit daunting. There are allusions to the Old Testament but not direct citations. The author of *Shepherd*, who was probably acquainted with the contents of the *Didache*, does not directly cite canonical scriptures by name, but he continually uses scriptural words and ideas, handling them lightly, and working them into new combinations. *Shepherd* is a valuable potential witness to the Christian canon, especially in the case of the four Gospels. Some have seen in the four feet of the couch in the Third Vision (13), namely that "the world too is upheld by means of four elements," the source of a patristic saying that there can be neither more nor fewer than four Gospels, because there are four regions of the world and four winds. It is actually quite surprising that no specific canonical scriptures are clearly cited, but there is a clear citation of the lost work called *Eldad and Modat* (*Vis.* 2. 3).

Because many scholars view the Letter of James as late, it is not usually observed that the *Shepherd* displays some quite remarkable echoes of that New Testament writing. Mention was made above about the theme of "double-mindedness" that is so prevalent in the *Shepherd* and that appears in the NT only in James. But a number of passages also convey a Jacobean practical approach to the Christian life. The reader is invited to peruse the contents of *Mandates* 9 and 11 with apparent resonances with the practical themes in James 4 and 3 respectively.

Reflection on the genre of the work, already addressed above, may help in this matter of seeing very few specific citations. That New Testament example of an apocalypse, appropriately bearing that very title (the *Apocalypse of Jesus Christ*), may be helpful in this regard. It has often been observed that the *Apocalypse* contains few if any clear citations from either Testament. Yet readers of that book cannot help but discern Scriptural themes that embed its narratives and visions and symbols. It does not directly quote that Old Testament apocalypse, the Book of Daniel, but what interpreter of it would venture to unravel its visions without serious attention given to Daniel? Therefore, the apocalyptic nature of the *Shepherd* may also yield themes and images from the Old and New Testaments without literally citing them. In a recent study of the *Shepherd*, Jonathon Lookadoo evaluates its genre and notes its differences with canonical apocalypses. He evaluates the similarities and differences and concludes that while the *Shepherd* "may not be one of the prototypes selected for early Christian apocalypses, the text remains comfortably within the formal boundaries of the apocalyptic genre" (*The Shepherd of Hermas. A Literary, Historical, and Theological Handbook*, 58).

CONCLUSION ABOUT THE *SHEPHERD*

As attested by its inclusion in Codex Sinaiticus and its evident popularity in the papyri codices read and shared among the laity of Christian congregations, the *Shepherd*, despite its length and its verbosity and its strangeness and its heavenly symbolic world, enjoyed an almost canonical authority from East to West because of its artless and simple but profound moral teachings. The imagery and apocalyptic nature may have appealed to people, even as the NT *Apocalypse* often has a popular appeal today. We should also not overlook, for example, the great popularity for centuries of the allegorical *Pilgrim's Progress*! Perhaps modern readers need to note that those "different" features so often mentioned in this chapter actually contributed to the work's popularity rather than detracting from it!

FURTHER READING ON *SHEPHERD OF HERMAS*

Batovici, Dan. "The Shepherd of Hermas as Early Christian Apocalypse" in *The Cambridge Companion to the Apostolic Fathers*, ed. M. Bird and S. Harrower, 290–308. Cambridge. Cambridge University Press, 2021.

Hellholm, David. "The Shepherd of Hermas" in *The Apostolic Fathers: An Introduction*, ed. W. Pratscher, 215–42. Waco, TX. Baylor University Press, 2010.

Lookadoo, Jonathon. *The Shepherd of Hermas. A Literary, Historical, and Theological Handbook*. London. T&T Clark, 2021.

Maier, H. O. *The Social Setting of the Ministry as Reflected in the Writings of Hermas, Clement and Ignatius*. Waterloo, ON. Wilfrid Laurier University Press, 1991.

Osiek, Carolyn. *The Shepherd of Hermas*. Hermeneia. Minneapolis. Fortress, 1999.

Pernveden, Lage. *The Concept of the Church in the Shepherd of Hermas*. STL 27. Lund, 1966.

Quasten, Johannes. "The Shepherd of Hermas" in *Patrology*, vol. 1. Notre Dame, IN. Christian Classics, 1983.

Reiling, Jannes. *Hermas and Christian Prophecy*. NovTSup 37. Leiden. E. J. Brill, 1973.

Snyder, G. F. *The Shepherd of Hermas*, vol. 6 of *The Apostolic Fathers*, ed. R. M. Grant. Camden, NJ. Nelson, 1968.

Taylor, Charles. *The Witness of Hermas to the Four Gospels*. Cambridge. Cambridge University Press, 1892.

Verheyden, Joseph. "The Shepherd of Hermas" in *The Writings of the Apostolic Fathers*, ed. P. Foster, 63–71. London and New York. T&T Clark, 2007.
Whittaker, Molly. *Der Hirt des Hermas*, 2nd ed. Die griechische christliche Schrifsteller. Berlin. Akademie-Verlag, 1967.
Wilson, J. Christian. *Toward a Reassessment of the Shepherd of Hermas. Its Date and Its Pneumatology*. Lewiston, NY. Edwin Mellen, 1993.

THE SHEPHERD OF HERMAS

As mentioned in the Introduction, Molly Whittaker suggested a new numbering of the *Shepherd*, with each chapter in the *Visions*, *Commandments*, and *Parables* numbered consecutively, for a total of 114 chapters. In addition to the traditional three divisions and sections, the Whittaker chapter numbering is also used.

First Vision

Chapter One

1.1 The person who raised me sold me to a certain Rhoda in Rome. After awhile I met her again and began to love her as a sister. 2 Later I saw her bathing in the Tiber and gave her my hand to lead her out of the river. When I saw her beauty, I began reasoning in my heart and said, "How fortunate I would be if I had a wife of such beauty and character!" My thought went thus far and no further. 3 A little later, on my way to Cumae, while praising the great splendor and power of God's creatures, I fell into a trance as I walked. A spirit then seized me and carried me through a deserted region where no person could make their way, since it was steep and broken into streams of waters. When I had crossed a river and came to level ground, I knelt down and began praying to the Lord and confessing my sins. 4 While praying I saw the heavens opened and that woman whom I had desired greeting me from heaven. "Greetings, Hermas!" 5 With my eyes fixed on her, I said, "Lady, what are you doing here?" She then replied, "I have been taken up to accuse you of your sins before the Lord." 6 I answered her, "Are you now my accuser?" "No" she said, "but listen to what I am about to tell you. The God who dwells in Heaven, the Creator of beings out of nothing, the one who increases and multiplies them for the sake of his holy church, is angry with you for sinning against me." 7 I answered her, "Have I sinned against you! In what way? Have I ever made an inappropriate remark to you? Have I not always thought of you as a goddess? Did I not always respect you as a sister? O Lady, why do you make these false accusations of wickedness and uncleanness against me?" 8 With a laugh she said to me, "In your heart has arisen the desire of evil. Surely you think it evil that an evil desire arises in the heart of an upright man. It is a great sin," she said, "yes, a great sin. For the upright man intends to do what is right. And in this aim to do the right thing his good name in heaven is secure and he finds the Lord looking favorably on every action of his, while those who pursue evil bring death and captivity on themselves, especially those who have set their affections on this age and boast in their riches and do not cling to the good things to come. 9 Their souls will be sorry for they have no hope. They have instead abandoned themselves and their life. As for you, pray to God and he will heal your sins, along with yours and those of your entire household and of all the saints."

THE SHEPHERD OF HERMAS

Chapter Two

1.2 After she spoke these words the heavens closed, and I sat trembling all over and upset. I thought to myself, "If even this sin is recorded against me, how then can I be saved? How will I appease God for the sins I committed? With what words will I ask the Lord for mercy?" 2 As I was pondering this in my heart, I saw before me a large white chair made of snowy white wool. Then there came an older lady, dressed in brilliant garments with a scroll in her hands. She was sitting alone and addressed me, "Greetings, Hermas!" While upset and weeping I said to her, "Greetings, Lady!" 3 She then said, "Why are you sad, Hermas? You are always so patient and slow to anger, always laughing. Why are you so downcast and not cheerful?" My answer was, "Because a very good woman tells me that I sinned against her." 4 Then she said, "May it not be for the slave of God! However, the thought about her did really enter your heart. For God's servants, such a thought leads to sin. It is an evil and shocking idea so far as a devout soul, already tried and tested, is concerned if there is a desire for evil action, especially for the self-controlled Hermas, who abstains from every evil desire and is full of all sincerity and great innocence."

Chapter Three

1.3 "But this is not the reason why God is angry with you. It is rather that you may convert your household that has sinned against the Lord and against you, their parents. But because of your love for your children, you do not admonish them, but allow them to fall into terrible ruin. This is the reason for the Lord's anger. But he will bring a remedy for all past evils committed by your family. Their sins and transgressions are the reason why you have fallen under the affairs of daily life. 2 But the great mercy of the Lord has taken pity on you and on your family and it will give you strength and establish you in his glory. But you must not be careless but encourage and strengthen your family. For just as a coppersmith by hammering his work secures mastery over it for his purposes, so also the righteous message spoken daily masters all evil. So do not let up but admonish your children, for I know if they repent with their whole heart, they will be inscribed with the saints in the books of life." 3 After these remarks she said to me, "Do you wish to hear me read?" "Yes I do, lady," I said. "Be attentive and hear about the glories of God." The great and marvelous things I heard I am unable to remember, for all her words inspired fear which no human being can endure. But her last remarks I do remember, for they were helpful for us and gentle. 4 "Behold the God of Hosts, who has created the world with his invisible power, strength, and surpassing wisdom, and who in his glorious good pleasure has clothed his creation with beauty and by his mighty word has firmly fixed the heavens and set the earth's foundations on the waters. In the wisdom and providence that is his alone he has founded his holy church and blessed it. Behold, he is removing the heavens, the mountains, the hills, and the seas, and all are becoming level for his elect, to fulfill the promise he made with great glory and joy, provided they keep the commandments of God which they have received in great faith."

Chapter Four

1.4 Now when she finished reading and rose from her chair, four young men came who took the chair and went away toward the east. 2 Then she beckoned me and, touching my breast, said, "Were you pleased by what I read?" To which I answered, "Yes, lady, the last part pleased me, but the first part was difficult and hard." She answered as follows, "The last part was for the upright, but the first part was for the Gentiles[1] and apostates." 3 As she was still speaking with me, two unknown men appeared, lifted her in their arms, and went away in the same direction as her chair to the east. However, she went away cheerfully and while going she said to me, "Be a man, Hermas!"

Second Vision

Chapter Five

2.1 While making my way to Cumae at the same time as the previous year, as I was walking, I remembered the last year's vision, and again the spirit seized me and carried me off to the same place as in the past. 2 So when I reached that place, I got down on my knees and began praying to the Lord and glorifying his name, because he had considered me worthy and made known to me my former sins. 3 After I rose from prayer, I saw before me the elderly lady I had seen the previous year, walking and reading a little scroll. Then she said to me: "Can you report these things to God's elect?" I said, "Lady, I cannot remember so many things. Give me the scroll and I will copy it." "Take it," she said, "and return it to me." I took it and went to some place in the field and copied everything letter by letter, for I could not distinguish the syllables. As I finished the last letters of the scroll, it was suddenly snatched from my hands, by whom I did not see.

Chapter Six

2.2 After fifteen days of my fasting and requesting the Lord, the knowledge of the writing was revealed to me. These things were what was written: 2 "Your offspring, Hermas, have rebelled against God and blasphemed against the Lord and have betrayed their parents by much evil-doing. Although they betrayed their parents, their betrayal has not benefited them. Instead, they have added lusts and improper sexual activities to their iniquities. In this way they made full the measure of their lawlessness. 3 Now make these things known to your children, every one of them, and to your wife who in the future is to be as your sister. She also fails to control her tongue with which she commits sin. However, after hearing these things she will control herself and will find mercy. 4 After you have made known to them these things the Master has commanded me to reveal to you, then all the sins that they previously committed will be forgiven. And all the saints who have sinned up to this day will be forgiven, if they repent whole-heartedly and rid themselves of double-mindedness from their heart. 5 For the Master has sworn by his glory about his elect, that if after this day has been determined there is any sin, they will not find salvation, because repentance for the righteous is at an end. The days of repentance for all the saints have reached their fullness, but for the Gentiles there is a possibility for repentance until the last day. 6 Therefore, tell the leaders of the church to rectify their ways in righteousness, that they may receive in full the promises with great glory. 7 Stand firm, therefore, you who do righteousness and be not double-minded, so that your entrance may be with the holy angels. Blessed are those of you who will endure the coming great tribulation and those who will not deny their life. 8 For the Lord has sworn by his Son that those who have denied their Lord have been rejected from their life; I mean those who are on the

---

[1]The translation of the plural *ethne* as "Gentiles" implies "unbelievers" here and throughout the book. Cf. Eph. 4:17; 1 Pet. 4:3. This practice occasionally appears in other AF and is frequent in the *Shepherd*.

point of denying him in the coming days. But to those who have formerly denied him, mercy has been given to them because of his great compassion."

Chapter Seven

2.3 "But you, Hermas, do not hold a grudge against your children any longer nor allow your sister to have her way, that they may be cleansed from their former sins. For by just discipline they will be disciplined, if you do not hold a grudge against them. For holding a grudge produces death. As for you, Hermas, you have had many trials of your own, because of the transgressions of your house and your lack of concern about them. But you were absorbed by other matters and entangled in your own evil doings. 2 However, your refusal to fall away from the living God, your simplicity and your great self-restraint are saving you. These things saved you, if you endure, and it is saving all who do the same and who walk in innocence and sincerity. These will gain the mastery over all evil and are going to endure unto everlasting life. 3 Blessed are all those who practice righteousness. They will not perish forever. 4 But say to Maximus: 'Behold, tribulation is coming. If it seems good to you, deny again'. The Lord is near to those who turn to him', as it is written in *Eldad and Modat*,[2] who prophesied to the people in the wilderness"

Chapter Eight

2.4 Brothers, a revelation was given to me in my sleep by a very handsome young man, who said: "Who do you think is the older lady from whom you took the little scroll?" "The Sibyl," I said. "No," he said, "you are mistaken." "Who is she then?" I said. "The Church," he said. "Why is she older?" I asked. "Because she was created before all things," he said. "This is why she is older and for her sake the world was formed." 2 After this I had a vision in my house. The older lady came and asked me whether I had already given the scroll to the presbyters. I said that I had not. "You have done well," she said, "for I have some words to add. When I complete all the words, through you they will be made known to all the elect. 3 Therefore, write two little scrolls, one for Clement and one for Grapte. Clement will then send it to the cities abroad since this is his job, and Grapte will admonish the widows and the orphans. But you will read it in this city together with the presbyters who lead the church."

Third Vision

Chapter Nine

3.1 Brothers, this was what I saw. 2 After much fasting and requesting the Lord to make clear to me the revelation he promised to show through the older lady, that very night she appeared to me and said, "Since you are in need, yet eager to know everything, go to the field where you are farming, and I will appear to you about the fifth hour and show you what you must see." 3 Then I asked her a question, "Lady, in what part of the field?" "Wherever you wish," she said. I chose a beautiful and secluded place, but before I could speak and tell her the place she said, "I will come wherever you wish." 4 And so, brothers, I counted the hours and came to the place where I had told her to come, when I saw an ivory couch set up. On the couch was placed a linen pillow and on top a linen cloth was spread out. 5 When I saw these things so arranged and that no one was

---

[2] An apocryphal book that no longer survives. The two prophets are mentioned in Num. 11:26.

in the place, I was astonished and seized with trembling and my hair stood on end and I was terrified, because I was alone. Then when I recovered, I remembered God's glory, took courage and knelt down, and once more I confessed my sins to the Lord. 6 Then she came with six young men whom I had also seen before and they stood by me. As I prayed and confessed my sins to the Lord, she listened. Then she touched me and said, "Hermas, stop saying all these prayers for your sins. Ask also for righteousness so that you may receive some of it in your house." 7 Then she raised me up by the hand and led me to the couch, saying to the young men: "Go and build." 8 After the young men departed and we were alone, she said to me, "Sit here." "Let the presbyters sit down first, lady," I said. "Do as I tell you," she said. "Sit down." 9 When I desired to sit down on the right side, she did not permit me, but indicated with her hand to sit on the left. As I was reflecting about this and was sad because she would not allow me to sit on the right, she said to me, "Are you sad, Hermas? The place at the right side is for others who have already pleased God and have suffered for the name. Many things remain for you to do before you sit with them. But continue in your sincerity, as you are now doing, and you will sit with them, as will all who do what they have done and who endure what they have endured."

Chapter Ten
3.2 "What have they endured?" I asked. "Listen," she said, "Floggings, imprisonments, great afflictions, crucifixions, and wild beasts for the sake of the name. For this reason, theirs is the right side of holiness, and for anyone who suffers for the name. The left side is for the rest. But the same gifts and the same promises are for both those sitting on the right and those sitting on the left. The only difference is that those who have suffered sit at the right and enjoy a certain glory. 2 Now you are eager to sit with those on the right, but you have many shortcomings. However, you will be purified from your shortcomings, as will all who are not double-minded, and will be cleansed from all their sins to this day." 3 After saying these things, she wished to go away, but I fell at her feet and asked her by the Lord to show me the vision she had promised. 4 So she took me again by the hand, raised me, and sat me on the couch at the left, while she sat down to the right. Then she raised a shining rod and said to me, "Do you see something great?" "Lady," I said, "I see nothing." Then she said to me, "Look! Do you not see before you a great tower built out of shining square stones upon the waters?" 5 The tower was being built in the shape of a square by the six young men who had come with her, but many other men were bringing along stones, some of them from the deep, others from the land, and they were distributing them to the six young men, who were taking them and building. 6 All the stones dragged from the sea they were placing in the building just as they were, for they had been shaped and fitted in the joint with the other stones. In fact they fit so closely with one another that the joints were not visible. The structure of the tower appeared to be of one single stone. 7 Of the other stones brought from the dry land, some they put into the building, while others were broken in pieces and thrown far away from the tower. 8 But many other stones were lying around the tower and were not being used in the building. Some of them were damaged, others had cracks, some were chipped, and some were white and round, and did not fit into the building. 9 I saw other stones thrown far from the tower and coming onto the road without staying on it but rolling to the wastelands. Other stones fell into the fire and were burned. Still others fell near the waters and yet were unable to roll into the water, even though they desired to roll and come to the water.

Chapter Eleven

3.3 After showing me these things, she wished to rush away. I said to her, "Lady, what good is it for me to see and not to know what these things mean"? "You are a crafty person!" she said. "You do wish to know about the tower." "Yes," I said, "so I may tell my brothers, lady, so they may have greater joy and with this message know the Lord with much glory." 2 She said, "Many will hear and some will rejoice for having heard, but some also will weep. But even if those listen and repent, they will also rejoice. Therefore, hear the parables of the tower; I will reveal everything to you. And do not bother me any more about the revelation, since these revelations are completed and fulfilled. Yet you will not cease asking for revelations, because you are shameless. 3 The tower which you see being built is I, the Church, who appeared to you now and previously. So ask me whatever you wish about the tower and I will reveal it to you, that you may rejoice along with the saints." 4 I said to her, "Lady, since once you considered me worthy of the whole revelation, reveal it." She said, "Whatever can possibly be revealed to you will be revealed. Only let your heart be with God and do not be double-minded about what you see." 5 Then I asked her, "Why, lady, is the tower built upon the waters?" "Yes," she said, "as I told you before, you keep seeking. With your enquiries you will find the truth. The reason why the tower is built on the waters is this: your life was saved and will be saved by water. The tower has been founded on the word of the almighty and glorious name, and it is held together by the Master's invisible power."

Chapter Twelve

3.4 I answered and said to her, "Lady, this is a great and marvelous thing. But, lady, who are the six young men who are building?" "These are the holy angels of God, the first to be created, to whom the Lord has committed his whole creation, to increase and to build up and to rule over all of creation. Through their agency the building of the tower will be completed." 2 "Who are the others who are dragging the stones?" "These too are God's holy angels, but these six are superior to them. With their help the tower will be completed and all will rejoice together around the tower and will give glory to God because the building of the tower has been completed." 3 I asked her, "Lady, I would like to know what is the destination and the meaning of the stones." She answered me, "It is not that you are worthier to receive the revelation than all the rest, for others are ahead of you and worthier, and it would be right for them to receive the revelation. But the revelation has been made that God's name may be glorified, and will be made to you and for those who are double-minded and those who question in their hearts whether this is so or not. Tell them that all these things are true and there is nothing outside the truth, but everything is strong and certain and firmly established."

Chapter Thirteen

3.5 "Hear now about the stones that go into the building. The square and white stones that fit in their joints are the apostles and overseers and teachers and deacons who have walked according to the holiness of God by ministering with purity and sanctity the office of overseers and teachers and deacons to God's elect. Some of them have fallen asleep and some are still living. They have always been in mutual agreement and are at peace with one another and listen to one another. For this reason their joints fit accurately in the building of the tower."2 "Who are the ones dragged from the sea to be put into the building, whose joints fit with the other stones already used in the building?" "These are the ones who have suffered for the name of the Lord." 3 "Lady, please let me know who are the other stones taken from the dry land." She said, "Those going into the building without being cut are the ones the Lord has approved, because they walk in the upright way of the Lord and strictly observe His commandments." 4 "Who are those that are brought and placed in the building?" "They are new in the faith and faithful. But they are admonished by the angels to do good, because evil was not found in them." 5 "Who are the ones they rejected and threw away?" "These are sinners but wish to repent because they will be useful in the building if they repent. They are not thrown far from the tower. Now those who are to repent will be strong in the faith when they actually do, provided they repent now, while the tower is still being built. But if the building is completed, they no longer have a place and will be excluded. Their only advantage is that they lie next to the tower."

Chapter Fourteen
3.6 "And those broken up into fragments and thrown far from the tower, do you wish to know about them? These are the children of lawlessness. They believed hypocritically and no wickedness ever left them. Because of this wickedness, therefore, they do not have salvation and are of no use for the building. That is why they have been broken into fragments and thrown far away, because of the Lord's anger and because they roused him to anger. 2 The many other stones which you see lying around not going into the building are the damaged stones, who knew the truth but failed to abide in it and did not associate with the saints. Therefore, they are useless." 3 "Who are the stones with cracks in them?" "They are those opposed in their hearts and not at peace with one another. They have only an appearance of peace, but when they leave one another, evil thoughts remain in their hearts. These are the cracks in the stones. 4 The stones that are chipped are for the most part believers, but a certain amount of lawlessness is lingering in them. Because of this they are chipped and not perfect in every respect." 5 "Lady, who are the white and round stones that do not fit into the building?" She answered and said to me, "How long are you going to be foolish and senseless? You ask all these questions but you understand nothing! These are those who have faith, but also are wealthy in this age. When persecution comes, they deny their Lord because of their riches and their business affairs." 6 I answered and said to her, "Lady, when will they be useful for the building?" "Whenever the riches that lead their hearts astray have been cut away from them," she said. "Then they will be useful to God. Just as the round stone cannot become square unless it is cut and loses something, so also the rich in this world cannot become useful for the Lord unless their riches have been cut out from them. 7 Know from your own experience. When you were rich you were useless, but now you are useful and beneficial to life. Become useful to God, for you yourself are taken from these same stones."

Chapter Fifteen
3.7 "The other stones which you saw thrown far from the tower, falling onto the road and rolling off it into waste lands, are believers, but in their double-mindedness have abandoned the true road, because they thought they could find a better one. So they wander in misery, walking through the wastelands. 2 Those falling into fire and burning are those who have completely rebelled against the living God, in whose hearts repentance no longer enters, because of their unbridled desires and the evil things they have performed. 3 Do you want to know who are the other stones that have fallen near the waters and are not able to roll into the water? They are the ones who heard the word

and wish to be baptized in the name of the Lord, but then change their mind when they recall the purity of the truth and return to pursue their evil desires." 4 So she finished her explanation of the tower. 5 Boldly I asked her yet another question whether these stones that have been thrown away and do not fit into the tower could ever repent and have a place in the tower. "They can repent," she said, "but they cannot fit into this tower. 6 They will fit into another inferior place, but only after they have been tormented and completed the days for their sins. But their place will be changed since they have partaken of the righteous word. Then it will also be their good fortune to be relieved of their torments, if they recall the evil deeds that they have done. But if they do not desire to repent, they will not be saved because of their hardness of heart."

Chapter Sixteen
3.8 When I finished asking her about all these things, she said to me, "Do you want to see something else?" Being eager to observe more, I was overjoyed to see. 2 She looked at me with a smile and said, "Do you see seven women around the tower?" "Yes, lady," I said. "This tower is being supported by them at the Lord's command. 3 Now hear about their functions. The first of them, with the strong hands, is called Faith; through her God's elect are saved. 4 The second, who is wearing a belt and looks like a man, is called Self-control; she is the daughter of Faith. Whoever follows her will be blessed in his life, because he will refrain from all evil deeds in the belief that by abstaining from every evil desire he will inherit eternal life." 5 "Who are the others, lady?" "They are the daughters of one another and are Sincerity, Knowledge, Innocence, Reverence, and Love. When you do all the deeds of their mother then you are able to live." 6 "Lady," I said, "I would like to know the power that each of them has." "Listen," she said, "to the powers they have. 7 Their powers are held by one another and they follow one another in the order in which they are born. Self-control is the daughter of Faith; from Self-control is born Sincerity, from Sincerity is Innocence, from Innocence is Reverence, from Reverence is Knowledge, from Knowledge is Love. Their deeds, therefore, are pure and reverent and divine. 8 Whoever serves these and succeeds in mastering their deeds will have a dwelling in the tower with God's saints." 9 Then I asked her about the times, if the consummation had arrived yet. But she cried out with a loud voice, saying, "Foolish man, do you not see that the tower is still being built? Whenever the building of the tower is finished, then will be the end. But it will be built quickly. Do not ask me anything more. This reminder and the renewal of your spirits is sufficient for you and for the saints. 10 But this revelation is not for you alone, but for you to make it known to everyone. 11 After three days (for you must understand this first), I command you, Hermas, to speak all the words I am about to tell you in the ears of the saints, so that when they hear and do them, they will be cleansed from their wickedness, and you along with them."

Chapter Seventeen
3.9 "Listen to me, children. I brought you up with great sincerity and innocence and reverence, through the Lord's mercy, who instilled righteousness in you, that you may be justified and sanctified from all wickedness and from all perversity. But you did not wish to cease from your wickedness. 2 Now hear me. Be at peace among yourselves, care for one another, and help one another. Furthermore, do not partake of God's creatures abundantly by yourselves, but share also with those who have less. 3 For some from the abundance of things to eat, bring sickness to their flesh and weaken it, while others who do not have enough to eat are weak in the flesh from lack of enough food and their body

wastes away. 4 So this failure to share is harmful to you who have and fail to distribute to those in need. 5 Look to the judgment to come. You who have more than enough should seek out those who are hungry as long as the tower is unfinished. For after finishing the tower, you will wish to do good and will not have an opportunity. 6 And so, you who pride yourselves on your wealth, beware lest those in need groan at any time and their groaning will rise up to the Lord, and you and your good things will be shut out from the door of the tower. 7 At this point it is to you who lead the church and to those who occupy the first seats that I speak. Do not be like sorcerers who carry their drugs in boxes, whereas you carry your drugs and poison in your hearts. 8 You are hardened and do not wish to cleanse your hearts. You do not wish to mix together your wisdom in a clean heart, that you may receive mercy from the great king. 9 Watch out, therefore, my children, lest these divisions deprive you of your life. 10 How do you expect to discipline the Lord's elect if you yourselves have no discipline? Therefore, instruct one another and have peace among yourselves, that I may take my stand before the Father joyfully and give an account of you to your Lord."

Chapter Eighteen
3.10 So when she finished speaking with me, the six young men who were builders came and took her to the tower, while four others picked up the couch and brought it to the tower. I did not see their faces, because they had turned away. 2 As she was going away, I asked her to reveal to me about the three forms in which she had appeared to me. "You have to ask someone to reveal these things." 3 In the former vision last year, brothers, she had appeared to me as a very old woman sitting on a chair. 4 In the second vision she had a more youthful appearance, but her hair was old, though she had spoken to me standing up, and she was more cheerful. 5 But in the third vision she was very youthful and very beautiful; only her hair was that of an old lady and toward the end she was very joyful and sitting on a couch. 6 I was deeply depressed, because I wished to know about this revelation. Now in a night-vision I saw the elderly lady saying to me: "Every question requires humility. Fast, therefore, and you will receive from the Lord what you ask." 7 So I fasted for one day, and that same night there appeared to me a young man, who said to me, "Why are you asking continually for revelations in your prayer? Be careful lest you injure your flesh by so many requests. 8 The present revelations are all you need. Can you see mightier revelations than those you have seen?" 9 Answering, I said to him: "Sir, I am only asking for a complete revelation in every detail about the three forms of the elderly lady." Answering me, he said, "How long are you going to be without understanding? It is your double-mindedness that makes you so and the failure to have your heart set toward the Lord." 10 Again I answered, "Well, sir, from you we will know these things more accurately."

Chapter Nineteen
3.11 "Hear," he said, "about the three forms which you are asking. 2 In the first vision why did she appear to you as an elderly lady sitting on a chair? Because your spirit was old and already wasting away and infirm because of your weakness and double-mindedness. 3 For just as older men, with no hope of renewing their youth, have nothing to look forward to except their sleep, so you also, weakened by temporal affairs, surrendered to indifference, instead of casting your cares on the Lord. Your understanding was broken and you have grown old with your sorrows." 4 "Sir, I would like to know why she was

THE SHEPHERD OF HERMAS

sitting in a chair." "Because every weak person sits in a chair because of weakness, that his weak body may find support. Here you have the symbolism of the first vision."

Chapter Twenty

3.12 "In the second vision you saw her standing, youthful in appearance and more cheerful than the former time, although with the body and hair of an old lady. Now listen also to this parable. 2 An old man who has given up hope because of his weakness and poverty is waiting for nothing more but the last day of his life. Then suddenly an inheritance is left to him, and he rises at the news, is exceedingly happy and gathers strength. He no longer lies down but stands up and his spirit is renewed, though it was broken by his former practices. He no longer sits but takes courage. In the same way you also were renewed when you heard the revelation the Lord made to you. 3 Because the Lord has had compassion on you and has renewed your spirits again, you put aside your weaknesses, strength returned to you, and you were empowered in the faith, while the Lord rejoiced at the sight of your strengthening. For this reason he showed you the building of the tower and will show you other things, if you continue with all your heart to be at peace among yourselves."

Chapter Twenty-One

3.13 "In the third vision you saw her as a younger lady, beautiful and cheerful, and her appearance was beautiful. 2 For a person soon forgets former sorrows when good news comes while he is grieving. He excludes everything except the good news he has heard; he gets strength to do good in the future; in his joy his spirit is renewed. And he is strengthened from then on to do what is good, and his spirit if renewed because of the news he has received. So your spirits have been renewed because of seeing these good things. 3 Because you saw her sitting on a couch means the position is secure, for the couch has four feet and stands firm, just as the world is supported by four elements. 4 Therefore, those who thoroughly repent with all their heart will be renewed and firmly established. You now have the complete revelation. Do not ask for anything more about a revelation, but if anything still is needed it will be revealed to you."

Fourth Vision

Chapter Twenty-Two

4.1 Brothers, this is what I saw twenty days after the former vision as a foreshadowing of the coming tribulation. 2 I was going into the country on the Via Campania. The place is about ten stadia off the public road and is easily reached. 3 As I was walking alone, I thanked the Lord for the revelations and visions he had shown me through his holy church and begged him to complete them. I begged him to strengthen me and to grant repentance to his servants who had stumbled, that his great and glorious name be glorified, since he considered me worthy to point out to me his marvelous wonders. 4 As I was glorifying him and giving thanks, a sound like my voice answered me, "Do not be double-minded, Hermas." I began to debate this with myself. "How can I be double-minded being so firmly established by the Lord and having seen such glorious things?" 5 So I approached a little closer, brothers, and behold, I saw a cloud of dust reaching up as to heaven, and I began to say to myself, "Is that cattle now approaching six hundred feet away from me and raising a cloud?" 6 As the cloud was getting bigger, I suspected it was something supernatural. The sun shone a little and, behold, I saw a huge beast something like a sea monster, with fiery locusts coming out of its mouth. The length of the beast was about a hundred feet and its head looked like a ceramic jar. 7 As I began to cry and to ask the Lord to deliver me from it, I remembered the word I had heard: "Hermas, do not be double-minded." 8 Then I put on the faith of the Lord and, remembering the wonderful things He had taught me, I faced the beast with courage. Then the beast came on in a rush capable of destroying a city. 9 I approached it and, for all its size, the monster only stretched itself on the ground, without doing anything but sticking out its tongue. In fact, it moved not at all until I had passed by it. 10 There were four colors on the beast's head: black, then the color of fire and blood, then gold, and finally white.

Chapter Twenty-Three
4.2 After I had gone approximately thirty feet past the beast, behold, a young woman met me, clothed like a lady coming from a bridal chamber, all in white and with white sandals, veiled down to the forehead. Her covering was a headband and her hair was white. 2 I knew from former visions that she was the church, and so I became more cheerful. She greeted me saying, "Greetings, my man." My greeting in turn was "Greetings, lady." 3 She responded to me, "Have you met anything?" "Lady," I said to her, "a sort of beast met me, capable of destroying people, but by the power of the Lord and his great mercy I escaped from it." 4 "Yes, indeed," she said, "you escaped because you cast your care on God and opened up your heart to the Lord, believing that you can be saved by nothing except his great and glorious name. Therefore, the Lord has sent his angel who has authority over the beasts, whose name is Thegri. He has shut its mouth, that it may not harm you. By your faith you have escaped a great tribulation, because at the sight of such a great monster you were not double-minded. 5 Depart, therefore, and explain to the Lord's elect his wonders and tell them that this beast is a symbol of the great tribulation that is to come. If you prepare in advance and repent before the Lord with all your heart, you will be able to escape it, provided your hearts become pure and sinless and you serve your Lord blamelessly the rest of the days of your life. Cast your worries on the Lord and he will direct them. 6 Believe in the Lord, you double-minded, because he can do all things and turns aside his wrath from you, while he sends plagues on you who are double-minded. Woe to those who hear these words and disobey! It would be better for them not to have been born."

Chapter Twenty-Four
4.3 I asked her a question about the four colors on the head of the beast. She answered and said, "Are you still curious about these matters?" "Yes, lady," I said. "Explain to me what this means." 2 "Listen," she said. "The black is this world in which you live. 3 The color of fire and blood means that this world must be destroyed by fire and blood. 4 You who flee this world are the gold section. For just as gold is tested by fire and becomes useful, so you also who live in the world are tried in it. So you who remain in it and pass through the flames will be purified. For just as gold casts off its dross, you also will cast off every sorrow and distress, becoming pure and useful for the building of the tower. 5 Finally, the white section is the age to come in which God's elect dwell, for those chosen by God for eternal life will be spotless and pure. 6 Do not stop speaking in the ears of the saints. You have also the foreshadowing of the great tribulation to come. But if you are willing, it will be nothing. Remember what was written before." 7 Having said these things she went away, but I did not see the place where she went, for there was a noise and I turned around in fear, thinking that the beast was coming.

Fifth Vision

Chapter Twenty-Five

5 As I was praying in my house and sitting on my bed, a man of glorious appearance entered. He was dressed like a shepherd, a white skin wrapped around him, with a bag over his shoulders and a staff in his hand. He greeted me and I returned his greeting. 2 Immediately he sat beside me and said, "I have been sent by the most venerable angel to live with you for the rest of your life." 3 Thinking he was here to test me, I said to him, "Who are you? I know to whom I was entrusted." He said, "Do you not recognize me?" "No," I replied. "I am the shepherd to whom you have been entrusted." 4 As he was still talking, his appearance changed and I recognized that he was the one to whom I had been entrusted. I was confused at once and fear took hold of me. I was completely overcome with sorrow for having answered him so wickedly and senselessly. 5 But he answered and said to me, "Do not be confused, but become strong in my commandments I am going to give you. For I was sent," he said, "to show you once more all that you saw before, the most important points that are useful to you. First of all, write down my commandments and parables. Write the rest in the order I will show you. The reason," he said, "why I command you to write first the commandments and parables is that you may have them to read at once and then keep them." 6 So I wrote the commandments and parables as he commanded me. 7 If you hear and keep them and walk in them and fulfill them with a pure heart, you will receive from the Lord everything He promised you. But if you hear them and do not repent, or even increase your sins, you will receive the opposite from the Lord. All these things the shepherd, the angel of repentance, commanded me to write as follows.

First Commandment

Chapter Twenty-Six

1 First of all, believe that God is one, who created all things and set them in order, and that He brought all things from non-existence into being, He who contains all things is himself uncontained. 2 Trust Him, therefore, and fear Him, and in this fear be self-controlled. Observe these things and cast away all wickedness far from you. Clothe yourself with every righteous virtue and you will live to God, if you observe this commandment.

Second Commandment

Chapter Twenty-Seven

2 He said to me, "Hold on to sincerity and be innocent, and you will be as infants who do not know the evil that destroys human life. 2 First of all, do not slander anyone and do not listen gladly to a slanderer. Otherwise, you the listener will share the sin of the slanderer, if you believe the slander you hear. For by believing it you also will hold something against your brother, and so you will be guilty of the sin of the slanderer. 3 Slander is evil; it is a restless demon, never at peace but always living in dissension. Abstain from it and you will always be on good terms with all people. 4 Clothe yourself with reverence in which there is no evil stumbling block, but which is all smooth and joyful. Do what is good and take from the fruit of your labors God's gift, giving generously to all who are in need, not debating about to whom you will and will not give. Give to everyone. God wishes that we give to everyone from His gifts. 5 Those who have received will give an

account to God why they received it and for what purpose. Those who receive in distress will not be judged, but those who receive under false pretenses will face condemnation. 6 Under these circumstances, the giver is innocent. Receiving from the Lord a ministry to perform, he did it with simplicity, without deciding to whom to give and not to give. The ministry, therefore, that is done with sincerity becomes glorious in God's sight. Therefore, the one who thus serves with sincerity will live to God. 7 Keep this commandment as I have spoken to you, so that you and your family may be found to be sincere and pure and innocent and blameless."

Third Commandment

Chapter Twenty-Eight
3 He then spoke to me again, "Love the truth and let nothing but truth come forth from your mouth, so that the spirit that God made to live in your flesh may be found to be true in the sight of all people. The Lord who dwells in you then will be glorified, for the Lord is true in his every word and there is no lie in him. 2 So liars reject the Lord and defraud him, since they do not return the deposit they received from him, a spirit that does not lie. If they return it to him as a liar, they defile the commandment of the Lord and become defrauders." 3 When I heard these things, I wept bitterly. When he saw me weeping, he said, "Why are you weeping?" "Because Lord," I said, "I do not know if I can be saved." "Why?" he said. "Because, Lord," I said, "I have never spoken a true word in my life. I always have lived craftily among everyone and portrayed my lie as the truth in the eyes of all people. At no time have I been contradicted by anyone, but they have trusted my word. How," I said, "can I live, Lord, after having done such things?" 4 "Your intentions are good and true," he said. "It was really your duty, as God's slave, to walk in the truth and not allow an evil conscience to dwell with the Spirit of truth. Neither ought you to cause sorrow to the revered and true Spirit." "Sir," I said, "I have never understood accurately these words." 5 "Well, now you are hearing them," he said. "Guard these things so that even the lies previously uttered in your daily affairs may become trustworthy, now that your present words have been found to be true. It is really possible for even these lies in your daily affairs to become trustworthy. For if you observe what you say and speak nothing but the truth from now on, you will be able to give yourself life. And whoever hears this commandment and avoids the wicked habit of lying will live to God."

Fourth Commandment

Chapter Twenty-Nine
4.1 "I command you," he said, "to guard your holiness. May it not enter your heart to think of someone else's wife, nor about sexual immorality nor any other such matter. If you do, you will commit a great sin. Always keep thinking about your wife and you will not fall into sin. 2 If this desire comes into your heart, you will go wrong and you will commit sin, and if any other wicked desire enters you heart. For a desire of this kind is a serious sin for God's slave and if anyone does such a wicked thing, he will bring death on himself. 3 Be then on your guard and keep away from this desire. Where reverence dwells, there in the heart of a just man lawlessness will not enter." 4 I said to him, "Lord, allow me to ask you a few questions." "Ask them," he said. "Lord," I said, "if a man is married to a wife who believes in the Lord and he discovers her in adultery, does he commit sin if he continues to live with her?" 5 "Before he finds out," he said, "he does not sin. But if her husband knows

about the sin, and she does not repent, but continues in her sexual immorality, he becomes guilty of her sin as long as he lives with her and is a partner in her adultery." 6 "Sir," I said, "what then is he to do, if the wife continues in her immorality?" "He should divorce her," he replied, "and remain single. But if he divorces her and marries another woman, he also commits adultery." 7 "But, Lord," I said, "if after the divorce the wife repents and wishes to return to her husband should he refuse to receive her?" 8 "No, indeed," he said. "If the husband does not receive her back, he sins and he commits a great sin. The sinner who has repented must be received back. But not many times, because there is but one repentance granted for God's slaves. To bring about her repentance, the husband ought not to marry. This is the practice required for a wife and husband. 9 Not only is it adultery," he said, "for a man to defile his flesh, but it is likewise adultery for anyone to act like the Gentiles. So if anyone continues in deeds like this and does not repent, avoid him and do not live with him. Otherwise you also will share in his sin. 10 This is why you were ordered to remain by yourselves, whether husband or wife be guilty, for in such cases repentance is possible. 11 I am not giving an excuse," he said, "that this may be the conclusion of the matter. I am saying that the sinner should sin no more. There is one who can provide healing for his former sin and he has authority over all things."

Chapter Thirty
4.2 Again I asked him saying, "Since the Lord has considered me worthy to have you live with me always, bear with me for a few more words, since I understand nothing at all and my heart has been hardened by my past deeds. Give me understanding, for I am very foolish and understand nothing at all." 2 He answered me and says, "I am in charge of repentance," he said, "and give understanding to all who repent. Do you not think," he said, "that this very act of repentance is itself understanding? Repentance," he said, "is a great understanding. For the man who has sinned then recognizes that he has done evil before the Lord; the deed he committed enters his heart, and he repents, never to commit evil again. Instead, he does good perfectly by humbling his soul and tormenting it, because he has sinned. Do you see now how repentance involves a great understanding?" 3 "Sir," I said, "following are the reasons why I am making accurate enquiries into everything. First, because I am a sinner and then because I do not know what works I must do to live, for my sins are many and various." 4 "You will live," he said, "if you keep my commandments and walk in them. Whoever hears these commandments and keeps them will live to God."

Chapter Thirty-One
4.3 "Sir, may I ask a further question?" I said. "Speak," he said. "Sir," I said, "I have heard from some teachers that there is no other repentance except the one when we went into the water and received forgiveness for our previous sins." 2 He said to me, "You have heard well, for such is the case. For the person who has received forgiveness of sins must no longer sin but live in purity. 3 However, since you are enquiring accurately into everything, I will also show this to you, without giving an excuse either to those who now believe or who are yet to believe in the Lord. For those who now believe or are yet to believe do not have any further repentance for sins, but they do have forgiveness of their former sins. 4 The Lord has provided repentance for those who were called before these days. For the Lord knows hearts and knows all things in advance, the weakness of human beings and the cunning of the Devil, the evil he will do to the slaves of God and his wickedness against them. 5 Therefore, the Lord in his exceeding mercy took pity on his creatures and provided this opportunity for repentance, and authority over this

repentance has been given to me. 6 But this I also say to you," he said. "After that great and holy call, if a man sins after severe temptation by the Devil, he has one repentance. But if he sins and repents repeatedly, it is no benefit for such a man, for only with difficulty will he live." 7 I said to him, "I was restored to life by hearing these things from you so accurately. Now I know that if I do not commit additional sins, I will be saved." "You will be saved," he said, "as well as all those who do these things."

Chapter Thirty-Two
4.4 Again I asked him, "Sir, since you have borne with me once, explain this also to me." "Speak," he said. "Sir," I said, "if a wife or husband should die and either one of them marries, does the one who marries sin?" 2 "There is no sin," he said, "but anyone who remains single brings greater honor for himself and great glory to the Lord. But even if one marries there is no sin. 3 Therefore, maintain your purity and holiness and live for God. Observe what I am telling you and am going to tell you from now on, from the day which you have been entrusted to me, and I will dwell in your house. 4 There will be forgiveness for your former transgressions, if you observe my commandments. There will also be forgiveness for all who observe these commandments and proceed in this purity."

Fifth Commandment

Chapter Thirty-Three
5.1 "Be patient and understanding," he said, "and you will rule over all evil works and do all righteousness. 2 For if you are patient, the Holy Spirit dwelling in you will be pure, not contaminated by any other evil spirit. Dwelling in a broad place, he will rejoice and be glad with the lodging where he finds himself. Thus, he will serve God with great cheerfulness, because he has his peace in himself. 3 However, if violent anger enters, the good spirit who is sensitive is immediately confined, since he does not have a clean habitation. He thus tries to withdraw from the place, for the evil spirit chokes him. He is unable to serve God as he wishes; he is polluted by the violent anger. For the Lord dwells amid patience, but the Devil in anger. 4 Therefore, if both spirits dwell in the same place, it is unprofitable and evil for the person in whom they dwell. 5 If you take a little wormwood and pour it into a jar of honey, is not all the honey spoiled? Even a great quantity of honey is ruined by the smallest amount of wormwood and its sweetness is lost. It is no longer pleasant to the owner because it has been mixed and it is no longer enjoyable. If no wormwood is put into the honey, it turns out to be sweet and becomes useful for the owner. 6 You thus see that patience is very sweet, far more than honey, and useful to the Lord. His dwelling is in patience, but anger is bitter and useless to Him. So if anger is mixed with patience, patience is spoiled and intercession with God is not useful." 7 "Sir, I would like to know how anger works to be on my guard against it," I said. "Yes, indeed," he replied. "If you and your house do not guard against it, you have destroyed all hope. So guard against it, for I will be with you. And all who repent with their whole heart will be protected from it. I will be with them and protect them, for all have been justified by the most holy angel."

Chapter Thirty-Four
5.2 "Hear now," he said, "about the inner working of the angry temper; how it is evil, and how it subverts God's servants by its working, leading them astray from righteousness. Now it does not lead astray those who are full of faith; neither is it able

to work against them, because the power of the Lord is with them, but it leads astray the empty-headed and double-minded. 2 For when it sees such people prospering, it inserts itself into that person's heart and, for no reason at all, the man or woman is embittered over worldly concerns, either about food or something trivial, or some friend, or about giving or receiving, or other such foolish matters. All these things are foolish and vain and senseless and unprofitable for God's servants. 3 But patience is great and sturdy, strong and powerful. It prospers widely; it is cheerful, joyous, carefree, glorifying the Lord at all times; it has no bitterness in itself, but in all circumstances it remains gentle and calm. So this patience dwells with those who hold the faith intact. 4 In the first place, an angry temper is foolish, frivolous, and senseless. Then bitterness arises from foolishness, from bitterness comes wrath, from wrath anger, and from anger rage. Finally, the rage that has in it such evil elements becomes a great and incurable sin. 5 For when all such spirits live in one vessel along with the Holy Spirit, it cannot hold them, but overflows. 6 Then the sensitive spirit that is not used to dwell with an evil one, nor with harshness, departs from a person of this kind and seeks to dwell with gentleness and quietness. 7 Then when he has left, the person in whom he dwelt becomes emptied of the righteous spirit; he is filled with evil spirits afterwards and is disorderly in all his actions, dragged here and there by evil spirits, blind to all good intentions. This is what happens to those given to a sharp temper. 8 Avoid a sharp temper, the most wicked spirit. Put on patience and oppose a temper as well as bitterness, and you will be found on the side of the reverence that is beloved by the Lord. Be sure, therefore, that you do not forget this commandment. For if you master this commandment, you will also be able to keep the other commandments I am about to give you. Be strong and empowered in their observance and may all those who wish to walk in them also be empowered."

Sixth Commandment

Chapter Thirty-Five
6.1 "In the *First Commandment*," he said, "I commanded you to guard faith, fear, and self-control." "Yes, sir," I said. "But now I wish to show also their powers, that you may know their individual power and inner working. Their effects are twofold, appointed for both the just and the unjust. 2 You must trust what is righteous, but distrust unrighteousness. For the righteous way is straight, but wickedness is a crooked path. So walk in the straight way and avoid the crooked way. 3 For the crooked way has no paths. Instead, there is nothing but waste lands and many obstacles; it is rough and full of thorns. So it is harmful to those who walk in it. 4 Those who take the straight way walk smoothly without stumbling, because it is neither rough nor thorny. Therefore, you see that it is better for you to walk in this way." 5 "Sir," I said, "it is on this way that I am pleased to walk." "Go, then," he said, "and anyone who turns to the Lord with a whole heart will also walk in it."

Chapter Thirty-Six
6.2 "Now hear about faith," he said. "There are two angels with man, one of righteousness and the other of wickedness." 2 "But how will I know their workings," I said, "because both angels are living with me?" 3 "Listen," he said, "and you will understand them. The angel of righteousness is sensitive and modest and gentle and calm. When this angel comes into your heart, he will immediately speak with you about righteousness, purity, holiness, self-control, every righteous work and glorious virtue. When all these thoughts enter your

heart, know that the angel of righteousness is with you. These are the deeds of the angel of righteousness. Believe him, therefore, and his deeds. 4 Now observe the deeds of the angel of wickedness. First of all, he is of a violent temper, bitter, and senseless, and his deeds are evil, overthrowing God's servants. Therefore, whenever this one enters your heart, recognize him from his deeds." 5 "Sir, I do not know how I will recognize him," I said. "Listen," he said. "When violent anger comes over you, or bitterness, know that he is in you. Then there arises the longing for excessive activities, extravagant things to eat and drink, numerous feasts, unnecessary luxuries, the desire for women, covetousness, arrogance, boasting, and a host of related excesses. Therefore, whenever these things arise in your heart know that the angel of wickedness is with you. 6 Therefore, since you know his deeds, depart from him and put no trust in him, because his deeds are wicked and harmful to God's servants. So here you have the workings of both angels. Recognize them and trust the angel of righteousness. 7 Stay away from the angel of wickedness, because his teaching is evil in every respect. For even if a person is faithful and the desire of this angel arises in his heart, that man or woman will inevitably commit some sin. 8 But again if a man or woman is very evil, when the deeds of the angel of righteousness enters his heart, they must necessarily do a good deed. 9 So you see," he said, "that it is good to follow the angel of righteousness and turn away from the angel of wickedness. 10 This commandment reveals the things about faith, that you may believe the deeds of the angel of righteousness and live to God by doing them. Believe that the deeds of the angel of wickedness are dangerous so if you do not do them, you will live to God."

Seventh Commandment

Chapter Thirty-Seven
7 "Fear the Lord and keep His commandments," he said. "Therefore, by keeping God's commandments you will be powerful in every deed, and your activity will be beyond criticism. Fear the Lord, then, and you will do all things well. This is the fear you must have to be saved. 2 But do not fear the Devil. By fearing the Lord you will rule over the Devil, for there is no power in him. Because there can be no fear of him in whom there is no power, but of him whose might is glorious there must be fear. For everyone who has power inspires fear, but the one who has no power is despised by everyone. 3 But fear the deeds of the Devil, because they are evil. If you fear the Lord you will fear the Devil's deeds. Do not do them but keep away from them. 4 Therefore, there are two kinds of fear. If you desire to do evil, fear the Lord and you will not do it. But if you wish to do good, fear the Lord and you will do it. So the fear of the Lord is powerful, mighty, and glorious. Fear the Lord, therefore, and live for him. All those who fear him and keep his commandments will live to God." 5 "Sir," I said, "why do you say about those who observe his commandments, 'They will live to God'?" "Because," he said, "all creation fears the Lord, but not all creation keeps his commandments. But life with God is for those who both fear him and keep his commandments, but there is no life in him for those who fail to keep his commandments."

Eighth Commandment

Chapter Thirty-Eight
8 "I have told you," he said, "that God's creations are twofold. Self-control also is twofold. For we have to restrain ourselves in some things and in others we do not." 2 "Inform me, sir," I said, "from what we should restrain ourselves and from what we should not."

THE SHEPHERD OF HERMAS

"Listen," he said. "Restrain yourself from evil and do not do it; from good, however, do not restrain yourself, but do it. For if you restrain yourself and keep from doing good, you commit a serious sin, but if you restrain yourself and abstain from doing evil, you perform a great act of righteousness. Therefore, refrain from all evil by doing good." 3 "What sorts of evil, sir," I said, "must we refrain from doing?" "Listen," he said. "From adultery and fornication, from lawless drunkenness, from wicked luxury, from excessive foods and extravagant wealth, boastfulness, pride, lying, slander, and hypocrisy, malice, and all blasphemy. 4 These deeds are the worst of all in the life of all human beings. From such deeds a servant of God must then restrain himself. The person who does not cannot live to God. Hear now about the consequences of such deeds." 5 "Sir," I said, "are there still other wicked deeds?" "Yes indeed, many that the servant of God must refrain from: theft, lying, fraud, false witness, covetousness, lust, deceit, vanity, arrogance, and such things like these. 6 Do you think such sins are very wicked indeed for servants of God?" he said. "A servant of God should refrain from all these excesses. Restrain from all of these that you may live to God and that you may be enrolled with those who refrain themselves from them. So these are the areas in which you should exercise self-control. 7 Listen now to what you should not refrain from," he said, "and what you ought to do. Do not refrain from the good, but do it." 8 "Sir, show me also the power of the good things," I said, "that I may proceed in them, and serve them, and by doing them I may be saved." "I will also tell you," he answered, "the deeds of the good that you are to do and from which you are not to hold back," he said. 9 "The first things are faith, fear of the Lord, love, harmony, righteous speech, truth, and endurance. There is nothing superior to these in human life. If a person observes these virtues and does not hold back from them, he will be blessed in his life. 10 Listen also to what follows from these: helping widows, visiting orphans and the poor, ransoming God's servants from their difficulties, showing hospitality (for benevolence occasionally is found in hospitality), not opposing anyone, being kind, being lower than all men, honoring the elderly, practicing righteousness, protecting the brotherhood, enduring insult, being patient, abstaining from grudges, comforting those who are weary, not rejecting those who have stumbled in the faith but winning them back and encouraging them, admonishing sinners, not oppressing debtors in their needs—all this and similar things. 11 Do you not think these things are good?" "Sir, there is nothing better than such deeds," I said. "Walk in them, therefore, and do not refrain from them," he said, "and you will live to God. 12 Observe this commandment: If you do good and not refrain from it, you will live to God, just as all those will live to God who do likewise. So also you will live to God, if you avoid doing evil and refrain from it. Whoever observes these commandments and walks in them will also live to God."

Ninth Commandment

Chapter Thirty-Nine
9 He said to me, "Cast off your double-mindedness and do not be of two minds when you ask anything from God. Do not say 'How can I ask and receive anything from the Lord after committing so many sins?' 2 Do not entertain such thoughts, but with your whole heart turn to the Lord and ask him without doubting. You will know his great compassion, for he will not forsake you, but will fulfill the request of your soul. 3 God is not like people who hold a grudge. He is without malice and shows compassion to His creation. 4 Cleanse your heart, therefore, from all the vanities of this age and of the vices mentioned above. Then ask of the Lord and you will receive all things. You cannot

fail to receive all you have requested, provided you ask the Lord without doubting. 5 However, if you doubt in your heart, you will not receive any of your requests. Those who doubt are of two minds before God and fail to receive any of their requests. 6 But those who are mature in the faith ask everything with reliance on the Lord and they receive, because they ask without doubting and being of two minds. Every double-minded person, if he does not repent, will be saved with difficulty. 7 Therefore, cleanse your heart of double-mindedness and clothe yourself with faith, because it is strong, and trust in God, confident that you will receive every request you have made. Now, having made it, if you did not receive your request, do not doubt because you did not receive your soul's request quickly. You probably received your request slowly because of some temptation or transgression of which you are not aware. 8 Therefore, do not cease that request of your soul. But if in your request you grow faint and doubt, blame yourself and not the one who gives. 9 Be on the alert against this double-mindedness, for it is evil and senseless and uproots many from the faith, even those strong in faith. For a divided mind is the daughter of the Devil and is exceedingly wicked for the servants of God. 10 Therefore, despise this double-mindedness and get the mastery over it in everything by clothing yourself with strong and powerful faith. For faith promises all things and perfects all things, but a divided mind without confidence in itself fails in everything it does. 11 You see, then," he said, "that faith comes from above from the Lord, and its power is great, whereas a divided mind is an earthly spirit from the Devil, not having any power. 12 Serve, therefore, the faith that has power and stay away from double-mindedness that lacks power, and you will live to God as well as all who think these things."

Tenth Commandment

Chapter Forty
10 "Remove sorrow from yourself" he said, "for it is the sister of both double-mindedness and an angry attitude." 2 "Sir," I asked, "how is it the sister of both? An angry attitude appears to me to be one thing, but double-mindedness something else and sorrow still different." "You are a foolish man," he said. "Do you not understand that sorrow is the worst evil of all the spirits and is very bad for God's servants? It destroys man more than all the spirits and crushes the Holy Spirit, and then again saves it?" 3 "I am a fool, sir," I said, "and I do not understand these parables. For how it can both destroy and save again? I do not understand this." 4 "Listen," he said. "Those who have never searched for truth nor inquired about God, but have simply believed, and have been involved in daily affairs and wealth and pagan associations and other concerns of this world, those who are involved in these things do not understand the parables about God because they are darkened by these things and are ruined and become barren. 5 Just as good vineyards unattended are made barren by thorns and weeds of different kinds when they are ignored, so people who have believed and then fall into these many diversions mentioned above lose their senses and do not understand anything at all about righteousness. For whenever they hear about God and the truth, their mind is distracted with their own affairs, and they perceive nothing at all. 6 But those who fear God and search for him and his truth and direct their hearts to the Lord learn it quickly and understand everything said to them, because they have the fear of the Lord in themselves. For where the Lord dwells, there also is great understanding. Therefore, cling to the Lord and you will understand and perceive all things."

Chapter Forty-One

10.2 "Listen, foolish one," he said, "to how sorrow crushes the Holy Spirit and then saves again. 2 Whenever a double-minded person engages in some effort and fails at it because of his double-mindedness, sorrow enters the man and grieves the Holy Spirit and crushes him. 3 Then again, when an angry attitude takes hold of a person over some issue and he becomes embittered, sorrow again enters the heart of the angry one, he is grieved by what he has done, and he repents because he has done evil. 4 This sorrow, therefore, appears to bring salvation, because he repented after having done the evil. Both actions grieve the Spirit, the double-mindedness, because it did not succeed in its effort, and the angry temper grieves the Spirit, because it did what is evil. Both are a cause for sorrow to the Holy Spirit, double-mindedness and an angry temper. 5 Therefore, remove sorrow from yourself and do not crush the Holy Spirit who lives in you, lest he intercede with God against you and then leave you. 6 For the Spirit of God who was given in this flesh endures neither sorrow nor distress."

Chapter Forty-Two

10.3 "Be clothed, therefore, with the cheerfulness that always finds favor with God and is acceptable to him, and then delight in it. Every cheerful person does good things and thinks good things and rejects sorrow. 2 But the sorrowful person always does evil. First, he does evil because he grieves the cheerful Holy Spirit, who has been given to man. Second, by grieving the Holy Spirit he behaves lawlessly because he neither prays nor confesses to God. For the intercession of a grieving man never has power to ascend to the altar before God." 3 "Why," I asked, "does the appeal of a grieving one not ascend to His altar?" "Because," he replied, "sorrow has sunk deep in his heart. When that sorrow is mixed with his appeal, it does not permit the appeal to ascend in holiness on the altar. For just as vinegar mixed together with wine does not taste pleasant, so also sorrow mixed with the Holy Spirit does not produce the same petition. 4 Therefore cleanse yourself from this evil sorrow, and you will live to God. All will certainly live to God who cast sorrow away and clothe themselves with all cheerfulness."

Chapter Forty-Three

11 He pointed out to me some men sitting on a bench and another man sitting on a chair. "Do you see the men sitting on the bench?" he said to me. "Yes, sir," I replied. "These men are believers," he said, "and the man sitting on the chair is a false prophet who destroys the understanding of God's servants. However, he corrupts the understanding of the double-minded, not of the believers. 2 These double-minded, therefore, come to him as a soothsayer and ask him about their future. That false prophet, without having in himself any power from a Divine Spirit, then speaks with them about their questions, in accordance with their evil desires, and fills their souls just as they wish. 3 Being empty, he gives empty answers to those who are empty. For whatever he is asked, his answer is directed to the emptiness of the person. However, some of the words he utters are true. For the Devil fills him with his own spirit, to see whether he can break down the righteous. 4 Therefore those who are strong in the faith of the Lord are clothed with truth and do not cling to such spirits but keep at a distance from them. But those who are double-minded repent frequently, consult soothsayers like the Gentiles, and bring a greater sin upon themselves by their idolatry. For the person who consults a false prophet about some matter is an idolater, empty of the truth and foolish. 5 For no spirit given by God has to be consulted, but speaks everything with the Godhead's power,

because it comes from above, from the power of the Divine Spirit. 6 But the spirit that is consulted and speaks according to the desires of men is earthly and fickle, without any power, and it does not speak at all, unless it is consulted." 7 "How, sir," I said, "is a man to know which of these is a prophet and which is a false prophet?" "Hear about both prophets," he said. "With what I am going to tell you, you can test the true and the false prophet. Test the man who has the Divine Spirit according to his life. 8 First, the man who has the Spirit from above is gentle and calm and humble. He abstains from all wickedness and the vain desires of this age, and considers that he is more lowly than all men. He does not give answers to questions either, nor does he speak by himself. Neither does the Holy Spirit speak when a man wishes him to speak, but he speaks when God wishes him to speak. 9 When a man who has the Divine Spirit enters a congregation of righteous men who have faith in God's spirit, and a petition is addressed to God by such a congregation, at that moment the angel of the prophetic spirit, who is assigned to this man, fills him and in the fullness of the Holy Spirit he speaks to the gathering as the Lord wishes. 10 In this way, therefore, the Divine Spirit will be made clear. This is the power of the Lord's divine spirit." 11 "Hear now," he said, "about the earthly spirit, that is empty and powerless and also foolish. 12 First, the person who appears to have this spirit exalts himself and wishes to have the seat of honor. Immediately he is impetuous and impudent and indulges in excess luxuries and in many other deceptions. He also receives payment for his prophecy and makes no prophecy unless he receives it. Can the Divine Spirit receive money for prophesying? It is impossible for a prophet of God to do this, but the spirit of such prophets is earthly. 13 Moreover, it does not approach gatherings of righteous men at all but avoids them. It clings to the men who are double-minded and to the empty, making prophecies to them in a corner, deceiving them by talking in accordance with their own desires, all in an empty manner, for their answers are empty. For the empty vessel placed with other empty vessels does not break, but they match one another. 14 But when he comes to a congregation filled with righteous men who have the Divine Spirit, such a man is emptied after their prayer of petition, the earthly spirit in fear departs from him and he is unable to speak and completely shattered, without saying a thing. 15 For, if you store wine and oil in a cellar and place an empty jar among the rest, when you wish to clear out the cellar, you will find the one you placed there still empty. In the same way, also, are the empty prophets. After entering the souls of righteous men, they are found to be exactly the same as when they entered. 16 The life of the two kinds of prophets has just been given to you. Test, then, by life and actions the man who says he is inspired. 17 Trust in the Spirit who comes from God and has power, but put no faith in the earthly and empty spirit, because there is no power in him; he comes from the Devil. 18 Hear, therefore, the parable I am going to tell you. Pick up a stone and throw it into the sky and see whether you can hit it. Or take a syringe full of water and squirt it up to the sky and see whether you can put a hole in it." "Sir," I said, "how can this be done? According to you, both of these actions are impossible." 19 "Just as these actions are impossible," he said, "so also are the earthly spirits powerless and weak. 20 Consider now the power that comes from above. A hailstone is the smallest of pebbles, but when it falls on a man's head, it causes considerable pain. Or consider a drop of fluid falling from a roof onto the ground and wears through a rock. 21 Therefore, see that the smallest objects falling from above have great power. So also the Divine Spirit that comes from above is powerful. Trust, therefore, in this Spirit, and keep away from the other."

Chapter Forty-Four

12.1 He said to me, "Remove every evil desire and clothe yourself with a good and reverent desire. For if you are clothed with this good desire, you will hate the evil desire and control it as you please. 2 For evil desire is fierce and is difficult to tame. It is fearsome in its wildness and exhausts people. In particular, if a servant of God falls into it out of ignorance, it dreadfully exhausts him. But it destroys those who are not clothed with good desire and are entangled with this world. Such people it hands over to death." 3 "Sir," I said, "what are the works of evil desire which hand a person over to death? Tell me, so I may avoid them." "Hear," he said, "about the deeds used by evil desire that brings death to the servants of God."

Chapter Forty-Five

12.2 "First of all is the desire for another man's wife or another wife's husband, or the desire for abundant wealth, for many extravagant foods and drinks, and for many other foolish luxuries. For every luxury is foolish and empty for the servants of God. 2 Such desires, then, are evil and bring death to the servants of God. This kind of evil desire is the daughter of the Devil. Therefore, one must abstain from evil desires and by this live to God. 3 Those who are dominated by them and do not resist finally die, since these desires are deadly. 4 Be clothed with the desire of righteousness and armed with the fear of the Lord and resist them. For fear of the Lord dwells in good desire. If evil desire sees you armed with the fear of God and resisting, it will flee far away and you will not see it, because it fears your weapons. 5 So after receiving the crown for your victory against it, come to the desire for righteousness and deliver it to the victory you have won. Serve the wishes of righteousness. If you serve and submit to a good desire, you will be able to overcome the evil desire and dominate it as you wish."

Chapter Forty-Six

12.3 "Sir," I said, "I want to know in what ways I should serve the good desire." "I will tell you," he said. "Practice righteousness and virtue, truthfulness and fear of the Lord, faith and gentleness and all similar good acts. By doing this you will be an acceptable servant of God and will live to Him. So all who are servants to good desire will live to God." 2 With this he completed the twelve commandments. He then said to me, "These are the commandments. Walk in them and encourage those who hear you, that their repentance may be pure for the remaining days of their life. 3 Fulfill diligently the ministry I have given you and work hard. You will find grace with those who are going to repent and they will be persuaded by your words. For I will be with you and will persuade them to obey you."

4 I said to him, "Sir, these commandments are great, good and glorious, and will gladden the heart of the one who is able to observe them. But I do not know whether these commandments can be kept by men, because they are so hard." 5 He answered me, "If you yourself are persuaded that they can be observed, you will do so easily and they will not be difficult, but if you have decided in your heart that they cannot be observed, you will not observe them. 6 But now I tell you: if you do not observe them but neglect them, neither you nor your children nor your house will be saved, since you yourself have already determined the impossibility for a human being to observe these commandments."

Chapter Forty-Seven

12.4 He said this with such great anger that I was confounded and very afraid of him. His appearance had so changed that no human being could stand up against his anger. 2 On seeing my utter distress and confusion, he began speaking to me more gently and cheerfully and he says, "Foolish man, senseless and double-minded! You do not realize how great and strong and marvelous is God's glory. It was for man that he created the world and it is to man that he has subjected all his creation, giving him the mastery over everything under the sky. 3 Now if man," he said, "is the master of all God's creation and has mastery of everything, certainly he can master these commandments. The man who has the Lord in his heart can master all things and all these commandments. 4 But those who have the Lord on their lips, while their heart is hardened, who are in fact far from the Lord, for them these commandments are difficult and hard to fulfill. 5 Put the Lord in your hearts, therefore, you who are empty and fickle in the faith. You will then know that nothing is easier or sweeter or more gentle than these commandments. 6 You who walk in the commandments of the Devil, commandments that are hard and bitter and cruel and licentious, be converted and do not fear the Devil, because he has no power over you. 7 I, the Angel of Repentance, who have overcome the Devil, will be with you. The Devil only causes fear, but his fear is of no force. Therefore, do not fear him and he will flee from you."

Chapter Forty-Eight

12.5 I said to him: "Sir, let me say a few words." "Say what you wish," he answered. "Sir," I said, "man is eager to keep God's commandments and there is not one who does not ask from the Lord to be strengthened by his commandments and to submit to them. But the Devil is harsh and overpowers them." 2 "The Devil" he said, "cannot overpower those who are servants of God with their whole heart and who hope in him. The Devil can wrestle with them but he is not able to defeat them. So if you resist him, he will flee from you in defeat and confusion. But empty men," he said, "fear him as if he had power. 3 When a man fills a large number of jars with good wine and among these jars there are a few that are partly empty, he does not pay attention to the full ones when he comes to his wine jugs, because he knows that they are full. But he is concerned lest the empty ones have turned sour, because empty jars quickly turn sour and the wine's good taste is destroyed. 4 In the same way the Devil comes and tempts all the servants of God. Those who are strong in the faith resist him and he departs from them, because he cannot find an entrance. So he then goes to the partly empty and, finding an entrance, he enters into them. Thus he accomplishes in them whatever he pleases and makes them his slaves."

Chapter Forty-Nine

12.6 "I, the Angel of Repentance, am telling you: Do not fear the Devil. For I have been sent," he said, "to be on the side of you who repent with your whole heart, and to strengthen you in the faith. 2 Believe in God, you who despair of your life because of your sins, you who add to your sins and make your life so burdensome. Trust that if you turn to the Lord with your whole heart and do righteousness for the rest of your life, serving him uprightly according to his will, he will provide a remedy for your previous failures and you will receive the power of mastering the Devil's snares. Do not be at all afraid of the Devil's threats, for they are as powerless as a dead man's tendons. 3 Hear this: fear him who has the power to save and to destroy. Observe all the commandments and you will live to God." 4 I said to him, "Sir, I have now been strengthened by all the upright demands of the Lord, because you are on my side. I know that you will break down all the Devil's power and we will have mastery over him and overcome all his works. Sir, I now hope, with the Lord's help, to observe these commandments you have given." 5 "You will observe them," he said, "if your heart is pure before the Lord. All those who also purify their hearts from the vain desires of this age will observe them and will live to God."

First Parable

Chapter Fifty
1 He said to me, "You know that you are God's slaves living in a foreign land, for your own city is a long distance from this one. Now, if you know your own city in which you live, why do you prepare fields here with expensive furnishings, buildings, and useless dwellings? 2 The person who secures such things in this city does not think of returning to his own city. 3 Foolish, double-minded and miserable person, do you not realize that these things are foreign to you and belong to somebody else and are in the control of another? For the ruler of this city will say, 'I do not want you to live in my city. Go out from it, for you do not live by my laws.' 4 So if you have fields, dwellings, and other property, what will you do with your field, your house and the rest of your belongings if you are thrown out by him? The ruler of this country will tell you justly, 'Either live according to my laws or leave my country.' 5 What are you going to do since you are subject to the law from your own city? For the sake of your fields what are you going to do with the rest of your belongings? Renounce your own law and follow the law of this city? Be careful because it may be against your interests to renounce your law. You may not be received if you wish to return to your city, because you have renounced the law of your own city and it will be closed to you. 6 Therefore, take care while living in a foreign land not to acquire more than what is needed. Be prepared, so that when the ruler of this city wishes to banish you for resisting his law, you can leave his city and enter your own and gladly without mistreatment observe your own law. 7 Be on your guard, you who serve the Lord and have Him in your heart. Remember the commandments of God and the promises he made and do his works. Be confident that he will fulfill his promises if his commandments are obeyed. Instead of fields, purchase souls who are afflicted, according to your ability. Take care of widows and orphans and do not neglect them. Spend your wealth and all your belongings that you have received from God on this kind of fields and houses. 9 This is why the Master made you rich, that you may carry out these ministries for him. It is far better to buy such lands and goods and houses, for you will find them when you return to your own city. 10 Such extravagance is good and makes one glad. It shows no sorrow and fear but is full of joy. Do not participate in the excesses of the Gentiles. They are of no profit for the slaves of God. 11 Instead, be involved in your own extravagance which can bring you joy. Do not counterfeit or touch what belongs to another or desire it. For it is evil to desire another person's goods. Rather do your own work and you will be saved."

Second Parable

Chapter Fifty-One
2 When I was walking in the country and considering an elm tree and a vine and reflecting on them and their fruits, the shepherd appeared and said to me, "What are you thinking about?" "I am thinking, sir," I said, "about the elm and the vine, that they are very well

suited to one another." 2 "These two trees," he said, "are intended as a symbol of God's slaves." "If only I could know what these trees you mention symbolize," I said. "You have the elm tree and the vine before your eyes?" he said. "Yes, sir," I answered. 3 "This vine," he said, "bears fruit, but the elm tree does not. However, this vine cannot bear fruit, unless it climbs up the elm. Otherwise, it spreads all over the ground. If it does bear fruit, it is rotten, because it has not been hanging from the elm. When the vine becomes attached to the elm, it bears fruit both from itself and from the elm. 4 So, you see that the elm yields fruit, not any less than the vine. It actually bears more." "How does it bear more, sir?" I said. "Because," he said, "the vine hanging on the elm yields abundant and healthy fruit, but if it is spread on the ground, it bears rotten fruit and little at that. This parable, then, applies to all the slaves of God, both to the poor as well as the rich." 5 "Lord," I said, "how is this the parable of the rich and the poor man? Let me know." "I will tell you," he answered. "The rich man has great riches, but as far as the Lord is concerned he is poor, because he is distracted by his wealth. His confession and his prayer to the Lord are quite limited. That which he does is small and weak and has no power from above. So when a rich man approaches a poor man and helps him with his needs, he has the assurance that what he does for the poor man will secure a reward from God, because the poor man is rich in his prayer to God and also in his confession. Therefore, the rich man does not hesitate to supply the poor man with everything. 6 On the other hand, the poor man who is helped by the rich man intercedes for him and gives thanks to God for his benefactor. And the latter is constantly concerned for the poor man, that he may not go lacking throughout his life. He knows that the poor man's intercession is acceptable and rich in God's sight. 7 Both fulfill their function as follows. The poor man intercedes—these are his riches—and gives them back to the Lord who supplied him. In the same way the rich man without hesitation provides the riches he received from the Lord for the poor. This is a great and acceptable work in the sight of God. He has wisdom with his riches, and out of the gifts of the Lord he works on the poor man's behalf and correctly fulfills the Lord's ministry. 8 From a human point of view the elm tree does not appear to bear fruit. But they do not know nor understand that in a drought the elm tree holds water and provides it to the vine. So the vine with an unceasing supply of water yields twice the amount of fruit, both for itself and also for the elm tree. So also the poor man who directs his prayer for the rich to the Lord completes their riches, while the rich ones, by supplying the needs of the poor, make up for what lacks in their souls. 9 Both of them in this way become partners in a righteous work. By doing this, you will not be abandoned by God, but will be recorded in the books of the living. 10 Blessed are those who possess this type of riches and understand that true riches are from the Lord. Those who understand this will also be able to do some good work."

Third Parable

Chapter Fifty-Two
3 He showed me many trees without leaves which all appeared withered to me. He said, "Do you see these trees?" "Yes, Lord," I replied, "I do. They are all withered and are alike." He answered, "These trees you see are the people living in this age." 2 "Why then" I said, "are they withered and are all alike?" "Because," he said, "in this age neither the upright nor sinners are distinguishable but they are both alike. For this age is winter for the righteous, and they do not stand out while they live with the sinners. 3 For just as in winter trees that have shed their leaves look alike and do not look dry as they are. Living so in this age neither the righteous nor the sinners can be distinguished, but all are alike."

Fourth Parable

Chapter Fifty-Three

4 Again he showed me a number of trees, some in bloom and some withered. He then said to me, "Do you see these trees?" "Yes, Lord," I said. "I see some that are blooming and some that are withered." 2 "Those that are blooming," he said, "are the righteous who are about to live in the age to come. For the age to come is summer for the righteous but is winter for sinners. When the Lord's mercy shines forth, then will God's slaves stand out, so all will recognize them. 3 Just as in summer the fruits of every single tree are evident and we know what they are, so will the fruits of the righteous be recognized, and it will be known that all are blossoming in that age. 4 Gentiles and sinners, the dry trees you saw, will be found to be withered and fruitless in that age. They will be burned as firewood and will be shown for what they are, because their deeds in their lifetime were wicked. The sinners will be burned because they sinned without repenting, but the Gentiles will be burned because they did not know their Creator. 5 Be fruitful, therefore, so that your fruit will be recognized in that summer. Avoid excessive types of business activities and you will not sin at all. For those who are engaged in multiple businesses also sin much, because they are distracted by their affairs and fail to serve their Lord. 6 How then" he said, "can such a person ask and receive anything from the Lord without serving as the Lord's slave? His slaves are those who will receive, but those who do not serve the Lord will receive nothing. 7 However, if a person is occupied with only one type of business, he can also serve the Lord. For his thoughts will not be corrupted and turned aside from the Lord. He will still serve Him by keeping his thoughts pure. 8 By doing this you can bear fruit in the age to come. So whoever does these things will bear fruit."

Fifth Parable

Chapter Fifty-Four

5 While I was fasting and sitting on a mountain and giving thanks to the Lord for all he had done for me, I saw the shepherd seated beside me and saying to me, "Why did you come here so early?" "Because I have a station, sir," I said. 2 "What is a station?" he said. "I am keeping a fast, sir," I said. "What is this fast you are keeping?" he said. "I fast, sir, just as I am accustomed," I said. 3 "You do not know how to fast to God," he said. "And this useless fast you are keeping for him is not a fast, either." "Why do you say this, sir?" I said. "I am saying that this is not a fast, as you think it is," he said. "I shall teach you what is a complete and acceptable fast to the Lord. Listen," he said. 4 "God does not wish vain fasting of this kind. When you fast thus for God's sake, you accomplish nothing for righteousness. Here is the fast you must keep for God. 5 Do not commit any wicked deed in your life and serve the Lord with a pure heart. Keep His commandments by walking according to his ordinances and do not let any evil desire enter your heart and believe in God. If you do this and fear him and refrain from every evil deed, you will live to God. And by doing this you will complete a fast that is great and acceptable to God."

Chapter Fifty-Five

5.2 "Hear the parable I am about to tell you related to fasting. 2 A man had a field and many slaves, and in a part of the field he planted a vineyard. Then he chose a dependable, respected, and honest slave, called him and said, 'Take this vineyard I planted and fence it in till I come, but do not do anything else to the vineyard. Obey this command and you will be free from me.' Then the owner of that slave went off on a journey. 3 When he had gone, the slave took the vineyard and fenced it in. After finishing it, he saw that the vineyard was full of weeds. 4 He thought to himself saying, 'I have done what my master commanded. I will cultivate the rest of the vineyard; it will look better after being dug. Without weeds it will yield more fruit, since the fruit will not be choked with weeds.' So he went and dug the vineyard and dug up all the weeds that were in it. Then the vineyard was very attractive and flourishing, without any weeds choking it. 5 After a while the master of the slave and of the field returned to his vineyard. When he saw that the vineyard had been fenced in properly and beyond this had been dug and cleared of weeds and that the vines were flourishing, he greatly rejoiced over the work of his slave. 6 So he called his beloved son who was his heir and his friends who were his advisors and told them what he had commanded his slave to do and what he found. They also were glad at the master's testimony about his slave. 7 He said to them, 'I promised freedom to this slave if he observed the order I gave him. He has kept my order and to my great pleasure, he also has done a good work in the vineyards. 8 Therefore, as a reward for this work he has done, I want to make him joint heir with my son, because when the good idea arose, he did not neglect it but did it.' With this the son of the master agreed that the slave should be a joint heir with him. 9 A few days later his master gave a banquet and sent him many items of food from the feast. The slave, however, took from the foods sent to him by his master only what was enough for himself and distributed the remainder to his fellow slaves. 10 Then the fellow slaves, in their joy at receiving the food, began praying for him to find even greater favor with his master, because he treated them so well. 11 When his master heard this, he once more was very pleased with his conduct. So once more he called together his friends and his son and reported to them what he had done with the food he had received. Those called together heartily approved that he should be made a joint heir with the son."

Chapter Fifty-Six
5.3 I said, "Sir, I do not understand these parables and cannot comprehend them, unless you interpret them to me." 2 "I will interpret everything to you," he said, "and everything I tell you I will make clear to you. Observe the commandments of the Lord and you will be acceptable to him. You will be enrolled in the number of those who keep His commandments. 3 But if you do some good over and above God's commandment, you will acquire the greater glory and will be held in much greater honor in the sight of God, with whom you are bound to be. Therefore, if you also perform these additional services, while keeping God's commandments, you will have joy, provided you keep them in accordance with my commandment." 4 I said to him, "Sir, whatever you command me I will observe, for I know that you are with me." "I will be with you, because you are zealous for doing good," he said. "I will be with you all who show the same zeal. 5 This fasting, which consists in the observance of the commandments of the Lord," he said, "is very good. This is how to observe the fast you intend to keep. 6 First, guard against every wicked word and every evil desire, and purify your heart from all the vanities of this age. If you observe these things, your fast will be complete. 7 You will do this: after doing what is written, on the day of your fast do not taste anything except bread and water. Add up the total cost for the food you eat on the day on which you desired to fast and give it to a widow or an orphan or someone in need. In this way you will become humble in soul, so that the one who receives because of your humility may satisfy his own soul and pray to the Lord for you. 8 If you fulfill your fast in the way I have just commanded, your sacrifice will be acceptable in the sight of God and this fast will be accounted as in your

favor, a service performed in this way is beautiful and joyous and acceptable before the Lord. 9 Keep these things thus with your children and your entire household. In keeping them you will be blessed, and all those who hear and keep them will also be blessed and will receive whatever they ask from the Lord."

Chapter Fifty-Seven

5.4 I urgently asked him to explain to me the parable of the field and the master and the vineyard and the slave who fenced in the vineyard and the fences and the weeds pulled out of the vineyard and the son and the friends who were advisors. For I understood that all these things were a parable. 2 He answered and said to me, "You are very arrogant in your questions. You do not have to ask anything at all, for if there is need of explanation, it will be given to you." I said to him, "Sir, if you do not explain what you show me, there is no use in my seeing it, since I do not understand what it means. Every time you tell me parables, without explaining them, I will be hearing for no purpose." 3 He answered me again and said, "Whoever is God's slave and has his Lord in his heart asks for understanding and he receives it. He interprets every parable and the words of the Lord told him in parables become known to him. But the weak and sluggish in prayer hesitate to ask the Lord. 4 But the Lord is abundant in his mercies and unceasingly gives to those who ask from him. Why do you not ask and receive understanding from the Lord? You have been strengthened by the holy angel, you have received such intercessions and you are not sluggish. So ask from the Lord and you will receive understanding." 5 I said to him, "Sir, I have you with me, I must ask and inquire of you, for you are showing me everything and now you are speaking with me. If I had seen and heard this without you, I would have asked the Lord to explain it to me."

Chapter Fifty-Eight

5.5 "I have told you just now," he said, "that you are crafty and obstinate in asking the interpretations of the parables. Since you are so stubborn, I shall interpret for you the parable of the field and all the rest that follows, so you can make them known to everyone. Now listen," he said, "and understand these things. 2 The field is this world. The lord of the field is the one who has created all things, and fitted things together, and given them power. The son is the Holy Spirit, and the slave is the Son of God, while the vines are the people he planted. 3 The fences are the holy angels of the Lord who keep His people. The weeds plucked from the vineyard are the transgressions of God's servants. The foods he sent from the feast are the commandments he gave to his people through his Son. The friends and advisers are the holy angels who were his first creation, and the departure of the master for a foreign land is the time left before his coming." 4 I said to him, "Sir, all this is marvelous and great and glorious. Really," I said, "I could not have understood these things. There is not another person, no matter how intelligent he is, able to understand them. Again, sir, explain what I am going to ask you," I said. "Ask whatever you wish," he said. "Why sir," I asked, "is the Son of God presented in the form of a slave in the parable?"

Chapter Fifty-Nine

5.6 "Listen," he said. "The Son of God is not presented in the form of a slave but is presented with great power and majesty." "How is that, sir?" I said. "I do not understand." 2 "Because," he said, "God planted the vineyard, that is he created he people and gave them over to his Son. The Son appointed the angels to watch over them. He himself cleansed many sins away by undergoing innumerable toils and labors, for nobody can dig a vineyard without toil and labor. 3 When he cleansed sins of the people, he showed them the paths of life and gave them the law which he received from his Father. 4 You see," he said, "that he himself is Lord of his people, receiving all power from his Father. Now, hear why the Lord took his Son and the glorious angels as advisors concerning the slave's inheritance. 5 The pre-existent Holy Spirit, the one who created all creation, God caused to dwell in the flesh of his choice. This flesh, then, in which the Holy Spirit lived, served beautifully the Spirit, and walked in holiness and purity, not defiling the Spirit in any way. 6 Therefore, because the flesh lived with strength and courage it was guided with beauty and purity by the Spirit and shared his toil and labor in everything. He associated it with the Holy Spirit, for the career of this flesh pleased the Lord because it had not been defiled while possessing the Spirit on earth. 7 Therefore, he took the Son and the glorious angels as advisors, in order that the flesh might have some place to live having served the Spirit and not appear to have lost the reward of its service. For all flesh in which the Holy Spirit has dwelt has been found undefiled and spotless will receive a reward. 8 Here you have the interpretation of this parable."

Chapter Sixty
5.7 "I am glad, sir," I said, "to hear this interpretation." "Hear now," he said. "Preserve this flesh of yours as clean and undefiled, in order that the indwelling Holy Spirit may bear witness to it and your flesh may be justified. 2 See that the idea never enters your heart that this flesh of yours is mortal and that you abuse it by some defilement. For if you defile your flesh, you also defile the Holy Spirit, and if you defile your flesh, you will not live." 3 "But if," I said, "before these words were heard there was some ignorance, how can a man who has defiled his flesh be saved?" "A remedy for previous ignorance is only possible to God," he said, "for he has all authority. 4 However, guard yourself now and the compassionate Lord will grant healing for your previous ignorance. In the future, defile neither flesh nor spirit, for both belong together, and one cannot be defiled without the another. Therefore, preserve both as clean and you will live to God."

Sixth Parable

Chapter Sixty-One
6.1 While sitting in my house and glorifying the Lord for all the things I had seen, I was considering the commandments that they were good and powerful and cheerful and glorious and able to save a person's soul. So I said to myself, "I will be blessed if I walk in these commandments; so will anyone who walks in them." 2 As I was saying this to myself, I suddenly saw him seated beside me. He said to me, "Why are you double-minded about the commandments I gave you? They are good. Put aside all doubt, clothe yourself with faith in the Lord, and walk in them, and I will empower you to keep them. 3 These commandments are profitable for those who are about to repent. For if they do not walk in them, their repentance is worthless. 4 You who repent should cast off the wickedness of this age which wears you down. If you put on every virtue of righteousness, you can observe these commandments and avoid committing any additional sins. If you do not add to your previous sins, you will walk in these commandments and live to God. All these things have been spoken to you by me." 5 After speaking these things he said, "Let us go into a field and I will show you the shepherds with their sheep." "Yes, sir," I said, "let us go." Going into a plain, he pointed out to me a young shepherd

dressed in a suit of yellow garments. 6 He was feeding a very large number of sheep, who were apparently well fed and frisky and skipping joyously here and there. The shepherd himself was cheerful with his flock and his whole appearance was joyful as he was running about among the sheep.

Chapter Sixty-Two
6.2 He said to me: "Do you see this shepherd?" "Yes, sir," I said. "This," he said, "is the angel of luxury and deception. He crushes the souls of God's servants and makes them turn away from the truth by deceiving them with evil desires through which they perish. 2 Consequently, they forget the commandments of the living God and walk in deceptions and worthless luxury. Thus are they led to destruction by this angel, some to death and some to corruption." 3 I said to him, "Sir, I do not know what this means: to death and to corruption." "I will tell you," he said. "The sheep you see happily skipping about are those who have been completely drawn away from God and have surrendered themselves to the desires of this age. For these persons there is no repentance unto life, because God's name is being blasphemed by them. Their life is death. 4 The sheep you see that are not skipping, but standing in one place and grazing, are those who have given themselves up to luxury and deception, but have not spoken any blasphemy against the Lord. They are those who have been led away from the truth. There is hope of repentance and of life for them. Their corruption, therefore, holds out some hope of renewal, but death means everlasting destruction." 5 Again we went forward a little distance, and he pointed out to me a shepherd, large and quite wild in appearance, dressed in a white goat's skin, with a bag on his shoulders. In his hands was a very rough staff with knots in it and a whip. His look was so fierce that I was afraid of him. 6 This shepherd was constantly receiving from a young shepherd the sheep that were frisky and well fed, but not skipping about, and he threw them into a place that was steep and full of thorns and briars. The sheep could not separate themselves from the thorns and thistles but became entangled in them. The sheep that were entangled in the thorns and thistles were very miserable, because they were being beaten by him. Being driven here and there, he gave them no rest, so those sheep had no peace at all.

Chapter Sixty-Three
6.3 When I saw them beaten like this and in misery, I was sorry for them. Such was their torment without any rest at all. 2 I said to the shepherd who was talking to me, "Sir, who is this heartless and bitter shepherd, so utterly without pity for these sheep?" "He is the angel of punishment," he said, "one of the upright angels entrusted with punishment. 3 He takes those who have wandered away from God and have walked in the desires and pleasures of this age and punishes them according to what they deserve with many dreadful punishments." 4 "I would like to know, sir," I said, "what these various punishments are." "I will tell you," he said. "The tortures and punishments are in this life. Some are punished with losses, some by poverty, some by various sicknesses, some by lack of any permanent dwelling, some from the insults of unworthy persons and sufferings of all kinds. 5 For many people who are unsettled in their plans set their hands at many things, but make no progress at all in them. They say that they are not doing well in their pursuits, but it does not occur to them that they have committed wicked deeds. Instead, they blame the Lord. 6 When they have suffered every affliction, they are handed over to me for good instruction and are strengthened in the faith of the Lord, and for the rest of their life they serve the Lord with a pure heart. Now, when they repent, they

recall the evil deeds that they committed and at that point they praise God. They declare that God is a just judge and that they each suffered according to their actions. From then they serve the Lord with pure hearts and prosper in all they do, receiving from the Lord everything they request. And then they praise the Lord because they were handed over to me and they no longer suffer any evil."

Chapter Sixty-Four
6.4 I say to him, "Sir, explain this yet to me." "What is it that you seek?" he said. "Sir," I said, "are those who live in luxury and deceit tortured for the amount of time that they lived in luxury and deceit?" "Yes, the same amount of time," he said. 2 "Sir," I said, "then they are tormented a very short time. They should be tormented seven times as long for living in luxury and forgetting God as they do." 3 He said to me: "You are foolish and do not understand the power of the torment." "If I did understand it, sir, I would not have asked you to explain it to me," I said. "Listen and I will tell you the power of both things. 4 The time of luxury and deceit is one hour, but an hour of torture has the power of thirty days. So if anyone indulges himself or allows himself to be deceived for a single day, a single day's torture has the power of a whole year. A man is tortured for as many years as were lived in luxury. Therefore, you see," he said, "that the period of indulgence and deceit is very short, but the period of punishment and torment is prolonged."

Chapter Sixty-Five
6.5 "Sir," I said, "I still do not understand fully about the period of deceit and indulgence and the period of torment. Give me a clearer explanation." 2 He answered me, "Your foolishness is persistent and you do not wish to purify your heart and serve God. Take care," he said, "lest the time be fulfilled and you are found to be foolish. Listen now," he said, "that you may understand as you wish. 3 The one who lives in indulgence and the man deceived for a single day, who does what he pleases, is clothed in much foolishness without realizing his performance. The next day he forgets what he did the day before. For indulgence and deceit have no memory, because of that foolishness in which they are clothed. But when punishment and torment are imposed on a man for a single day, it is as punishment and torment for a whole year. For punishment and torment have long memories. 4 So the man who is punished and tormented for a whole year remembers at last his luxury and deceit, and he knows that he suffers evil for that reason. Consequently, every one given to indulgence and deception is tormented in this way, because, though he had life, he gave himself up to death." 5 "What kinds of indulgence," I said, "are harmful, sir?" "Every deed performed with pleasure is luxurious for a man," he said. "For example, the sharp-tempered man, by giving satisfaction to his passion, is self-indulgent. So the adulterer, the drunkard, the slanderer, the liar, the envious, the robber, and anyone who commits similar sins, gives way to his individual vice. Consequently, he is self-indulgent in his action. 6 All these selfish acts are harmful to God's servants. It is for these deceits that those who are punished and tormented suffer. 7 However, there are acts of indulgence that bring salvation to human beings. For there are many persons who are given to indulgence in their good actions, who are carried away by the pleasure this gives them. This kind of indulgence, then, is advantageous for God's servants and secures life for this type of man. Whereas, the harmful luxuries mentioned above brings them punishment and torment, and if they continue without repenting they bring death on themselves."

Seventh Parable

Chapter Sixty-Six

7 After a few days, I saw him in the same plain where I had also seen the shepherds, and he said to me, "What are you looking for?" "I have come here, sir," I said, "to have you command the punishing shepherd to leave my house, because he is afflicting me very much." "You have to be afflicted," he said. "Such is the command of the glorious angel in your regard," he said. "For he wants you to be put to the test." "What have I done, sir, that is so wicked that I must be handed over to this angel?" I said. 2 "I will tell you," he said. "Your sins are innumerable, but not so numerous that you must be handed over to this angel. However, your household has committed many sins and iniquities, and the glorious angel is embittered by their deeds. This is why he has given orders that you should be afflicted for a while, that they also may repent and cleanse themselves of all worldly desires. When they repent and are cleansed, then the angel will cease from punishment." 3 I said to him, "Sir, even if they have committed acts to anger the glorious angel, what have I done?" "They cannot be otherwise afflicted," he said, "unless you, the head of the whole household, suffers affliction. For if you suffer affliction, they also will necessarily be afflicted, but if you fare well, they suffer no affliction at all." 4 "But look, sir," I said. "They have repented with the whole heart." "I also know," he said, "that they have repented with the whole heart. Do you think, then, that there is immediate remission from sin with repentance? Not at all. The one who repents must torment his soul and be thoroughly humble in all his actions and afflicted in a variety of ways. If he endures the afflictions that come to him, full mercy will be granted by the creator of all things, who also has given him strength and who will grant healing. 5 This God will do when he sees the heart of the one who repents from all wickedness. But it is to the benefit of you and your house that you be afflicted now. What more do I need to say to you? You must be afflicted in accordance with the orders of that angel of the Lord who handed you over to me. Give thanks to the Lord also that you were considered worthy beforehand of some indication of the affliction destined for you. By knowing it in advance you will endure it with bravery." 6 I said to him, "Sir, be with me and I will be able to endure every affliction." "I will be with you," he said, "and I will also ask the punishing angel to send you milder afflictions. However, you must be afflicted a short time and then be restored once more to your house. Only continue in your humble service to the Lord with a pure heart as well as your children and your house. Walk in the commandments I have given you, and it will be possible for your repentance to be strong and pure. 7 If you observe these commandments, together with your whole house, all affliction will pass from you. So will it leave all who walk in these commandments of mine."

Eighth Parable

Chapter Sixty-Seven

8.1 He showed me a great willow tree that spread over plains and mountains, and under its shelter came all those called by the name of the Lord. 2 The glorious and exceedingly tall angel of the Lord stood by the willow with a mighty sickle. He was lopping off branches and distributing them to the people in the shelter of the willow. He also distributed small rods, about two feet long. 3 After everyone had received rods, the angel put aside his sickle, yet the tree was as sound as when I had first seen it. 4 I wondered at this to myself and said, "How can the tree be healthy after so many branches have been lopped off?" The shepherd said to me, "Do not wonder that the tree remains sound after so many branches have been lopped off. Wait until you have seen everything and the meaning will be made clear to you." 5 The angel who had distributed the rods summoned them back. In the order in which they had received the rods they were summoned to him, and each returned his rod to him. The angel of the Lord received them and examined them carefully. 6 From some he took rods withered and apparently worm-eaten. To those who had returned such rods he gave orders to stand by themselves. 7 Others returned rods that were dry but not worm-eaten. These people he also ordered to stand aside. 8 Others returned rods that were half-dry and they stood at the side. 9 Another group returned rods with cracks in them and they stood apart. 10 Another group handed over rods green and cracked and stood by themselves. 11 Others gave him rods half-green and half-cracked and stood by themselves. 12 Others brought him rods two-thirds green and one-third dry and stood by themselves. 13 Others returned rods two-thirds dry and one-third green and stood by themselves. 14 Others handed over their rods almost totally green with a very small portion dry, just the end; there were cracks in them also. Then they stood by themselves. 15 The rods of others were green only in a very small portion and the rest were dry. They also stood by themselves. 16 Others came and brought rods that were green just as they had received them from the angel. The majority of the crowd returned rods of this kind. With them the angel was exceedingly pleased. They also stood by themselves. 17 Others returned rods that were green with buds on them. They also stood by themselves and the angel was likewise very pleased with them. 18 Others returned rods that were green with buds on them, and the rods seemed to have some fruit. The people whose rods were found in this condition were very joyous. The angel also rejoiced over them and the shepherd was very glad for them.

Chapter Sixty-Eight
8.2 The angel of the Lord ordered crowns to be brought. When the crowns were brought apparently made of palm leaves, he crowned those who had returned rods with buds and some fruit and sent them to the tower. 2 He also sent the rest of them to the tower, those who had returned rods that were green and budding without fruit, giving them a seal. 3 On their way to the tower they all had the same clothes, white as snow. 4 He also sent off those who had returned rods that were green as when they received them, after giving them white clothes and seals. 5 Finishing this, the angel said to the shepherd: "I am going away so send these persons to dwell in their place within the walls as they deserve. Send them off only after examining carefully their rods. Scrutinize them carefully and be sure no one slips by you," he said. "But if someone does go by you, I will put him to the test upon the altar." With these words to the shepherd he departed. 6 After the departure of the angel, the shepherd said to me, "Let us take the rods of all and plant them. Perhaps some of them may live." I said to him, "Sir, how can these dry rods live?" 7 He answered and said, "This tree is a willow and clings to life. So if they are planted and get a little moisture, many of the rods will live. Then we will also try to pour water on them. If any of them can live, I will join in its joy. But if it cannot live, it will be found that I was not negligent." 8 The shepherd ordered me to call them just as they stood. They came up row by row and returned their rods to the shepherd. Receiving them, the shepherd planted the rods in rows. After planting them, he poured so much water on them that the rods could not be seen in the water. 9 After he had watered the rods, he said to me, "Let us go and after a few days we will return and look at all the

THE SHEPHERD OF HERMAS

rods. For He who created this tree wishes all who have taken branches from it to live. I also hope that the majority of these rods will live, now that they received moisture and have been watered."

Chapter Sixty-Nine

8.3 I said to him, "Sir, tell me what this tree is. I am puzzled about it, because so many branches have been cut and it is healthy and does not look like anything has been cut from it. Therefore, this really puzzles me." 2 "Listen," he said. "This great tree that covers plains and mountains and the whole earth is the law of God that is given to the whole world. This law is the Son of God proclaimed to the ends of the earth. The people under its shelter are those who have heard the proclamation and believed in him. 3 The great and glorious angel is Michael, who has authority over this people and is their guide. For it is he who gives the law into the hearts of believers. He examines closely the ones to whom he gave it to see whether they have kept it. 4 You can see the rods of each individual person for they are the law. You see that many rods have been made useless, so you know that all these persons failed to keep the law. You will also see their dwelling." 5 "Sir," I said to him, "why did he send some to the tower, while he left some behind?" "He left behind in my power those who violated the law they received from him, to see whether they will repent. But those who have already satisfied the law and have kept it he keeps under his own authority." 6 "Sir," I said, "who are those who are crowned and gone into the tower?" "They who are crowned are those who have wrestled with the Devil and defeated him. They are the ones who suffered for the law. 7 The others who also have returned green rods with buds but without fruit have endured persecution for the law, but have not suffered; however they did not deny their law. 8 Those who returned their green rods as they received them are holy and righteous and walk especially in purity of heart, keeping the commandments of the Lord. The rest you will know when I examine closely the rods that were planted and watered."

Chapter Seventy

8.4 After a few days, we came to the place and the shepherd sat in the place of the great angel, while I took a position beside him. He says to me: "Tie an apron around you and wait on me." So I put on a clean apron of sackcloth and was ready to wait on him. 2 "Call the men," he said, "whose rods were planted in the order each presented the rods." And I went into the plain and called everyone. They all stood group by group. 3 He says to them, "Let each one pull up his rod and bring it to me." 4 The first to return them were those who had dry and chipped rods, and so they were found as dried and chipped. He ordered them to stand to the side. 5 Those who had dry but not chipped rods then returned them. Some returned the rods green, but some returned them dried and chipped, as if by woodworms. So he commanded those who had returned them green to stand aside, but those who returned them dried and chipped were to stand with the first group. 6 Then those who had half-dried and cracked rods returned them. Many of them gave back green rods without cracks, but some green rods with buds and fruit on the buds like those who were crowned and entered the tower. But some returned them dry and worm-eaten, others dried but not worm-eaten, while some were half-dry and had cracks. And he commanded each one of them to stand aside, some in their own groups and others apart.

Chapter Seventy-One
8.5 Then those who had green rods with cracks returned them. Since these all had green rods, they stood in their own group. The shepherd was pleased with them because their rods had all changed and had lost their cracks. 2 Then those who had half-green and half-dry rods also returned them. The rods of some were found to be completely green, of others half-dried, of others still dried and worm-eaten, but some were green and had buds. All these were sent, each to his rank. 3 Then those whose rods were two-thirds green and one-third dry returned them. Many of them returned green rods, many returned half-dried rods, and the rest dried and worm-eaten rods. All these stood in their ranks. 4 Then those who had rods two-thirds dry and one-third green returned them. Many of them returned half-dried rods, but some returned dry and worm-eaten rods; some rods half-dried with cracks; a few returned green ones. All these persons stood in their ranks. 5 Those who had rods with a very small dry portion and cracks returned them. Of this number some returned them green and others green with buds. These also went off to their group. 6 Then those who had rods with very little green, but otherwise dry, returned them. In this group more were discovered to have rods that were green with buds and fruit on the buds, while the rest of the rods were completely green. The shepherd was extremely happy with those whose rods were found like this. They all then departed, each to his own group.

Chapter Seventy-Two
8.6 After looking closely at all the rods, the shepherd says to me, "I told you that this tree is hardy. Do you see," he said, "how many have repented and were saved?" "Yes, I do," I said. "It is," he said, "that you may recognize that the abundant mercy of the Lord is great and glorious and that he has granted his Spirit to those worthy of repentance." 2 "Why is it, sir," I said, "that all do not repent?" "The Lord has granted repentance to those whose heart is about to become pure and who will serve him with their whole heart. But lest his name again be blasphemed, he has not granted repentance to those whose deceit and wickedness he saw, for they were repenting hypocritically." 3 I said to him, "Now, sir, explain what sort of persons they are and where is the dwelling of those who returned their rods. In this way believers who have received the seal but have broken it and failed to keep it intact, may realize what they have done and repent. Then they will receive a seal from you and will praise the Lord for having had mercy on them and for sending you to renew their spirits." "I will tell you," he said. 4 "The persons whose rods were discovered to be dry and worm-eaten are apostates and traitors to the church, who blaspheme the Lord by their sins. Furthermore, they were ashamed of the name of the Lord by which they were called. Therefore, these persons are lost to God. You see that not one of them has repented, though they heard what you told them at my command. From persons of this kind life has departed. 5 Those also are like those who returned dry rods, not worm-eaten. For they are hypocrites, who introduce strange doctrines and pervert God's servants. In particular, they pervert sinners by not allowing them to repent, but dissuade them by foolish doctrines. However, there is hope of repentance for them. 6 And you see that many of them have repented since you spoke my commandments to them and more will repent. But those who will not repent have lost their life. However, those of their number who have repented have become good and they dwell within the first walls, some even ascending the tower. So you see," he said, "that repentance from sins brings life, but failure to repent means death."

Chapter Seventy-Three

8.7 "And hear also about those who returned half-dried rods with cracks in them. Those whose rods were half-dry throughout are double-minded people, neither alive nor dead. 2 Those who are half-dry and have cracks are double-minded and slanderers. They are never at peace with one another and always are causing dissensions. But repentance is possible for them also. You see," he said, "that some of them have repented, and there is still remaining in them," he continued, "a hope of repentance. 3 All of this group who have repented," he said, "also have a dwelling in the tower. However, those who were slower in their repentance dwell in the walls, while those who do not repent, but persist in their deeds, will die the death. 4 Those who have returned their rods green but cracked always were faithful and good, but there was a little jealousy among them about being first and about one's glory. All of these are foolish, competing with one another about being first! 5 But these also, after hearing my commandments, purified themselves and soon repented, since they are good. Their dwelling, therefore, is in the tower. But if any turn aside again to dissension, they will be cast out of the tower and will lose their life. 6 Life belongs to all who keep the Lord's commandments. Now in the commandments there is nothing about being first nor any honor but about man's patience and humility. So the life of the Lord is with these kinds, but death is among those who cause dissension and are transgressors."

Chapter Seventy-Four

8.8 "Those who gave up rods half dry and half green are the persons absorbed in their business, who fail to cling to the saints. For this reason one half are living and the other half are dead. 2 So many who have heard my commandments have repented. Those that repented have a dwelling in the tower, but some of them have fully fallen away. They, therefore, have no repentance, for they blasphemed the Lord and denied him on account of their business affairs. Consequently, they destroyed their life by their wicked practices. 3 Many of this group were double-minded. These can still have repentance, provided they repent in good time. Then they will have a dwelling in the tower. Even if they repent rather slowly, they will dwell within the tower. But if they do not repent, they also have lost their life. 4 Those who returned rods two-thirds green and one-third dry are the persons who denied the Lord on various occasions. 5 Many of this group have repented and returned to the tower to dwell. However, many fell away from God completely and these finally lost their life. And some of this group were doubters at heart and caused dissensions and they have repentance, if it comes in good time and if they do not continue in their passions. But if they do continue in their deeds, they also will bring death on themselves."

Chapter Seventy-Five

8.9 "Those who returned their rods as two-thirds dry and one-third green are those who had been faithful but became rich and made a name among the Gentiles. They put on an arrogant demeanor, became haughty, and so abandoned the truth and did not cling to the righteous. Instead, they lived in the manner of the Gentiles and among them, a life more agreeable to them. However, they did not fall away from God, but clung to the faith, without doing the works of faith. 2 Many of them repented and their dwelling was in the tower. 3 But others who lived and associated constantly with the Gentiles were corrupted by their vanities to fall away from God and act in the manner of the Gentiles and such persons are considered as Gentiles. 4 Others in this group were double-minded and had no hope of being saved because of their deeds. Others again were double-minded and caused schisms among themselves. There is still repentance for those who doubt because of their actions. However, their repentance must be swift if they will have a dwelling within the tower. But death is near for those who do not repent and remain in their pleasures."

Chapter Seventy-Six
8.11 "Those who returned their rods green, but dry-tipped and cracked, were always good, faithful, and glorious in the sight of God, but they committed a least sin out of small desires or because they had petty quarrels with one another. The majority quickly repented on hearing my words and their dwelling was in the tower. 2 But some were double-minded, and in their doubts they created greater dissension. Still there is yet a hope of repentance for them, because at all times they were good, and one of them is hardly likely to die. 3 Those who returned their rods dry, with only the slightest touch of green, are believers, but their deeds were done in iniquity. However, they never fell away from God and bore the name gladly. In their houses they also graciously received God's servants. So when they heard of this repentance, they repented without hesitation and now they are performing all virtue and righteousness. 4 Some of them also suffer, bearing distress gladly, knowing their former deeds. The dwelling of all these persons, therefore, is in the tower."

Chapter Seventy-Seven
8.11 After finishing the explanations of all the rods, he said to me: "Go and tell everyone to repent and live for God. The Lord in His mercy has sent me to grant repentance to all, although some are unworthy because of their deeds. But in His patience the Lord wishes those who were called through his Son to be saved." 2 I said to him, "Sir, I hope that those who have heard this will repent. I am quite sure that each one who realizes the things they have done will repent out of fear of God." 3 He answered and said, "Those who repent with their whole heart and cleanse themselves of all the wickedness just mentioned, without also adding to their former sins, will receive from the Lord healing for their former sins. If they are not double-minded in fulfilling my commandments, they will live to God. But those who add to their sins and return to the desires of this age will bring death on themselves. 4 But you should walk in my commandments and live to God. Whoever walks in these commandments and acts uprightly will live to God." 5 After showing and telling me all these things, he said, "I will show you the rest of these things in a few days."

The Ninth Parable

Chapter Seventy-Eight
9.1 After I wrote the commandments and the parables of the shepherd, the angel of repentance came and said, "I want to point out to you what the Holy Spirit has shown you while speaking to you in the form of the church. For that Spirit is the Son of God. 2 Since you were too weak in the flesh, these things were not explained to you by an angel. When you were empowered by the spirit and you grew in enough strength to see an angel, then the building of the tower was revealed to you by the church. You have looked at everything in a good and reverent way, as shown from a virgin. Now instruction is being given you by the same spirit through an angel. 3 You are to learn everything from me more accurately. This is why I was assigned by the glorious angel to dwell in your house, that you may have powerful insight into everything, without any fear as before." 4 Then he led me off to Arcadia to a certain breast-shaped mountain and set me down on the peak of the mountain. From here he showed me a huge plain with twelve mountains around it, each with a different shape. 5 The first was black as pitch;

THE SHEPHERD OF HERMAS

the second was barren, with no vegetation; the third was full of thorns and thistles; 6 the fourth had plants half-dried, the top of the grass green, but the part near the roots dry, while some of the vegetation scorched by the sun; 7 the fifth mountain had green vegetation, despite the fact that it was rough; the sixth mountain was full of crevices, some of them small and some large. However, the crevices contained plants, not very flourishing and apparently wilted. 8 The seventh mountain contained healthy vegetation and it was flourishing everywhere, with all kinds of cattle and birds feeding on it. And the more the cattle and birds fed, the more did the vegetation on that mountain blossom. And the eighth was full of springs and every kind of creature of the Lord was provided with water from the springs on that mountain. 9 But the ninth mountain was completely empty of water and an utter wasteland. However, there were wild beasts and deadly serpents that destroy men. The tenth mountain had huge trees, having complete shade, and under cover of them sheep were resting and chewing their cud. 10 The eleventh mountain was covered with fruit-bearing trees, each adorned with various fruits, and a person seeing this fruit would desire to eat from it. The twelfth mountain was all white and its sight was attractive, most beautiful in itself.

Chapter Seventy-Nine
9.2 In the middle of the plain he pointed out to me a huge white rock rising out of the plain. The rock was higher than the mountains, square-shaped, large enough to hold the entire world. 2 It was old and a gate had been cut out of it, but this gate seemed to have been cut recently. The glow of the gate was so greater than the sun that I marveled at its brilliance. 3 In a circle around the gate stood twelve virgins. The four that stood at the corners appeared to be more glorious than the others, though the others also seemed glorious. They stood at the four parts of the gate, two virgins each with two virgins between them. 4 They were dressed in linen tunics and had beautiful belts. Their right shoulders were uncovered as if they were about to carry a load. They were prepared, cheerful, and eager. 5 After seeing this I said to myself that I was looking at something great and glorious. But again I was at a loss to explain how these virgins, delicate though they were, stood there bravely, ready to hold up the whole heaven. 6 Then the shepherd said to me, "Why are you debating with yourself and why are you so perplexed and making yourself sad? Do not try, as though you were intelligent, to understand things you cannot comprehend, but ask the Lord so you may receive the intelligence to understand them. 7 You cannot see what is behind you, but you see what is before you. So leave alone what you cannot see and do not bother yourself. Master what you do see and do not concern yourself about the rest. Everything I show you I will explain to you. Therefore, consider the rest."

Chapter Eighty
9.3 I saw six men coming who were tall and glorious and similar in form, and they called a multitude of men. The others who were also advancing were tall, handsome, and strong. The six men commanded them to build a tower on top of the gate. The noise of the men who were coming to build the tower was extraordinary, for they were running back and forth around the tower. 2 The virgins who were standing around the tower told the men to hurry up and build the tower. The virgins stretched out their hands as though they were about to take something from the men. 3 The six men ordered stones to come up from an abyss for the building of the tower. Then ten bright, uncut, and square stones came up. 4 Then the six men called to the virgins and commanded them to carry all the stones for the building of the tower, walk through the gate, and pass them on to the men

who were about to build the tower. 5 Then the virgins loaded the first ten stones that came out of the abyss upon one another and carried them together, one stone at a time.

Chapter Eighty-One
9.4 In the same position in which they stood around the tower, the ones who seemed strong enough got under the corners of the stone and carried it, while the others got up under the sides. This is how they carried all the stones. They carried them through the gate as they had been hidden and passed them on to the men in the tower. Once they had the stones, they began building. 2 The tower was built on top of the huge stone over the gate. Then those ten stones were joined together and covered the whole rock and became the foundation for the building of the tower. The rock and gate were the support of the whole tower. 3 After the ten stones twenty-five others came out of the abyss. These were also carried by the maidens like the first, and were joined together in the building of the tower. After these stones there came up thirty-five more, and they were joined together like the rest in the building of the tower. Then forty more came up and also all these were put into the building of the tower. There were thus four stories in the foundations of the tower. 4 Then they ceased coming up from the abyss and the workers also ceased for a while. Then once more the six men ordered a multitude of the crowd to bring along stones from the mountains for the building of the tower. 5 Then stones of various colors were brought from all the mountains. They had been cut by the men and handed to the virgins, who carried them through the gate and passed them on for the building of the tower. And when the various stones were placed into the building, they changed their color and all of them became white. 6 However some stones given by the men for the building did not become white but turned out to be of the same color as when they were being put into the building. For they had not been handed over by the virgins, nor had they been carried through the gate. 7 These stones were not suitable for the building of the tower. When the six men saw that the stones were not suitable, they ordered them to be removed and carried down to the particular place from where they had been brought. 8 And they said to the men who were bringing in the stones, "You must not bring any stones into the building. Place them beside the tower for the virgins to carry them through the gate and hand them over for the building. For if these stones are not carried by the hands of the virgins, they cannot change their colors. And so do not," they said, "labor in vain."

Chapter Eighty-Two
9.5 On that day the building was finished, but the tower was not completed; additions still had to be made, and there was a pause in the building. The six men gave orders to the builders to leave for a short while and rest, but to the virgins their orders were not to depart from the tower. It seemed that they had been left there to guard the tower. 2 After the departure of everyone to rest, I said to the shepherd, "Why is it, sir, that the building of the tower has not been completed?" "It cannot be completed," he said, "unless the lord of the tower comes and inspects the building to find out whether some stones are decayed. Then he will change them, for the tower is being built according to his will." 3 "Sir," I said, "I would like to know what the building of this tower means. I would like to know about the rock and the gate and the mountains and the virgins and the stones that have come out of the abyss uncut and yet have gone into the building. 4 And why are ten stones first put into the foundations, then twenty-five, then thirty-five, and then forty? I would also like to know about the stones that went into the building and were taken out

again and put back in their original place. Put my soul at ease about all these matters, sir, and explain them to me." 5 "If it turns out that you are not idly curious," he said, "you will understand everything. For after a few days we will come and you will see the rest of what is happening to this tower. Then you will understand all the parables accurately." 6 So after a few days we came to the place where we had been sitting and he said to me, "Let us go to the tower because the owner is coming to examine it." So we went to the tower, but absolutely no one except the virgins was with him. 7 And the shepherd asked the virgins if the master of the tower had arrived. And they replied that he intended to come to inspect the building.

Chapter Eighty-Three
9.6 And behold after a short while I saw an array of many men coming. And in the midst there was a man so tall that he rose above the tower. 2 The six men in charge of the building were walking with him on his right and his left. All those in charge of the building were with him and many other distinguished people were around him. The virgins who kept watch over the tower ran forward and kissed him and began to walk beside him around the tower. 3 The very tall man examined the building carefully, even handling some individual stones. Taking a rod in his hand, he struck each individual stone placed in the building. 4 After he hit them, some stones became black as soot, some became rough, some showed cracks, some were chipped, some were neither white nor black, some were rough and did not fit into the other stones, and some had many stains. These were the various appearances of the rotten stones found in the building. 5 Therefore, he ordered all these stones to be removed from the building and placed beside the tower and other stones were to be brought in and used as replacements. 6 The builders asked him from what mountain he wished the stones to be carried and used in their place. But he did not command stones to be carried from the mountains. Instead, he commanded them to be brought from a nearby plain. 7 When the plain was dug up, brilliant square stones were found and also some that were rounded. And any stones that were in the plain were all brought in and carried through the gate by the virgins. 8 The square stones were cut and put into the place of those that had been removed. The round stones were not put into the building, because they were too hard to cut and it took too long. But they were placed beside the tower, because they were about to be cut and placed in the building, for they were very bright.

Chapter Eighty-Four
9.7 When he had finished, the glorious man who was the lord of the whole tower, called the shepherd and put him in charge of all the stones lying next to the tower, which had been thrown out of the structure, and said to him, 2 "Clean these stones carefully and put them in the building of the tower, and use those that can fit in with the others. Throw those that do not fit far away from the tower." 3 After ordering the shepherd he left the tower in the company of those with whom he had come, but the virgins remained standing around the tower watching it. 4 I said to the shepherd, "How can these stones again be used in the building after being rejected?" He answered and said, "Do you see these stones?" "I do, sir," I said. "I will trim the majority of these stones," he said, "and put them in the building where they will fit in with the rest of the stones." 5 "But, sir, how can they fill the same space, after being trimmed?" I asked. He answered and said, "Those that are too small will find a place in the middle of the building, but those that are larger will be put on the outside and will hold them together." 6 After speaking these things he

said to me, "Let us go and after two days we will return and clean these stones and put them into the building. For everything around the building must be cleaned, in case the master should suddenly come. He will be angry if he finds the things around the tower are dirty and that these stones have not gone into the tower. It would then appear to the master that I am careless." 7 So after two days, when we returned to the tower, he said to me, "Let us inspect all the stones and determine the ones that can go into the building." I said to him, "Sir, let us inspect them."

Chapter Eighty-Five
9.8 At first we inspected the black stones and we found that they were the same as when they were taken out of the building, so the shepherd ordered that they be moved away from the tower. 2 Then he inspected the rough ones, and many of these he took and trimmed and ordered the virgins to take and put them into the building. So the virgins took them and put them in the middle of the building, but the rest he ordered to be placed with the black stones, since they also turned out to be black. 3 Then he inspected the stones with cracks. Many of these he cut and ordered that they be carried into the building by the virgins. They were placed on the outside of the walls because they turned out to be especially strong, but the rest could not be trimmed because of the excessive number of cracks. For this reason they were cast aside away from the tower's structure. 4 He next looked at the stones that were chipped. Among them many turned out to be black and had developed large cracks. So he commanded that these be put aside with the rejected stones. But those left over he cleaned and cut and commanded to be put into the building. And the virgins took up these stones and fitted them into the middle of the tower's structure, for they were rather weak. 5 His inspection next turned to the half white and half black stones, many of which turned out to be black. He ordered that these also be taken out with the rejected stones. All the rest proved to be white and were taken up by the virgins, and since they were white, they could be fitted into the building by the virgins themselves. They were then placed on the outside, because they turned out to be sound and able to support those placed in the middle, for not one of them was completely chipped. 6 Then he examined the hard and rough ones. A few of these were rejected, because they could not be trimmed and proved to be very hard. However, the rest were trimmed and taken up by the virgins to be placed into the middle of the tower's structure, since they were rather weak. 7 Then he inspected the spotted stones. Very few of them had been blackened and had to be thrown away with the rest. The remainder were glistening and sound and those were fitted into the building by the virgins. Because of their strength, they were placed on the exterior.

Chapter Eighty-Six
9.9 Then he went to inspect the round white stones and said to me, "What are we to do with these stones?" "How am I to know, sir?" I said. "Do you not notice anything about them?" he said. 2 "Sir, I do not have this skill. I am not a stone mason and do not understand." "Do you not see," he said, "that they are very round? And if I wish to square them, I will have to cut off a great amount? However, some of them have to be put into the building." 3 "Well, sir," I said, "if some have to be put into the building, why do you bother? Choose those you want for the building and fit them into it." He then chose from these stones the larger and brilliant ones and cut them. Then the virgins took them and fitted them into the exterior parts of the building. 4 And the rest were taken and put away in the plain from where they had been carried. However, they were not rejected,

"because" he said, "there is still a small part of the tower to be built. The master of the tower is very anxious to have these stones fitted because they are very bright." 5 Twelve women of most beautiful form were then called. They were dressed in black and belted. Their shoulders were exposed and their hair was hanging loose. These women seemed to me to be wild. The shepherd ordered them to take up the stones rejected from the building and to carry them back to the mountains from where they were taken. 6 They picked up and cheerfully carried away all the stones and put them in the place whence they had been taken. After all the stones had been picked up and there was not a single one lying around the tower, the shepherd said to me, "Let us walk around the tower to see whether there is any defect in it." So I walked around it with him. 7 At the sight of the tower's beauty of structure he was extremely happy, for it was so beautifully constructed that I envied it when I saw it. It was built as if it were a single stone with only one joint. The stone looked as if it had been cut out of the rock, for it seemed to be of one stone.

Chapter Eighty-Seven
9.10 As I was walking with him, I was happy at this beautiful sight. The shepherd said to me, "Go and bring plaster and fine clay to fill up the holes left by the stones taken and put into the building. Everything around the tower must be smooth." 2 I did as he told me and brought these to him. "Help me" he said, "and the work will soon be finished." Then he removed the imprints on the stones that had gone into the building and gave orders to sweep around the tower and to make it clean. 3 And the virgins took brooms and removed all the rubbish taken out of the tower, washed the site with water, and made it pleasant and attractive. 4 Then the shepherd said to me, "Everything," he said, "has been cleaned. Whenever the lord comes to inspect his tower, he will have nothing for which to blame us." With these words he wished to leave. 5 But I took hold of him by his bag and began requesting him in the Lord's name to explain what he had shown me. He said to me, "I am busy for a little while. Then I will explain everything. Wait here for me until I return." 6 I said to him, "What will I do here while I am by myself?" "You will not be alone," he said, "for these virgins will be with you." "Put me in their care," I said. The shepherd called them and said to them, "I am entrusting this person to you until I return." Then he left. 7 So I stayed alone with the virgins, who were quite cheerful and gracious to me, especially the four most distinguished ones.

Chapter Eighty-Eight
9.11 The virgins said to me, "The shepherd will not return today." "Then," I said, "what will I do?" "Wait for him until tomorrow. If he comes, he will speak with you, and if he does not, stay with us here until he comes." 2 I said to them, "I will wait for him until tomorrow. But if he does not come, I will go home and return early in the morning." They answered and said, "You have been put in our care, so you cannot leave us." 3 "Where will I stay?" I said. "You will spend the night with us as a brother, not as a husband," they said. "For you are our brother and in the future we intend to stay with you, because we love you very much." However, I was ashamed to stay with them. 4 Then the one who seemed to be the leader began to kiss and embrace me. And when the others saw her kiss and embrace me they also began to kiss me and lead me around the tower in play. 5 At this I also became like a young man and played with them. Some formed a chorus; some were dancing; others were singing. I kept silent as I moved in their company around the tower, thrilled to be with them. 6 When evening came, I wanted to go home. However, they did not let me, but detained me. So I stayed with them for the night and slept near

the tower. 7 The virgins spread their linen tunics on the ground and made me lie down in the midst of them. Yet they did nothing at all except to pray. I also prayed without ceasing, not less than they. The virgins rejoiced at such a prayer on my part. I remained there with them until the next day at the second hour. 8 Then the shepherd came back and said to the virgins, "Have you done him any harm?" "Ask him," they said. "Sir," I said, "I was delighted to stay with them." "What did you have for dinner?" "Sir," I said, "our meal all night was the words of the Lord." "Did they treat you well," he asked. "Yes, sir," I said. 9 "What do you want to hear first?" he asked. "Sir," I said, "I would like to ask you questions in the order in which you pointed things out to me and to have you give explanations in the order of my questions." "Just as you wish," he said. "I will explain them to you and I will hide absolutely nothing from you."

Chapter Eighty-Nine
9.12 "First of all, sir," I said, "show me this: What is the rock and the gate?" "This rock and this gate," he said, "is the Son of God." "But, sir," I said, "how is it that the rock is ancient, but the gate is new?" "Listen," he said, "and understand why, O foolish man. 2 The Son of God is before all His creation and he is counselor to his Father for his creation. For this reason the rock is ancient." "But, sir, why is the gate new?" I said. 3 "Because," he said, "He has been revealed in the last days of its completion. And for this reason the gate is new. In this way those who are about to be saved enter the kingdom of God through it. 4 Do you not see," he said, "that the stones that have entered through the gate go into the building of the tower, whereas those that have not entered are cast off to their own place?" "Yes, sir," I said. "For that reason nobody enters the kingdom of God if they have not received the name of his Son. 5 For if you desire to enter a city that has a wall all around it with only one gate, you cannot possibly enter without going through that gate." "How else, sir," I said, "could one enter?" "In the same way that you cannot enter a city, except through this gate, so no human being can enter the kingdom of God, except through the name of his beloved Son. You saw," he said, "the crowd of people building the tower?" "Yes, sir," I said. "Those people," he said, "are all glorious angels. By them the Lord is surrounded like a wall. But the gate is the Son of God. This is the one entrance to the Lord. Therefore, no one will enter to him except through his Son. 7 You have seen," he said, "the six men and the glorious and great man in their midst, the one who walked around the tower and rejected the stones from the building?" "Yes, sir," I said. 8 "The glorious man," he said, "is the Son of God, and those six are the glorious angels who guard him on the right and on the left. None of these glorious angels," he said, "will enter before God without him. Whoever does not receive his name will not enter into the kingdom of God."

Chapter Ninety
9.13 "And about the tower," I said, "what is it?" "This tower," he said, "is the church." 2 "And who are these virgins?" "These," he said, "are holy spirits. No man will be found in the kingdom of God unless they clothe him with their clothing. For if he only receives the name, without receiving clothing from them, it is of no use to him. These virgins are the powers of the Son of God. If you bear the name without his power, you are bearing the name in vain. 3 Now the stones you saw cast out," he said, "are those who bore the name, but did not put on the virgins' clothing." "What kind of garment is this clothing of theirs?" I said. "The names themselves," he said, "are their clothing. Anybody who bears the name of the Son of God is also bound to bear their names. Even the Son himself bears the names of these virgins. 4 All the stones," he said, "that you saw going into the building of the tower and given over by the hands of the virgins to remain in the

building are clothed with the power of these virgins. 5 For this reason you see that the tower has been made as a monolith from the rock. And those who believe in the Lord through his son, and clothed themselves with these spirits, will be one spirit and one body and with a single color to their garments. And those who bear the names of the virgins will dwell in the tower." 6 "Now, sir," I said, "why are these rejected stones cast out? They also have come through the gate and were placed in the building by the hands of the virgins." "Since you are concerned," he said, "and inquire carefully, I will tell you about the rejected stones. 7 They all received the name of the Son of God as well as the power of the virgins. On receiving these spirits, they received power and accompanied the servants of God, sharing one spirit and one body and one clothing, for they had the same mind and practiced righteousness. 8 After some time they were seduced by the beautiful women you saw wearing black garments, with uncovered shoulders and hair hanging down loosely and beautiful figures. When they saw them they were filled with desire for them, clothed themselves with their power, and shed the power of the virgins. 9 Therefore, they were ejected from the house of God and handed over to those women. But those who were not led astray by the beauty of these women remained in the house of God. Now," he said, "you have the interpretation of the rejected stones."

Chapter Ninety-One
9.14 "Now, sir," I said, "what if these men, in spite of their condition, should repent and put off their desire for these women and return to the virgins? Suppose also that they walk in their power and in their deeds. Will they not enter God's house?" 2 "They will enter," he said, "if they cast aside the deeds of these women and assume the power of the virgins, so as to walk in their deeds. That is the reason for a pause in the building, so they could repent and return to the building of the tower. However, if they do not repent, then others will enter and they themselves will be finally rejected." 3 At all this I gave thanks to the Lord that he had mercy on all who call on his name and that he had sent the angel of repentance to us who had sinned against Him. I gave thanks that he had renewed our spirit and that now, when we were lost without hope of life, he had renewed our life. 4 "Now, sir," I said, "explain why it is that the tower is not built on the ground, but on the rock and the gate." "Are you still foolish and without understanding?" he said. "I have to ask all the questions, sir," I said, "because I am unable to understand anything. All these matters are awesome and glorious and difficult for people to understand." 5 "Listen," he said. "The name of the Son of God is great and incomprehensible and supports the whole world. Now if all of creation is supported by the Son of God, what do you think of those called by him, who bear his name and walk in his commandments? 6 Do you see the kind of persons He supports? Those who bear his name with their whole heart. Therefore, he has become their foundation and gladly sustains them, because they are not ashamed to bear his name."

Chapter Ninety-Two
9.15 "Show me, sir," I said, "the names of the virgins and of the women dressed in black garments." "Hear," he said, "the names of the stronger virgins standing at the corners. 2 The first one is Faith, the second is Self-Control, the third is Power, and the fourth is Patience. The others standing between them are called: Simplicity, Innocence, Purity, Cheerfulness, Truth, Understanding, Harmony, and Love. The one who bears these names and that of the Son of God can enter into the kingdom of God. 3 Hear also," he said, "the names of the women with the black garments. Four of these are more powerful. The first is Unbelief, the second is Self-Indulgence, the third Disobedience, and the fourth Deceit.

The ones following them are called Sorrow, Wickedness, Licentiousness, Short Temper, Lying, Foolishness, Slander, and Hatred. The servant of God who bears these names will see the kingdom of God but will not enter it." 4 "Who are these stones, sir," I said, "that have been taken out of the abyss and that fit into the building—what are they?" "The first ten put into the foundations," he said, "are the first generation. The twenty-five are the second generation of righteous men; the thirty-five are God's prophets and His ministers; the forty are the apostles and the teachers of the proclamation of the Son of God." 5 "Why, sir," I said, "did the virgins carry these stones also through the gate and deliver them for the building of the tower?" 6 "These first stones," he said, "bore these spirits. They were never at all separated from one another, neither the spirits from men, nor the men from the spirits. Their spirits remained with them until they slept. If these spirits had not remained with them, they would have been of no use for the building of this tower."

Chapter Ninety-Three
9.16 "Sir, show me something else," I said. "What do you want to know?" he said. "Why," I said, "did the stones that bore these spirits go up from the abyss, and why were they put into the building?" 2 "They had to ascend," he said, "through water in order to be made living. Otherwise, if they had not laid aside the death of their former life, they could not enter the kingdom of God. 3 Those who slept received the seal of the Son of God and entered the kingdom of God. For a man is dead before he receives the name of the Son of God, but when he receives the seal, he lays aside death and receives life. 4 The seal, therefore, is the water. They go down dead into the water and come out of it living. Therefore, this seal was proclaimed to them and they made us of it to enter the kingdom of God." 5 "Then why, sir," I said, "did the forty stones come out of the abyss with them, if they already had the seal?" "Because" he said, "the apostles and teachers who preached the name of the Son of God, after having been laid to rest in power and faith in the Son of God, preach also to those who have fallen asleep before them. To the latter they themselves passed on the seal of the preaching. 6 So they went down with them into the water and came up again. But the apostles and teachers, although alive, went down and returned alive. But those who had been laid to rest before them went down dead and came up alive. 7 With the help of the apostles and teachers they were made alive and came to know the name of the Son of God. For this reason they rose up with them and were fitted together into the building of the tower along with them, built into it without being cut. They slept in righteousness and great purity but did not have this seal. Now you have the interpretation of these matters also." "I have it, sir," I said.

Chapter Ninety-Four
9.17 "Now then, sir, tell me about the mountains. Why are some of one shape and color and others of other shapes and colors?" "Listen," he said. "These twelve mountains are the twelve tribes that inhabit the whole world. To these the Son of God was proclaimed through the Apostles." 2 "But why are they of different colors? Explain to me, sir, why the mountains are some of one shape and others of another." "Listen," he said. "These twelve tribes that inhabit the earth are twelve nations. They differ in understanding and in mind. The varieties of mind and understanding among the nations correspond to the different mountains. I will show you the conduct of each." 3 "First, sir," I said, "show why, although the mountains are of such different colors, when their stones are fitted into the building they all become of one bright color, like those that come up out of the depth." 4 "Because," he said, "all the nations that dwell under the heavens, after hearing and believing, are called by name of the Son of God. So when they received the seal, they

have one understanding and one mind. Their faith and love make them one and, along with the name, they bear the spirits of the virgins. For this reason, the construction of the tower became bright as the sun and shown of one color. 5 But after they entered the same place and became one body, some of them defiled themselves and were cast out from the society of the righteous to become what they formerly were, only much worse."

Chapter Ninety-Five
9.18 "Sir," I said, "how did they become worse, after coming to know God?" "The person who does not know God," he said, "and commits wickedness receives some punishment for his wickedness, but the person who has known God should no longer do wicked actions and must do good. 2 So if the person who knows God ought to do good but still does evil, certainly he commits a greater wickedness than the person who does not know God. For this reason those who have not known God and act wickedly are condemned to death, whereas those who have known God and have seen His mighty works, and yet act wickedly for the second time, will be punished and will die forever. In this way the church of God will be cleansed. 3 You yourself have seen the stones removed from the tower and handed to the wicked spirits, to be cast out along with them. So to leave one body of the cleansed, so also did the tower become as one stone after its cleansing. In the same way it will be with the church of God after the cleansing, after the wicked have been cast out, namely the hypocrites, blasphemers, and persons who are double-minded and perpetrators of various crimes. 4 After the removal of these people, the church of God will become one body, with one understanding, one mind, one faith and one love. Then, too, the Son of God will be glad and rejoice in their midst because he has received his people as clean." "All these things, sir," I said, "are great and glorious. Again, sir," I said, "explain to me the power and conduct of each of the mountains, so that every soul who trusts in the Lord may hear and praise his great, marvelous, and glorious name." "Listen," he said, "to the variety of the mountains and of the twelve nations."

Chapter Ninety-Six
9.19 "Out of the first black mountain come believers of this kind: apostates and blasphemers against the Lord, betrayers of the servants of God. Repentance is impossible for them but there is death and for that reason they also are black, because their kind is lawless. 2 From the second mountain, the bare one, comes this kind of believer: hypocrites and teachers of wickedness. These also are like the first, not having the fruit of righteousness. For as their mountain is fruitless, so men of this kind have the name but are devoid of faith. There is no fruit of truth in them. To these, then, repentance is offered, if they repent promptly, but, if they delay, their death will be with the former." 3 "Sir, why is repentance possible for these, but not for the former? Their deeds are about the same." "The reason why repentance is possible for the second group," he said, "is that they have not blasphemed their Lord, nor have they betrayed God's servants. But from a desire of gain they each taught others the passions of sinners. But they will pay a penalty. Repentance is still offered to them, because they have not become blasphemers nor betrayers."

Chapter Ninety-Seven
9.20 "From the third mountain having thorns and thistles, these believers come: the rich and those involved in many business affairs. The thorns are the rich and the thistles are those involved in varied business affairs. 2 These persons who are involved in those business affairs do not cling to the servants of God, but wander off and are choked by

their activities. The rich have difficulty clinging to the servants of God, because they fear that they may ask them for something. Such people, therefore, will enter the kingdom of God only with difficulty. 3 So for these persons it is just as hard to enter the kingdom of God as it is to walk among thorns in bare feet. 4 But repentance is still possible for all of these, but it has to be swift. Since they were formerly idle, they now have to hasten back to former days and do something good. If they repent and do something good, they will live to God. But if they continue in their activities, they will be handed over to those women who will put them to death."

Chapter Ninety-Eight
9.21 "From the fourth mountain with the many plants, green at the top but dried at the roots, and some scorched by the sun, come believers like this: the double-minded who have the Lord on their lips but not in their hearts. 2 Because of this their foundations are dry and without strength; only their words are alive, but their works are dead. Persons like this are neither alive nor dead. They resemble the people who are double-minded. These are neither green nor dry; they do not live, neither are they dead. 3 Just as these plants wither at the sight of the sun, so also do the double-minded worship idols in their cowardice and are ashamed of the name of their Lord when they hear of affliction. 4 Therefore, people like this are neither alive nor dead. But they also, if they quickly repent, will be able to live. But if they do not repent, they are already handed over to the women who take away their life."

Chapter Ninety-Nine
9.22 "From the fifth mountain with green but rough plants, come these kind of believers: faithful but slow learners and opinionated and self-satisfied. Although they want to know everything, they know nothing at all. 2 Because of their arrogance, understanding has left them and foolishness and ignorance has entered into them. They praise themselves, like having wisdom, and they wish to volunteer as teachers, although they are ignorant. 3 So because of this arrogance, many who exalt themselves have been made empty by their haughtiness. For stubbornness and empty confidence are a mighty demon. Of this group many have been rejected, although some have understanding once they realized their own foolishness. 4 For the rest of them repentance is possible, for they have not become wicked, but merely have become senseless and foolish. If they repent, these people will live to God. But if they do not repent, they will dwell with the women who do them harm."

Chapter One Hundred
9.23 "Those who come out of the sixth mountain, with the large and small rifts and wilted plants in the rifts, are of this kind. 2 Those with the same rifts are people who have grudges with one another and because of their slanders have withered in the faith. However, many of this group have repented. The rest will repent when they hear my commandments, for their slanders are small and they repent quickly. 3 Those with large cracks persist in their slanders and hold grudges in their anger against one another. These have been thrown out of the tower and have been rejected from its building. Such ones will live only with difficulty. 4 Now our God and Lord of all things has power over all his creation and shows no malice against those who have confessed their sins but is merciful. How is it that a corruptible man who is full of sins can show malice against another as if he were able to destroy and to save? 5 I, the angel of repentance, say to you who live

in such division: Put this away, repent! And the Lord will heal your former sins if you cleanse yourselves from this demon. If not, you will be handed over to him for death."

Chapter One Hundred One
9.24 "From the seventh mountain, in which there are green and healthy plants and with which the whole mountain is flourishing, where every kind of cattle and the birds of the sky feed on the plants, and where the plants on which they feed thrive all the more, are these believers: 2 people who are at all times simple and innocent and blessed, holding no grudge against one another; and who are always rejoicing in God's servants and clothed with the holy spirit of these virgins. These from their labors are merciful to every person and help them, without reproach or hesitation. 3 The Lord, on seeing their simplicity and childlike innocence, has filled them through the labors of their hands and favored them in their every deed. 4 I, the angel of repentance, say to you who are like this to remain this way, and your descendants will never be obliterated. For the Lord has approved you and has inscribed you in our number. All your descendants will dwell with the Son of God, for you have received from his Spirit."

Chapter One Hundred Two
9.25 "From the eighth mountain, where there are many springs, are those who watered all the Lord's creation, the believers are these: 2 apostles and the teachers who preached to the whole world and those who teach the word of the Lord with reverence and purity; people who do not turn aside at all for evil desire, but walk at all times in righteousness and truth as they received the Holy Spirit. So their path lies with the angels."

Chapter One Hundred Three
9.26 "From the ninth mountain, deserted and having serpents and wild beasts that destroy human beings, the believers are these: 2 the stones with stains are the deacons who ministered wickedly and robbed widows and orphans of their livelihood and who make a living for themselves out of the ministry they have received. If they persist in the same desire, they die with no hope of life, but if they turn from their ways and fulfill their ministry in a holy manner, they will be able to live. 3 The stones with a rough surface are those that denied their Lord and did not return to Him. Barren and wasted, they did not cling to the servants of God, but went their lonely ways and are destroying their own souls. 4 These men are like a vine, left by itself on a fence, that gets no care and is wasted by weeds. Eventually it becomes wild and is no longer of any use to the master. In the same way these have given themselves up in despair and becoming wild, have become useless to their Lord. 5 Repentance is possible for these people, if it happens that they have not denied (the Lord) from their heart. But if it is found that one of these men has denied from the heart, I do not know whether he can live. 6 I am not saying for the present that one who denies can receive repentance, for it is impossible for a man to be saved who intends to deny his Lord. But there is a possibility for those who denied him in the past to repent. So if one intends to repent, let him do so quickly before the tower is completed. Otherwise, he will be destroyed by the women. 7 Now the chipped stones are deceitful persons and slanderers. They are also the wild beasts you saw on the mountain. The remarks of these people hurt and slay a man just as the wild beasts hurt and kill with their poison. 8 These are broken in their faith, because of their behavior toward one another. However, some of them have repented and been saved. The others of the same

kind can be saved if they repent. But if they do not repent, they will be put to death by those women who have the power."

Chapter One Hundred Four
9.27 "From the tenth mountain, where there are trees providing shelter to some sheep, comes this kind of believers: 2 overseers friendly to strangers and who receive the servants of God into their homes gladly without any hypocrisy. They have given shelter constantly by their own ministries to the poor and widows and have conducted themselves purely. 3 Therefore, they will be given shelter by the Lord at all times. Those who act in this way are glorious before God and their place is now with the angels, if they continue to the end in their service to the Lord."

Chapter One Hundred Five
9.28 "From the eleventh mountain, where are the trees full of all kinds of fruit, the believers are these: 2 those who have suffered for the name of the Son of God, who suffer cheerfully with their whole heart, and who have laid down their lives." 3 "But, sir," I said, "why do all the trees bear fruit, but some of them are more beautiful fruit than others?" "Listen," he said. "All who ever suffered for his name are glorious before God and all their sins are forgiven, because they suffered for the name of the Son of God. Now listen and I will tell you why their fruits are different and why some of them surpass others. 4 All who were brought before authorities and examined and tortured but did not deny when called before the magistrates, but suffered cheerfully are more glorious before the Lord and their fruit is superior. But those who were cowards and lost and in doubt, who reasoned in their hearts whether to deny or confess, yet finally suffered, the fruit of these persons is less, because this suggestion occurred to them. 5 Take care if you have had such decisions not to allow it to remain and you die to God. You who have suffered for his name ought to glorify God, because he has considered you worthy to bear his name that all your sins be healed. 6 Therefore, consider yourselves blessed, and consider that you have done a great deed, if any of you suffers for God. The Lord is bestowing life on you and you are not aware of it for your sins were heavy, but if you had not suffered for the name of the Lord, you would have died to God for these sins. 7 These things I say to you who have hesitated about denial and confession. Confess that you have the Lord, lest denying him you be handed over and put in prison. 8 If Gentiles punish their slaves for denying their master, what do you think the Lord who has power over all things will do to you? Remove these thoughts from your hearts that you may live forever to God."

Chapter One Hundred Six
9.29 "From the twelfth white mountain the believers are these: they are innocent as infants into whose hearts no evil enters and they do not know what wickedness is, but always continue in their innocence. 2 These undoubtedly live in the kingdom of God, because they have not defiled in any way the commandments of God. All the days of their lives they have innocently persisted with the same mind. 3 You who will remain steadfast," he said, "and will be like infants, without evil guile, and will be more glorious than all those mentioned. Every child is glorious in God's sight and comes to him before all others. Blessed are you who have removed wickedness from yourselves and are clothed with innocence, and you will live to God before all the rest." 4 When he had finished the parables of the mountains, I said to him, "Now, sir, explain to me the stones removed

from the plain and placed in the building in place of the stones taken out of the tower. Explain also the round stones put into the building and those that are still round."

Chapter One Hundred Seven
9.30 "Listen to all these things," he answered. "The stones removed from the plain and placed in the building of the tower to replace those that were rejected are the roots of this white mountain. 2 Since the believers from this mountain were found innocent, the Lord of the tower gave orders that the believers from the base of this mountain be put in the building of the tower, for he knew that these stones will remain bright and not one of them will become black.[3] 3 But if he had added some from other mountains, it would have been necessary for him to come back to the tower to purify it. However, it was found that all these persons who believe and are destined to believe are white, for they are of the same kind. Blessed are they because they are innocent. 4 Now I will tell you about those brilliant and round stones, all taken from this white mountain. First, I must tell you why they were found as round. Their riches blinded their minds to the truth and obscured it. However, they have never departed from the true God and no evil word came from their mouths, but whatever was righteous and worthy of the truth. 5 So when the Lord saw their frame of mind and that they could favor the truth and remain virtuous, he ordered their riches to be cut off from them. But he did not remove their riches completely, so they could do some good with what was left them. They will live to God, for they are from a good kind. Consequently, they have been trimmed a little and placed in the structure of the tower."

Chapter One Hundred Eight
9.31 "However, the other stones that remained round and were not fitted into the building, because they have not yet received the seal, were returned to their own place, for they were found to be round. 2 This age and its empty riches needed to be cut away from them. Then they will dwell in the Kingdom of God. They must enter God's Kingdom for God has blessed this innocent kind. Not a single one of this kind will perish. For although one or the other may sin because of the Devil's temptation, he will quickly return to his Lord. 3 I, the angel of repentance, consider you all fortunate who are innocent as infants, because your part is good and honorable before God. 4 I declare to all of you who have received the seal: maintain your innocence, do not bear grudges, do not continue in your wickedness nor in the bitterness of your past offenses. Be of one spirit and heal those evil schisms. Remove them from yourselves, that the Lord of the flock may rejoice in them. 5 And he will if he finds all the sheep healthy. But woe to the shepherds if he finds any of the sheep scattered. 6 And if the shepherds themselves are found scattered, what will they say to the master of the flock? They cannot say that they were scattered because of the sheep. No one would believe them. It is beyond belief that a shepherd could suffer from the sheep. Their punishment will instead be greater because of their lie. I am also a shepherd, and I have a serious obligation to give an account for you."

Chapter One Hundred Nine
9.32 "Therefore, heal yourselves while the tower is being built. 2 The Lord dwells among those who love peace and he is far from the quarrelsome and from those who are given to wickedness. Return to him that spirit intact as you received it. 3 Suppose you give to

---

[3] Most of the rest of the *Shepherd* is from a Latin version compiled from several medieval Latin texts.

the cleaner a whole new garment. You want to receive it back intact. Will you receive it if the cleaner returns it torn? You will instantly be angry and cover him with abuse, saying: 'I gave you a whole garment. Why did you tear it and ruin it? Because of the tear you made in it, it cannot be used.' Surely you will say all this to the cleaner for the tear he made in your garment? 4 Now if you are so upset about your garment and complain about not receiving it back intact, what do you think the Lord will do to you? He gave you his Spirit intact and you return it to him completely useless, so that it is of no use to its Lord. For it became useless after it had been destroyed by you. Surely the Lord of that spirit will punish you with death for this act of yours." 5 "Evidently," I said, "he will punish everyone who bears grudges." "Do not trample on His mercy," he said. "Pay honor to him for he is patient with your sins, and he is not like you. Repent, then, for it is good for you."

Chapter One Hundred Ten
9.33 "All these things written above I, the shepherd, the angel of repentance, have declared and spoken to God's servants. So if you believe and hear my words and walk in them and correct your ways, you will be able to live. But if you persist in wickedness and continue to bear malice, remember that no one of this type will live to God. All these things I had to say have been said to you." 2 The shepherd also said to me, "Have you asked me all your questions?" "Yes, sir," I said. "Why, then, did you not ask me about the marks left by the stones put back in the building which we filled in." I said, "I forgot, sir." 3 "Hear about this now. They are those who have heard my commandments now and have repented with all their heart. When the Lord saw that they had done a good and pure repentance, and that they were able to continue in it, he ordered that their former sins be wiped out. These marks were their sins which have been smoothed over so that they no longer are visible."

Tenth Parable

Chapter One Hundred Eleven
10.1 After I had written this book, the angel who handed me over to the shepherd came to the house I was in and sat on my couch, and on his right hand stood the shepherd. Then he called me and said, 2 "I handed you over with your house to this shepherd, so you could be protected by him." "Yes, sir," I replied. "So if you want to be protected from all trouble and violence; if you want success in every good work and word; if you want every virtue of righteousness, walk in the commandments I gave you, and with them you can overcome all wickedness. 3 For when you keep his commandments, every desire and pleasure of this age will be under your control and success will accompany you in every good undertaking. Imitate his perfection and moderation and tell all that he is highly regarded and that his dignity is great in the sight of the Lord. Tell all, likewise, that he is a mighty ruler and powerful in his office. Over the whole world authority over repentance has been put in his hands alone. Surely you see that he is powerful. However, you despise the maturity and moderation that he shows you."

Chapter One Hundred Twelve
10.2 I said to him, "Ask him, sir, if I have done anything contrary to his command, anything offensive to him since he came to my house." 2 "I know," he said, "that you have done and are going to do nothing against his command. I say these things for your

perseverance, for his report about you has been good. Tell these things to others, that those who repent or who are going to repent should have the same attitude as you. Then he will give a good report about them to me, and I to the Lord." 3 "Sir," I said, "I also make known to everybody the mighty acts of the Lord. It is my hope that all who committed sin in the past will readily repent on hearing these things, and thus regain their life." 4 "Continue in this ministry," he said, "and complete it. All who complete his commandments will have life. Indeed, such a person will be held in high honor by the Lord. Anyone who does not keep his commandments runs away from his own life, besides acting against him. Furthermore, he who does not keep his commandments delivers himself to death and is guilty of his own blood. I remind you to keep his commandments and you will have a cure for your sins."

Chapter One Hundred Thirteen
10.3 "I sent these virgins to live with you because I saw that they were friendly with you. So now you have helpers to be better able to keep His commandments. For the observance of these commandments is impossible without the help of these virgins. Though I see they are glad to be with you, I will nevertheless command them not to leave your house at all. 2 As for you, clean your house thoroughly, for they will gladly live in a clean dwelling. They are pure, chaste, and industrious, and all of them are highly regarded by God. So if they have a clean dwelling in your house, they will remain with you. But if the slightest impurity creeps in, they will instantly go away from your house, for these virgins have not the slightest love for any impurity." 3 "Sir," I said to him, "I hope that I will please them and that they will always be glad to live in my house. Just as this person to whom you handed me over finds no fault in me, so neither will they." 4 He said to the shepherd, "I am sure that the servant of God wants to live, and will keep these commandments, and will house these virgins in a clean dwelling." After saying these things, he handed me over again to the shepherd and called the virgins and said to them, "Because I am sure that you are glad to live in this man's house, I entrust him and his household also to you. So do not depart from his house at all." They were glad to hear these words.

Chapter One Hundred Fourteen
10.4 Then he said to me, "Carry out your ministry courageously. Proclaim to everyone the Lord's mighty works and you will be favored in this ministry. Everyone who walks in these commandments will then live and will be happy in his life, but whoever disobeys them will not live and will be unhappy in his life. 2 Tell all who can do right not to lack in good works and that this is beneficial to them. Now I say that every person should be helped out in his difficulties. Because a person who is in need and endures difficulties in his daily life is in anguish and misery. 3 The person who rescues another from misery obtains great joy for himself. For the man who is troubled by this kind of misfortune suffers the same torment as the man who is in chains. Indeed, many who are incapable of enduring such misfortunes take their own lives. Therefore, the one who knows the misery of such a person, and does not relieve him, commits a serious sin and becomes guilty of his blood. 4 Therefore, all you who have received from the Lord should do good works, lest while you delay doing them, the building of the tower is completed. For your sakes the building of the tower has been suspended. If you do not act quickly to do right, the tower will be completed and you will be shut out." 5 After speaking to me, he rose from the couch and left, taking the shepherd and the virgins with him, and telling me that he would send the shepherd and the virgins back to my house.

CHAPTER THREE

The Letter of Clement of Rome to the Corinthians

EMERGENCE AND RECOGNITION

It should be recognized at the outset in studying this work that no author is mentioned in the document itself. The reputed author of the letter that we call "First Clement," however, gained a rather notable reputation in early Christianity. The writer Hegessipus, who visited Rome during the days of Bishop Anicetus (155–66), refers to a letter that Clement wrote to the Corinthians during the Domitian persecution, around 96 CE. That is at least what Eusebius wrote because we do not possess any of Hegessipus' actual writings (*EH* 3.16; 4.22). Eusebius also informs us that Bishop Dionysius of Corinth mentions around 170 that this letter was read during the liturgy there (*EH* 4.23). The famous Irenaeus of Lyons cites a list of Roman bishops that mentions Clement, in addition to Linus and Anacletus, as succeeding the "apostles" whom they had personally known. He adds that during the time of Clement the church in Rome wrote a letter to the church in Corinth with the purpose of restoring the peace because of a sort of spiritual rebellion that had taken place there (*Haer.* 3.3.3). Toward the end of the second century, another "Clement," this time from Alexandria often referred to the letter in his work called the *Stromata*, sometimes attributing its authorship to an earlier Clement, but sometimes simply stating that the letter came from the church in Rome.

In the early third century, Tertullian claimed that Clement was ordained in Rome by none other than the Apostle Peter. Then the celebrated Origen of Alexandria and Caesarea identified Clement with the fellow worker of the Apostle Paul mentioned in Phil. 4:3. Eusebius also followed Origen in this same identification. By the fourth century, Epiphanius was attempting to reconcile this statement with Irenaeus' earlier placing of Clement in Rome. He wrote that although Peter had ordained Clement, he had surrendered his place and thus the latter to Linus (*Panarion* 27.6). Earlier Clement of Rome had been immortalized in the first surviving Christian "novel" eventually known as the *Pseudo-Clementines*. In this anti-Pauline and Jewish-Christian work, Clement relates his pagan origins, his conversion to the Christian faith, and his journeys with Peter in the eastern Roman Empire. Much of this drama centered on their conflict with the notorious Simon Magus who was mentioned originally in Acts 8. A much later tradition refers to Clement being martyred, but this is unlikely since such a fate had not been mentioned by anyone until this writing emerged. This literature helped in eventually assigning an entire set of additional works supposedly authored by him. The book that we are introducing here, however, is the only one that can be confidently linked with him, although it is not at all an absolute certainty that he was its original author.

THE MANUSCRIPT EVIDENCE

The fifth-century manuscript known as Codex Alexandrinus (A) contains the Septuagint, the New Testament, and after the Apocalypse of John, the two works known as First and Second Clement. As we shall see later, "Second Clement" is not a letter and is not by Clement! Most scholars conclude that the scribe and those who authorized the copying of this manuscript codex intended by this addition that their New Testament canon should include these two "Clements." The second major Greek manuscript that includes Clement is the codex discovered by Philotheos Bryennios in the Jerusalem monastery library of Constantinople in the 1870's and published in 1883. This Codex 54 was removed to Jerusalem soon thereafter. The colophon states that it was copied by a scribe named Leon in 1056 and includes other AF like the *Letter of Barnabas*, the long recension of Ignatius, and the long lost *Didache*! This codex helped to fill in the missing spaces and chapters in Codex Alexandrinus, especially the last eight chapters of 2 Clement. There is also available a Latin translation of 1 Clement as well as another manuscript in Syriac and two in Coptic.

THE CONTENTS OF 1 CLEMENT

The letter is labeled as "First" only because it was handed down with another non-epistolary "homily" that was called "Second Clement." As was mentioned previously, no sender or author is named in the letter. Harnack referred to it as: *The Letter of the Roman Church to the Corinthian Church from the Era of Domitian (1 Clement)*. See "Harnack" in the Bibliography.

While the nature of the letter appears to some readers as rambling and rather disjointed, the following overall structure may commend itself to readers. There are two major sections: (1) chapters 1–38 and (2) chapters 40–65. The first section consists of a broad examination of the chief theme, namely the situation in Corinth where some presbyters had been deposed. The second section then implements the theme with specific instruction about the leaders, namely the apostles, overseers, and deacons. Within that overall structure, the chapters develop generally along the following lines.

After a rather full greeting that could rival Paul's in his letter to the Romans, the substance of chapters 1–3 recalls "the vile and unholy schism" that was stirred up in Corinth by "reckless and headstrong persons" who promoted discord, rebellion, and disorder. The root problem that led to all these troubles was labeled as jealousy. In the narrative style of a synagogue sermon, examples are then provided of the severe results of such jealousy, the examples being taken both from canonical scriptures and the recent history of the community. The luminaries Peter and Paul were victims of such jealousy as well as "a great multitude of the elect" (6.1) sufferers in the community. This suffering has been traditionally viewed as a reference to the recent results of the persecution under Domitian, although this is not certain.

The cure for this schismatic activity is clear. God desires repentance and obedience, faith and humility, meekness and peace, as well as a genuine harmony marked by the fear of God (chs. 7–21). He will fulfill His promise of the resurrection, but only to those who fear Him. Therefore, we must draw near with pure lives to him who from the beginning of the ages has justified his people through faith (chs. 22–32). Modern readers are sometimes surprised at Clement's analogy of the mythical phoenix bird to illustrate the resurrection (25). The author even calls it "a paradoxical sign" and along with the biblical example of Job it illustrates to the author the reality of the resurrection. The message is that God has imbedded even in the natural order clear signs that point to the divine order. Since God worked in creation, this faith does not imply that we are to neglect good works that must still accompany our faith. Even angels submit to the Father's will, so also must we. Faith does not imply that there is no struggle. We must make such an effort to receive the promised blessings, and the way we receive them is through a focus on Jesus Christ (chs. 33–6).

After this long essay on the solution to his readers' problems, the author then turns to the real subject of the letter, the issue of the rebellion in the church and its proposed solution. The readers are exhorted to mutual submission and service through examples from military service and from the role of members in a body. Under the Old Covenant (although the expressions Old Covenant or Testament are not used) the priestly hierarchy was ordained by God. In this age God also ordained and sent his son, Jesus Christ, who ordained his apostles and they in turn ordained overseers and deacons as servants in the Church. Those apostles also set forth a program for an orderly succession to those offices, but this order and succession has been torn apart in this church when the overseers and deacons were so wickedly and wrongly removed (chs. 37–44). This serious deposition of the rightly constituted authorities was a serious persecution of just people that had wounded the members of Christ. "Clement" appeals to the earlier example of Paul's rebuking the offenders in his own (first) Letter to the Corinthians. As love was so abused and then commended in that letter (ch. 13), so love again in Corinth must be restored to its rightful place and role in this congregation. The "rebels" must seek forgiveness by recognizing that the common good is far more important than their own personal agendas. The leaders of the rebellion must seek forgiveness by recognizing what is best for the group as far more important than their personal agendas and they must then submit again to the leaders by accepting their correction (chs. 45–8). The writer's church in Rome will pray that God will protect and preserve the number of the elect. That prayer (chs. 59–61) is a beautiful model of combining praise, thankfulness, and intercession that crosses the boundaries of the second century to reach down through the ages of the history not only of the church in Corinth but of all subsequent ages. The letter closes with another exhortation toward peace. While its end arrives with the naming of the necessary carriers of the letter, a final moving doxology and blessing provide a most eloquent conclusion to the letter (chs. 62–5).

THE NATURE OF THE LETTER

Readers who are familiar with the varying lengths of NT letters are rightly surprised by the extreme length of First Clement. They should still be reminded that it is not an essay with the added trappings of a letter (Hebrews?) but is in actuality a true letter. Remember that it actually comes from a church (in Rome) not from an individual (like Clement). There were real circumstances that prompted its composition, and those behaviors are directly addressed in the letter. This argues against its nature as a supposed "fictive letter" composed as an essay to address a desired subject. The letter, like its younger sister's homily (2 *Clem.*19.1), serves as an "appeal" (63.2). This word was used to appeal to a king or other arbiter to make a decision on the merits of the argument. The community is to decide on rebellion in its midst and to deal with that problem!

As was mentioned earlier, similar to biblical examples in a synagogue homily, hearers (the letter would have been read out to the congregation) would be expected to respond to the vices and virtues in these examples and apply them to their own situation. While there is no clear evidence that the author was a Jewish Christian, he clearly indicates that his "Christian" worldview must have been rooted in the scope and traditions of Hellenistic Judaism. The specific issues were those found in what could be called anachronistically a "Christian church," but the rhetoric still breathes Jewish themes and answers to problems that are not simply Jewish or Greek, but are found in the humanity shared by all peoples and their cultures.

THEOLOGY IN THE LETTER

Writers on "Clement" through the years have often attempted to detect any indications of doctrinal aberration among the recipients, often those similar to Gnostic tendencies. But as one reads about the proposed "doctrinal deviants," such philosophical and theological worldviews simply do not emerge. It is not so much their "orthodoxy" that has gone astray as their "orthopraxy." The detection of such philosophical tendencies is, in this writer's opinion, read *into* the text rather than read *from* the text. As mentioned above, the doctrine of the resurrection is taught and utilized but not because the problem makers were denying the fact of the resurrection, as was the case earlier in Corinth (1 Cor. 15:12). The troublemakers were guilty of sinful and prideful behavior, not because they were denying the doctrinal tenets of the faith. There is simply no theological polemic that is clearly conveyed in the letter. Now it is true that bad behavior is often traced to bad theology, but Clement does not focus on the philosophical and theological issues that are often the favorite topics of those who desire to see these issues on the ground floor of the Corinthian church.

Along the way, however, the author(s) of the letter do reveal some basic theological views that are very important, whatever the practical problems may be. For example, the letter makes extensive use of the scriptures, drawing on the world view behind those scriptures. His quoting of most of the "Servant Song" in Isaiah 53 actually serves to portray the humility of the Messiah. Why? Because the troublemakers were being anything but humble! Justification by faith is grounded not primarily in Paul but in the creation of the world. The relationship between faith and works would be pleasing to both Pauline sympathizers and lovers of the Letter of James because works must follow faith (chs. 32–33). Abraham's faith is not his only claim to fame, but he is offered as an example of one who practiced righteousness because of his faith (31.2).

Therefore, the work is clearly *not* devoid of theology. Consider the following. The language about God is the language of the OT and the Jewish synagogue. God is "the Almighty" and "the all-seeing Master" (55.6); the "Creator and Lord of all things" (33.2); "the Father of the ages, the All Holy One" (35.3); "the Father and Creator of the whole world" (19.2); "the King of the ages" (41.2), who "embraces all things" (28.4). His activity in the world displays his love of harmony (20.11). He is made known as "the Creator and overseer of every spirit" (59.3). To his people he is as a "gentle and merciful Father" (29.1), and "the protector and defender of those who minister to his all holy Name" (45.7). Such language might be unoffensive to Jews, but the following echoes also with followers of Jesus. "Do we not have one God and one Christ and one Spirit of grace poured out upon us?" (46.6). See also the statement that at least carries

Trinitarian implications. "As God lives and the Lord Jesus Christ lives and the Holy Spirit, the faith and the hope of the elect" (58.2).

In regard to the person of Jesus, a clear allusion to His pre-existence is in the statement that he speaks through the Holy Spirit in the OT Scriptures (22.1). A similar reference is found in the words "Jesus Christ was sent forth from God" (42.1). He is never directly called God, but His deity is implied when He is described as "the scepter of God's majesty" (16.2), who showed us as in a mirror the very face of God (36.2). The letter speaks of Christ as "the High Priest of our offerings, the benefactor and helper of our weakness" (36.1). "Through him we taste the knowledge of immortality" (36.2), "the full knowledge of God's glorious name" (59.2), and through him we have access to the Father (7.4). This is language that would be cherished by later Nicene theologians.

And there is even more about the Holy Spirit. In times past he inspired the message of the prophets (8.1, 45.2). In the present he is the living power poured out upon the Church (46.6). His indwelling was the source of the many virtues which had formerly even distinguished this church in Corinth (2.3). The writer also claims that his own words were written "through the Holy Spirit" (63.2), a statement that is probably not intended to be taken on the same level as scripture authors, but is profound nonetheless.

Previously mentioned has been the use of the salvific teaching of justification and the relationship of faith to works in both salvation and sanctification. Enough evidence then has been cited to show that "Clement" was no mere moralist, devoid of the theological grounding that makes morality even possible!

SCRIPTURAL INTERPRETATION IN CLEMENT

Many early church writers have gained a reputation, often richly deserved, for allegorical or extremely typological exegesis. While Rahab's red thread in Josh. 2:18 is handled typically (12.7), the author really does not engage in the allegorical interpretation that so marked those in the later "Alexandrine" school (e.g., Origen) over against the "Antiochene" literalist school (e.g., Gregory of Nyssa). Clement's exegesis, while not profound and detailed, is simple and straightforward, and some later writers might even call it rather bland. For example, there is no major takeover of the ritual practices of Judaism as being forerunners of Christ.

Personal examples from the Old Testament abound, but not because of their allegorical importance. A veritable plethora of OT worthies are paraded before the reader, outdistancing in number and scope that famous "Hall of Faith" in Hebrews 11. Women, of whom only one is mentioned in Hebrews, are listed in greater number alongside the many men, such as Miriam (4.11), female martyrs (5.1–6.2), and Rahab (12.1, 3). The positive examples of Esther and the post-biblical Judith are also commended for their courage and virtue (55.3–6). Unlike Hebrews, which only lists positive exemplars of faith, unsavory characters like Dathan and Abiram (4.12) are cited because their factionalism was one of the problems being addressed in Corinth.

In his use of what we call "canonical scripture," our author does make use of the gospel tradition, although not by citing any Gospel author by name (13.2; 46.8), but sometimes simply referring the words to "Jesus." Clement is also our earliest Christian witness to the teachings found in the NT Letter to the Hebrews. Many examples could be cited, but none clearer than his references to Jesus as "priest," a theme dependent on that

NT book. As just one example, see his clear use of Heb. 1:3-13 in 36.2–5. The extremely valuable work by Hagner on Clement's use of scripture should be consulted on all these matters (see bibliography).

SIGNIFICANCE OF 1 CLEMENT IN REFERENCE TO ROME

As has been often noted, Clement is never named in the letter. The sender seems simply to be the church in Rome. No "bishop/overseer" writes as an authoritative person issuing an encyclical. The author does not wish to pronounce on matters related to the authority of "the Roman see," but all must acknowledge that the author was not what was later called a "pope" or as part of a Roman "curia." It is acknowledged by all that no monarchical episcopate existed in Rome at that time. As in other churches, there was undoubtedly a collegial leadership of what would be called "presbyters" or "overseers." Even the word "bishop" should be avoided because of its monarchical or monepiscopal nuances, although that does appear in the slightly later writings of Ignatius. The list of successive bishops found in Irenaeus, for example, appear to be creations of the late second century, not existing in the previous century. In this regard, it is fascinating to take notice of the almost prescient observation in 44.1, that "our apostles also knew, through our Lord Jesus Christ, that there would be strife about the office of the *episkopos*," rendered either as "overseer" or "bishop." Because the word "bishop" carries later "episcopal" connotations, the practice in the translation is to render the Greek noun as "overseer." Neither current liturgical nor non-liturgical traditions should look confidently at this letter to either shore up or to attack other church succession traditions.

In regard to the Roman Catholic approach to these matters, some have discerned in 1 Clement "unequivocal proof" of the primacy of the Roman Church. While there is no categorical assertion of that primacy, "the very existence of the Epistle is in itself a testimony of great moment to the authority of the Roman Bishop. The Church of Rome speaks to the church of Corinth as a superior speaks to a subject" (Quasten, 46). Whatever be one's view on these issues, both sides need to heed what the letter says and also not insist that it says more than it does.

THE PROBLEM OF THE DATE

Before turning to the lasting practical value of 1 Clement for succeeding generations, it would be advised to consider one more "academic" issue, namely, the dating of this letter. As was mentioned in the first paragraphs of this chapter, the traditional and almost universally accepted date for this letter is around 95–96 CE during the persecution of Christians under the Emperor Domitian. This dating is based on a remark by Eusebius over two hundred years later. But what if Eusebius was simply wrong, as has been shown in other observations he made? Also, why is it that "the sudden misfortunes and setbacks" referenced in 1.1 have to be the Domitian persecutions? A summary of an alternative idea about the date follows.

Father Thomas Herron has effectively argued for a much earlier date of around 70 CE (see bibliography). His argument relies heavily on the account in the present tense of what looks like in chapters 40–1 to be a fairly detailed description of the sacrifices in the Jerusalem Temple. It is striking that "Clement" uses the present tense in these chapters. While it is possible that a "historical present" could be employed, the fact that he contrasts the Divine command to perform those sacrifices in the past tense with the description of the ritual in the present tense argues that they were still going on at the time of his writing. It is a fact that is not debated that the Jerusalem Temple was destroyed in 70 CE and not rebuilt. The point then is that the writing would not have taken place in 96 CE but at least twenty-five years earlier.

So what about the Domitian persecution? There is some real question about whether or not that persecution ever really took place on an empire wide basis. The idea is based on faulty evidence and even if it did take place, why must that general expression in 1.1 ("sudden misfortunes and setbacks which have fallen on us") be referring to it? Finally, as has been noted before, the church rule by presbyters with no reference at all to the monepiscopacy described by Ignatius in 110 CE also argues for an earlier date. That date would be nearer the time that such a type of church government existed, namely when the Pauline epistles were written prior to 70 CE. Herron's evidence supporting this can be explored in his 1988 volume (Herron, 11–28). His conclusions were affirmed by Tugwell (89, 102) and they have been viewed with favor by a few other authors (see Batovici, 305–7). Whether or not Herron is correct in his analysis, the date does not alter any of the conclusions previously reached in the chapter or in what follows.

VALUE OF 1 CLEMENT

The history of the beginning of the Christian movement can be easily constructed from the facts supplied by the NT writings. The stage of growth which it had reached toward the end of the second century is amply illustrated by the writings of Irenaeus, Tertullian, and Clement of Alexandria. But for that intermediate period, which is sometimes called the sub-apostolic age, the available sources for first-hand or eyewitness evidence are very slight. One of the main values of this Epistle of Clement is that it is one of those eyewitnesses and possibly the earliest one. 1 Clement helps us to understand better this earliest period, or as some have called it, the sub-apostolic age. The work actually is a witness to a period not necessarily marked by original thought, but rather by a diligent commitment to preserve intact the Christian doctrine and practice that were handed down by the apostles. The evidence supplied by this genuine literary treasure is quite sufficient to dispose of the old idea, possibly inherited from the nineteenth-century German, Ferdinand Baur, that the second-century church was the result of a compromise (thesis-antithesis-synthesis) between Jewish and Pauline sectors who in the first century were quite antagonistic.

Another great German scholar of the early church, Adolph von Harnack, provided as a gift to his students a major work on Clement recently translated into English. Harnack began his book with the following effusive estimates of its value.

> Next to the transmission of the New Testament is the most important foundational document that we have received from the earliest history of the church: the so-called 1 Clement, that is, the extensive letter from the Roman church, the congregation of the capital of the world, to the Corinthian church, the congregation of the Greek metropolis. ... This letter forms directly the foundation for the study of the ancient

history of the church. ... From here arises the necessary conclusion that the study of ancient church history must begin with 1 Clement, since there is no other foundational document that is able to compete with its historical significance.

(Harnack, 3–4)

On a more practical note, Tugwell concludes his treatment of Clement with the following well-chosen words.

The general success of the letter indicates that his message was widely received as having a permanent and universal relevance. And it shows that, long before Augustine espoused a tolerant and a comprehensive view of the church, there was a recognized belief that individual spiritual prowess was less important than remaining humbly and peaceably in the institutional church, looking towards Christ in faith, hoping for salvation for oneself and for one's fellow Christians, praying for mercy upon all sinners, and putting up with everyone and everything in charity.

(Tugwell, 102)

Thus, a lasting lesson from the book is that it could be safely said that the theme of "harmony" (Greek *homonoia*), which is used no less than fourteen times by the author, is one of the greatest values that Clement conveys to later readers. Anyone familiar with the strife that marks much contemporary church ministry recognizes that its message is needed, not only in the second century, but down until today.

FURTHER READING ON FIRST CLEMENT

Batovici, Dan. "Was 1 Clement Written during the Reign of Domitian?" in *Die Daiterung neutestamentlicher Pseudepigraphen*, ed. Wolfgang Grünstäudl and Karl Schmidt, 297–312. Tübingen. Mohr Siebeck, 2021.

Clarke, W. K. L. *The First Epistle of Clement to the Corinthians*. London. SPCK, 1937.

Grant, R. M. and H. H. Graham. *First and Second Clement*. The Apostolic Fathers, vol. 2. New York. Nelson, 1965.

Gregory, Andrew. "Clement. An Introduction" in *The Writings of the Apostolic Fathers*, ed. Paul Foster, 21–31. London and New York. T&T Clark, 2007.

Hagner, Donald A. *The Use of the Old and New Testaments in Clement of Rome*. Leiden. E. J. Brill, 1973.

Harnack, Adolph Von. *The Letter of the Roman Church to the Corinthian Church from the Era of Domitian. 1 Clement*. Edited and Translated by Jacob N. Cerone. Eugene, OR. Pickwick Publications, 2021.

Herron, Thomas J. *Clement and the Early Church of Rome*. Steubenville, OH. Emmaus Road Publishing, 1988.

Knopf, R. *Die Lehre der zwölf Apostel. Die zwei Clemensbriefe*. Tübingen. Mohr Siebeck, 1920.

Lightfoot, Joseph Barber. *The Apostolic Fathers, Part 1. S. Clement of Rome*. 2nd ed., vol. 2. London. Macmillan, 1890. Repr. Grand Rapids. Baker, 1981.

Peters, Janelle. "1 and 2 Clement" in *The Cambridge Companion to the Apostolic Fathers*, ed. Michael Bird and Scott Harrower, 186–207. Cambridge. Cambridge University Press, 2021.

Quasten, Johannes. "Clement of Rome. Epistle to the Corinthians" in *Patrology*, vol. 1. Notre Dame, IN. Christian Classics, 1983.

Welborn, Lawrence, L. "On the Date of First Clement." *Biblical Research* 29 (1984). 25–54.

FIRST CLEMENT

The congregation of God that is sojourning in Rome to the congregation sojourning in Corinth, those who are called and sanctified through the will of God in our Lord Jesus Christ. May grace and peace from Almighty God through Jesus Christ be yours abundantly.

Chapter One
Brothers, because of the sudden misfortunes and setbacks which have fallen on us, one after another, we confess that we have been somewhat delayed in turning our attention to the matters in dispute, and especially to the vile and unholy schism among you. It is alien and foreign to those who have been called by God. Started by a handful of reckless and headstrong persons, it has been inflamed to such a level of madness that your name, once so well known and loved and revered by all, has suffered a severe damage. 2 There was a time when everyone who lived among you thought highly of your virtuous and stable faith, admired the sweet gentleness of your Christian piety, proclaimed abroad your unbounded hospitality, and praised the perfection and soundness of your knowledge. 3 You did all things impartially and walked according to the commands of God, submitting to your leaders and properly respectful of the presbyters in your community. You instructed the minds of your young people toward moderation and modesty. You exhorted young ladies to do all things with a blameless, respectful, and pure conscience. And you taught married women to show affection to their husbands as they should, under the rule of submission, and to manage their homes with piety and much discretion.

Chapter Two
Every one of you used to walk in humility of mind, without arrogance, submitting rather than demanding submission, giving more gladly than receiving,[1] satisfied with the provisions supplied by God. You heeded his words, careful to keep them within, and his sufferings were before your eyes. 2 Thus to all were granted a deep and rich peace and an unceasing desire to do good, and there came on everyone a full outpouring of the Holy Spirit. 3 You were filled with his holy will and in devoted confidence and reverent faith you stretched out your hands to Almighty God, begging him to be gracious to your unconscious shortcomings. 4 Day and night you kept up your efforts for the entire brotherhood, so that with mercy and compassion, the number of his chosen ones might be saved. 5 You were sincere and innocent and forgiving toward one another. 6 Every faction and schism was hated by you. You wept for the failings of your neighbors and considered their shortcomings as your own. 7 You had no regrets for any good you have done and were ready to undertake every kind of good deed.[2] 8 Adorned with the conduct of virtue and honor, you performed all your duties with a reverent awe of God. The commandments and righteous ordinances of the Lord were written upon the tablets of your heart.[3]

Chapter Three
All glory and greatness were given to you, and what was written was fulfilled. "My beloved was eating and drinking, and then grew large and fat and kicked."[4] 2 From

---

[1] Acts 20:35.
[2] Titus 3:1.
[3] Prov. 7:3.
[4] Deut. 32:15.

this came jealousy and envy, quarreling and division, persecution and disorder, war and captivity. 3 Thus those who are dishonorable rose up against the honorable ones, the disreputable against the reputable, the foolish against the wise, the young ones against the older ones. 4 The reason why righteousness and peace are far removed is because each one has abandoned the reverential awe of God, becoming blind to the things of his faith, not walking in the ways of his commandments, and not living worthy of Christ. Instead, each one walks according to the desires of his evil heart, yielding to an unrighteous and impious jealousy, through which also death entered into the world.[5]

Chapter Four

For it is written thus:

> And it came to pass after some days that Cain offered a sacrifice to God from the fruits of the earth, and Abel also offered from the first born of the sheep and their fat. 2 And God looked with favor on Abel and his gifts, but he did not pay attention to Cain and his sacrifices. 3 And Cain was greatly annoyed and his face became downcast. 4 And God said to Cain, "Why are you distressed and why is your face downcast? If you have offered correctly but not divided correctly, have you not sinned? 5 Be at ease; you can repel it, but you must control it." 6 And Cain said to Abel his brother, "Let us go into the field." And it happened while they were in the field that Cain rose up against Abel his brother and killed him.[6]

7 You see, brothers, that jealousy and envy brought about the murder of a brother. 8 Because of jealousy our father Jacob fled from the face of Esau his brother. 9 Jealousy caused Joseph to be persecuted to death, and to be enslaved. 10 Jealousy compelled Moses to flee from the face of Pharaoh, King of Egypt, when he was asked by his countryman, "Who made you a judge or ruler over us? Do you wish to kill me as you killed the Egyptian yesterday?" 11 Through jealousy Aaron and Miriam were excluded from the camp. 12 Jealousy brought down Dathan and Abiram alive into Hades because they rebelled against Moses the servant of God. 13 Because of jealousy David was envied not only by the Philistines, but was persecuted also by Saul, King of Israel.[7]

Chapter Five

Leaving the ancient examples, let us come to the heroes nearer our times. Let us consider the noble examples of our own generation. 2 Through jealousy and envy our greatest and holiest pillars were persecuted and endured to the death. 3 Let us put before our eyes the good apostles. 4 Peter, because of unrighteous jealousy, underwent not one or two but many troubles, and having given testimony he then went to his well-deserved place of glory. 5 Because of jealousy and strife Paul pointed out the way to the reward for endurance: 6 Being chained seven times, he was also banished and stoned; he preached in the East and in the West and received a noble reputation for his faith. 7 He taught righteousness to the whole world, and having reached the limits of the West, and given testimony before rulers, passed from this world and was taken up to the holy place, having become a notable example of endurance.

---

[5] Wis 2:24.
[6] Gen. 4:3-8.
[7] The previous seven verses refer to events in Gen. 27; Gen. 37; Exod. 2; Num. 12; Num. 16; 1 Sam. 18.

Chapter Six

Besides these men who lived such holy lives, there was a great multitude of the elect who suffered many torments because of jealousy and became the finest example among us. 2 It was because of jealousy that women were paraded as Danaids and Dircae and killed after they had suffered horrible and cruel indignities. They maintained the race of faith to the finish and, despite their physical weakness, won the noble reward. 3 Jealousy separated wives from their husbands and changed the saying of our father Adam, "This is now bone of my bone and flesh of my flesh."[8] 4 Jealousy and strife have destroyed great cities and uprooted mighty nations.

Chapter Seven

These things, beloved, we are writing, not only as warning you, but also as reminding ourselves. For we are in the same arena, and the same contest lies before us. 2 For this reason let us abandon empty and silly concerns, and let us come to the renowned and holy rule of our tradition. 3 Let us see what is good and pleasing and acceptable in the sight of him who made us. 4 Let us look intently on the blood of Christ and realize how precious it is to his Father, since it was poured out for our salvation and brought the grace of repentance to the whole world. 5 Let us review all the generations and learn that from generation to generation the Master has given an opportunity for repentance to all who would return to him. 6 Noah preached repentance and those who obeyed were saved.[9] Then Jonah announced destruction to the Ninevites and they repented of their sins, sought God in prayer and received salvation, although he was alienated from God.[10]

Chapter Eight

The ministers of God's grace preached on repentance through the Holy Spirit. 2 And the Master of all things himself spoke of repentance with an oath, "For as I live, says the Lord, I desire not the death of the sinner but his repentance."[11] He added a good announcement, 3 "Repent, O house of Israel, from your wickedness. Say to the sons of my people: 'If your sins reach from the earth to heaven, and if they are redder than scarlet and blacker than sackcloth but you return to me with all your heart and say, 'Father, I will listen to you as a holy people'."[12] 4 And in another place he speaks this way,

> Wash and cleanse yourselves, put away wickedness from your souls before my eyes, cease from your wickedness, learn to do good, seek justice, rescue the oppressed, give a judgement for the fatherless and justice to the widow, and come and let us consider together, says the Lord. If your sins be as scarlet, I will make them white as snow, and if they be as crimson, I will whiten them as wool. And if you are willing and listen to me, you shall eat the good things of the earth, but if you are unwilling and do not listen to me, a sword will devour you, for the mouth of the Lord has spoken these things.[13]

---

[8]Gen. 2:23.
[9]Gen. 7.
[10]Jonah. 3.
[11]Ezek. 33:11.
[12]Ezek. 33?
[13]Isa. 1:16-20.

5 Wishing that all his beloved ones should share in repentance, he established it by his almighty will.

Chapter Nine
So let us obey his magnificent and glorious will. Let us become petitioners of his mercy and kindness and prostrate ourselves and turn to his mercies. Let us abandon fruitless toil and strife and the jealousy which leads to death. 2 Let us fix our eyes on those who have perfectly served his magnificent glory. 3 Let us consider Enoch, who was found righteous in his obedience, and was transported and his death was not found.[14] 4 Noah was found to be faithful through his service. He proclaimed a new birth for the world, and through him the Master saved the living creatures who entered in harmony into the ark.[15]

Chapter Ten
Abraham, who was called "the friend,"[16] was found faithful by becoming obedient to God's words. 2 It was through obedience that he went out from his country, and from his family and from his father's house. It was by leaving a small country and a weak family and a small house that he hoped to inherit the promises of God. For he says to him, 3

> Depart from your country and from your family and from your father's house to the land which I will show you, and I will make from you a great nation, and I will bless you, and I will magnify your name, and you will be blessed. And I will bless those who bless you, and I will curse those who curse you, and through you all the families of the earth will be blessed.[17]

4 And again, when he separated from Lot, God said to him:

> Lift up your eyes and look from the place where you are now, to the north and to the south and to the east and to the west. For all the land which you see I will give to you and to your seed forever. 5 And I will make your seed as the dust of the earth. If a man can count the dust of the earth, then can your seed also be counted.[18]

6 And again he says: "God brought Abraham forth and said to him, 'Look up to the heaven and count the stars if you can count them. So will your seed be.' And Abraham believed God and this was reckoned to him for righteousness."[19] 7 Because of his faith and hospitality a son was given him in his old age, and through obedience he offered him as a sacrifice to God on the mountains which he showed him.[20]

Chapter Eleven
Because of his hospitality and piety Lot was saved from Sodom, when the entire region was judged by fire and brimstone. The Master made clear that he does not abandon

---

[14]Gen. 5:24; Heb. 11:5.
[15]Gen. 6:8; Heb. 11:7.
[16]Isa. 41:8; Jas. 2:23.
[17]Gen. 12:1-3.
[18]Gen. 13:14-16.
[19]Gen. 15:5-6.
[20]Gen. 22.

those who hope in him, but delivers to punishment and torment those who turn away. 2 For as his wife was going out with him, being of a different mind and not continuing in harmony, she was made a sign. She became a pillar of salt to this day, so that all may know that the double-minded and those who question God's power come into judgment and become a warning sign to all generations.[21]

Chapter Twelve
Because of her faith and hospitality Rahab the harlot was saved. 2 When the spies were sent by Joshua the son of Nun to Jericho, the king of the land recognized that they had come to spy out their country, so he sent out men to capture them, intending to put them to death as soon as they were seized. 3 The hospitable Rahab, however, hosted them and hid them upstairs under some stalks of flax. 4 So when the king's men arrived and said, "The men spying on our land came to you; bring them out, for the king commands it," she answered, "Yes, the men whom you are seeking came to me, but they left immediately and are already on their way back," and then she pointed them in the opposite direction. 5 Then she said to the men, "I am definitely convinced that the Lord your God is handing this country over to you, for the fear and the terror of you have come upon all the inhabitants. Therefore, when you do take the country, save me and my father's house." 6 They said to her, "It shall be certainly as you have said. Therefore, when you learn that we are coming, gather all your family together in your house, and they will be saved. But anyone who is found outside the house will perish." 7 In addition, they gave her a sign that she should hang something red from her house, making it clear that through the blood of the Lord redemption will come to all who believe and hope in God. 8 You see, dear friends, not only faith but also prophecy was found in this woman.[22]

Chapter Thirteen
Let us, therefore, be humble-minded, beloved, putting aside all boasting and conceit and foolishness and anger, and let us do what is written, for the Holy Spirit says, "Let not the wise man boast in his wisdom, nor let the strong man boast in his strength, nor the rich man in his riches, but let him who boasts boast in the Lord, to seek him and to do what is just and right."[23] We should especially remember the words which the Lord Jesus spoke, when he taught gentleness and patience. 2 For he spoke thus:

> Be merciful that you may receive mercy. Forgive that you may be forgiven. As you do, so will it be done to you. As you give, so will it be given to you. As you judge, so will you be judged. As you are kind, so will you be treated kindly. With what measure you measure, with the same it will be measured to you.[24]

3 By this commandment and by these demands let us strengthen ourselves to walk obediently to his holy words, being humble-minded, for the holy word says: 4 "Upon whom shall I have regard but for the meek and gentle and the one who trembles at my sayings."[25]

---

[21]Drawn from Gen. 19.
[22]Drawn from Josh. 2.
[23]Jer. 9:23-24.
[24]Matt. 5:7; 6:14-15; 7:1-2, 12.
[25]Isa. 66:2.

Chapter Fourteen

And so, brothers, it is right and holy for us to obey God rather than follow those who in arrogance and disorder are the leaders in an abominable jealousy. 2 For we will suffer no ordinary harm, but run a very great danger, if we rashly trust ourselves to the desires of men who aim at strife and faction, to alienate us from what is good for us. 3 Let us be kind to one another after the model of the compassion and sweet character of the one who made us. 4 For it is written, "The kind shall remain inhabitants of the land, and the innocent shall be left upon it, but the lawbreakers will be entirely destroyed from off it."[26] 5 And again he says, "I saw the wicked lifted up and exalted as the cedars of Lebanon. Then I passed by and behold, he was no more. So I sought for his place, but did not find it. Guard innocence and behold uprightness, for there is a remnant for the peaceful man."[27]

Chapter Fifteen

And so let us cling to those who are practicing peace with piety and not to those who desire peace with hypocrisy. 2 For He says in one place, "This people honors me with their lips, but their heart is far from me."[28] 3 And again, "They bless with their mouth, but they curse with their heart."[29] 4 And again he says, "They loved him with their mouth, and they lied to him with their tongue, and their heart was not right with him, nor were they faithful to his covenant."[30] 5 For this reason, "Let the deceitful lips which speak iniquity against the righteous man become speechless."[31] And again,

> May the Lord destroy all deceitful lips, the tongue that boasts, and those who say, 'Let us magnify our tongue, our lips are our own, who is lord over us'? 6 Because of the misery of the poor and the groaning of the needy, I will now arise, says the Lord, I will place him in safety; 7 I will deal boldly with him.[32]

Chapter Sixteen

For Christ is with the humble, not with those who exalt themselves above his flock. 2 The scepter of God's majesty, our Lord Jesus Christ, came not with the pomp of boasting or of arrogance, although he was mighty, but he was humble, as the Holy Spirit spoke about him. For he says, 3

> Lord, who believed our report, and to whom is the arm of the Lord revealed? We announced in his presence that he is as a child, as a root in thirsty ground. There is no beauty in him, nor glory, and we have seen him, and he had neither form nor beauty, but his form was without honor, inferior to the form of men. He was a man living in stripes and hardships, and knowing how to endure weakness, for his face was turned away, and he was dishonored and not credited. 4 This is he who bears our sins and

---

[26] Prov. 2:21-22; Ps. 37:9.
[27] Ps. 37:35-37.
[28] Isa. 29:13; Matt. 15:3.
[29] Ps. 62:4.
[30] Ps. 78:36-37.
[31] Ps. 31:18.
[32] Ps. 12:4-6.

suffers pain for us, yet we regarded him as subject to pain and stripes and affliction. 5 But he was wounded for our sins, he was bruised for our iniquities. The punishment for our peace was upon him, and by his wound we are healed. 6 We all went astray like sheep; everyone went astray in his own way. 7 And the Lord delivered him up for our sins, and he did not open his mouth because of his affliction. Like a sheep he was led to the slaughter, and as a lamb dumb before its shearer he does not open his mouth. In his humiliation justice was taken away. 8 Who will declare his genealogy? For his life is taken away from the earth. 9 For the iniquities of my people he came to his death. 10 And I will give the wicked for his burial, and the rich for his death, because he did no iniquity, nor was deceit found in his mouth. And the Lord desires to purify him from his wound. 11 If you make an offering for sin, your soul shall see a seed with long life. 12 And the Lord desires to take away the torment of his soul, to show him light and to form him in understanding, to justify a righteous man who serves many. And he himself will bear their sins. 13 Because of this he will inherit many, and will share the spoils of the strong, because his soul was delivered to death, and he was counted among the lawless. 14 And he bore the sins of many, and for their sins he was delivered up."[33]

15 And again he himself says, "But I am a worm and not a man, a reproach among men, and the outcast of the people. 16 All who saw me mocked me, they spoke with their lips, they shook their head, 'He hoped in the Lord, then let him deliver him, let him save him, seeing that he delights in him'."[34] 17 You see, beloved, what is the example given to us. For if the Lord thus humbled himself, what should we do who through him have come under the yoke of his grace?

Chapter Seventeen
1 Let us become imitators also of those who went about "in goatskins and sheepskins,"[35] preaching the coming of Christ. We speak of Elijah and Elisha, and also Ezekiel, the prophets, and in addition to those of renown. 2 Abraham was greatly renowned and was called the "Friend of God," and fixing his gaze on the glory of God, says in his humility, "I am just dust and ashes."[36] 3 It is also written about Job, "And Job was righteous and blameless, a genuine worshiper of God, keeping himself from every evil."[37] 4 But he accuses himself, saying, "No one is pure from defilement, not even if his life is for a single day."[38] 5 Moses was called "faithful in all his house,"[39] and through his service God judged Egypt with their plagues and torments. But even he, when he was greatly honored, did not utter proud words, but when the oracle was given to him at the bush, said, "Who am I, that you are sending me? I am feeble in speech and slow of tongue."[40] 6 And again he says: "But I am only steam from a pot."[41]

---

[33] Isa. 53:1–12.
[34] Ps. 22:6–8.
[35] Heb. 11:37.
[36] Gen. 18:27.
[37] Job 1:1.
[38] Job 14:4–5 (LXX).
[39] Num. 12:7; Heb. 3:2.
[40] Exod. 3:11; 4:10.
[41] Source unknown.

Chapter Eighteen

What shall we say of the illustrious David, to whom God said: "I found a man after my own heart, David the son of Jesse, in eternal mercy I anointed him."[42] 2 But even he says to God,

> Have mercy on me, O God, according to your great mercy, and according to the multitude of your tender mercies blot out my iniquity. 3 Wash me even more from my iniquity, and cleanse me from my sin; for I know my iniquity, and my sin is always before me. 4 Against you only have I sinned, and have done evil before you, that you may be justified in your words, and may overcome when you are judged. 5 For, behold, I was conceived in iniquities, and in sins did my mother bear me. 6 For, behold, you have loved truth. The dark and hidden things of your wisdom you have made clear to me. 7 You will sprinkle me with hyssop, and I will be cleansed; you will wash me, and I will be whiter than snow. 8 You will cause me to hear joy and gladness; the bones that have been humbled shall rejoice. 9 Turn away your face from my sins and blot out all my iniquities. 10 Create a clean heart in me, O God, and renew a right spirit within me. 11 Cast me not away from your face and take not your Holy Spirit from me. 12 Restore to me the joy of your salvation and strengthen me with your guiding spirit. 13 I will teach the lawless ones your ways, and the unholy will be converted to you. 14 Deliver me from the guilt of blood, O God, the God of my salvation; 15 my tongue will rejoice in your righteousness. Lord, you will open my mouth, and my lips will declare your praise. 16 For if you had desired sacrifice, I would have given it; with whole burnt offerings you will not be pleased. 17 A sacrifice to God is a crushed spirit; a crushed and humbled heart God will not despise.[43]

Chapter Nineteen

The humility and obedient lowliness of so many men of such great renown have made us better, and not only us, but likewise our fathers before us and all who have received his words in fear and truth. 2 Sharing, therefore, in their great and glorious deeds, let us run toward the goal of peace which from the beginning has been handed down to us.[44] And let us fix our gaze on the Father and Creator of the whole world, and hold fast to his magnificent and excellent gifts of peace and kindness to us. 3 Let us see him with our mind and let us look with the eyes of the soul on his patient intention. Let us realize how free from anger he is toward his whole creation.

Chapter Twenty

The heavens move at his direction and are subject to him in peace. 2 Day and night complete the course assigned by him neither hindering each other. 3 Sun and moon and the choirs of stars revolve in harmony according to his command in the orbits assigned to them, without any deviation. 4 The earth, bearing fruit at his bidding in the proper seasons, brings forth abundant food for men and animals and all the living beings that dwell on it, without dissent and without altering any of his arrangements. 5 The unsearchable depths of the abysses and the indescribable regions of the lower world are

---

[42] 1 Sam. 13:14.
[43] Ps. 51:1-17.
[44] Cf. Heb. 12:1-2.

subject to the same decrees. 6 The basin of the boundless sea, gathered together in one place according to his plan, does not overrun the barriers appointed to it, but behaves as he ordered it. 7 For he said. "Thus far will you come, and your waves will be broken within you."[45] 8 The ocean, limitless to men, and the worlds beyond it are regulated by the same decrees of the Master. 9 The seasons, spring and summer and fall and winter, give way in turn, one to the other, in peace. 10 The winds from the different quarters, each in its proper season, perform their service without hindrance. The ever-flowing springs, made for enjoyment and for health, without fail offer their breasts to sustain the life of mankind. The very least of the animals come together in harmony and in peace. 11 The great Creator and Master of the universe commanded all these things to be at peace and to be in harmony. He does good to all things, and more abundantly to us who have found refuge in his mercies through our Lord Jesus Christ. 12 To whom be glory and majesty forever and ever. Amen.

Chapter Twenty-One
Take care, beloved, lest his many benefits turn into a judgment upon all of us. This will happen if we do not do in harmony the virtuous deeds pleasing to him, to lead lives worthy of him. 2 For he says somewhere, "The Spirit of the Lord is a light, searching the depths within."[46] 3 Let us see how near he is, and that nothing of our thoughts or plans we make escapes him. 4 It is right, then, that we should not turn away from his will. 5 It is better to offend foolish and senseless men who exalt themselves and boast in the arrogance of their reason, rather than offend God. 6 Let us fear the Lord Jesus Christ, whose blood was given for us; let us respect our leaders; let us honor the presbyters; let us teach the young the instruction of the fear of God. Let us guide our women toward what is good. 7 Let them demonstrate a habit of purity, let them exhibit an unfaltering will to be gentle. Let them display the control of their tongue by their silence. Let them show their love, not with partiality but in holiness equally to all who fear God. 8 Let your children receive the instruction which is in Christ, let them learn how humility is powerful with God, how strong is a pure love, how the fear of him is lovely and great and saves all who live in it in holiness with a pure understanding. 9 For he is a searcher of thoughts and desires. His breath is in us, and whenever he wishes he will remove it.

Chapter Twenty-Two
Faith in Christ confirms all these things, for he himself through the Holy Spirit thus calls us to himself:

> Come, children, listen to me and I will teach you the fear of the Lord. 2 Who is the man who desires life, and who loves to see good days? 3 Keep your tongue from evil, and your lips from speaking deceit. 4 Turn away from evil and do good; 5 seek after peace and pursue it. 6 The eyes of the Lord are upon the righteous and his ears unto their prayer. But the face of the Lord is against those who do evil, to destroy any remembrance of them from the earth. 7 The upright person cried out, and the Lord heard him, and rescued him out of all his afflictions.[47]

---

[45] Job 38:11.
[46] Prov. 20:27.
[47] Ps. 34:11-17, 19.

8 "The troubles of the righteous are many, but mercy will surround those who hope in the Lord."[48]

Chapter Twenty-Three
The compassionate and beneficent Father has pity on those who fear him, and with gentleness and kindness bestows his favors on those who approach him with a sincere mind. 2 So let us not be double-minded, nor let our soul conceive false ideas about his extraordinary and glorious gifts. 3 May that scripture be far from us where it says,

> Miserable are the double-minded who doubt in their soul and who say, 'These things we have heard even in the days of our fathers, and behold, we have grown old, and none of these things has happened to us.' 4 O foolish ones, compare yourselves to a tree. Take a vine: first it sheds its leaves, then there comes a bud, then a leaf, then a flower, and after that the unripe grape, then the full bunch.[49]

You see how in just a short time the fruit of the tree becomes ripe. 5 Truly his plan will be fulfilled swiftly and suddenly, as the scripture testifies, "He will come suddenly and not delay; and the Lord will come suddenly to his temple, the Holy One whom you await."[50]

Chapter Twenty-Four
Let us consider, beloved, how the Master always points out to us the coming resurrection of which he declared the Lord Jesus Christ as the first fruits when he raised him from the dead.[51] 2 Let us take note, beloved, about the resurrection that is about to occur. 3 Day and night show us this resurrection. The night falls asleep and the day then rises. The day departs and the night then returns. 4 Observe also the crops. How and in what way does the sowing take place? 5 The sower went forth and threw into the earth each of his seeds.[52] These seeds, falling to the earth as dry and bare, then decay, but then from their decay the greatness of the Master's providence raises them up, and from the one seed many more grow and bear fruit.

Chapter Twenty-Five
Let us consider the paradoxical phenomenon which takes place in the East, in the regions near Arabia. 2 For there is a bird which is called the Phoenix. This bird, the only one of its kind, lives five hundred years. As the time when its dissolution through death is near, it makes a tomb of frankincense and myrrh and other spices, which it enters when its time is completed, and then it dies. 3 As its flesh decays a worm is born, which is nourished by the secretions of the dead bird and it then grows wings. When it grows strong, it picks up that tomb in which are the bones of its predecessor and carries them from the country of Arabia to Egypt, to the city called Heliopolis. 4 Then in the daytime, when all are looking, it flies to the altar of the sun, and deposits them there, and thus it

---
[48] Ps. 32:10.
[49] Source unknown. Cf. 2 Clem. 11:2-3.
[50] Mal. 3:1; cf. Isa. 13:22 (LXX).
[51] 1 Cor. 15:20.
[52] Mark 4:3.

hastens back. 5 When the priests examine the records of the times, they then discover that it has come at the end of the five-hundredth year.

Chapter Twenty-Six
Do we then think that it is so great and marvelous if the Creator of all things will bring about a resurrection of those who served him in holiness, with the confidence of good faith, when he thus shows the greatness of his promise even if it is through a bird? 2 For it says somewhere, "You will raise me up and I will praise you,"[53] and "I lay down and slept and I arose because you are with me."[54] 3 And again, Job says, "You will raise up this flesh of mine which has endured all these things."[55]

Chapter Twenty-Seven
With this hope, therefore, let our souls be bound to him who is faithful in his promises and righteous in his judgments. 2 He who commanded us not to lie how much more will he not lie. For nothing is impossible for God, except to lie. 3 Let faith in him, therefore, be rekindled in us, and let us consider that all things are near to him. 4 By the word of his majesty he has set up all things, and by a word he is able to overturn them. 5 "Who shall say to him, 'What have you done?' Or who will stand against the might of his power?"[56] When he wishes and as he wishes, he will do all things and nothing decreed by him will fail. 6 All things are before him, and nothing is hidden from his will. 7 "The heavens show forth the glory of God, and the firmament declares the work of his hands. Day to day it utters speech, and night to night it proclaims knowledge. And there are no words nor sounds, whose voices are not heard."[57]

Chapter Twenty-Eight
Seeing, therefore, that all things are seen and heard, let us fear him and abandon the unclean desires for evil deeds, that we may be shielded by his mercy from the coming future judgments. 2 For where can any of us flee from his mighty hand? And what world will welcome any one of those who desert him? 3 For the Scripture says in some place, "Where will I go, and where will I hide from your face? If I ascend to heaven, you are there. If I journey to the ends of the earth, there is your right hand. If I make my bed in the abyss, your spirit is there."[58] 4 Where then can someone go or escape from him who embraces all things?

Chapter Twenty-Nine
Let us come before him, therefore, with a devout soul, lifting pure and undefiled hands to him, loving our gentle and merciful Father who has made us his chosen portion. 2 For thus it is written: "When the Most High divided the nations, when he scattered the sons of Adam, he set up the boundaries of nations according to the number of the angels of God. His people, Jacob, became the portion of the Lord; Israel became the allotment

---

[53] Ps. 28:7.
[54] Ps. 3:5.
[55] Job. 19:26.
[56] Wis. 12:12.
[57] Ps. 19:1-3.
[58] Ps. 139:7-8.

of his inheritance."[59] 3 And in another place it says, "Behold, the Lord takes to himself a nation from the midst of the nations, as a man takes the firstfruits from his threshing floor, and from that nation will come forth the Holy of Holies."[60]

Chapter Thirty
Since then we are a portion of the Holy One, let us do everything that belongs to holiness, fleeing from evil speech and abominable and impure embraces, from drunkenness and from revelry, and loathsome lusts, foul adultery, and loathsome pride. 2 "For God," he says, "resists the proud but gives grace to the humble."[61] 3 Let us then join with those to whom grace is given from God. Let us be clothed with harmony in meekness of spirit and humility, keeping ourselves far from all gossip and evil speech, being justified by deeds and not by words. 4 For he says, "He who speaks much must also hear much, or does he who speaks eloquently think that he is righteous? 5 Blessed is the man born of a woman who has a short life. Be not full of words."[62] 6 Let our praise be with God, and not from ourselves, for God hates those who praise themselves. 7 Let the witness of our good deeds be given by others, as it was given to our fathers, who were righteous. 8 Audacity and arrogance and presumption belong to those who are cursed by God; gentleness and humility and meekness belong to those who are blessed by God.

Chapter Thirty-One
Let us, then, cling to his blessing, and let us see what are the paths of blessing, and let us call to mind the events from the beginning. 2 Why was our father Abraham blessed? Was it not because he performed righteousness and truth through faith? 3 Isaac, knowing the future in confidence, was willingly led forth as a sacrifice. 4 Jacob went out from his own country with humility because of his brother, and departed to Laban and served him, and the scepter of the twelve tribes of Israel was given to him.[63]

Chapter Thirty-Two
Whoever examines each example sincerely will recognize the greatness of the gifts given by him. 2 For from him come priests and Levites who minister at the altar of God. From him comes the Lord Jesus according to the flesh; from him come the kings and rulers and leaders of Judah. And the other scepters are in no small honor either, as God promised, "Your seed will be as the stars of heaven."[64] 3 They were all glorified and magnified, not through themselves or their own works or the good deeds which they did, but through his will. 4 And we also, having been called through his will in Christ Jesus, are not justified by ourselves, or by our own wisdom or understanding or piety or the works we have done in holiness of heart, but through that faith by which the Almighty God has justified all from the beginning, to whom be glory for all ages. Amen.

---

[59] Deut. 32:8-9. LXX: "sons of God"; Hebrew: "sons of Israel."
[60] Deut. 4:34; 14:2.
[61] Prov. 3:34; Jas 4:6; 1 Pet. 5:5.
[62] Job 11:2-3 (LXX).
[63] Gen. 15: 22; 28 referenced in the chapter.
[64] Gen 15:5; 22:17; 26:4.

Chapter Thirty-Three

What then should we do, brothers? Should we abstain from doing good and abandon love? May the Master never allow this to happen to us, but let us be diligent to complete every good work with fervor and zeal. 2 For the Creator and Lord of all things himself takes joy in his works. 3 For in his incomprehensible might he has established the heavens, and by his unsearchable wisdom he has set them in order. He separated the earth from the surrounding water and placed it on the solid foundation of his own will. He called into existence the animals that move about in it by his own command. Having prepared the sea and the living beings that are in it, he then enclosed them by his own power. 4 Over all he formed man with his holy and pure hands, the most excellent and greatest in intelligence, stamped with his own image. 5 For God spoke thus, "Let us make man according to our image and likeness. So God made man, male and female he made them."[65] 6 Having finished all these things, he praised and blessed them and said, "Increase and multiply."[66] 7 Let us recognize that all the righteous have been adorned with good works. So the Lord himself, adorning himself with good works, rejoiced. 8 Having this model, therefore, we should follow his will without hesitation. Let us do the work of righteousness with all our strength.

Chapter Thirty-Four

The good laborer receives the bread of his labor with confidence; the lazy and careless one does not look his employer in the eye. 2 We must, therefore, be eager in doing good, for all things come from him. 3 He warns us in advance, "Behold the Lord comes, and his reward is before his face, to pay each according to his work."[67] 4 He therefore urges us who believe in him with all our heart not to be lazy nor careless in every good work. 5 Let our glorying and our confidence be in him; we should be subject to his will. Let us consider the whole multitude of angels, how they stand before him, ministering his will. 6 For the Scripture says, "Ten thousand times ten thousand stood before him, and thousands of thousands were ministering to him, and they cried, 'Holy, Holy, Holy, Lord of hosts the whole creation is full of his glory'."[68] 7 We, therefore, gathering together in harmony in our conscience, also should cry out fervently with one voice to him, that we may share in his great and glorious promises. 8 For he says, "Eye has not seen, nor ear has heard, nor has it entered the heart of man, what things the Lord has prepared for those who wait for him."[69]

Chapter Thirty-Five

How blessed and marvelous are the gifts of God, beloved. 2 Life in immortality, brilliance in righteousness, truth in boldness, faith in confidence, self-control in holiness, and all these things fall within our understanding. 3 And what then shall we say of the things that are being prepared for those who wait? Only the Creator and Father of the ages, the All Holy One, knows their quantity and beauty. 4 Let us strive, therefore, to be found in the number of those who wait for him, that we may share in the promised gifts. 5 But how

---

[65] Gen. 1:26-27.
[66] Gen. 1:28.
[67] Isa. 40:10; Rev. 22:12.
[68] Dan. 7:10; Isa. 6:3.
[69] 1 Cor. 2:9.

shall this be, beloved? If our mind is fixed through faith toward God; if we seek what is pleasing and acceptable to him; if we perform what is proper to his faultless will and follow the way of truth, casting from us all injustice and lawlessness, covetousness, strife, both malice and deceit, both gossiping and evil speaking, hatred of God, both arrogance and boasting, vanity and inhospitality. 6 For those who do these things are hateful to God, and "not only those who do them, but also those who approve them." 7 For the Scripture says,

> But to the sinner God says: "Why do you declare my righteous deeds and take my covenant in your mouth? 8 You who hate discipline and have cast away my words behind you. If you see a thief, you run with him, and with adulterers you have had a share. Your mouth has been full of evil and your tongue has woven plans of deceit. You sat to speak slander against your brother and have placed a stumbling block against your mother's son. 9 These things have you done, and I was silent. You have thought, O lawless man, that I will be like you. 10 But I will convict you and set you against your own face. 11 So understand these things, you who forget God, lest he seize you like a lion, and there will be no one to deliver you. 12 The sacrifice of praise will glorify me, and there is a way by which I will show him the salvation of God."[70]

Chapter Thirty-Six
This is the way, beloved, through which we found our salvation, Jesus Christ, the high priest of our offerings, the benefactor and helper of our weakness.[71] 2 Through him let us gaze into the heights of heaven. Through him we see mirrored his spotless and glorious countenance. Through him the eyes of our heart have been opened. Through him our foolish and darkened understanding springs up into the light. Through him the Lord decided that we should taste the knowledge of immortality. "Who, being the brightness of his majesty is so much greater than the angels as he has inherited a more excellent name."[72] 3 For it is so written, "Who makes his angels spirits, and his ministers a flame of fire."[73] 4 But regarding his son the Lord has spoken thus, "You are my Son; this day I have begotten you. Ask me and I will give you the Gentiles for your inheritance, and the end of the earth for your possession."[74] 5 And again he says to him, "Sit at My right hand until I make your enemies a footstool for your feet."[75] Who then are the enemies? Those who are wicked and oppose his will.

Chapter Thirty-Seven
Therefore, men and brothers, let us be his soldiers with all earnestness under his faultless commands. 2 Let us consider those who are enrolled under our leaders, how well-ordered, how readily, and how obediently they carry out commands. 3 Not all are commanders, or tribunes, or centurions, or in charge of bands of fifty. But each one in his own order

---

[70] Ps. 50:16-23.
[71] Cf. Heb. 3:1; 2:18.
[72] Heb. 1:3-4.
[73] Heb. 1:7; Ps. 104:4.
[74] Ps. 2:7-8; Heb. 1:5.
[75] Ps. 110:1; Heb. 1:13.

carries out the commands issued by the king and the officers. 4 The great cannot exist without the small, nor the small without the great. There is a certain organization and it is useful to all. 5 Let us consider our own body. The head without the feet is nothing, and so also the feet without the head are nothing. The smallest members of our body are necessary and useful to the whole body. But all parts work together and unite in a single obedience, so that the whole body can be saved.[76]

Chapter Thirty-Eight
Therefore, let our whole body be saved in Christ Jesus, and let each one submit to his neighbor, according to the gift bestowed on each. 2 Let not the strong neglect the weak and let the weak respect the strong. Let the rich man supply the needs of the poor, and let the poor man give thanks to God, because he has given him someone to supply his needs. Let the wise show his wisdom not in words but in good deeds. Let the humble not testify to his own humility, but allow others to give witness about him. Let him who is pure in the flesh be so without arrogance, knowing that it is another who grants him this self-control. 3 Let us consider, brothers, the material from which we were made; who and what we are who have come into the world; from what kind of grave and what darkness our Maker and Creator brought us into the world and prepared his benefits for us even before we were born. 4 We who have all these things from him ought to thank him in every way. To him be glory forever and ever. Amen.

Chapter Thirty-Nine
Ignorant, unlearned, foolish, and untaught men laugh at us and ridicule us, wishing to exalt themselves in their own thoughts. 2 For what can a mortal do? Or what is the power of one born on earth? 3 For it is written,

> There was no shape before my eyes, but I heard breathing and a voice. 4 What then? Shall a mortal be pure before the Lord? Or will a man be blameless in his deeds if he does not believe in his servants, and finds defects in his own messengers? 5 Even heaven is not pure in his sight. Away you who live in clay dwellings, from which is the same clay we ourselves were made. He struck them like a moth, and between morning and evening they ceased to exist. They perished without being able to help themselves. 6 He breathed on them, and they died, because they did not have wisdom. 7 Call out if there is anyone to hear you, or if you will see any of the holy angels. For wrath destroys the foolish and jealousy kills the one who is deceived. 8 I have seen the foolish taking roots, but their dwelling was immediately consumed. 9 Let their children be removed from safety. Let them be ridiculed in the gates of their inferiors, and there will be none to deliver them. For the righteous will eat what was prepared for them, and they will not be delivered from those who are evil.[77]

Chapters Forty
Therefore, since these things are clear to us and having searched the depths of the divine knowledge, we should do everything that the Master commanded us to do at the appointed times. 2 He commanded that the offerings and the services should be done diligently and

---

[76] 1 Cor. 12:21.
[77] Job 4:16-18; 15:15; 4:19–5:5.

not carelessly or out of order, but at the designated times and the seasons. 3 Where and by whom he wants them to be done, he determined by his supreme will, so that all things should be done devotedly according to his good desire and acceptable to his will. 4 Therefore, those who make the offerings at appointed times are acceptable and blessed, for they follow the instructions of the Master and cannot do wrong. 5 For the proper services have been given to the High Priest, and to the other priests the appropriate offices have been assigned, and upon the Levites the appropriate ministries are imposed. The layperson is bound by the rules for the laity.

Chapter Forty-One
Let each of you, brothers, in his own proper order give thanks to God, maintain a good conscience, and not transgress the designated rule of his ministry, but do these things with reverence. 2 Not just anywhere, brothers, are the continuous daily sacrifices to be offered, as well as the freewill offerings or the sin and trespass offerings, but only in Jerusalem. And even there the offering is not made in every place, but only in front of the sanctuary at the altar, with the offerings first inspected for blemishes by the High Priest and the previously mentioned attendants. 3 Those who do anything contrary to the duty imposed by him have the penalty of death. 4 You see, brothers, the more knowledge we have been given, the more we are exposed to danger.

Chapter Forty-Two
The apostles received the gospel for us from the Lord Jesus Christ and Jesus Christ was sent forth from God. 2 Christ, therefore, is from God and the apostles are from Christ. Both then came in order by the will of God. 3 Receiving their commands, therefore, and being confident through the resurrection of our Lord Jesus Christ, and persuaded by the word of God, and with full assurance from the Holy Spirit, they went forth preaching the gospel that the kingdom of God was about to come. 4 Preaching, therefore, throughout the country and the cities, they appointed their firstfruits, after testing them by the Spirit, to be overseers and deacons for those who would believe. 5 And this was not something novel, since many years before things were written about overseers and deacons. Thus, the scripture says in one place, "I will establish their overseers in righteousness and their deacons in faith."[78]

Chapter Forty-Three
And how amazing is it if they, who had been entrusted in Christ from God with such a work, appointed the persons we previously mentioned? Even the blessed Moses, "a faithful servant in all his house,"[79] recorded in the sacred scrolls all the things commanded him. And the other prophets followed him, testifying with him to the laws given by him. 2 For when jealousy arose about the priesthood and the tribes quarreled as to which of them should be honored with that glorious name, he commanded the leaders of the twelve tribes to bring him rods inscribed with the name of each tribe.[80] He took them and bound them together and sealed them with the rings of the tribal leaders and placed them in the tabernacle of witness upon the table of God. 3 Closing the tabernacle, he

---
[78]Isa. 60:17 (LXX).
[79]Num. 12:7; Heb. 3:5.
[80]This account is derived from Numbers 17.

sealed the keys as well as the doors. 4 And he said to them, "Brothers, the tribe whose rod blossoms is the one God has chosen to be priests and to minister before him." 5 When morning came he called together all Israel, six hundred thousand men, and showed the seals to the heads of the tribes, and opened the tabernacle of witness, and brought out the rods. And the rod of Aaron was the only one to have blossomed but also to be bearing fruit. 6 What do you think, beloved? Did not Moses know ahead of time that this would take place? He certainly knew. But so that no disorder would arise in Israel, he did it this way so the name of the true and only God would be glorified, to whom be glory forever and ever. Amen.

Chapter Forty-Four
Our apostles also knew, through our Lord Jesus Christ, that there would be strife about the office of the overseer. 2 For this reason having received this full foreknowledge, they appointed those previously mentioned, and then gave them a permanent character, so that when they died, other approved men would succeed them in their ministry. 3 Those, therefore, were appointed by the apostles or afterwards by other reputable men, with the consent of the whole church. These who ministered blamelessly and in humility to the flock of Christ, peaceably and nobly, and who were commended for many years by all, we consider are not justly deposed from their ministry. 4 It will be no small sin if we depose from the overseer's office men who have blamelessly and in holiness offered up their gifts. 5 Blessed are the presbyters who have gone before, since they enjoyed a fruitful and perfect departure, for now they need not fear that anyone will remove them from the position assigned to them. 6 For we see that, despite their good conduct, you have forced some men from a ministry which they conducted blamelessly and honorably.

Chapter Forty-Five
Brothers, be eager and zealous for the things that relate to salvation. 2 You have studied the scriptures which are true and given by the Holy Spirit. 3 You know that nothing unjust or contrary to truth has been written in them. You will not find that righteous men have been expelled by holy men. 4 The righteous were persecuted, but by the wicked. They were imprisoned, but by unholy men. They were stoned by transgressors; they were killed by men who had embraced a foul and wicked envy. 5 Although suffering such things, they endured nobly. 6 What shall we say, brothers? Was Daniel cast into the lions' den by those who feared God? 7 Or were Hananiah, Azariah, and Mishael shut up in the fiery furnace by men who participated in the great and glorious worship of the Most High?[81] May it never be! Who, then, were the ones who did these things? They were hateful men, filled with all evil, who were roused to such fury that they tortured those who served God in holiness and purity of purpose. They did not know that the Most High is the protector and defender of those who minister to his all holy Name with a pure conscience. To him be glory forever and ever. Amen. 8 But those who endured confidently inherited glory and honor, and were exalted and inscribed by God in their own memorial forever and ever. Amen.

---

[81]These incidents are described in Dan. 2 and 6.

Chapter Forty-Six

And so, brothers, we also must cling to models such as these. 2 For it is written, "Cling to the holy ones, for they who cling to them shall become holy ones."[82] 3 And again in another place it says, "With an innocent man, you will be innocent; and with an elect man, you will be elect; but with a perverse man, you will be deal perversely."[83] 4 Let us cling, then, to the innocent and the righteous, for these are God's elect. 5 Why are there quarrels and ill will and dissensions and factions and war among you? 6 Do we not have one God and one Christ, and one Spirit of grace poured out upon us, and one calling in Christ?[84] 7 Why do we wrench and tear apart the members of Christ, and revolt against our own body, and reach such folly as to forget that we are members of one another? Remember the words of our Lord Jesus, 8 for He said, "Woe to that person! It would be better for him if he had not been born, rather than to cause one of my elect to stumble. It would be better for him that a millstone be tied to him and that he be cast into the sea, than he should pervert one of my chosen."[85] 9 Your schism has corrupted many, has thrown many into despair, and all of us into sorrow, and your faction continues!

Chapter Forty-Seven

Take up the epistle of the blessed Paul the apostle. 2 What did he first write to you at the beginning of his preaching the gospel? 3 In truth, he wrote to you a letter in the Spirit about himself and Cephas and Apollos, because even then you were split into factions.[86] 4 But that factiousness involved you in less guilt, since you were partisans of highly reputed apostles, and of a man approved by them. 5 But consider now who they are who have corrupted you and diminished the respect you had because of your esteemed reputation for brotherly love. 6 It is disgraceful, beloved, very disgraceful and unworthy of your training in Christ, to hear that the secure and ancient church of the Corinthians because of one or two people, is revolting against its presbyters. 7 And this report has come not only to us, but also to those who are opposed to us, so that blasphemies are uttered against the name of the Lord because of your foolishness, and you are exposing yourselves to danger.

Chapter Forty-Eight

Therefore, let us quickly remove this and fall down before the Master and weep, imploring him to be merciful and reconciled to us, and restore us to the honored and holy practice of brotherly love. 2 For this is the gate of righteousness that opens to life. As it is written, "Open to me the gates of righteousness that I may enter through them and confess the Lord. 3 This is the gate of the Lord; the righteous will enter through it."[87] 4 Although many gates are opened, the one through righteousness is the one in Christ. All are blessed who enter by this gate and pursue their way in holiness and righteousness, accomplishing all things without disorder. 5 Let a person be faithful, let them be able to utter knowledge, let him be wise in discerning words, let him be pure

---
[82] Source unknown.
[83] Ps. 18:25-26.
[84] Eph. 4:4-6.
[85] Matt. 26:64; Luke 17:2.
[86] 1 Cor. 1:12.
[87] Ps. 118:19-20.

in deeds. 6 For the more he appears to be, the more should he be humble, seek the common good for all and not just his own.

Chapter Forty-Nine

Let him who has love in Christ do Christ's commandments. 2 Who can explain the bond of God's love? 3 Who can recount the greatness of its beauty? 4 The height to which love lifts us is inexpressible. 5 Love unites us to God; love covers a multitude of sins.[88] Love bears all things and endures all things. There is nothing vulgar in love, nothing arrogant. Love knows no schism, does not rebel, does all things in harmony. All of God's elect have been perfected in love. Without love nothing is pleasing to God.[89] 6 In love the Master received us; out of the love he had for us, Jesus Christ the Lord gave his blood for us by the will of God, and his flesh was for our flesh, and his life was for our lives.

Chapter Fifty

You see, beloved, how great and wonderful is love, and that its perfection is beyond explanation. 2 Who is good enough to be found in it except those whom God makes worthy? Let us pray, therefore, and beg from his mercy to be found in love, without human partisanship and blameless. 3 All the generations from Adam to this day have passed, but those who were perfected in love by the grace of God live among the saints. They will be revealed at the judgment of the kingdom of Christ. 4 For it is written, "Enter into your rooms for a little while, until my wrath and anger pass by, and I will remember a good day and will raise you up out of your graves."[90] 5 Blessed are we, beloved, if we obey God's commandments in the harmony of love, that our sins may be forgiven through love. 6 For it is written, "Blessed are they whose iniquities are forgiven, and whose sins are covered. Blessed is the man whose sin the Lord does not take into account, and in whose mouth is found no deceit."[91] 7 This blessing came to those who were chosen by God through Jesus Christ our Lord, to whom be glory forever and ever. Amen.

Chapter Fifty-One

Whatever we have done wrong, and whatever we have done through the plots of the adversary, let us hope that it will be forgiven us. Even those who were the leaders of rebellion and schism must look to the common hope. 2 For those who live in awe and love prefer that they, rather than their neighbors, should undergo sufferings, and they more willingly suffer their own condemnation than the loss of that harmony which has been taught us nobly and righteously. 3 It is better for a man to confess his sins than to harden his heart, as the heart of those who rebelled against Moses, the servant of God, was hardened, and the judgment on them was publicly seen. 4 For they went "down into Hades alive" and "death will shepherd them."[92] 5 Pharaoh and his army and all the leaders of Egypt, both the chariots and their riders, were plunged into the Red Sea and perished for no other reason than that their foolish hearts were hardened, after the signs and wonders in the land of Egypt were done through God's servant Moses.[93]

---

[88] 1 Pet. 4:8.
[89] Cf. 1 Cor. 13:4-7.
[90] Isa. 26:20; Ezek. 37:12.
[91] Ps. 32:1-2; Rom. 4:7-9.
[92] Num. 16:33; Ps. 49:14.
[93] Exod. 14:23.

Chapter Fifty-Two

Brothers, the Master of the universe is in need of nothing. He requires nothing from anyone, except that praise be made to him. 2 For the chosen one, David, says, "I will confess to the Lord, and it will please him more than a young calf with horns and hoofs. Let the poor see it and rejoice."[94] 3 And again he says, "Sacrifice to God a sacrifice of praise, and render to the Most High your vows. Call upon me in the day of your affliction, and I will deliver you, and you will glorify me."[95] 4 "For a broken spirit is a sacrifice to God."[96]

Chapter Fifty-Three

For you know, beloved, and well understand the Holy Scriptures, and you have studied the sayings of God. Therefore, we write these things only as a reminder. 2 For when Moses ascended the mountain and spent forty days and forty nights in fasting and humiliation, God said to him, "Moses, Moses, descend quickly, for the people whom you brought out of Egypt have committed iniquity.[97] They have quickly gone astray from the way which you commanded them and have made images for themselves." 3 And the Lord said to him, "I have spoken to you once and twice, saying, 'I have seen this people and, behold, they have a stiff neck. Let me destroy them and I will extinguish their name from under heaven, and I will make you a great and marvelous nation, more numerous than this one.'" 4 And Moses said: "No Lord! Pardon the sin of this people or blot me also out of the book of the living." 5 O what great love! O what incomparable perfection! The servant speaks boldly to the Lord and asks forgiveness for the multitude or he requests that he himself be blotted out with them.

Chapter Fifty-Four

Who then among you is noble? Who is compassionate? Who is filled with love? 2 Let him say, "If because of me there is rebellion and strife and schisms, I will leave. I will go wherever you wish and will do what is commanded by the multitude, only allow the flock of Christ to have peace with its appointed presbyters." 3 He who does this will win for himself great glory in Christ and every place will welcome him, for "the earth is the Lord's and its fullness."[98] 4 Thus have they done and will do who fulfill their obligations as citizens of God without regret.

Chapter Fifty-Five

And now let us take examples from the Gentiles also. Many kings and rulers, when a period of plague occurred, followed the advice of oracles and handed themselves over to death, in order to rescue the citizens by their own blood. Many left their own cities that these might be divided no more. 2 We know that many among us have given themselves to chains in order to redeem others. Many have surrendered themselves to slavery and provided food for others with the purchase price they received. 3 Many women, strengthened by the grace of God, have accomplished many heroic deeds. 4 The blessed Judith, when the city was besieged, asked permission from the elders to be allowed to go

---

[94] Ps. 69:30-32.
[95] Ps. 50:14-15.
[96] Ps. 51:17.
[97] The following is drawn from Exo. 32:7-10; 31-32; Deut. 9:12-14.
[98] Ps. 24:1.

into the foreigners' camp. 5 By handing herself over to danger for love of her country she went out for the people who were besieged, and the Lord delivered Holofernes into the hand of a woman.[99] 6 No less did Esther, who was perfect in faith, put herself in danger to save the twelve tribes of Israel that were about to be destroyed.[100] For through fasting and humility she petitioned the all-seeing Master, the God of the ages, who seeing the humility of her soul, rescued the people for whom she had faced danger.

Chapter Fifty-Six
Therefore, let us also intercede for those who fall into some transgression, that gentleness and humility be given to them, so that they may yield not to us but to God's will. For in this way there will be for them a fruitful and perfect and compassionate remembrance with God and the saints. 2 Let us receive instruction, beloved, and not be irritated by it. The admonition which we give to one another is good and most beneficial, for it joins us to the will of God. 3 For the holy word speaks in this way: "With discipline did the Lord discipline me, and he did not deliver me to death. 4 For whom the Lord loves he disciplines, and whips every son whom he receives."[101] 5 For it says, "The righteous one will discipline me with mercy and correct me, but let not the oil of sinners anoint my head."[102] 6 And it says again,

> Blessed is the man whom the Lord has corrected, and do not despise the admonition of the Almighty, for he causes pain and again restores him. 7 He struck and his hands then healed. 8 Six times he will deliver you from troubles, and in the seventh time evil will not touch you. 9 In famine he will deliver you from death, and in war he will free you from the hand of the sword. 10 And he will hide you from the scourge of the tongue, and you will not be afraid when evils come. 11 You will laugh to scorn the unrighteous and lawless, and you will not fear wild beasts. 12 For wild beasts will be at peace with you. 13 Then you will know that your house will be at peace, and the habitation of the tent you inhabit will not fail. 14 And you will know that your seed will be numerous and your children will be like all the grass of the field. 15 And you will enter the grave like ripe grain harvested in its season, or like a heap of sheaves on the threshing floor gathered at the appointed time.[103]

16 You see, beloved, how great is the protection given to those who are disciplined by the Master. For he disciplines as a good father, that we may receive mercy through his holy discipline.

Chapter Fifty-Seven
You, therefore, who laid the foundation of rebellion, submit to the presbyters, and accept the discipline that leads to repentance, bending the knees of your heart. 2 Learn to be submissive, laying aside the boastful and proud insolence of your tongue. It is better for you to be considered as "little ones" but honorable within the flock of Christ than appear prominent and be cast out from his hope. 3 For his all-virtuous Wisdom speaks this way.

---

[99]Drawn from Judith 8–12.
[100]Drawn from Esther 4–7.
[101]Prov. 3:12; Heb. 12:6.
[102]Ps. 141:5.
[103]Job 5:17-26.

Behold I will bring forth to you the words of my spirit, and I will teach you my word. 4 Because I called and you did not obey, and I put forth my words and you paid no attention but considered my counsel useless and disobeyed my warnings. Therefore, I will also laugh at your destruction, and I will rejoice when ruin comes upon you and when confusion suddenly overwhelms you and catastrophe descends like a whirlwind, or when affliction or a siege comes. 5 For it will come to pass when you call upon me I will not hear you. The wicked will seek me and not find me. For they hated wisdom and did not choose the fear of the Lord. Neither would they heed my advice but mocked my reproofs. 6 For this reason they will eat the fruits of their own way and will be filled with their own impious deeds. 7 Because they treated unjustly the young, they will be killed, and judgment will destroy the ungodly. But he who hears me will dwell securely in hope and will be at rest without fear of any evil.[104]

Chapter Fifty-Eight
1 Let us, therefore, obey his all-holy and glorious name, and escape the threats spoken about the disobedient long ago by Wisdom, that we may dwell in confidence in the most sacred name of his majesty. 2 Take our advice, and there will be nothing for you to regret. For as God lives and the Lord Jesus Christ lives and the Holy Spirit, the faith and hope of the elect, so will the one who with humility of mind and ready gentleness and has obeyed without turning back the decrees and commandments given by God be enrolled and chosen among the number of those who are saved through Jesus Christ, through whom is the glory to God forever and ever. Amen.

Chapter Fifty-Nine
But if some disobey the words spoken by him through us, they should know that they will involve themselves in no little transgression and danger. 2 But we ourselves will be innocent of this sin and will ask with fervent prayer and petition that the Creator of all will keep unharmed the counted number of his elect in the entire world, through his beloved Servant Jesus Christ, through whom he called us out of darkness into light, and from ignorance to the full knowledge of his glorious name. 3 Grant us, Lord, to hope in his name, the source of all creation. Open the eyes of our heart to know you, who alone is the highest among the high ones, who remains holy among the holy ones. You humble the pride of the proud ones. You destroy the conceits of the nations, lifting up the humble and humbling the exalted. You are the one who makes both rich and poor, who kills and who brings to life, who is the sole benefactor of spirits and the God of all flesh. You look into the regions of the abyss. You see into the works of humans. You are the helper of those in danger, the Savior of those who are hopeless, the Creator and overseer of every spirit. You multiply nations on earth and from them you have chosen those who love You through Jesus Christ your beloved Servant. Through him you have taught us, sanctified us, and honored us. 4 We ask you, Master, to be our helper and protector. Save those of us who are afflicted, show mercy to the humble, raise up the fallen, show yourself for those who are in need, heal the sick, return the wanderers among your people, feed the hungry, ransom our prisoners, raise up the weak, encourage the despondent. Let all the Gentiles know that you alone are God, and that Jesus Christ is your Servant, and that we are your people and the sheep of your pasture.[105]

---

[104]Prov. 1:23-33.
[105]The references to Jesus as "Servant" (*pais*) in this chapter probably recall the "Servant" of Isaiah 52–53.

Chapter Sixty

For you have made plain the eternal order of the world through the works you have completed. You, Lord, created the inhabited world. You who are faithful in all generations, upright in your judgments, wonderful in strength and majesty, wise in your creation, and intelligent in establishing your works, good in what is seen, and kind to those who trust in you as well as merciful and compassionate. Forgive our sins and unjust deeds, our trespasses and faults. 2 Count not every sin of your male and female slaves, but cleanse us with your truth, and make our steps straight that we may walk in holiness and justice and simplicity of heart and be able to do those things that are good and well-pleasing before you and our rulers. 3 Yes, Master, make your face shine on us in peace for our good, that we may be protected by your powerful hand and rescued from all sin by your uplifted arm, and also deliver us from those who hate us unjustly. 4 Grant harmony and peace to us and to all who inhabit the earth, just as you gave it to our fathers, when they called on you reverently in faith and truth, so that we may be saved, and grant that we may be obedient to your omnipotent and excellent name, and to our rulers and leaders on earth.

Chapter Sixty-One

You, Master, have given the authority of the kingdom to them through your all-powerful and indescribable might, that we by recognizing the glory and honor you have given to them, may also be subject to them and in no way resist your will. Give to them, Lord, health, peace, harmony, and stability that they may administer without failing the rule which you have given to them. 2 For you, heavenly Master, King of the ages, have given to the sons of men glory and honor, and authority over the things on earth. Direct their plans, Lord, according to what is good and acceptable before you, that by administering with piety in peace and gentleness the authority granted them by you they may experience your mercy. 3 You who alone can do these good things for us and more abundant things, we praise you through the High Priest and Benefactor of our souls, Jesus Christ, through whom be glory and majesty both now and for all generations and for all ages. Amen.

Chapter Sixty-Two

And we have written enough to you, men and brothers, about what is fitting in our religion and beneficial for a virtuous life for those who desire to lead their lives in godliness and righteousness. 2 We have touched on faith and repentance and sincere love and self-control and moderation and endurance to remind you to please the all-powerful God in righteousness and truth and patience, in harmony, without malice, in love and peace with gentleness, just as our previously mentioned fathers in humility were pleasing to God by being humble-minded toward the Father who is both God and Creator to all people. 3 And we brought to mind these matters with great pleasure, since we are well assured that we are writing to men who are faithful and of the highest reputation and who had looked carefully into the sayings of God's teaching.

Chapter Sixty-Three

Having considered so many and such great examples, therefore, it is right that we bow our necks and adopt an attitude of obedience, so that abandoning this futile rebellion we may without blame reach the goal set before us. 2 For you will provide us joy and gladness if we obey what you have written through the Holy Spirit and remove the wicked anger that is expressed by jealousy, according to the appeal for peace and harmony we have made in this letter. 3 We have sent trustworthy and prudent men, who have lived among us blamelessly from youth to old age, and they will be witnesses between you and us. 4 We have done this so that you may know all our concern has been and remains that you may quickly establish peace.

Chapter Sixty-Four
Finally, may the omniscient God and Master of the spirits and the Lord of all flesh, who chose both the Lord Jesus Christ and us through him to be his special people, give to every soul who calls upon his great and holy name faith, reverence, peace, endurance and patience, self-control, purity and moderation, that they may be found well-pleasing to his name through our High Priest and Benefactor, Jesus Christ. May glory and majesty, power and honor, be to him, both now and for all ages. Amen.

Chapter Sixty-Five
Send back quickly to us our messengers Claudius Ephebus and Valerius Vito and Fortunatus, in peace with joy, in order that they may report as soon as possible the peace and harmony which we pray for and desire, that we may more quickly rejoice in your stability. 2 The grace of our Lord Jesus Christ be with you and with all in every place who have been called by God through him, to whom be glory, honor, power and majesty and eternal dominion to God, from eternity to eternity. Amen.

CHAPTER FOUR

Introduction to 2 Clement

In 1627 a gift from the Patriarch of Constantinople, Cyril Lucaris, for the monarch, Charles I, arrived in England. It was a large codex copied in the fifth century, later dubbed Codex A, that contained the entire Old and New Testaments with the books of 1 Clement and 2 Clement at the end. The manuscript broke off at 2 *Clem.* 12.5, the rest of the contents being lost. These two books appeared later in what was the first collection of books that went by the name "Apostolic Fathers," published by the French scholar, J. B. Cotelier in 1672. Subsequent editions of this collection continued to include these two works attributed to "Clement of Rome." The role of 2 Clement in that corpus of writings was strengthened by its presence in a codex of early church writings discovered by Philotheos Bryennios in Constantinople around 1873. To the delight of scholars, this codex included the eight chapters of 2 Clement that were missing in Codex A.

Many introductions to the "Second Letter of Clement" open with words like the following. "This work is neither written by Clement nor is it a letter." Then often follows a statement that the work is the earliest Christian sermon outside the New Testament. Even though overshadowed by its "Big Sister" (1 Clement), this shorter document appears in all editions of the Apostolic Fathers. Yet, few writers, ancient or modern, cite or allude to 2 Clement when compared to the greater attention given to other works among the AF. "Second Clement is probably the most overlooked and least appreciated of the writings of the Apostolic Fathers" (Ehrman, I, 154).

Patristic scholars, however, have not ignored 2 Clement. English commentaries include the magisterial work of J. B. Lightfoot in his multi-volume set on the AF. The first one-volume commentary in English is by Christopher Tuckett in the Oxford Apostolic Fathers series. The published dissertation by Karl Paul Donfried is a monograph on 2 Clement that offers many comments on the text. Your author has issued his own contribution as well. Students of this book await the major commentary in the Hermeneia series by James A. Kelhoffer.

MANUSCRIPT TRADITION OF 2 CLEMENT

Two Greek manuscripts preserve what we call 2 Clement along with 1 Clement. The codex called Alexandrinus (A) dates from the fifth century CE while the Hierosolymitanus 54 codex was copied in 1056 CE. Second Clement also appears with 1 Clement in a Syriac manuscript (*c.* 1170). Codex Hierosolymitanus, referred to as Codex H or the Constantinople Codex, is now housed in the Library of the Monastery of the Holy Sepulcher in the Old City of Jerusalem (MS 54). The codex contains such AF as the

Clements, Barnabas, the longer recension of the Ignatius letters, and the only surviving Greek manuscript of the Didache. A colophon states that the manuscript's completion was in 1056 CE with the name of the scribe as "Leon scribe and sinner." While mostly confirming the text of A in the first eleven and a half chapters, Codex H is not as reliable as the earlier manuscript.

Did the author of 2 Clement leave any further footprints among surviving manuscripts? A ninth-century codex mentioned by Photius, the Patriarch of Constantinople, contained these two "Clements" bound in one volume with the Epistle of Polycarp to the Philippians. This small codex, however, has not survived.

Codex A preserves the earliest form of the text. The Greek text has been utilized for well over a century and was the one published by Lightfoot. No Latin manuscript witnesses to 2 Clement survive from antiquity through the Middle Ages. This absence in the West should not be surprising since all the surviving witnesses had their origin in the eastern Mediterranean. Latin versions have not been found and it appears not to have been widely known in the West.

USE OF 2 CLEMENT IN ANTIQUITY

In addition to the small number of 2 Clement manuscripts, a few ancient Christian writers either allude to or cite it, but much fewer than the many attestations to 1 Clement. **Irenaeus** in the late-second century provides (*Haer.* 3.3.3) a summary of 1 Clement and refers to a description of fiery judgment which is not found there. The language, however, is quite similar to such a description in 2 Clement (see 7.6; 16.3; 17.5). In his commentary on John (*Comm. Jo.* 2.34.207), **Origen** before 250 CE utilized language quite similar to the famous expression in 2 *Clem.* 1.1. "what we should think about the son of God." The allusion remains illusory at best. **Eusebius** provides the earliest clear attestation to 2 Clement: "a second letter is ascribed to Clement, but we do not have the same knowledge of its recognition as the former, because we do not know if the ancient writers used it." Eusebius does not classify 2 Clement in any of the four categories in which he placed Christian literature: (1) Recognized Books; (2) Disputed Books; (3) Rejected Books; (4) Heretical Books. Toward the end of the fourth century, the authors of the *Apostolic Canons* (8.47.85) describe a list of what it calls "our books, that is the books of the New Testament" which includes "two epistles of Clement." **Severus** of Antioch (*c.* 513–18) in a polemical work (*Adv. Joannem*) cites verbatim the opening verses of 2 Clement (1.1–2) and credits them as from Clement. By the sixth century, the reticence of Eusebius about its Clementine authorship had evidently disappeared. **Photius**, ninth-century Patriarch of Constantinople, has one of the most extensive descriptions of 2 Clement. While he appreciated the high Christology of the book, he was concerned about its use of non-canonical writings, an issue that has been one of the controversial aspects of the work.

This manuscript evidence attests to a high value given to 2 Clement in various corners of the growing Christian world, some even viewing it as part of the NT canon. While attestation by individual writers may go back to the second century, some "citations" may be only hopeful at best. Certainly by the fourth century the work was well-known and came to be viewed as a *letter* written by *Clement*, both suppositions which are now widely questioned.

AUTHORSHIP AND PROVENANCE OF 2 CLEMENT

Despite the evidence of Codex Alexandrinus and the attribution to Clement since the fourth century, no one today identifies its author as "Clement of Rome." The differences in style are such that their origin from different authors is undoubtedly an accurate assessment. The author of 1 Clement is dependent on Paul and makes very little use of Jesus traditions, while the author of 2 Clement shows little evidence of Paul but makes extensive use of Jesus *logia*. These differences, however, do not imply there was no possible connection between the documents.

One cannot isolate the author of 2 Clement from its place of origin. The idea of a Middle Eastern origin is based on its presence in a Syriac manuscript. Although a universal consensus today is that we cannot know the personal identity of the author, we should not be completely agnostic about its origin. Lightfoot argued that the original setting of the "sermon"—as he called it—was in Corinth, although he did not suggest the name of an author. He based his argument on the athletic language used in 7.1–2. "So then, my brothers, let us compete, knowing that the competition is at hand, and that many are arriving by boat for corruptible prizes, but not all are crowned, except those who have trained hard and competed well. Let us therefore compete that we may all be crowned." The importance of the verb "arriving by boat" is crucial to this claim. The original audience addressed by the speaker was probably in Corinth. If the homily was delivered in that city, we have an explanation of two facts. *First*, the allusion to the athletic games and the Isthmian festival are couched in language quite natural if addressed to Corinthians, but not so if spoken elsewhere. When the preacher refers to the crowds that "land" to take part in the games, we can conclude that this was delivered in the general area where these contestants landed. *Secondly*, this hypothesis best explains the preservation of the document since it was early associated with the traditional Epistle of Clement and came to be attributed to the same author. How did this happen? The First Epistle was read from time to time in the Church of Corinth. This message was first preached, if my view is correct, to these same Corinthians. It was not an *extempore* address but delivered from a manuscript. It was considered of sufficient value to be carefully preserved and was occasionally read to the Corinthian congregation like the other Epistle of Clement.

Lightfoot's key argument is the use of the verb "arriving by boat." "Clement" is obviously making an analogy with the athletic games, which Paul also does in 1 Cor. 9:24-27. The analogy draws from actual events and the specific use of that nautical verb. This conveys a vivid message to Clement's original hearers, aware of their location near to the Isthmian games.

Donfried offers a sustained argument (4–7) for viewing this verb and the overall passage as indicating a Corinthian locale.

> Lightfoot's argument makes sense. For 2 Clement 'sailing' is used to mean a coming to shore and the reason it is unnecessary to name the city is because the persons addressed by 2 Clement are in that city .... It is most probable that the congregation in Corinth clearly understood the reference in question as referring to the Isthmian games in their city and that it was so intended by the author of 2 Clement (6).

This is the only use of the verb in the AF, and its only use in the NT is in Lk. 8:26. These examples of the verb argue for a literal meaning in chapter 7 with the analogy used for Christians "sailing toward port" for spiritual contests. As Paul referred to literal running and then bridged to a metaphorical meaning in his analogy, so Clement does the same in a vivid manner that would have been rhetorically effective with his hearers.

This Corinthian origin of the book suggests the provenance of the work. Why was it preserved with the document we call 1 Clement? And *why* was it in the archives and preserved with its larger companion? I suggest that it was closely associated with 1 Clement from the beginning because it had a connection with the issue in Corinth that originally prompted Clement to write.

Donfried's argument is persuasive, although it has not encountered wide acceptance among many scholars.

> 1 Clement was written from Rome about 96–98 CE to the Corinthian church in the hope of ending a schism which had developed there after some persons had succeeded in removing the presbyters from office. The intervention of 1 Clement was successful and these presbyters who had been removed from office were in probability reinstated. It is our thesis that shortly after their reinstatement these presbyters wrote a hortatory discourse, known to us as 2 Clement, which one of them read to the Corinthian congregation assembled for worship. Because both 1 and 2 Clement had together averted a severe crisis in the life of this congregation they were preserved together by the Corinthians (7).

Donfried does not argue that the "author" of 2 Clement is identical with the proposed Clement of the first letter. His proposal actually makes such an identity impossible. But that there exists a plausible connection between the two not only arises from their close association in the tradition but is supported by some additional factors.

Since 1 Clement was preserved in the Corinthian church and 2 Clement with it, it is logical that the latter was also appreciated by the Corinthians. References in 1 Clement indicate that it is an appeal to bring back presbyters who had been removed (1 *Clem.* 2.1; 37; 42–44). 2 Clement is thus a hortatory address originating with presbyters who had been removed and now reinstated. The speaker in 19.1 asks that the congregation repent in light of God's grace to them. "For as a compensation I ask you to repent with all your heart, giving yourselves salvation and life." He asks for compensation because he has been wrongly removed from office. That compensation is not monetary but consists of a heart-felt repentance.

The issue of disobeying the presbyters appears in 17.5–6. Describing the unrepentant, he writes. "Woe to us, because it was you, and we did not realize it, nor did we believe; and we did not obey the presbyters when they spoke to us about our salvation." 1 *Clem.* 57.1 says that his readers "must submit to the presbyters ... and repent." One of its main admonitions is a thoroughgoing call to repentance. What 1 Clement asked for in general terms, because the Roman church had only heard about the problem, 2 Clement carries out specifically because the presbyters were very aware of the sin.

Each author (1 *Clem.* 63.2; 2 *Clem.* 19.1) refers to his own writing as an "appeal" to obey "what has been written." With this expression 1 Clement describes his own previous words, while it is unclear if 2 Clement is doing the same or if it is a reference to the Scriptures. 2 Clement is thus an "appeal" from the Corinth presbyters to their congregation. That which enabled the presbyters to make their "appeal" was the prior "appeal" from the Roman congregation so the presbyters were able to urge their fellow believers "to heed what was written."

Has Donfried finally solved the *Sitz im Leben* of 2 Clement? Perhaps he has offered the best possible explanation for what he called the "setting of Second Clement in early Christianity." If Donfried's theory is accepted, and if 1 Clement is dated to the mid-'90s, then 2 Clement would be dated near the turn of the century, although admittedly most scholars date the work well into the second century (i.e., between 130 and 150).

THE GENRE OF 2 CLEMENT

What "type" of document is 2 Clement? Being labeled as a "letter" or an "epistle" does not arise from any features in the document itself. Many have noted that it lacks all the features of the epistolary genre such as a salutation and postscripts and also never refers to itself in the terms of a letter.

The scholarly consensus is that 2 Clement is a sermon, although some authors prefer the term "homily." Others are more careful about 2 Clement's label as a "sermon" or "homily." It is clear that 2 Clement was originally delivered orally (19.1) to a gathered congregation who had presbyters as their leaders (17.3, 5). Early in the document (2.1) is a quotation of an extended text from Isaiah which has often been assumed to be the text of the sermon. Finally, the fervent exhortations throughout certainly would seem to embody the "exhortation" that we have come to expect in a sermon.

A few scholars are not convinced about "sermon" as its genre. After correctly concluding that it is not a letter, Tugwell writes.

> The modern practice of calling it a 'homily' is, however, not entirely accurate. His appeal is distinguished from the exhortations given by the presbyters, in a way which strongly suggests that its author is not himself a presbyter (17.3). Is he perhaps an official reader or *lector*? The speaker identifies himself in 15.1 as giving the congregation counsel, and as hoping to gain salvation for himself hereby, must be the author. The best parallel I can suggest is the message *Hermas* presents himself as having received by divine revelation, which he is charged to read to the congregation in Rome (*Vis.* 2.4, 8.3). Hermas also nowhere presents himself as being a presbyter, and he speaks of presbyters as if they are a class to which he does not belong (*Vis.* 2.4). Conceivably the 'preacher' of *2 Clement* was in a similar position.
>
> (Tugwell, 136)

More recently, the scholar who has written the most about the book concluded that "2 Clement may then be a sermon, but it is not a homily in the stricter sense of being a sermon in the form of a detailed interpretation of a specific scriptural text" (Tuckett, 22). In an NT description of an address that could be called a homily, the previous chapters of Hebrews 1–12 are referred to in 13:22 as a "message of exhortation." This same expression is also used by the synagogue leaders in Acts 13:15 to describe the expected homily to follow the reading of the law and the prophets. That expression is nowhere used as a self-description in 2 Clement. While exhortation is certainly involved in 2 Clement, the way in which the reader describes his address is by an entirely different set of terms.

In 2 *Clem.* 15.1 the speaker says that "I do not think that the advice I have given about self-control is unimportant." This noun, which appears only here and in *Barn.* 21.2, means "advice, counsel" and in both places appears to be a self-description of each work. The word "advice" (*sumboulia*) refers to the advice contained within the address and is not intended as a description of the work as a whole. Another descriptive term is used by the speaker in 19.1. "I am reading you an *appeal* (*enteuxis*) to pay attention to what has been written ..." This noun means "petition, request," and seems to be a general description of the appeal that has been made in chapters 1–18. The word is also used in 1 *Clem.* 63.2 to describe Clement's non-sermonic "appeal" to the church in Corinth.

James A. Kelhoffer cites Donfried as an ally in questioning the "sermon" genre assigned for 2 Clement. Donfried had earlier concluded that "the term homily is so vague and ambiguous that it should be withdrawn until its literarily generic legitimacy has been demonstrated" (26). Donfried's concerns have largely fallen on deaf ears, however, and he offered no alternative genre than simply a "hortatory address."

In conclusion, I suggest that we discard the terms "sermon" or "homily" as the genre of 2 Clement and look to ancient rhetoric for guidance. One of the three types of speeches was "deliberative" in its rhetorical goal. This suggestion is supported by the self-designation of the address as a *sumboulia* (15.1), a term with rhetorical connections. As was previously mentioned, the self-designation of the "speech" as an appeal also reflects a rhetorical usage. Another transliterated term, *paraenesis*, has been applied to this type of address.

It is evident that scholars have failed to identify 2 Clement with an identifiable class of writings that we call a "sermon." Therefore, the use of the term to describe Second Clement should be abandoned. What should we then call 2 Clement? Perhaps it is simply a "hortatory address" delivered in a particular *Sitz im Leben*, namely a Christian congregational setting.

THE OPPONENTS IN SECOND CLEMENT

Some writers have thought the enemies addressed by the speaker were Gnostics. That bold assertion has proven quite unjustified, especially in recent years. Simon Tugwell observed: "Similar claims recur in certain forms of Gnosticism, but there is no sign in our text of any of the distinctive tenets of Gnosticism or of the typically Gnostic sophism used to justify evading the challenge of martyrdom" (Tugwell, 143).

Tuckett has even questioned the use of the word "Gnostic" as a "catch-term" in this early period. He observes that to merit the title literary works "should include the idea that the creation of the material world is the work of a being other than the supreme God and that the world is essentially something alien (and bad) from which one should seek to escape." Second Clement lacks this emphasis. The lack of ethical seriousness addressed in the book "does not clearly point to a Gnostic background. Not all Gnostics were necessary libertines, and not all libertines were necessarily Gnostics" (Tuckett, 55). What is clear is that the importance of ethical behavior is under threat, but such threats are not necessarily presented by Gnostics.

Who then were the "opponents"? We simply should not seek to identify them by any philosophical or theological label. There were persons within the group who were bothering the believers with their teaching. "Now if they alone were doing these things (seeking pleasure), it could be endured; but now they persist in teaching evil to innocent souls, knowing that both they and their listeners will receive double punishment" (10.5). They do display some "libertine" tendencies and ignore any future consequences for their behavior. If we must put a modern label on them, they could be called something akin to "Antinomians." Such opponents can also be discerned in some writings of the NT.

THE USE OF "SCRIPTURE" IN 2 CLEMENT

2 Clement exhibits a rich and varied use of writings considered as authoritative by the author. The book incorporates more references to other "sources" than any other work among those included in the AF. In chapters 2–17 there are twenty-five citations or clear allusions to previous texts, one for every four verses. Many are recognizable as to their source but a few are uncertain. The terms "Old Testament" and "New Testament" as well as "Apocrypha" and "canon" are used in this discussion, even though the speaker himself would not recognize their meaning at the time.

RECEPTION HISTORY OF "JEWISH" TRADITIONAL BOOKS

There are around fourteen quotations and allusions to OT books in 2 Clement. The quotations of a text are often accompanied by a formula such as the name of the author or the familiar expression "the scripture said." Allusions are references to a text that involve a greater measure of freedom but maintain enough of the language for most readers to identify the source. These can be summarized as follows: 2.1 (Isa. 54:1), clearly a quotation; 3.5 (Isa. 29:13); 6.8 (Ezek. 14:14-20), clearly an allusion; 7.6 and 17.5 (Isa. 66:24); 13.2 (Isa. 52;5); 14.1a (Ps. 71:5, 17 LXX); 14.1b (Jer. 7:11); 14.2 (Gen. 1:27); 15.3 (Isa. 58:9); 16.3 (Mal. 3:19; Isa. 34:4); 17.4–5 (Isa. 66:18). Two citations are drawn from what probably is an unknown Jewish source: (1) 11.2–4, which is cited as "scripture" in 1 *Clem.* 23.3. Lightfoot suggested that it is from the lost book, *Eldad and Modat*, mentioned by Herm. *Vis.* 2.3.4; and (2) 11.7. These citations are preceded by a formula including the verb "says" except in 2.1 and 17.5. The "speakers" of the cited text are identified as God (15.3), the Lord (13.2; 17.4–5), and the "scripture"(14.1–2).

Six of the OT quotations are from the LXX text of Isaiah, which probably assumes that the author had access to a manuscript of that book. Other quotations are also close to the LXX, but some vary slightly. The purpose of citing these texts is almost always hortatory, with 2.1 and 14.1–2 ("scripture") utilized to make a specific theological point.

THE JESUS *LOGIA*

Seven quotations have close parallels to the sayings of Jesus in the canonical Gospels. These are: 2.4 (Matt. 9:13; Mark 2:17; Luke 5:32), 3.2 (Matt. 10:32; Luke 12:8), 4.2 (Matt. 7:21; Luke 6:46), 6.1 (Matt. 6:24; Luke 16:13), 6.2 (Matt. 16:26; Mark 8:36); 9.11 (Matt. 12:50; Mark 8:35; Luke 8:21), and 13.4 (Matt. 5:44; Luke 6:27-28). Each of these is introduced by some citation formula (except 6.2). As in the OT citations, the verb used is the present tense "says" (except 9.11, "said"). As the speaker in these formulas, Jesus is referred to as Christ (3.2); Lord (6.1); and God (13.4). An interesting feature is how the quotation in 2.4 is traced to "another scripture" and raises the possibility of at least one written Gospel that was utilized. Apart from 2.4, it is difficult to be dogmatic about the specific sources of these quotations, whether written or oral. While the Matthean tradition is discernable, sometimes the quotation is closer to Luke (e.g., 3.2 and 4.2).

As with the OT quotations, the purpose in citing these sayings is almost always to exhort his hearers about ethical behavior. In keeping with the speaker's stress on a "payback" owed to God and Christ, hearers are to learn from Jesus to confess with their deeds, not just with their mouths (3.2; 4.2). A follower of Jesus does the will of the Father (9.11). To be inconsistent in one's words and deeds is to blaspheme the name of Christ (13.4). Consistent with the hortatory thrust of the discourse and with the quotations from the OT, these citations of Jesus *logia* promote obedient behavior in a disciple of Jesus. This type of behavior is essential for entering into the life that is both now and is to come.

Some words in 11.7 are cited as scripture by Paul in 1 Cor. 2:9 ("ear has not heard nor eye seen nor the heart of man imagined"), but the statement is similar to Isa. 64.4 and does not prove dependence on Paul. A general response among scholars to the question of Pauline citations has been a rather firm "no." Some possible allusions to Pauline texts appear in a few places, such as the athletic analogies in chapter 7 (see 1 Cor. 9:24-47).

Donfried's general conclusion is worth consideration as to Clement's general naming of his authoritative sources. "Given the whole of 2 Clement, we note three sources of authority: τὰ βιβλία (the Jewish Scriptures), ὁ κύριος (especially with reference to the Jesus *logia*), and οἱ ἀπόστολοι (including Paul)" (Donfried, 95).

In summary, it can be said that 2 Clement uses Jesus material that has been shaped by Matthew and Luke, but also contains Jesus tradition that may originate elsewhere. Other possible sources are Ephesians and Hebrews, but these similarities are not enough to be convincing. A safe conclusion is that the author used Matthew and Luke but use of Hebrews is doubtful. A final observation is that 2 Clement preserves what is probably the earliest Christian reference to both Old and New Testaments together in 14.2: "the scrolls and the apostles" (τὰ βιβλία καὶ οἱ ἀπόστολοι).

RECEPTION HISTORY OF "APOCRYPHAL" TEXTS

At least four quotations in are taken from non-canonical sources (4.5; 5.2–4; 8.5; 12.2–6). The speaker in the citation is sometimes the "Lord," but in 5.4 it is Jesus and in 12.6 no personal subject is expressed. In contrast to the prominent use of the present tense of λέγειν in the "Jesus" sources, the use of εἶπεν is prominent in 4.5; 5.4; and 12.2. While the oral nature of the sayings is stressed, in 8.5 a written source is mentioned, where the speaker utilized what has been called an "apocryphal gospel."

While three of these have similar ideas to some gospel texts (e.g., 8.5 in Luke 16:10–12), the quotation in 12.2–6 has no NT parallels. It may be from the "Gospel of the Egyptians" but has some interesting echoes also in the *Gospel of Thomas* 22. The reference to "the apostles" (14.2) probably is what Justin Martyr called "the memoirs of the apostles," namely the canonical gospels.

The citations are often inserted after introducing a theme. A hortatory theme is then followed by a hortatory allusion. In 3.1 the theme is a summary of chapter 1. Then 3.2 is a quote from the Gospels supporting the points previously made. The exhortation is found in verses 3–4 and is followed by a quotation from a text in Isaiah. This pattern is followed in chapters 4, 6, 7, 8, 9, 11, and 13. At two points a quotation is given and an explanation of that quote is attempted (chapters 2 and 12). The citations play no role in an extended argument as in the NT (e.g., Rom. 4; Gal. 3; or Rom. 9–11). The texts are cited in either an illustrative or supportive function, and most often after an exhortation. The appeal to the authority of the Jewish and Christian traditions is not only to illustrate but to provide authoritative support for what is being said.

THE THEOLOGY OF SECOND CLEMENT

The speaker is not a "theologian" as such. While there is theological reflection, it is ethical behavior rather than nuanced theology that concerns the author. It is better to discern the "message" of the book within an overall theological framework. How do the author's theological beliefs help to shape his main "message," that is, that believers must render a "payback" to God for his great salvation (1.3, 5; 9.7; 15.2)? What was later called *orthodoxy* is important to him, but it is *orthopraxy* that is his main concern.

Theology Proper

The God of 2 Clement has acted in the past, is active in the present, and will act decisively in the future ("Eschatology"). He is the Creator (15.2) and the author of a new creation as well. God sent his son on his mission of salvation (1.4–8; 20.5). God is described not abstractly but as the one who saves (9.7), who cares for his people (2.3), who is benevolent (15.5), and is willing to give (15.3–5). These "attributes" are not presented abstractly but in connection with His relationship to others. Some expressions do convey traditional theological attributes. God is all-knowing (9.9) and is the only God (20.5) who is invisible to the created eyes (20.5). He is the Father and the god of truth (3.1; 19.1).

Christology

The pre-existence of the Son is evident (14.1–2) but is expressed in his relation to the also pre-existent Church. Jesus is the one sent to save "us" and that is expressed by God sending his mercy by Jesus' suffering for us (1.4–8). The verbs for calling (1.8; 2.4; 10.1; 16.1) and saving (1.4–7; 10.1) and teaching (4.5; 8.4; 17.3) are all used of both God and Christ with no distinction. In the opening passage (1.1), Christ is thought of as God and exercises the eschatological role of judge. The familiar Jesus *logion* of loving one's enemies is introduced as something that "God says." The exact relationship between Father and Son is not expressed as in later Nicene theology. If God and Jesus are not identical, they are inseparable; Jesus simply shares in the divine identity. In his final benediction (20.5) the author calls Jesus the "Savior" and then couples that with "Founder," a possible reflection of the Christology of Hebrews.

Pneumatology

The teaching about the Spirit is one of the most controversial aspects of the book. The word πνεῦμα is virtually confined to chapter 14, where it appears five times. As his other doctrines are related directly to his ethical concerns, the references to the Spirit are all found in a Christological context. Jesus was "spirit" before he "became flesh" (9.5), and currently Jesus in heaven is again equated with "spirit" (14.4). Absent is any clear reference to the presence of the Spirit among believers.

The relevance of 2 Clement to later trinitarian discussions is that his description of the Godhead operates within the ancient Jewish concept of monotheism. It would be anachronistic to expect that he would use Nicaean terms and attempt to distinguish between the "persons" of Father, Son, and Holy Spirit. Clement does associate the Son with the Father's divine identity. The few and at times unclear references to the "Spirit" make any claims to offer an incipient trinitarianism as unwise at best. While some divine characteristics may be discerned in his few references to the "Spirit," it is best to view

Clement's Godhead without any clear inclusion of a divine person called the Holy Spirit. I recommend that the best we can say is that Clement's theology reflects a distinctively "dyadic shape."

Ecclesiology

What 2 Clement says about the church is also connected to Christ and the spirit. The preexistent and spiritual church was united with Christ (14.1) and came to earth as the "flesh of Christ" (14.3). Apart from its appearance in chapter 14, the only reference to the "church" is in 2.1. The barren woman in the Isaiah citation in chapter 2 is equated with the church who also was barren before she produced offspring. In a rather muddled explanation, he further asserts that the "flesh" is the antitype of the genuine reality, which again is the Spirit (14.3). The purpose of all this discussion is not to formulate a developed ecclesiology but again to emphasize the importance of ethical behavior.

Eschatology

The author could claim the modern label of "futurist." He has a surprisingly current discussion of the "two ages" (6.3; 19.3–4). In reference to God's appearing (12.1; 19.3–4) he mentions the future "kingdom of God" (also 12.1). While there is no reference to the NT term *parousia*, God's future judgment is vividly described (16.3; 17.6) with Jesus as judge (1.1). Entering God's future kingdom (5.5; 6.9; 9.6; 11.7; 12.1) will be through the resurrection (9.1; 19.3) and the passing of the heavens and earth (16.3). The speaker handles the issue of the delay in the second coming by reference to an apocryphal text (11.1–5). With the aid of a similar text (12.1–6) he declares that the time of that coming will be when "outside" (body) and "inside" (soul) are the same as well as male and female differences are removed and an original unity restored. He has no teaching about the nearness of the *parousia*, but he does counsel its expectation. He exhorts ethical behavior consistent with the future expectation. As long as we are in this world (8.1–2), we have an opportunity for salvation (9.7) because God is kind (16.1).

Soteriology

Christ has brought salvation by the giving of "light," by his recognition of recipients as "sons," and by "saving" the lost (chapter 1). The importance of Christ's "passion" is mentioned in terms that later would be called "atonement." In 3.1 this saving action was based on his "mercy." Christ's "saving" is not only mentioned in an early chapter (1.4, 7), but also in 2.7; 3.3; and 9.5. Chapter 2 also conveys a "then-now" theme echoing a pattern of the "before and after" aspects of salvation. In addition to these "past" references to salvation, there exist many other texts that clearly imply that salvation depends on a proper behavioral response in the present, thus focusing this aspect of salvation in the future (8.2; 13.1; 14.1; 15.1; 17.2; and 19.3). Therefore, the current "praxis" of soteriology cannot be separated from its "completed" nature, although it is related to that past event. The references to keeping the seal of baptism "pure" (6.9; 7.6) and to a sort of "redemptive almsgiving" that is as good as repentance must also be viewed in this light. Another soteriological doctrine is the importance of "repentance." The verb *metanoeo* (8.1–13; 9.8) and the noun *metanoia* (8.2; 16.4) describe the expected continual actions of the saved. The speaker is also a sinner in need of this repentance (8.2–3; 18.2). Roman Catholic commentators view this section as "a direct testimony to the *paenitentia secunda*, that is, penance for sins committed after baptism" (Quasten, 56). All this extensive praxis is an appropriate response to grace given to the hearers in the salvation secured through Christ.

Theological Praxis

The main "theological message" is what I call the "Theological Praxis." That central "message" is that believers have an ongoing obligation to render "pay-back" or "repayment" to Christ or God (2 *Clem.* 1.3, 5; 9.7; 15.2). This "repayment" is rendered in the form of "works" as the proper response to God's grace. Failure by ungrateful believers to repay Christ would put them at risk of their salvation and liable to eternal punishment (17.5–7). Being "saved" is both the result of God's gracious initiative (1.4; cf. 1.7; 2.7; 3.3; 9.2, 5) and as something that needs to be realized through reciprocity (8.2; 14.1; cf. 4.1–2; 13.1; 14.2; 15.1).

Some authors describe 2 Clement as an example of "moralism" at best, if not an outright denial of salvific grace. Another critical assessment was made by the author T.F. Torrance, who summarizes his critical assessment of the "doctrine of grace" in 2 Clement by declaring that the book is "the least evangelic of all the writings of the so-called Apostolic Fathers" (Varner, 42).

As a counter-balance to Torrance, James A. Kelhoffer has contributed a number of articles exploring important features of 2 Clement. "Reciprocity as Salvation. Christ as Salvation Patron and the Corresponding 'Payback' Expected of Christ's Earthly Clients according to the Second Epistle of Clement" has informed the following observations about the book's applied theology. The article analyzes the concept of "payback" or "repayment" (*antimisthia*) that … "believers owe to Christ. As a corollary, I propose that a likely purpose for *Second Clement* was to convince a Christian audience that the benefits of salvation come with recurring obligations to Christ, their salvific patron" (Kelhoffer, 456).

J. B. Lightfoot called attention to a parallel idea expressed by the author of Ps. 116:12-14. "What will I return to the LORD for all his goodness to me? I will lift up the cup of salvation and call on the name of the LORD. I will fulfill my vows to the LORD in the presence of all his people." The LXX in Ps. 115:3a employs a verb which conveys this sentiment of the psalmist's desire to pay back the Lord for his gracious blessings. While this verb does not appear in 2 Clement, a similar noun, *antimisthia*, conveys the crux of the author's message. This noun appears in 1.3, 5; 9.7; 11.6, and 15.2. The word is without a pre-history to the NT but appears there in 2 Cor. 6:13 in a positive sense and in Rom. 1:27 in a negative sense. This noun has been found thus far only in Christian writers and conveys the reciprocal nature of a **"requital based upon what one deserves, recompense, exchange,** either in the positive sense of *reward* or the negative sense *penalty*, depending on the context" (BDAG, 90). This word occurs at the very beginning of the book with his vivid description of God's grace in salvation (1.6–8).

Kelhoffer suggests that possible precedents in the NT for this approach to balancing grace with orthopraxy are in such passages as Matt. 6:14-15; 22:11-14; Rom. 15:27; and 1 John 3:16. He concludes that a likely purpose is "to convince a Christian audience that the benefits of salvation come with obligations to Christ, their salvific patron" (Kelhoffer, 433).

The idea of pay-back for grace is consistent with the relationship between "faith" and "works" in James, as well as with the teaching of Paul, who wrote about a "faith working through love" (Gal. 5:6); the necessity of "good works" (Eph. 2:10; Titus 3:8); that believers should prove themselves worthy of Christ (Col. 1:10; 1 Thess. 2:12); expected fruitful deeds in their lives (Phil. 1:11); and emphasized that the final judgment of believers would be according to their works (Rom. 2:6-10). The message about salvific grace abounds in 2 *Clem.* 1. Anything that he then says about "payback" must be understood in light of that opening chapter.

The Christian life as marked by obedience is the dominant theme in 2 Clement. What motivated the author's strong emphasis on obedience and proper behavior? The saving action of Christ is stressed in salvation, liberation from darkness, and offering a status of being God's sons as the result of Christ's death. Something, however, is missing. The only NT aspect that is lacking is the presence of the Spirit, which was typical for early Christians (e.g., Gal. 5:25). If a Corinthian context is valid for 2 Clement, the church must have shed much of the spiritual exuberance which was so evident in the first letter to the Corinthians.

THE INTEGRITY AND STRUCTURE OF SECOND CLEMENT

Some authors argue that 19.1–20.4 do not belong to the original sermon which is 1.1–18.2, 20.5. Some evidence can be assembled for this approach. Verbal differences between the sections include (1) the address is always "brothers" in 1–18, while "brothers and sisters" are addressed in 19.1 and 20.2; (2) the speaker refers to his address as "advice" in 15.1 while in 19.1 it is an "appeal"; (3) the major term *reward* appears five times in the first section but is absent in the "appendix"; (4) terms mentioned at the end such as *piety* in 19.1 and *religious* in 20.4 are absent in the earlier part; and (5) words expressing the same idea such as *commandment* in 3.4; 4.5 are delivered by a different word like *instruction* in 19.3.

Some of the differences above (such as "5") can be explained as an author's variation in his vocabulary, and do not demand a different author. Theological differences have also been discerned between the sections. The idea of God's prevenient grace (1.8; 15.3–5) appears to be absent in the appendix. It is also possible that the two chapters were part of a different address later attached to 1–18 with 20.5 forming the conclusion when it was placed beside 1 Clement.

These arguments are persuasive, but not all writers see such serious differences between 1–18 and 19–20. It could be that these chapters are the concluding *peroratio* of the entire discourse. While acknowledging differences between the sections, Tuckett concludes "that the argument against the literary unity of the present text is not completely watertight" (27). There are also a number of expressions that unite the ideas between the sections. For example, "wholehearted repentance" in 8.2 and 19.1; "Father of truth" in 3.1 and 20.5; hearers saving both themselves and the speaker in 15.1 and 19.1; and the metaphor of athletics in 7.1–4 and 20.2. While it is true that the signature word *antimisthia* does not appear in 19–20, another related word reflecting "recompense," *misthos*, appears five times in 1–18 (1.5; 3.3; 9.5; 11.5; 15.1) and twice in 19–20 (19.1; 20.4). Finally, the appeal in 19.1 is "to pay attention to what has been written." While scripture has been appealed to quite often in chapters 1–18, this expression is best viewed as describing "what has been written" in the present discourse, namely, chapters 1–18.

The argument that there were originally two separate documents, 1–18 and 19–20, is simply overdrawn. The most striking difference is the switch to "brothers and sisters" in

19.1; 20.2, which, however, could be part of the strategy of the speaker in focusing on his application to all of his hearers present. The issue, however, may not be that crucial to decide. Since the document has come down to us as a whole, we should still consider it as a whole discourse. The approach here is to view 19–20 as a concluding *peroratio*, functioning as a summary appeal on the basis of what has gone before.

The lack of an overall thematic and logical construction is evident to many readers. One can discern, however, that the decisive past salvific events are strongly emphasized in chapters 1–2. Ethical and hortatory concerns, although not limited to chapters 3–14, are quite prominent there. A move to an eschatological thrust can be discerned in chapters 15–18 with the conclusion comprising chapters 19–20. Viewing 19–20 as a summary-conclusion, a suggested outline is:

I. The Role of Jesus Christ in Salvation 1.1–2.7
II. The Obedient Response of Believers 3.1–14.5
    A. The need to respond to Christ's work 3.1–4.5
    B. A Christian's struggles in the world 5.1–7.6
    C. An appeal for obedient living 8.1–13.4
    D. The church as the body of Christ 14.1–5
III. The Urgent Response to Christ 15.1–18.2
    A. Appeal to righteousness and holiness 15.1–5
    B. General appeals for repentance 16.1–18.2
IV. Summary and Conclusions 19.1–20.5

FURTHER READING ON THE "SECOND LETTER OF CLEMENT"

Donfried, K. P. "The Theology of 2 Clement." *Harvard Theological Review* 66 (1973). 487–501.
Donfried, Karl P. *The Setting of Second Clement in Early Christianity*. Leiden. E. J. Brill, 1974.
Grant, R. M. and H. H. Graham. *First and Second Clement*. The Apostolic Fathers, vol. 2. New York. Nelson, 1965.
Kelhoffer, James A. "Reciprocity as Salvation. Christ as Salvific Patron and the Corresponding 'Payback' Expected of Christ's Earthly Clients According to the Second Epistle of Clement." *NTS* 59 (2013). 433–56.
Lightfoot, Joseph Barber. *The Apostolic Fathers, Part I. S. Clement of Rome*. 2nd ed., vol. 2. London. Macmillan, 1890. Repr. Grand Rapids. Baker, 1981.
Parvis, Paul. "2 Clement and the Meaning of the Christian Homily" in *The Writings of the Apostolic Fathers*, ed. Paul Foster, 32–41. London and New York. T&T Clark, 2007.
Peters, Janelle. "1 and 2 Clement" in *The Cambridge Companion to the Apostolic Fathers*, ed. Michael Bird and Scott Harrower, 186–207. Cambridge. Cambridge University Press, 2021.
Quasten, Johannes. "The So-Called Second Epistle of Clement" in *Patrology*, vol. 1. Notre Dame, IN. Christian Classics, 1983.
Tuckett, Christopher. *2 Clement. Introduction, Text, and Commentary*. Oxford Apostolic Fathers. Oxford. Oxford University Press, 2012.
Varner, William. *Second Clement. An Introductory Commentary*. Eugene, OR. Cascade Books, 2020.

SECOND CLEMENT

Chapter One
Brothers, we must think of Jesus Christ as of God, as "the Judge of the living and the dead."[1] And we ought not to undervalue our salvation, 2 for when we undervalue him, we also hope to receive little. And those who listen as if it is a little matter are sinning, and we also are sinning if we do not recognize from where and by whom and to what place we were called, and what great suffering Jesus Christ endured for our sake. 3 What repayment, then, should we give to him, or what fruit should we offer that is worthy of what he has given us? And what holy deeds do we owe him? 4 For he gave us the light; as a Father he has called us "sons;" he saved us when we were perishing. 5 What praise, then, will we give him, or what payback for what we received?

6 We were maimed in our understanding, worshiping stones and wooden objects and gold and silver and copper, the products of men, and our whole life was nothing else than death. We were thus covered with darkness and our sight was filled with mist, but we have received our sight, by his will we have cast off the cloud that covered us. 7 For he had pity on us and he saved us by his mercy, even though he had seen in us great error and destruction, when we had no hope of salvation except what comes from him. 8 For he called us when we did not exist, and out of nothing he willed us into existence.

Chapter Two
"Rejoice, O barren woman, who bears no children; break forth and shout, you who have no labor pains; because the deserted woman has more children than she who has a husband."[2] In saying, "Rejoice, O barren woman, who bears no children," he spoke about us, for our church was barren before children were given to her. 2 And when he said, "cry, you who have no labor pains," he means this: that we should offer up our prayers sincerely to God, and not grow weary like women who are giving birth. 3 And when he said, "the deserted woman has more children than the one who has a husband," he meant that our people seemed to be deserted by God, but now that who have believed have become more than those who seem to have God. 4 And another Scripture also says, "I came not to call the righteous ones, but sinners."[3] 5 He means that those who are perishing must be saved, 6 for that is a great and marvelous thing, to support not those things that are standing but those that are falling. 7 So also Christ desired to save the perishing, and he saved many by coming and calling us who were already perishing.

Chapter Three
Seeing, then, because he has shown mercy towards us—first, that we who are living do not sacrifice to the dead gods, nor do we worship them, but through him we have come to know the Father of truth—what is the true knowledge about him if it is not refusing to deny him through whom we have come to know him? 2 And he himself also says, "Whoever acknowledges me before men, I will acknowledge him before my Father."[4] 3 This, therefore, is our reward, if we acknowledge him through whom we were saved. 4 But how do we acknowledge him? By doing what he says and not disobeying his

---

[1] Acts 10:42; 1 Pet. 4:5.
[2] Isa. 54:1; cf. Gal. 4:27.
[3] Matt. 9:13; Mark 2:17; Luke 5:32.
[4] Matt. 10:32; Luke 12:8.

commandments and honoring him not only with our lips but "from all our whole heart and all our whole mind."[5] 5 And he also says in Isaiah, "This people honors me with their lips, but their heart is far from me."[6]

Chapter Four
Let us, therefore, not just call him Lord, for this will not save us. 2 For he says, "Not everyone who says to me, 'Lord, Lord,' will be saved, but only the one who practices righteousness."[7] 3 So then, brothers, let us acknowledge him in our deeds by loving one another, by not committing adultery nor slandering one another nor being jealous, but by being self-controlled, compassionate, and good. And we ought to sympathize with one another, and not love money. By these actions we should acknowledge him, and not by their opposites. 4 And we must not fear men but rather God. 5 Because of this, you who do these things, the Lord said, "If you are gathered with me in my breast, but do not obey my commandments, I will throw you out and will say to you. 'Depart from me; I do not know where you are from, you who commit iniquity'."[8]

Chapter Five
For which reason, brothers, let us turn away from our temporary sojourn in this world, and do the will of him who called us, and let us not fear to depart from this world. 2 For the Lord says, "You will be like lambs in the midst of wolves."[9] 3 But Peter answered and said to him, "What if the wolves tear apart the lambs?" 4 Jesus said to Peter, "Let the lambs have no fear of the wolves after their death, and have no fear of those who kill you, and can do nothing more to you, but fear him who after your death has power to cast body and soul into the hell of fire."[10] 5 And be assured, brothers, that our temporary stay in this world of the flesh is a little thing and lasts a short time, but the promise of Christ is great and wonderful, and brings us rest in the coming kingdom and eternal life. 6 What then will we do to secure these things except to lead a holy and righteous life, and regard these worldly things as not our own, and not desire them? 7 For when we desire to acquire these things, we fall away from the right path.

Chapter Six
Now the Lord says, "No servant is able to serve two masters."[11] If we desire to serve both God and Mammon it is harmful to us. 2 "For what is the advantage if someone gains the whole world but loses his soul?"[12] 3 Now this age and the coming one are two enemies. 4 This age speaks of adultery and corruption and love of money and deceit, but that age renounces these things. 5 Therefore, we cannot then be the friends of both, but we must renounce this age in order to make the most of that one. 6 We think that it is better to hate the things that are here, because they are insignificant and short-lived and corruptible, but to love those things that are good and incorruptible. 7 For if we do the will of Christ we will find rest. On the other hand, nothing will rescue us from eternal punishment if we

---

[5]Mark 12:30.
[6]Isa. 29:13; cf. Matt. 15:8; 1 *Clem.* 15:2.
[7]Matt. 7:21.
[8]Source unknown. Cf. Matt. 25:41ff.
[9]Matt. 10:16; Luke 10:3.
[10]Cf. Matt. 10:28; Mark 8:36.
[11]Luke 16:13; Matt. 6:24.
[12]Matt. 16:26; Mark 8:36; Luke 9:25.

disobey his commandments. 8 And the scripture also says in Ezekiel, "Even if Noah and Job and Daniel arise, they will not rescue their children in the captivity."[13] 9 Now even if such righteous men as these are not able to save their children by their own righteous deeds, with what confidence will we enter the kingdom of God, if we do not keep our baptism pure and undefiled? Or who will be our advocate if we are not found to have holy and righteous deeds?

Chapter Seven
So then, my brothers, let us compete, knowing that the competition is at hand, and that many are arriving by boat for corruptible prizes, but not all are crowned, except those who have trained hard and competed well. 2 Let us therefore compete that we may all be crowned. 3 Let us run the straight course, the incorruptible competition, and let many of us sail to it and compete, that we may also be crowned. And if we all cannot receive the crown, let us at least come close to it. 4 We must remember that if someone taking part in the contest for a corruptible prize is found to be unfair, he is flogged, disqualified, and thrown out of the stadium. 5 What do you think? What will he suffer who cheats in the contest for what is incorruptible? 6 Concerning those who have not kept the seal he says, "Their worm will not die and their fire will not be quenched and they will be a spectacle for all flesh."[14]

Chapter Eight
Therefore, while we are on earth, let us repent. 2 For we are clay in the hand of the craftsman. For in the same way as the potter, if he makes a vessel, and it becomes misshapen or breaks while it is in his hand, he reshapes it; but if he has already put it into the kiln, he no longer is able to mend it. So also, as long as we are in this world, let us repent with all our heart from the wicked deeds which we have done in the flesh, that we may be saved by the Lord while we still have time to repent. 3 For after we have departed from the world, we are no longer able there to confess or to repent anymore. 4 So, brothers, if we have done the will of the Father and have kept the flesh pure and have observed the commandments of the Lord, we will receive eternal life. 5 For the Lord says in the Gospel, "If you have not kept what is small, who will give you what is great? For I tell you that whoever is faithful in what is little is faithful also in what is much."[15] 6 He means this then: keep the flesh pure and the seal unstained, so that we may receive eternal life.

Chapter Nine
And let none of you say that this flesh is not judged nor rises again. 2 Understand this. In what condition were you saved? In what condition did you receive your sight, if not while you were in this flesh? 3 We must therefore guard the flesh as a temple of God. 4 For just as you were called in the flesh, you will also come in the flesh. 5 If Christ the Lord who saved us, although he was originally spirit, became flesh and called us, so we will also receive our reward in the flesh. 6 Therefore, let us love one another, so that we all may come into the kingdom of God. 7 While we have time to be healed, let us give

---
[13] Ezek. 14:14.
[14] Isa. 66:24; Mark 9:44, 46, 48.
[15] Luke 16:10-12.

INTRODUCTION TO 2 CLEMENT

ourselves to God who heals us, making a payback to him. 8 What sort? Repentance from a sincere heart. 9 For he is the one who knows all things beforehand and knows what is in our heart. 10 Therefore, let us then give him eternal praise, not only from the mouth, but also from the heart, so that he may receive us as sons. 11 For the Lord also said, "My brothers are these who do the will of my Father."[16]

Chapter Ten

So, my brothers, let us do the will of the Father who called us, that we may live, and let us rather pursue virtue, and let us give up malice as the forerunner of our sins, and let us flee ungodliness lest evil things overtake us. 2 For if we are eager to do good, peace will pursue us. 3 For this reason it is not possible for a person to find peace, when they bring in human fears and prefer the present pleasures to the coming promise. 4 For they do not know what great torment the present pleasure brings, and what delight the coming promise brings. 5 And if they alone were doing these things it could be endured, but now they continue teaching evil to innocent souls, not realizing that both themselves and their hearers will receive a double punishment.

Chapter Eleven

Let us therefore serve God with a pure heart, and we will be righteous; but if we do not serve him because we do not believe the promise of God, we will be miserable. 2 For the prophetic word also says, "Miserable are the double-minded who doubt in their heart, saying, 'We heard all these things long ago and in the time of our fathers, but waiting day to day, we have seen none of them'. 3 O foolish ones! Compare yourselves to a tree; consider a vine; first it sheds its leaves, then comes a bud, after these things a sour grape, then the full bunch. 4 So also my people have had turmoils and troubles; but then they will receive the good things."[17] 5 Therefore, my brothers, let us not be double-minded, but let us endure in hope, so that we may also receive the reward. 6 For faithful is the one who promised to pay to each person the reward of his deeds.[18] 7 Therefore, if we do what is right before God we will enter into his kingdom, and we will receive the promises "that ear has not heard, nor eye seen, nor has it entered the human heart."[19]

Chapter Twelve

Therefore, let wait hourly for the kingdom of God in love and righteousness, since we do not know the day of God's appearing. 2 For when the Lord himself was asked by someone when his kingdom will come, he said, "When the two will be one, and the outside is like the inside, and the male with the female is neither male nor female."[20] 3 Now "the two are one" when we speak to each other in truth, and there is one soul in two bodies with no hypocrisy. 4 And by "the outside is like the inside" he means this: "the inside" is the soul, and "the outside" is the body. Therefore, just as your body is visible, so let your soul be evident by your good deeds. 5 And by "the male with the female is neither male nor female" he means this: that when a brother sees a sister he

---

[16] Matt. 12:50; Mark 3:35; Luke 8:21.
[17] Source unknown. Cf. 1 *Clem.* 23:3-4.
[18] Heb. 10:23.
[19] 1 Cor. 2:9.
[20] Cf. *Gospel of Thomas* 22.

should not think of her as a female, nor she of him as a male. 6 When you do these things, he says, the kingdom of my Father will come.

Chapter Thirteen
Therefore, brothers, let us at once repent. Let us exercise self-control for our good, for we are full of much foolishness and wickedness. Let us wipe off from ourselves our former sins and repent with all our soul so we may be saved. Let us not be people-pleasers and let us not desire to please ourselves alone by our righteousness, but also those who are outside, so that the Name not be blasphemed because of us. 2 For the Lord says, "My name is always blasphemed among all the Gentiles,"[21] and again, "Woe to him on whose account my name is blasphemed."[22] Why is it blasphemed? Because you do not do what I desire. 3 For the Gentiles, when they hear from our mouth the sayings of God, they marvel at their beauty and greatness. Then, when they find out that our deeds are not worthy of the words we speak, they turn from then on to blasphemy, saying that it is a myth and a delusion. 4 For when they hear from us that God says: "It is no credit to you if you love those who love you, but it is a credit to you if you love your enemies and those that hate you."[23] When they hear these things, they marvel at this extraordinary goodness. But whenever they see that we not only do not love those who hate us but not even those who love us, they laugh scornfully at us, and thus the Name is blasphemed.

Chapter Fourteen
So then, brothers, if we do the will of God our Father, we will belong to the first church, the spiritual one which was created before the sun and moon. But if we do not obey the will of the Lord, we will be among those of whom the scripture says, "My house has become a den of bandits."[24] So let us choose, therefore, to belong to the church of life, so that we may be saved. 2 Now I do not imagine that you are not ignorant that the living church is the body of Christ. For the scripture says, "God made mankind male and female."[25] The male is Christ, the female is the Church. Also the scrolls and the apostles say that the church belongs not to the present, but has existed from the beginning; for she was spiritual, as was also our Jesus, but he was manifested in the last days that he might save us. 3 And the church, which is spiritual, was manifested in the flesh of Christ, showing us that if any of us guard her in the flesh without corruption, he will receive her back again in the Holy Spirit. For this flesh is a copy of the Spirit. Therefore no one who has corrupted the copy will partake in the original. So, then, he means this, brothers: "guard the flesh, so that you may partake of the Spirit."[26] 4 Now if we say that the flesh is the church and the Spirit is Christ, then the one who abuses the flesh has abused the church. Such a person, therefore, will not partake of the Spirit, who is Christ. 5 So great is the life and immortality this flesh is able to partake of, if the Holy Spirit is joined with it, no one is able to express or to speak of the things "which the Lord has prepared" for his chosen ones.

---

[21]Isa. 52:5.
[22]Source unknown.
[23]Luke 6:32, 35.
[24]Jer. 7:11; Matt. 21:13.
[25]Gen. 1:27.
[26]Source unknown.

Chapter Fifteen

Now I think that I have not given unimportant advice about self-control, which if anyone follows he will have no regret, but will save both himself and me his advisor. For it is no small reward to turn to salvation a wandering and perishing soul. 2 For this is the return which we can pay back to God who created us, if the one who speaks and hears both speaks and hears with faith and love. 3 Let us, therefore, remain righteous and holy in our faith, that we may boldly ask God, who says, "While you are speaking I will say, 'Behold am I here'."[27] 4 For this saying is the sign of a great promise, for the Lord says that he is more ready to give than we are to ask. 5 Let us then share in such great kindness, and not begrudge ourselves the gaining of such good things, for as great is the pleasure that these words bring to those who do them, so severe is the condemnation they bring to those who disobey.

Chapter Sixteen

So, brothers, as we have received no small opportunity to repent, while we have time, let us turn to the God who calls us, while we still have the one who accepts us. 2 For if we renounce these pleasures and conquer our soul by not doing its evil desires, we will receive Jesus' mercy. 3 But you know that the day of judgment is already approaching like a burning oven and some of the heavens will melt and the whole earth will be like lead melting in a fire,[28] and then both the hidden and the open deeds of people will be made visible. 4 Charitable giving is therefore as good as repentance from sin. Fasting is better than prayer, but charitable giving is better than both; and love "covers a multitude of sins,"[29] but prayer from a good conscience rescues from death. Blessed is everyone who is found to be full of these things, for charitable giving lightens the burden of sin.

Chapter Seventeen

Therefore, let us repent with our whole heart, so that none of us perish. For since we have commands that we should do this, to tear men away from idols and to instruct them, how much more must we save from perishing a soul who already knows God? 2 Let us then help one another, and bring back those who are weak in goodness, so that we may all be saved, and turn each other around and exhort each other. 3 And let us not only appear to believe and pay attention now, while we are being exhorted by the presbyters, but also when we have returned home, let us remember the commandments of the Lord, and let us not be dragged aside by worldly desires. Rather by coming here more frequently, let us attempt to progress in the commands of the Lord, so that we may all think the same way and be gathered together for life. 4 For the Lord said, "I am coming to gather together all the nations, tribes, and languages."[30] Now by this he means the day of his appearance, when he will come and rescue us, each one according to his deeds. 5 And the unbelievers will see his glory and power, and they will be astonished when they see the sovereignty of the world given to Jesus; and they will say, "Woe unto us, because it was you, and we did not know it or believe it, and we did not obey the presbyters who proclaimed to us about our salvation." "And their worm will not die and their fire will not be quenched,

---

[27] Isa. 58:9.
[28] Isa. 34:4.
[29] 1 Pet. 4:8; cf. Prov. 10:12; Jam. 5:20.
[30] Isa. 66:18.

and they will be a spectacle for all flesh."[31] 6 He means the day of judgment, when they will see those who were ungodly among us and who perverted the commands of Jesus Christ. 7 But the righteous who have done good, who endured torture, and who hated the pleasures of the soul, when they see those who have gone astray and denied Jesus by words or deeds punished with terrible torment in unquenchable fire, will give glory to their God, saying that there will be hope for him who has served God with his whole heart.

Chapter Eighteen
Let us then also be among those who give thanks, who have served God, and not among the ungodly who are judged. 2 For I myself also am completely sinful, and I have not yet fled from temptation, but while still in the midst of the devil's tools, I am endeavoring to pursue righteousness, so that I may have the strength at least to come near to it, while in fear of the coming judgment.

Chapter Nineteen
So then, brothers and sisters, following the God of truth, I am reading you an appeal to pay attention to what has been written, so that you may both save yourselves and the one who is the reader among you. For as a payback I ask you to repent with all your heart, giving yourselves salvation and life. For when we do this, we will set a goal for all the younger ones, who wish to devote themselves to piety and the goodness of God. 2 And we should not be displeased or be indignant in our foolishness when anyone admonishes us and turns us from unrighteousness to righteousness. For sometimes, when we do evil, we do not know it because of the double-mindedness and faithlessness that in our breasts, and we are darkened in our understanding by useless desires.[32] 3 Let us then practice righteousness, so we may be saved at the end. Blessed are those who obey these instructions; although they may suffer evil for a short time in this world, they will reap the immortal fruit of the resurrection. 4 So then, the godly person should not grieve if he endures misery at this present time; a blessed time awaits him. He will live again with the fathers above and will rejoice in an age when there is no sorrow.

Chapter Twenty
May it not disturb your mind when we see unrighteous being wealthy and God's servants being oppressed. 2 Let us then have faith, brothers and sisters. We are competing in the contest of the living God and being trained in the present life, so that we may be crowned in the coming one. 3 None of the righteous has received their fruit quickly but they wait for it. 4 For if God paid the wages of the righteous quickly, we would immediately be engaged in business and not in godliness, for we would appear to be righteous when we were not pursuing piety but gain. Because of this, divine judgment punishes a spirit which is not righteous and burdens it with chains. 5 To the only invisible God,[33] the Father of Truth, who sent forth to us the Savior and Founder of immortality, through whom he revealed to us the truth and the heavenly life, to him be the glory for ever and ever. Amen.

---

[31] Isa. 66:18, 24.
[32] Cf. Eph. 4:18.
[33] 1 Tim. 1:17.

CHAPTER FIVE

Ignatius

"The letters of St. Ignatius of Antioch give us an unusually intimate picture of the mind of a heroic and tragic churchman of the early second century" (Tugwell, 104). This sentence is truly *multum in parvo* about a man who wrote a lot in a very short time. Like a meteor that appears brightly to us without revealing its history and its future travels, Ignatius bursts into the world of western Asia Minor, shines brightly, and then is gone. His letters, however, were kept and treasured by some that we know about (e.g., Polycarp). They were even condensed and then lengthened by later admirers, but today we have them as they came from him, with their truly profound combination of orthodoxy and pathos.

Most of the authors of the books that we call the "Apostolic Fathers" are actually shrouded in mystery, and what is often mentioned about them is based purely on tradition. The exception to that anonymity are the authors Polycarp and Ignatius. Polycarp was not only the undisputed author of a letter attributed to him, but also is the subject of a rather full martyrdom account which we will later consider. Polycarp also received a letter from the other more well-known author Ignatius of Antioch. In his seven surviving letters we do not learn a lot about his background, but we do learn a lot about his mind and heart and his intensely personal views about both life and death!

In dealing with the period of Trajan (98–117 CE), Eusebius in the fourth century mentions Ignatius, whom he calls the second successor of Peter as the bishop of Antioch (*EH* 3.36.5–11). Our author was taken as a prisoner from his church in Antioch of Syria to Rome where he evidently suffered martyrdom. On the way, he was allowed enough leisure to write letters in Smyrna to the Ephesians, the Magnesians, the Trallians, and the Romans, while he was temporarily staying there in personal communication with Polycarp the bishop. The three remaining letters, to the Philadelphians, to the Smyrnaeans, and to Polycarp, were written during the next stage in his journey from Troas, where again he tarried for a time, before crossing the sea for Europe. The place of writing in each case is determined from notices in the letters themselves.

Ignatius always greets his readers as "Ignatius who is also called Theophorus." The latter word literally means "god-bearing" or "inspired." But since the word is not found as a personal name before Ignatius, it is probable that the name was coined by him or for him. In the following translations, it is rendered "God-bearer" as a sort of nickname.

THE COLLECTION OF LETTERS

The collection of letters from Ignatius is first attested by one of his correspondents, Polycarp of Smyrna (*Pol.* 13.2). Ignatius has the unenviable reputation of experiencing both a later condensation and also an expansion of his work. Until the seventeenth century, a collection of these missives, in both Latin and Greek, was well known. Six extra letters eventually were shown to be spurious, but finally what is now called the "middle recension" won the day. Archbishop Usher and Nicolaus Videllius discovered this recension as a corpus in actual manuscripts, confirming what was before simply a literary hypothesis. By 1689 the seven which we now have were printed, and these have been published as the "genuine letters" from the nineteenth century until the present day. The collection of the seven is not in the order that they appear in the manuscripts but in the order they are mentioned by Eusebius (*EH* 3.36.1–10). The first four were written from Smyrna, while the last three from Troas. It is interesting that the order of the letters begins with the longest one to the Ephesians and ends with the shortest one to Polycarp.

THE "ENEMIES" OF IGNATIUS

Ignatius does not speak of the Roman guards to which he was chained or the Roman Empire as his enemies, despite referring to those soldiers as "leopards" (*Ign. Rom.* 5.2). He is far more concerned with the internal spiritual affairs within the six churches and with the one bishop/overseer he addresses. His struggle was against groups of professing Christians whose view threatened the saving nature of the passion and death of Christ. He actually rejects any possible future efforts of the Roman church to which he writes to somehow intercede and save him from a martyr's death. He viewed his impending death as the ultimate justice of his cause.

Who were the spiritual enemies endangering the churches that he sought to expose and defeat in his correspondence? To the groups he opposes, Ignatius attributes both a denial of the reality of Christ's flesh and therefore of his death and resurrection (see *Trallians* and *Smyrnaeans*) and a Judaizing point of view (*Magn.* 8–10; *Phld.* 6–9). An interesting debate has arisen over the question whether Ignatius is combating a tendency which combines Docetism and Jewish practices, or two separate enemies. It is simply difficult to find any known group that fits this framework. Antidocetist polemics are also found in passages about Judaism (*Magn.* 9.1; 11; *Phld.* 6.1).

Ignatius does not use the term *docetist*, but he does use the corresponding Greek verb (*dokeo*) when he writes that these people teach that Jesus suffered only "in appearance" (*Smyrn.* 2; 4.2). The docetist opponents deny that Christ was of the human line of David (*Smyrn.* 1.1; *Trall.* 9.1), and that he "truly" suffered under Pontius Pilate, died, and rose again (*Smyrn.* 1.1, 2; 2. 1, 2; *Trall.* 9.1,2).

Their attitude to the church also consists in opposing some of the outward physical ceremonies, such as abstaining from the eucharist and the liturgy, because they deny that the eucharist is the flesh of Christ (*Smyrn.* 7.1) and they have no regard for outward love (*Smyrn.* 6.2). They additionally reject the authority of the overseer, challenge the presbyters, and do not respect the deacons (*Smyrn.* 8.1; *Trall.* 2–3). Finally, they are swollen with pride (*Trall.* 7.1), which is based on their rank (*Smyrn.* 6.1). Since they are neither presbyters nor deacons, what rank can this be? It seems from *Trall.* 5.1–2 and *Smyrn.* 6.1 that they boast of knowing heavenly secrets, angelic hierarchies, and throngs of celestial powers, possibly due to ecstatic experiences. The reference here must be to "charismatics" who claimed a special authority because of their supposed ability to receive revelations, while also criticizing their overseer, who strangely sometimes "remains silent" (*Ign. Eph.* 6.1; *Phld.* 1.1), probably because he does not have the so-called proper charismatic gifts.

In *Smyrn.* 5.1, these problem causers are dissuaded neither by prophecies nor by Moses' law, which probably means that they do not affirm that the OT foretells the events of the physical incarnation, suffering, and death of Jesus. In *Phld.* 8.2, Ignatius recalls a debate that he had with some of them (in Antioch?) where they claimed that if they did not find it in the "ancient records" (i.e., the Scriptures) they do not believe that it is in the Gospel. The disagreement here is certainly on the Messianic or Christological interpretation of the OT Scriptures. They sound quite legitimate when they state that anything about Christ must be proved by correct exegesis. Ignatius simply responds: "for me, the ancient records are Jesus Christ" (*Phld.* 8.2). In general, he makes little use of the Scriptures in his letters, especially the OT, which is not his best response, in this writer's opinion.

If the Jews are a separate group from the docetists, which is the best approach, Ignatius opposes those who live according to Judaism but who profess "false doctrines or old fables that are useless" (*Magn.* 8.1). The "Judaizing" mentioned in 8.1 is not quite as clear. It appears to be too strong an attachment to the Hebrew scriptures, particularly the prophets (also *Magn.* 9.2). This is similar to what he condemns in *Phld.* 8.2, which also reflects a position attacked as docetic. His attack on Sabbath observance in *Magn.* 9.1 stresses the contrast between what he calls "ancient customs" and our "new hope." Here the adversaries do not necessarily observe the Sabbath, but in the same sentence he again exposes the docetists! Sometimes the accusations against the Judaizers seem to suppose only their attachment to the Hebrew scriptures. If these letters had the format of tractates instead of letters, maybe a greater consistency could be seen in all this apparent diversity.

In the end, the Judaizers and the docetists seem to be different opponents. Perhaps also he may not have had direct contact with the Judaizers and depended on reports about them in these congregations, which may explain some of his occasional confusing rhetoric.

THE SCRIPTURES OF IGNATIUS

In his letters Ignatius cites the OT only three times (*Eph.* 5.3; *Magn.* 12; *Trall.* 8.2). In the first two, he precedes the quotation with the familiar NT expression, "it is written." An allusion to Isa. 66:18 may be detected in *Magn.* 10.3. An observation can be offered that his low view of Jews and Judaism could be affected by his apparently scant appreciation of those "Jewish" scriptures.

Ignatius' familiarity with the events in the Gospel accounts is evident. He almost presages in *Trall.* 9.1–2 the "Jesus events" later mentioned in the Apostles' Creed. More concrete references to Synoptic Gospel texts, however, are harder to find. The few possible allusions seem to be to the Gospel of Matthew. A number of references to the Fourth Gospel are quite possible. See, for example, the probable reference to John 6:33 in *Eph.* 5.2, to John 1:14 in *Eph.* 7.2, and to John 5:19 in *Magn.* 7.1. In this last matter of Johannine citations, attention should be given to the ancient patristic tradition concerning his relationship to the Apostle John that was mentioned by both Irenaeus and Eusebius.

The following quotation appears in *Smyrn.* 3.2. "For when he came to those who were with Peter, he said to them, 'Take hold on me and handle me and see that I am not a bodiless daimon.' And as soon as they touched him they believed, being closely united with his flesh and spirit." Eusebius cites this "citation" as coming from an unknown source (*EH* 3.36), and Jerome thought that it was from the *Gospel to the Hebrews* (*Vir Ill* 2). A simpler explanation is that Ignatius was simply providing a loose paraphrase of Luke 24:40 and borrowing the word "believed" from John 20:29.

An examination of these possible "quotations" of canonical scriptures leaves one with the impression that most are more like allusions or even echoes rather than quotations.

This may be due to the fact that these letters were written in transit and not allowing immediate access to the written texts. In other words, Ignatius is referring to these texts by memory. In the text of his letters that follow, many of the footnoted "quotations" are not clearly citations from the biblical book. When this is the case, the source of the allusion is preceded by a "cf." See, for example, the footnotes to *Trall.* 8.2 and 12.3. The perceptive reader may also wonder at times if we have been too generous in even suggesting some of his statements as possible scriptural allusions.

IGNATIUS AND THE "BISHOP"

One of the most striking and "famous" features in the Ignatian letters, especially for modern readers who come from a non-liturgical context, is his frequent emphasis on the ecclesiastical role of the "bishop" and his council of leaders. The word is intentionally singular, because there is no indication of a plurality of presbyters and bishops in a church, but what looks like the role of a monarchical bishop who ruled over a number of congregations that were in a larger city.

The bishop is the earthly representative of God and Christ (*Eph.* 4.1–6.2; *Trall.* 2.1–3.3; *Smyrn.* 8.1–9.2). The words "harmony" and "unity" are code words for being submitted to the bishop (*Eph.* 13.1–2; *Philad.* 8.1–2). Those who resist such submission are guilty of "strife" and "division" (*Philad.* 8.1; *Magn.* 6.2). Public prayer is to be led by the bishop as well as the celebration of the Eucharist (*Eph.* 5.2; *Smyrn.* 8.1). Neither baptism nor the agape or love feast should proceed without him (*Smyrn.* 8.2). Surprisingly, there seems to be only one reference to preaching by the bishop: a "message" mentioned in *Ign. Polyc.* 5.1.

This prominent role of the monarchical bishop is quite evident in the writings of Ignatius, and thus is evident as early as the first decade of the second century! This strong emphasis on the "bishop" does not appear to be evident in the surviving writings of other AF up until the mid-second century. It can be argued, however, that this absence of evidence in other contemporary writers does not necessarily imply the evidence of absence about this role of the bishop in other contemporary churches.

The reader of the following Ignatian letters may be surprised that I have chosen not to render the Greek word *episkopos* as "bishop." Whatever one's ecclesiastical background all should agree that the later semantic associations that accompany the English word "bishop" were not intended either in the New Testament or even by Ignatius. This is despite his lofty view of the role of the *episkopos* as the spiritual head of a local church, with "presbyters" and "deacons" under him. It is still too early in church history for the *episkopos* to be viewed as the "metropolitan" spiritual leader of a diocese with priests under him in the individual local churches. Therefore, I have rendered the word as "overseer," a meaning with a long history from the Attic period down through the first century of the Christian era (*Cambridge Greek Lexicon*, I, 573). I have resisted the effort to translate *presbuteroi* as "priests" by simply using the transliteration "presbyters." The word *diakonoi* is rendered by the transliteration "deacons."

THEOLOGY OF IGNATIUS

In the Christology of Ignatius God the Father has revealed himself through Jesus Christ his Son and the Logos/Word (*Magn.* 8.2). He pre-existed in God and was with the Father before the worlds. "Jesus Christ ... came forth from one Father and was with the one and returned to the one" (*Magn.* 7.2). Christ was in God before time, invisible, and it was for us he became visible (*Ign. Polyc.* 3.2). As the Logos he came forth from the silence of God, which means that he is revealed to the world in the incarnation, through which he comes forth from the Father to reveal himself (*Eph.* 7.2).

Ignatius' Christology often consists of a refutation of the previously mentioned Docetism, which regarded Christ as a spiritual being, not truly human but one who "seems" (*dokeo*) to be that way. Ignatius offers a special emphasis on the real humanity and the bodily being of Christ. Christ was conceived in the womb of Mary; he is from the seed of David and of the Holy Spirit; he was born and was baptized (*Ign. Eph.* 18. 2). He was truly born of a virgin (*Smyrn.* 1.1): "Jesus Christ ... was of the line of David, the son of Mary who was truly born and ate and drank; who was truly persecuted under Pontius Pilate and was truly crucified and died in the sight of those in heaven and on earth and under the earth. 2 Moreover, He was truly raised from the dead by the power of his Father" (*Trall.* 9.1–2). He was "truly nailed in the flesh for our sakes" (*Smyrn.* 1.2); "He was in the flesh even after the resurrection; and when he came to Peter and his company ... they touched him, and they believed" (3.2). Ignatius declares in Christ the dualism of flesh and spirit. Through the flesh he is born of Mary and mortal. Through the spirit he is without beginning; he is life and he is God. In a word, he is God come in the flesh.

The union of man and God in Christ is not precisely defined by Ignatius. Christ is called *theos*, although He is distinct from the Father. Even in His incarnation Jesus is called God (*Eph.* 18.2; *Rom.* 3.3). Christ is our God not only insofar as He lives in us, but absolutely. Again, Jesus Christ is not only our God or God for us, he is very God. "I give glory to Jesus Christ the God who made you so wise" (*Smyrn.* 1.1). In *Eph.* 18.2, the designation "God" is given to Christ absolutely.

The work of Christ consisted in giving man a knowledge of the true God. Jesus Christ is the "Logos" of God who came forth from the silence of God (*Magn.* 8.2). God became manifest in the flesh to prove the newness of undying life and the destruction of death. The passion of Christ and His blood shed for us are the pledge of this renewal of humanity. Ignatius offers no explanation of this mystery, either of the benefit of Christ's suffering or of the manner in which this is communicated to believers. He lays great stress on the suffering of Christ and on what it secures. This is explained when we remember not only that he was refuting Docetism but also that this aspect of Pauline theology was of fundamental importance.

The Spirit stands in opposition to the flesh. This was an important article of faith to Ignatius. The flesh is man while the Spirit is a principle which comes from God and works in man, searching out his hidden secrets (*Philad.* 7.1). The Spirit inspires the spiritual man, and Ignatius himself is conscious of being so inspired. "It was the preaching of the Spirit who spoke *by my mouth*" (implied, *Philad.* 7.2).

Believers are the "building of God the Father, you are being carried up to the top by the crane of Jesus Christ, which is the cross, and the rope of the Holy Spirit" (*Eph.* 9.1). Such tropes often amaze the modern reader who may struggle at times to clearly "see" the analogy. Ignatius counsels the Magnesians to remain united in flesh and spirit by faith and love, in the Son, the Father, and the Spirit (*Magn.* 13.1). The Spirit is named along with the Logos (*Smyrn.* inscr.). The apostles were obedient to "the Christ and the Father and the Spirit" (*Magn.* 13.2). It is not difficult to recognize this as an early effort at expressing what became the trinitarian baptismal formula.

Christianity, in opposition to Judaism, is the life of Christ in us (*Smyrn.* 4.1), which is manifested through faith and love (*Ign. Eph.* 14. 1). This life is the fruit of the Spirit in contrast with the flesh. Ignatius even goes to the length of declaring, "No one professing faith commits sin" (*Eph.* 14. 2), although this is not much different from what we read in 1 John 3:4–6.

Ecclesiology is also expressed in the above terms. As Christ is joined to the Father so the church is joined to Christ (*Eph.* 5.1), for Christ is in every believer (15.3). He "breathes incorruptibility into the church" (17.1). He is the High Priest to whom is committed the holy of holies. To him alone the secrets of God are disclosed. He is the door of the Father through which Abraham, Isaac, and Jacob, the Prophets, the Apostles, and the Church can enter (*Philad.* 1.9). Ignatius is also the first Christian writer to apply the transliterated word "catholic" to the church (*Smyrn.* 8.2). The meaning is the "universal" rather than the local assembly. The later *Martyrdom of Polycarp* also utilizes the word in this sense (8.1; 19.2).

Every AF spoke of the *eschaton*, and so did Ignatius. The time of the end is at hand. "These are the end times" (*Eph.* 11.1). All those who believe in Christ will rise again (*Trall.* 9.2). The believers are members of Christ through His cross and passion. The head cannot exist apart from the members, so in the end there will be unity, God himself being that unity (*Trall.* 11.2). There is no evidence of chiliasm and no vivid apocalyptic imagery. The things of heaven are mentioned only in the abstract (*Trall.* 5.2), and with them the angelic orders. Of such things Ignatius made no special claims but observed, "as for the invisible matters, pray that they may be revealed to you" (*Ign. Polyc.* 2.2).

CONCLUDING OBSERVATIONS ABOUT IGNATIUS

Allen Brent (*Ignatius of Antioch*) has encouraged a fresh look at some of the peculiar features of Ignatius' drama and his relationship with Polycarp, who preserved his letters for posterity. He argues that Ignatius in his letters to other churches re-interpreted church order, the eucharist, and martyrdom against the background of the Second Sophistic in Asia Minor by utilizing the cultural material of a pagan society. Brent pays special attention to the procession of Ignatius through Asia Minor in light of the secular processions of his day. His acts and aspirations would have been unintelligible to a reader who did not participate in the civic culture of the early second century. He recounts these circumstances and the cultural context in which Ignatius constructed what became the historic church order of Christendom. Brent also defends the authenticity of the Ignatian letters by showing how the circumstances of Ignatius' condemnation at Antioch and departure for Rome fit well with what we can reconstruct of the internal situation of the church of Antioch in Syria at the end of the first century. Ignatius is described as a controversial figure arising in the context of a church at war with itself. Ignatius constructs out of the conflicting models of church order that were available to him one model founded on a single overseer/bishop that he commends to the Christian communities through which he passed in chains as a condemned martyr prisoner.

In regard to those letters, what lent greater authority to them was Ignatius' impending and certain martyrdom. His epistles, written in an abrupt and scattered style, overloaded with metaphors, and to some readers almost incoherent, are yet endowed with a fervent faith and passionate joy as he faced martyrdom. With such overwhelming love for Christ, many observers have concluded that they are one of the best expressions of the Christian faith in the second century.

At the same time, many modern readers simply have a hard time encountering the rhetorical style in his letters. The reasons for this usually center around three issues: (1) the almost macabre eagerness with which he anticipates his martyr's death; (2) his rather harsh attacks on Jews who in the NT are still "beloved for the sake of the fathers"; and (3) his elevation of the overseer/bishop to a position demanding absolute submission. While answers and justifications have been offered for all three of these, we still consider each of them a less than admirable characteristic for someone who was and still is held in such high esteem. It is not enough to conclude that no one is perfect. Perhaps the distance of centuries is the best explanation why both great traits and unlovely characteristics can both be present in some of these ancients. Perhaps that is also true of us! We simply should not try to make him a modern pastor but rather accept and appreciate him for all that he did and accomplished in the early second century.

We also need to look past some of those unlikeable traits and focus more on his admirable qualities. This chapter opened with an eloquent comment about this man who was both a heroic and a tragic churchman. We return to that same author now at the end for a helpful perspective we should not overlook in his character.

Those who read his letters will find it hard to doubt the intensity of his love for God and his utter fidelity to the gospel and to the church. Over and over again he expresses his yearning to 'attain God' or 'attain Jesus Christ' (Eph. 12.2; *Mag.* 14.1; *Trall.* 12.2; 13.3; *Rom.* 2.1; 4.1; 5.3, 9.2; *Sm.* 11.1, *Pol.* 7.1). These extraordinary letters, drained from him on his way to his death, reveal a hunger for God and a passionateness unlike anything that we find elsewhere in the writings of the Apostolic Fathers.

(Tugwell, 125)

FURTHER READING ON IGNATIUS OF ANTIOCH

Bammel, C. P. Hammond. "Ignatian Problems." *Journal of Theological Studies* 33 (1982). 62–97.

Barrett, C. K. "Jews and Judaizers in the Epistles of Ignatius" in *Jews, Greeks and Christians*, ed. R. Hammerton-Kelly and R. Scroggs, 220–44. Leiden. E. J. Brill, 1976.

Brent, Allen. *Ignatius of Antioch: A Martyr Bishop and the Origin of Episcopacy*. London. T&T Clark, 2009.

Corwin, Virginia. *St. Ignatius and Christianity in Antioch*. New Haven. Yale University Press, 1960.

Foster, Paul. "The Epistles of Ignatius of Antioch" in *The Writings of the Apostolic Fathers*, ed. Paul Foster, 81–107. London and New York. T&T Clark, 2007.

Grant, R. M. *Ignatius of Antioch*. The Apostolic Fathers, vol. 4. Camden, NJ. Nelson, 1966.

Lightfoot, J. B. *The Apostolic Fathers, Part II. S. Ignatius. S. Polycarp*, 2nd ed., vol. 3. London. Macmillan, 1889. Repr. Grand Rapids. Baker, 1981.

Maier, Harry O. *The Social Setting of the Ministry as Reflected in the Writings of Hermas, Clement and Ignatius*. Waterloo, On. Wilfrid Laurier University Press, 1991.

Schoedel, W. R. "Are the Letters of Ignatius of Antioch Authentic?" *Religious Studies Review* 6 (1980). 196–201.

_____. *Ignatius of Antioch. A Commentary on the Letters of Ignatius of Antioch*. Hermeneia. Philadelphia. Fortress, 1985.

_____. "Polycarp of Smyrna and Ignatius of Antioch" in *ANRW* 2.27.1, 272–358. Berlin and New York. De Gruyter, 1993.

To the Ephesians

Ignatius, who is also called "God-bearer," to the Church of Ephesus in Asia, blessed with greatness through the fullness of God the Father, having been predestined from eternity to eternal abiding and unchanging glory forever, united and chosen through a true suffering by the will of the Father and of Jesus Christ our God, the church worthy of blessing. Heartfelt greetings in Jesus Christ and with blameless joy.

Chapter One

I have welcomed in God your greatly beloved name, which is yours by reason of your natural goodness according to the faith and love in Jesus Christ our Savior. You are imitators of God, with hearts inflamed through the blood of God, you have done perfectly the work that fell to you to do. 2 For you were eager to visit me when you heard that I was on my way from Syria, in chains because of our common name and hope and longing, with the help of your prayers, to face the wild beasts in Rome successfully and so to become a disciple. 3 Therefore in God's name I received your whole community in the person of Onesimus, your overseer in the flesh, a man whose love is beyond all power to express. I beg of you to love him in Jesus Christ and to be like him to a man. May he be blessed who gave you the grace to have and to deserve such an overseer.

Chapter Two

Concerning my fellow servant Burrhus, your deacon by the will of God and a man blessed in every way, I ask that he continue with me to your honor and that of your overseer. Crocus also, who is worthy of God and of yourselves, I have received as an exemplar of the love you bear me. He has been a great comfort to me in every way. May the Father of Jesus Christ reward him with his grace, and not only him but Onesimus, Burrhus, Euplus and Fronto, for in them I saw the love of all of you. 2 If I am worthy of it, may I have joy in you always. And so it is fitting for you to glorify Jesus Christ in every way, who has given you glory so that you may be made complete by submitting to the overseer and the presbytery and be made holy in every way.

Chapter Three

I am not ordering you as though I was someone, for I have not yet been made perfect in Jesus Christ, even though I am a prisoner for his name. But now I am beginning to be his disciple and speak to you as my fellow disciples. For I have need of being trained by you in faith, counsel, endurance, and patience. 2 Since love will not permit me to be silent about you, I am so bold to beg you to be in harmony with God's mind. For Jesus Christ, our inseparable life, is the mind of the Father, and the overseers appointed to the ends of the earth are of one mind with Jesus Christ.

Chapter Four

Thus it is proper for you to agree, as you do, with the mind of the overseer. For your presbyters, who are worthy of the name and worthy of God, like the strings of a lyre, are in harmony with the overseer. Hence it is that in the harmony of your minds and hearts Jesus Christ is sung. 2 Make each of you into a choir, so that with one voice and one mind, taking up the song of God, you may sing in unity with one voice through Jesus Christ to the Father, and he may hear you and recognize you through your good deeds as members of his Son. It is good for you, therefore, to be in perfect unity that you may always be partakers of God.

Chapter Five

And if I in a short time have such spiritual and not merely human fellowship with your overseer, all the more do I consider you happy who have become one with him, as the church is one with Jesus Christ and as Jesus Christ is one with the Father, so that all things may be harmonious in unity. 2 Let no one be deceived. If a person is not within the sanctuary he is deprived of the bread of God. For if the prayer of one or two has such force, how much greater is that of the overseer and of the whole church. 3 Anyone, therefore, who fails to assemble with the others has already shown his pride and set himself apart. For it is written, "God resists the proud."[1] Let us be careful, therefore, not to oppose the overseer, so that we may be in submission to God.

Chapter Six

And when a man notices that the overseer is silent, all the more he should stand in awe of him. For, whoever the Master sends to run his house, we ought to receive him as we would receive the one who sent him. It is evident, therefore, that we ought to regard the overseer as we would the Lord himself. 2 I should tell you that Onesimus himself praises you for your orderly behavior in God, because all of you are living according to truth and because among you no heresy dwells. Indeed, you do not so much as listen to anyone unless he speaks truthfully of Jesus Christ.

Chapter Seven

There are some who have a way of bearing the name in deceit and wickedness while doing things unworthy of God. Such people you must avoid as you would wild beasts, for they are mad dogs that bite when you are not on your guard. You must beware of them, for they are hard to tame. 2 There is one physician of both flesh and spirit, begotten and yet unbegotten, God in man, true life in death, both from Mary and from God, first able to suffer and then beyond suffering, Jesus Christ, our Lord.

Chapter Eight

Let no one, therefore, deceive you as being wholly given to God, since you are not deceived. For when no passion rooted within you has an established power to torment you, you are certainly living according to God. As a humble sacrifice for you I offer myself for you Ephesians, for your church which will be remembered for the ages. 2 Carnal men can no more do the works of the spirit than those who walk in the spirit do the things of the flesh[2]; nor can faith do the things of unfaithfulness nor infidelity the things of faith. For you do all things in Jesus Christ, even those things which you do according to the flesh are spiritual.

Chapter Nine

I have learned that some strangers holding to evil teaching have passed your way, but that you have not allowed them to sow their seeds among you and have stopped your ears lest you should receive what was sown by them. Like the stones of a temple, cut for a building of God the Father, you are being carried up to the top by the crane of Jesus Christ, which is the cross, and the rope of the Holy Spirit. And your faith has drawn you up and love has been the way leading to God. 2 You are all fellow pilgrims, carrying with you God and his

---

[1] Prov. 3:34; Jas. 4:6; 1 Pet. 5:5.
[2] Rom. 8:5, 8.

temple; you are bearers of Christ and of holy things, adorned with the commandments of Jesus Christ. And through this letter I celebrate with you, to be of your company, to rejoice with you because you love nothing human in life, but God only.

Chapter Ten
And pray constantly for all people, for there is hope of their repentance that they may reach God. Give them the opportunity to learn from you, at least by your deeds. 2 When they are angry with you, be gentle; to their arrogance show humility, to their blasphemies your prayers, to their error by your steadfastness in faith, to their bullying by your gentleness. Do not be eager to imitate them. 3 By our gentleness, show that we are their brothers. Let us rather be eager to imitate the Lord. Let us see who can be the more wronged, who the more cheated, who the more rejected, in order that no weed planted by the devil may be found in you, but that with complete holiness and self-control you may abide in Christ Jesus in the flesh and in the spirit.

Chapter Eleven
These are the end times. And so let us feel shame and fear the patience of God, lest it turn in judgment against us. Either let us fear the wrath that is coming or else let us love the grace that is here—one or the other as long as we are found in Jesus Christ unto true life. 2 Without this nothing should appeal to you. In him I bear my chains about me like spiritual pearls; and in these with your prayers—in which I trust always to have a share—may I rise again. Then I may be found to share the lot of the Ephesian Christians who have always agreed with the apostles by the power of Jesus Christ.

Chapter Twelve
I know who I am and to whom I am writing. I am a condemned man; you have received mercy. I am in danger; you are secure. 2 You are the passage for those on the way to die for God. You are fellow initiates with Paul the sanctified, who received a witness, who was worthy of blessing. May I be found in his footsteps when I reach God; in his every letter he mentions you in Christ Jesus.

Chapter Thirteen
Be eager, therefore, to assemble more frequently to give thanks and glory to God. For when you gather frequently, the powers of Satan are destroyed and his danger is dissolved in the harmony of your faith. 2 There is nothing better than peace by which every warfare is abolished by those in heaven and on earth.

Chapter Fourteen
You are aware of all these truths if you have faith and love in Jesus Christ. This is the beginning and end of life; faith is the beginning and the end is love and God is the two of them brought together in unity. After these comes whatever else makes up nobility of character. 2 No one who professes the faith commits sin, and no one hates who possesses love. A tree is known by its fruit,[3] and in the same way those who profess to belong to Christ will be seen by what they do. For what is needed is not mere present profession but being found in the power of faith at the end.

---

[3] Matt. 12:33.

Chapter Fifteen

It is better to be silent and to exist than to speak and not exist. It is good to teach, if the one who speaks also acts. There is one teacher who spoke and it happened.[4] And even the things he did in silence are worthy of the Father. 2 The one who possesses the word of Jesus is truly able to hear even his very silence, that he may be perfect, and may both act as he speaks, and be known by his silence. 3 Nothing is hidden from the Lord and even the things we have kept hidden are near to him. Let us do all things, therefore, as though he were dwelling in us, that we may be his sanctuaries and he in us as our God,[5] and indeed he is. And it will be clearly seen before us that we love in a righteous way.

Chapter Sixteen

Do not be deceived, my brothers. Those who corrupt families will not inherit the kingdom of God.[6] 2 If those who do these things according to the flesh die, how much worse is the one who with bad doctrine corrupts the divine faith for which Jesus Christ was crucified. Such a person is filthy and will depart into the unquenchable fire; so also will the one who listens to him.

Chapter Seventeen

Because of this the Lord received the ointment on his head,[7] that he might breathe incorruptibility into the church. Do not be anointed with the stench of the teaching by the prince of this age, lest he take you away captive from the life set before you. 2 Why do we not all become wise by receiving the knowledge of God which is Jesus Christ? Why do we foolishly perish by being ignorant of the gracious gift which the Lord has truly sent?

Chapter Eighteen

My spirit is a humble offering for the cross, which is a stumbling block to those who have no faith, but to us salvation and eternal life. Where is the wise man? Where is the debater?[8] Where is the boasting of the so-called intelligent? 2 For our God Jesus Christ was, according to God's plan, conceived by Mary from the seed of David and of the Holy Spirit. He was born and baptized in order that he might purify the water by his suffering.

Chapter Nineteen

The virginity of Mary and her giving birth and also the death of the Lord escaped the notice of the ruler of this age—three mysteries loudly proclaimed which were accomplished in the silence of God. 2 How, then, did he appear to the ages? A star shone in the sky brighter than all other stars and its brightness was indescribable and its novelty caused astonishment. And the rest of the stars, along with the sun and the moon, formed a chorus to that star, but the light of the star by itself outshone all the rest. It was a puzzle to know the origin of this novelty unlike anything else. 3 Consequently all magic was dissolved and every bondage of evil disappeared. Ignorance was destroyed and the ancient kingdom was ruined, when God appeared in human form to give us newness of eternal life. What had

---

[4]Ps. 33:9.
[5]Cf. 1 Cor. 3:16.
[6]1 Cor. 6:9.
[7]Matt. 26:7; Mark 14:3.
[8]1 Cor. 1:20, 23.

been prepared by God received a beginning. From then all things were set in commotion because of the plan for the abolition of death.

Chapter Twenty
If Jesus Christ finds me worthy through your prayer and if it should be his will and still more if the Lord should reveal it to me, in a second small letter which I plan to write to you, I will explain more fully what I have merely touched upon. This is the divine plan of becoming the new man Jesus Christ who is of the race of David involving his faith and his love, according to his passion and resurrection. 2 Especially (I will do so) if the Lord makes known to me that you come together one by one in common through grace in one faith, and in Jesus Christ, who was of the seed of David according to the flesh, being both the Son of man and the Son of God, so that with undivided mind you may obey the overseer and the presbyters, breaking one bread which is a medicine of immortality and an antidote to take that we might not die but live forever in Jesus Christ.

Chapter Twenty-One
I am giving my life for you and for those to the honor of God you sent to Smyrna. From here I am writing to you, thanking the Lord and loving Polycarp as I also love you. Remember me as Jesus Christ remembers you. 2 Pray for the church in Syria—from which I am the least of the faithful there—for I am being led away a prisoner to Rome, for so I was judged worthy to be found honorable to God. Farewell in God the Father and in Jesus Christ our common hope.

To the Magnesians

Ignatius, who is also called "God-bearer," to the church that is blessed with the grace of God the Father through Christ Jesus our Savior, in whom I greet the church in Magnesia near the Maeander. I wish you heartfelt greetings in God the Father and in Jesus Christ.

Chapter One
Having heard of the perfect order of your love for God, it is with great joy and in the faith of Jesus Christ that I have decided to communicate with you. 2 Since I have been honored with a name so dear to God, in the chains I bear about with me I sing the praise of the congregations. And I pray that the congregations may have unity in the flesh and spirit of Jesus Christ, who is our constant life. This union in faith and love is to be preferred to all else and especially union with Jesus and the Father. Through him if we endure all the abuse of the ruler of this age we will reach God.

Chapter Two
It was possible for me to see you through your devout overseer Damas and the worthy presbyters, Bassus and Apollonius, and my fellow servant and deacon Zotion. May I continue to have joy in him, since he is obedient to the overseer as to the grace of God and to the presbytery as to the law of Jesus Christ.

Chapter Three
It is not proper for you to take advantage of your overseer because of his age. You should show him all respect according to the power of God the Father. I understand that the holy presbyters so do. They do not take advantage of his apparent youthful appearance, but

they yield to him as to one who is wise in God—not merely to him but to the Father of Jesus Christ, who is the overseer over all. 2 To the honor of him who loves you, you must obey without any hypocrisy. For in this case one does not so much deceive an overseer who is seen but cheats the one who is unseen. In such a case one must give an account not to a man, but to God who knows the hidden things.

Chapter Four
Therefore, it is not fitting only to be called Christians, but also to be such. So also there are those who call one an overseer but do everything without him. Such people, it appears to me, are not acting in good conscience, for they do not assemble validly as commanded.

Chapter Five
Seeing that all things have an end, two things are set together, death and life, and each of us is to depart to his own place. 2 As there are two currencies, one from God and the other from the world, and each with its own stamp, so the unbelieving have the stamp of the world, but the believers are those who in love have the stamp of God the Father through Jesus Christ. And if we are not ready to die through him to his suffering, his life is not in us.

Chapter Six
In the people I mentioned I have observed in faith and have loved your whole congregation. So I exhort you to be careful to do all things in God's harmony, the overseer sitting in the place of God and the presbyters in the place of the council of the apostles, and the deacons especially dear to me, entrusted with the ministry of Jesus Christ, who was with the Father before the ages and appeared to us at the end. 2 All should respect one another in conformity with God's character. No one should regard his neighbor according to the flesh, but love one another always in Jesus Christ. Let there be nothing among you to divide you, but be unified with the overseer and with those who preside, as an exemplar and lesson of incorruptibility.

Chapter Seven
So just as the Lord was united with the Father and did nothing apart from the Father, either through himself or through the apostles, so you should do nothing without the overseer and the presbyters. Nor should you try to make a thing out to be reasonable, merely because it seems so to you personally. Let there be one prayer, one petition, one mind, one hope in love, in blameless joy which is Jesus Christ, concerning whom nothing is superior. 2 All of you should run together as into one Divine sanctuary, as upon one altar, upon one Jesus Christ, who came forth from one Father and was with the one and returned to the one.[9]

Chapter Eight
Do not be deceived by either false doctrines or old fables that are useless. For if we live according to Judaism we admit that we have not received grace, 2 because the holiest prophets lived according to Christ Jesus. For this reason they were persecuted. But they were inspired by his gracious gift so that the disobedient became fully assured that there

---

[9]Cf. John 16:28.

is one God who manifested himself in Jesus Christ his Son, who is his Word proceeding from silence, and who in all things was pleasing to the one who sent him.

Chapter Nine
Those who were brought up in the old ways have come to possess a new hope, no longer observing the Sabbath, but living in the observance of the Lord's Day, on which also our life has sprung up again by him and by his death. Although some deny him, we are found the disciples of Jesus Christ our only Teacher, by whose mystery we have obtained faith and therefore endure. 2 How will we be able to live apart from Him, whose disciples the prophets themselves in the spirit waited for him as their Teacher? And therefore the one whom they righteously awaited has come and raised them from the dead.

Chapter Ten
And so let us not fail to perceive his kindness, for were he to act toward us as we do toward him, we would no longer exist. So by becoming his disciples, let us learn to live according to Christianity. No one with any other name than this can belong to God. 2 Put away, therefore, the bad leaven that has become old and sour, and turn to the new leaven which is Jesus Christ. Be salted in him, lest any of you becomes rotten, for by your odor will you be judged. 3 It is absurd to preach Jesus Christ and to practice Judaism. For Christianity did not believe in Judaism, but Judaism in Christianity, in which every tongue that believes in God has been gathered together.[10]

Chapter Eleven
I am writing these things, beloved, not because I have heard that any among you are practicing Judaism. But small as I am in comparison with you, to forewarn you against being snared by the hooks of worthless opinions. May you be fully convinced of the birth and the suffering and the resurrection that took place during the time of the governor Pontius Pilate. These things were truly and certainly done by Jesus Christ our hope. From this hope may none of you be turned aside.

Chapter Twelve
I hope I may have joy in you in every way, if only I am worthy. It is true that I am in bonds, but in comparison with any of you who are free I am no one. I know that you are not conceited, for you have Jesus Christ in you. Rather when I praise you I know that you are blushing; as it is written, "The upright man is his own accuser."[11]

Chapter Thirteen
Be eager, therefore, to be secure in the commandments of our Lord and his apostles, that whatever you do you may prosper in body and spirit, in faith and love, in the Son and Father and Spirit, in the beginning and in the end, along with your most worthy overseer and the presbytery—a spiritual crown that so fitly crowns him—and your godly deacons. 2 Be obedient to your overseer and to one another, as Jesus Christ in his human nature was to the Father and as the apostles were to Christ and the Father. In this way there will be both fleshly and spiritual unity.

---

[10] Cf. Isa. 66:18.
[11] Prov. 18:17.

IGNATIUS

Chapter Fourteen
I have exhorted you briefly, because I know that you are filled with God. Remember me in your prayers, so that I may reach God, and also the church in Syria, of which I am unworthily a member. I need your united prayer and love in God, if the church in Syria is to be refreshed with dew through your church.

Chapter Fifteen
The Ephesians greet you from Smyrna, where I am writing to you. They are with me, like yourselves, for the glory of God, and have been an unfailing encouragement to me. Also Polycarp, the overseer of the people of Smyrna, and all the other congregations greet you in the honor of Jesus Christ. Trusting that you may remain in the harmony of God, farewell to you who possess an undivided spirit which is Jesus Christ.

To the Trallians

Ignatius, who is also called "God-bearer," to the holy church in Tralles in Asia. Beloved, you are by God, the Father of Jesus Christ, the elect and worthy of God, outwardly and inwardly at peace through the passion of Jesus Christ, in whom we have hope through our resurrection unto him. I greet you in the fullness of God, as the apostles used to do, and I wish you every joy.

Chapter One
By the will of God and of Jesus Christ your overseer, Polybius, has visited me here in Smyrna. He informs me that by nature more than by habit you are blameless in understanding and unwavering in your endurance. Despite the bonds I bear for Christ Jesus, he filled me with such encouragement that through him I was able to envision your whole community. 2 Accepting your spiritual kindness through him, I thanked God to find, as I had heard, that you are imitators of God.

Chapter Two
For it seems to me that, when you are obedient to the overseer as you would be to Jesus Christ, you are living, not in a human way, but according to Jesus Christ, who died for us that by faith in his death you might escape death. 2 You must continue, then, to do nothing apart from the overseer. Be obedient also to the presbyters as to the apostles of Jesus Christ, our hope, in whom we will be found if only we live in him. 3 As ministers of the mysteries of Jesus Christ, the deacons should please all in every way they can, for they are not merely ministers of food and drink but are the servants of the church of God. They must guard against all reproaches as they would of fire.

Chapter Three
In the same way all should respect the deacons as they would Jesus Christ, just as they respect the overseer as representing the Father and the presbyters as the council of God and the college of the Apostles. Apart from these there is nothing that can be called a church. 2 In such matters I am sure you feel as I do, for I have received a sample of your love in the person of your overseer who is here with me. His behavior is a great lesson and his meekness is his power. I am sure that even the unbelievers think highly of him. 3 Because I love you I treat you gently, but on his behalf I could write more sharply.

However, since I am a prisoner, I have not felt myself to be in a position to command you as though I were an apostle.

Chapter Four
By the grace of God I am not lacking in wisdom, but I mark my words, lest I perish by boasting. Indeed I must be more afraid than ever of paying attention to those who flatter me. Their words only serve to punish me. 2 I long to suffer, but I do not know if I am worthy. To most people my sincerity is not apparent, but for my part it is becoming irresistible. My prayer is for humility, by which the prince of this age can be overcome.

Chapter Five
It is not that I am unable to write to you about heavenly realities, but I am afraid that since you are infants I might do you harm.[12] Please share my convictions, else you may be choked by what you cannot swallow. 2 I myself do not pretend to be a disciple merely because I am in chains and can comprehend mysteries such as the ordered hierarchy of angels and principalities and the visible and invisible worlds.[13] Many things we must lack if we are not to lose God.

Chapter Six
Then I exhort you to leave alone the foreign plant of heresy and keep entirely to Christian food. Not I but the love of Jesus Christ is speaking. 2 For the heretics mix poison in with Jesus Christ, as men can administer a deadly drug with sweet wine without giving a hint of their wickedness. So that without thought or fear of the fatal sweetness a man can drink his own death.

Chapter Seven
Be on your guard against such people. This will be possible if you are not arrogant and if you keep close to Jesus Christ and the overseer and the ordinances of the apostles. 2 Anyone who is within the sanctuary is clean and anyone who is outside is unclean, which means that no one who acts apart from the overseer and the presbyters and the deacons has a clear conscience.

Chapter Eight
Not that I have heard of anything about this among you. I guard you as ones whom I love, for I foresee the snares of the devil. So put on the armor of patience and refresh yourselves in faith, that is in the body of the Lord, and in love, that is in the blood of Jesus Christ. 2 Let no one look down on his neighbor. Let not the folly of a few give an opportunity to the pagans to criticize your pious community. "Woe unto him through whom my name is blasphemed before others without cause."[14]

Chapter Nine
So be deaf when anyone speaks to you apart from Jesus Christ, who was of the line of David, the son of Mary who was truly born and ate and drank; who was truly persecuted under Pontius Pilate and was truly crucified and died in the sight of those "in heaven and

---
[12]Cf. 1 Cor. 3:1-2.
[13]Cf. Col. 1:16.
[14]Cf. Isa. 52:5.

on earth and under the earth." 2 Moreover, he was truly raised from the dead by the power of his Father. In like manner his Father will raise up through Christ Jesus those of us who believe in Him. Apart from Him we have no true life.

Chapter Ten
If, as the godless say in the sense that they are without faith, he merely seemed to suffer—it is they themselves who merely seem to exist—why am I in chains? And why do I pray that I may be thrown to the wild beasts? I die, then, to no purpose. I then bear false witness against the Lord.

Chapter Eleven
Therefore, avoid the evil branches that bring forth deadly fruit. Merely to taste such fruit is to meet a sudden death. Such are not the plants of the Father. 2 If they were they would appear as branches of the cross and their fruit would be immortal. It is by the cross and by his suffering that he invites you who are his members. The head cannot be born without the members, since it was God himself who promised to keep them together.

Chapter Twelve
I am writing these greetings from Smyrna. With them goes the others from God's congregations who are with me. They have been of encouragement to me in many ways, both physical and spiritual. 2 My bonds, which I bear with me for the cause of Jesus Christ and as a prayer that I may reach God, are my exhortations to you. Persevere in harmony with one another and in common prayer together. All of you and particularly the presbyters must help to keep up the overseer's spirit out of honor for the Father and Jesus Christ and the apostles. 3 I beg you to give heed in love to what I say, so that my letter may not be taken as evidence against you. Pray for me, for by the mercy of God I stand in need of your love, if I am to be worthy of the end that I am eager to meet and am not found to be disqualified.[15]

Chapter Thirteen
The Smyrnaeans and Ephesians greet you in love. Remember in your prayers the church in Syria of which I am a member, unworthy I am as the least among them. 2 Farewell in Jesus Christ. Be obedient to your overseer, and to the presbyters as well, as to the commandment. With undivided heart let each and all of you love one another. 3 My life is offered for you both now and when I reach God. I am not yet out of danger, but the Father through Jesus Christ can be trusted to answer both my request and yours. May we be found in him blameless.

To the Romans

Ignatius, who is also called "God-bearer," to the church on which the majesty of the most high Father and Jesus Christ his only Son has shown mercy; to the congregation beloved and enlightened by the faith and love of Jesus Christ our God, through the will of Him who has willed all things to exist—the church in the place of the district of the Romans which holds the preeminence. I greet you in the name of Jesus Christ, the Son

---

[15] Cf. 1 Cor. 9:27.

of the Father. You are a church worthy of God, worthy of honor, blessing and praise, worthy of reaching God, a church without blemish, which holds the preeminence of the community of love, obedient to the law of Christ, bearing the Father's name. To you who are united in flesh and spirit to every commandment of his, being filled with the grace of God and with every foreign color filtered out, I wish every blameless joy in Jesus Christ, our God.

Chapter One
In answer to my prayer and beyond all I asked for, I have at last seen the faces I have longed to see. As I am in chains for Christ Jesus, I hope to greet you, if only he counts me worthy to reach my goal. 2 I will know that the beginning is providential if, in the end, I am to obtain the inheritance without hindrance. For I am afraid of your love; it may do me wrong. For it is easy for you to have your way, but it will be hard for me to reach God if you do not spare me.

Chapter Two
I would have you think of pleasing God,[16] as indeed you are doing, rather than men. For never again will I have an opportunity like this of reaching God; nor can you ever have any better work credited to you, if only you remain silent. If only you say nothing on my behalf, I am a word of God. But, if your love is for my body, I will be once again a mere voice. 2 You can do me no greater kindness than to allow me to be poured out as an offering to God while the altar is still prepared. Thus forming yourselves into a chorus of love, you may sing to the Father in Jesus Christ that God deemed the overseer of Syria worthy of being transferred from the rising to the setting sun. It is good to be setting, leaving the world for God, that I may rise in Him.

Chapter Three
You have never envied anyone. You have taught others. I trust that what you have taught and commanded to others will remain in force. 2 Pray only that I may have outward and inward strength, not only in word but in desire, that I may not be a Christian merely in name but in fact. For if I am one in fact, then I may be called one and be faithful long after I am no longer visible to the world. 3 Nothing merely visible is good, for our God, Jesus Christ, is visible more now that he is hidden in the Father. Christianity is not a matter of persuasiveness, but of greatness when it is hated by the world.

Chapter Four
I am writing to all the congregations to tell them all that I am to die for God with all my heart, if only you do not hinder me. I implore you not to show your goodwill at the wrong time. Please let me be food for the wild beasts since through them I can reach God. I am God's wheat; I am being ground by the teeth of the wild beasts that I may end as the pure bread. 2 If anything, entice the wild beasts to become my tomb and to leave nothing of my body undevoured so that I may be no bother to anyone when I am dead. I will be truly a disciple of Jesus Christ when the world can no longer see my body. Pray, then, to the Lord for me, so that by these means I may be a sacrifice to God. 3 I do not command you like Peter and Paul did. They were apostles; I am a condemned man. They were free;

---

[16]Cf. 2 Thess. 2:4.

I am still a slave. But if I suffer, I will become the free man of Jesus, and will rise again as a free man in him. But now in chains I am learning to desire nothing.

Chapter Five

I am already fighting with beasts on my journey from Syria to Rome. On land and at sea, by night and by day, chained with ten leopards around me, or at least with a band of guards who grow worse the better they are treated. Their mistreatments, however, make me a better disciple. But it is not because of this I am justified.[17] 2 May I find my joy in the beasts that have been prepared for me. My prayer is that they will be prompt with me. I will entice them to devour me quickly and not be timid to touch me, as has happened with some. And if when I am ready, they hold back, I will provoke them to attack me. 3 Bear with me; I know what is best for me. I am now beginning to be a disciple. May nothing visible or invisible prevent me from reaching Jesus Christ. Fire and cross and battles with wild beasts, the breaking of bones and mangling of members, the grinding of my whole body, the wicked tortures of the devil; let these come upon me, but only that I may reach Jesus Christ!

Chapter Six

Neither the kingdoms of this world nor the ends of the earth are of any use for me. I would rather die for Jesus Christ than rule the ends of the earth. I seek for Jesus Christ who died for us. My love is for him who rose for us. The pains of birth are upon me. 2 Bear with me, brothers. Do nothing to prevent this new life. Do not wish me to die. Do not give to the world a man whose heart is fixed on God. Do not entice me with material things. Allow me to receive the pure light, for when I reach it, I will be fully a human being. 3 Allow me to be an imitator of the suffering of my God. Let those who hold him in their hearts understand what I long for, knowing what I am choosing, and share my feelings.

Chapter Seven

The ruler of this age is eager to tear me to pieces, to weaken my will that is fixed on God. Let none of you who are watching the battle assist him. Come in rather on my side, for it is the side of God. Do not speak for Jesus Christ but desire the world. 2 Let envy have no place among you. And even when I am come, if I should urge you, pay no attention to what I say; believe, rather, what I am writing to you now. For alive as I am at this moment of writing, my longing is for death. Desire within me has been crucified[18] and no flame for material things is left. Only the living water[19] speaks within me saying, "Hasten to the Father." 3 I have no taste for the food that perishes nor for the pleasures of this life. I want the bread of God which is the flesh of Christ, who was of the seed of David; and for drink I desire his blood which is love that cannot be destroyed.

Chapter Eight

I desire no longer to live a purely human life, and this desire can be fulfilled if you agree. Make this your choice if you yourselves would be chosen. 2 I make my petition in a few words. Please believe me; Jesus Christ will make it clear to you that I speak the truth, for

---

[17] 1 Cor. 4:4.
[18] Cf. Gal. 6:14.
[19] Cf. John 4:10, 14.

he was the mouth without deceit through which the Father truly spoke. 3 Beg for me that through the Holy Spirit that I may not fail. I have not written to you according to the manner of men, but according to the mind of God. If I die, it will prove you loved me; if I am rejected, it will be because you hated me.

Chapter Nine
Remember in your prayers the church of Syria, which now in my place has God for its shepherd. Jesus Christ, along with your love, will be its only overseer. 2 For myself, I am ashamed to be called one of them, for I am not worthy, being the last among them and a miscarriage.[20] If I reach God, I will be someone only by his mercy. 3 My spirit salutes you, and with it the love of the congregations which welcomed me in the name of Jesus Christ. They treated me as more than a passing pilgrim; for even the communities that did not lie along the route I was taking went before me from city to city.

Chapter Ten
I am writing this letter to you from Smyrna by the hands of the Ephesians, who deserve all praise. Among many others who are with me there is my dear friend Crocus. 2 I trust you have come to know those who went ahead of me from Syria to Rome for the glory of God. Please tell them that I am not far away. All of them are worthy of God and of yourselves. You will do well to help them in every way. The date of this writing is the ninth day before the calends of September. Farewell until the end in the endurance of Jesus Christ.

To the Philadelphians

Ignatius, who is also called "God-bearer," to the congregation of God the Father and of Jesus Christ in Philadelphia of Asia. You have received mercy and are firmly established in harmony with God and with enduring joy in the suffering of our Lord and through abundant mercy you have been given full assurance of his resurrection. I greet you by the blood of Jesus Christ. Your church is to me a cause of unending and unbroken joy. It will be even more so, if all of you continue to be at one with the overseer and with his presbyters and with the deacons, who have been appointed according to the mind of Jesus Christ. All of you have been securely established through his Holy Spirit according to his own will.

Chapter One
I have learned that your overseer obtained his ministry for the whole community, not by any effort of his own or of others nor out of vanity, but through the love of God the Father and of the Lord Jesus Christ. I have been amazed at the gentleness of a man who can do more by his silence than others by speaking. 2 He has been attuned to the commandments like a harp to its strings. And so my soul blesses his Godly mind, knowing how virtuous and perfect it is, how steadfast and calm, living in all gentleness from the living God.

---

[20] 1 Cor. 15:8-9.

Chapter Two

Therefore, children of the light of truth, flee from schisms and false teachings. As sheep do, follow wherever the shepherd leads. 2 For there are many seemingly trustworthy wolves who snare God's runners by wicked pleasure, but they will have no place in your unity.

Chapter Three

Avoid the poisonous weeds which grow where Jesus Christ does not cultivate the soil, for they are not the Father's planting. Not that I have found any division among you, only the filtering of impure elements. 2 For all who belong to God and Jesus Christ are with the overseer, and those who repent and return to the unity of the Church will belong to God to live in accordance with Jesus Christ. 3 Make no mistake, brothers. If any follow a schismatic, they will not inherit the kingdom of God.[21] If anyone follows an alien opinion, he does not agree with the Passion.

Chapter Four

Be zealous, therefore, to have one eucharist. For there is one flesh of our Lord, Jesus Christ, and one cup that brings unity through His blood. There is one altar, as there is one overseer together with the presbytery and deacons, my fellow workers. So that whatever you do, do in the name of God.

Chapter Five

My brothers, I am overflowing with love for you, and with immense joy I am watching over you, not I but Jesus Christ for whom I am in chains—for I am even more afraid that I am far from perfection. However, your prayer to God will perfect me, so that I may gain the inheritance that God's mercy has assigned me, if only I take refuge in the Gospel as in the body of Jesus and in the apostles as the presbytery of the church. 2 Let us also love the prophets, for it was they who anticipated the Gospel and hoped in him and awaited him. And by believing in him they were saved in the unity of Jesus Christ, saints worthy of love and admiration. They were testified by Jesus Christ and numbered with us in the gospel of our common hope.

Chapter Six

But if anyone expounds Judaism to you, do not listen to him. It is better to hear about Christianity from one who is circumcised than about Judaism by one who is not. But if either fails to preach Jesus Christ, they are for me tombstones and graves inscribed with the names of men. 2 Flee from the tricks and traps of the ruler of this age, else you be worn out by his schemes and grow weak in your love. Assemble all of you together instead, in unity of heart. 3 I thank my God that my conscience is clear, for there is no one among you who can claim, privately or openly, that I have been a burden to him in any matter, great or small. I pray that nothing that I have said may be viewed as evidence against any to whom I have spoken.

---

[21]Cf. 1 Cor. 6:9-10.

Chapter Seven

There may be some who according to the flesh sought to deceive me, but the spirit from God is not deceived. He knows from where it comes and to where it goes, and he exposes what is hidden.[22] I cried out among you and I spoke with a loud voice, the voice of God: "Give heed to the overseer, the presbytery and the deacons." 2 When I said this, there were those who suspected that I knew ahead of time of the division among you. But he is my witness, for whom I am in chains, that I knew of this from no human source. It was the Spirit who proclaimed these words: "Apart from the overseer let nothing be done. Guard your flesh as a temple of God. Love unity. Flee from divisions. Be imitators of Jesus Christ as he is of his Father."

Chapter Eight

As for me, I did my part like a person appointed to bring about unity. For where there is division or anger, God does not dwell. Now the Lord forgives all who repent, so long as their repentance turns to union with God and to the council of the overseer. I have faith in the grace of Jesus Christ, who will break all your bonds. 2 I urge you to do nothing in a party spirit but everything in accordance with Christ's teaching. There are some saying, "If I do not find it in the ancient records, I do not believe in the gospel." When I said: "It is written," they replied: "That is just the question." But for me, Jesus Christ is the ancient records and his cross and death and resurrection and faith through him are the sacred ancient records. Through these, with your prayer, I desire to be justified.

Chapter Nine

The priests are good, but still better is the high priest, to whom is entrusted the Holy of Holies and to whom alone the mysteries of God were entrusted. He is the door of the Father[23] through which Abraham and Isaac and Jacob and the prophets and the apostles and the Church all enter. All these are bound together into the unity of God. 2 But what distinguishes the Gospel is that it is about the coming of the Savior, our Lord Jesus Christ, his suffering and his resurrection. The beloved prophets proclaimed about him. The gospel is the consummation of immortality. All these things together are good as long as you believe with love.

Chapter Ten

The news has reached me that, thanks to your prayer and the concern you showed in Christ Jesus, that the church of God in Antioch of Syria is at peace. I feel that you ought, as a church of God, to choose a deacon to go there as God's ambassador, for the glory of the name and to congratulate them when they gather together. 2 Blessed in Christ Jesus is the man who is considered worthy of this ministry and will also be honored. You can do this for the name of God if only you choose, just as the congregations that are near sent deacons or presbyters and even overseers.

Chapter Eleven

The deacon, Philo of Cilicia, a man of good testimony who is now ministering to me by the word of God, and Rhaius Agathopus, a chosen person of Syria who gave up his

---

[22]Cf. John 3:8; 1 Cor. 2:10.
[23]Cf. John 10:7, 9.

present occupations to follow me, join in speaking highly of you. I give thanks to God for your kindness in receiving them with the kindness which the Lord shows to you. But may the grace of Jesus Christ forgive those who treated them disrespectfully. 2 The love of the brothers in Troas greets you. I am writing from there by the hand of Burrhus, who was sent by the Ephesians and Smyrnaeans to accompany me as a pledge of respect. The Lord Jesus Christ will honor them who hope in him in body, soul and spirit, in faith, love, and harmony. Farewell in Christ Jesus, who is our common hope.

To the Smyrnaeans

Ignatius, who is also called "God-bearer," to the congregation of God the Father and of the beloved Jesus Christ which is at Smyrna in Asia. I wish you every joy in a blameless spirit and the word of God. Your church has been mercifully blessed with every spiritual gift and is lacking in none, filled with faith and love, most worthy of God, and fruitful in holiness.

Chapter One

I give glory to Jesus Christ, the God who has made you so wise. I am well aware that you have been made complete in an unwavering faith, nailed in body and spirit to the cross of our Lord Jesus Christ and established in love by the blood of Christ. You are thoroughly convinced that he was of the family of David according to the flesh and the Son of God by God's will and power, truly born of the virgin and baptized by John in order that all righteousness might be fulfilled by him.[24] 2 He was truly nailed for us in the flesh under Pontius Pilate and Herod the tetrarch. From his most blessed suffering we are the fruit, so that through his resurrection he might raise eternally in the one body of his church a standard for the holy faithful ones, whether among Jews or Gentiles.

Chapter Two

For he suffered all these things for us, that we might be saved. And he truly suffered and just as truly raised himself from the dead. He did not suffer merely in appearance, as some of the unbelievers say, they themselves being only in appearance, for it will happen to them just as they think, since they will bodiless and demonic.

Chapter Three

For I know that even after his resurrection he was in the flesh and I believe this to be true. 2 For when he came to those who were with Peter, he said to them, "Take hold on me and handle me and see that I am not a bodiless phantom."[25] And as soon as they touched him they believed, being closely united with his flesh and spirit. For this reason they despised death and even showed themselves to be beyond death. 3 After his resurrection he ate and drank with them like anyone with a body, although he was spiritually united with the Father.

Chapter Four

Although I know you agree with these things, beloved, I am advising you. I am guarding you against the wild beasts in human form. If possible, you should not even meet with

---

[24]Cf. Matt. 3:15.
[25]Cf. Luke 24:39.

them, let alone welcome them. Instead you must pray for them, so that difficult as it is, they may somehow repent. But Jesus Christ, who is our true life, has authority over this. 2 If the things done by our Lord were merely in appearance, then I am in chains only in appearance. Then why did I give myself up to death, to fire, to the sword, and to the wild beasts? To be near to the sword is to be near to God. To be among the beasts is to be with God, as long as it is in the name of Jesus Christ. I endure all so I can suffer along with him, for he who is perfect man empowers me.

Chapter Five
There are some who deny him, because they do not know him, or rather they are denied by him, being advocates of death and not truth. These have not been persuaded by the prophecies, nor the law of Moses, nor until now by the Gospel nor by the sufferings of any one of us. 2 For they think of us as they think of him. For what is the use of a man thinking well of me, if he blasphemes my Lord by denying that he was clothed in flesh? Anyone who denies this denies him altogether, as one clothed in a corpse. 3 I do not think it right for me to set down the names of such men, since they are unbelievers. May I not record them until they repent concerning the passion, which is our resurrection.

Chapter Six
Let no one be deceived. Judgment is prepared even for heavenly beings, and the glorious angels and rulers, visible or invisible, if they do not believe in the blood of Christ. He that can receive this, let him receive it.[26] Let no one be haughty because of his position, for faith and love are all, and nothing is preferable to them. 2 Consider how contrary to the mind of God are those with false views about the grace of Jesus Christ that has come to us. They have no regard for love, none for the widow, nor for the orphan, nor for the oppressed, none for the man in prison, or the hungry or the thirsty. They abstain from the eucharist and from prayer because they do not admit that the eucharist is the flesh of our Savior Jesus Christ, the flesh which suffered for our sins and whom the Father raised in his kindness.

Chapter Seven
Therefore those who deny the good gift of God perish in their contentiousness. It would be more to their advantage to love, so that they also may rise up. 2 It is good for you to keep away from such people and not even to speak of them in private or in public. It is better to pay attention to the prophets and especially to the gospel in which the passion is shown to us and the resurrection is accomplished.

Chapter Eight
Shun divisions as the beginning of evils. All of you should follow the overseer as Jesus Christ does the Father, and the presbytery, as you would the apostles. Respect the deacons as you would the command of God. Without the overseer, let no one perform any of the functions that pertain to the church. Let that eucharist be valid which is offered by the overseer or by one to whom the overseer has designated. 2 Wherever the overseer appears, there let the people be. Wherever Jesus Christ is, there is the "catholic" church. It is not lawful to baptize or have a love feast without the consent of the overseer. But whatever has his approval is pleasing to God, so that whatever you do will be trustworthy and valid.

---

[26] Matt. 19:12.

Chapter Nine

It is reasonable for us from now on to come to our senses and while there is still time to repent to God. It is good to know God and the overseer. One who honors the overseer is honored by God. One who acts without the knowledge of the overseer is serving the devil. 2 Therefore, by grace may all things abound to you in grace, for you are worthy. You have refreshed me in every way, and may Jesus Christ refresh you. Whether I was absent or present, you loved me. May God reward you. You will reach him one day, if you endure all things for his sake.

Chapter Ten

It was good of you to welcome Philo and Rhaius Agathopus as deacons of God, for they followed me for the sake of God. They give thanks to the Lord for you because you refreshed them in every way. Nothing will ever be lost to you. 2 My spirit is given in exchange for you and also my bonds, which you did not despise nor were you ashamed of them. Neither will Jesus Christ, who is the perfect hope, be ashamed of you.

Chapter Eleven

Your prayer has reached the Church in Antioch of Syria, to which I unworthily belong, for I am the last of all. I come from there in chains which are pleasing to God, and I greet you all. By the divine will I was counted worthy that, through your prayer, I might reach God. This is not through any merit of mine, but by the grace of God; and I pray that the final grace may be given me. 2 If your work may be perfect in earth and heaven, you should have your church appoint for God's honor an ambassador of God to go to Syria to rejoice with them. For they are in peace after recovering their greatness and having restored to them their corporate life. 3 It seemed to me a deed worthy of God for you to send someone from you with a letter, that he might join with them in giving glory for the tranquility that has come upon them from God and for the fact that they have attained the harbor through your prayers. Being perfect calls on you to think perfect things.[27] For those wishing to do good, God is ready to help you do it.

Chapter Twelve

The love of the brothers who are at Troas greets you. I am writing from here through the hand of Burrhus, whom you and your brothers from Ephesus sent along with me. Burrhus has refreshed me in so many ways. I could wish that everyone would imitate him, for he is a model in God's ministry, and grace will repay him in every way. 2 I greet your overseer so worthy of God and your godly presbytery and my fellow servants, the deacons, individually and all in common in the name of Jesus Christ, and in his flesh and blood, in his passion and resurrection in body and spirit, in oneness with God and with you. Grace be to you, mercy, peace and endurance always.

Chapter Thirteen

I greet the families of my brothers with their wives and children and the virgins who are called widows. I wish you farewell in the power of the Father. Philo, who is with me, greets you. 2 I greet the family of Gavia, and I pray that she may be rooted in faith and a love in both flesh and spirit. I greet Alce, a name dear to me, and Daphnus the incomparable and Eutecnus and all by name. Farewell in the grace of God.

---

[27] Cf. Phil. 3:15.

To Polycarp

Ignatius, who is also called "God-bearer," to Polycarp, overseer of the congregation of the Smyrnaeans, or rather who has as overseer God the Father and Lord Jesus Christ. I wish you heartiest greetings.

Chapter One

I was glad to learn that your mind is grounded in God as upon an immovable rock, but I rejoice exceedingly to be judged worthy of seeing your blameless face. May it bring me joy in God. 2 I urge you by the grace with which you are clothed to press on in the race and exhort all people so that they may be saved. Do justice to your position with constant care for your practical and spiritual duties. Be focused on unity for nothing is better than this. Help others along as the Lord helps you. Bear with all out of love, just as you are doing. 3 Devote yourself to unceasing prayers. Ask for more understanding than you have. Keep your spirit awake and on watch. Follow God in speaking to each one as an individual person. Like an athlete in perfect condition, bear with all who are sick. Where there is more labor, there is much gain.

Chapter Two

There is no credit for loving good disciples. The real task is by gentleness to bring to submission those who trouble you. Not every wound is healed with the same plaster. Where the pains are fever, give relief with cold compresses. 2 In all things be wise as the serpent and at all times be as innocent as the dove.[28] You are made of flesh and spirit so that you may be able to treat gently whatever appears to you; as for the invisible matters, pray that they may be revealed to you. In this way nothing will be lacking, and you will abound in every spiritual gift. 3 The age is in need of you, if it is to reach God, as pilots need winds and as a storm-tossed sailor needs a harbor. Be self-controlled, like God's athlete; the prize is immortality and eternal life, of this you have no doubt. In every respect I am a ransom for you, and my chains which you loved.

Chapter Three

There are some who seem trustworthy enough, but who teach strange doctrines. Do not let them disturb you. Stand firm like an anvil struck by a hammer. A great athlete will take a beating and yet will conquer. We ought to patiently bear all things especially for God's sake, so that he will bear with us. 2 Become more diligent than you are. Understand the times. Wait for Him who is beyond time, the timeless one, the invisible one who became visible for our sake, the one who cannot be handled, the one beyond suffering who suffered for us and who endured in every way for us.

Chapter Four

Do not allow the widows to be neglected. After the Lord, you should be their guardian. Let nothing be done without your consent; and continue at present to do nothing yourself without God's consent. Be firm. 2 Let your gatherings be held more frequently. Seek out all by name, 3 and do not treat with contempt the slaves, whether male or female. At the same time, they should not be conceited, but rather serve faithfully for the glory of God, so that they may receive from God an even better freedom. Lest they become slaves of their own desires, they should not long to obtain freedom at the public cost.

---

[28] Matt. 10:16.

Chapter Five

Flee from dishonest practices, but rather give a message about such things. Tell my sisters to love the Lord and to be content with their companions in flesh and spirit. In the same way tell my brothers in the name of Jesus Christ to love their wives as the Lord loves the church.[29] 2 If anyone is able to remain in a state of purity to the honor of the flesh of the Lord, let him remain so without boasting. If he boasts, he is lost; if it is known to others than the overseer he is ruined. It is proper for men and women to marry with the consent of the overseer, so that the marriage may be according to the Lord and not due to lust. Let all be done to the honor of God.

Chapter Six

Pay attention to the overseer, in order for God to pay attention to you. I am a ransom for those who obey the overseer, presbyters, and deacons. May it be granted to me to be with them in God. Train together, run and suffer together, rest and get up at the same time, as God's stewards, assistants and servants. 2 Please the one whom you serve as soldiers, for from him you receive your wages.[30] May none of you be found as a deserter. Let your baptism be always your shield, your faith a helmet, your love a spear, your endurance as armor.[31] Let your works be your down payments, so that you may receive the wages that are due to you. In humility be patient with one another, as God is with you. May I rejoice in you always.

Chapter Seven

I have been told that the church in Antioch of Syria has found peace through your prayer. I also have become very encouraged and without anxiety in God—if only through suffering I reach God, so that by means of your prayers, I may prove to be a disciple. 2 Polycarp, you have been so blessed by God and it is appropriate for you to call a council to elect someone who is especially dear and resolute and qualified to be called God's runner. Let him be appointed to go to Syria that he may glorify your tireless love, to the glory of God. 3 A Christian is not his own master since he belongs to God. When you complete this work, it will be God's and yours. I trust in his grace that you are ready for a good work in the service of God. Because I know your eagerness for the truth, I have exhorted you briefly.

Chapter Eight

It has been impossible for me to write to all the congregations, because I am sailing at once from Troas to Neapolis, as God's will commands. And so I ask you, as one who knows the mind of God, to write to the congregations on this side and have them do likewise. Those who can should send messengers by land, and let others send letters by those messengers, so that you may have the glory of a work that will never be forgotten, as you deserve. 2 I greet all of you by name, not forgetting the wife of Epitropus with all who serve her and her children. I greet Attalus whom I love, and the one who is thought fit to go to Syria. Grace will be with him forever and with Polycarp who sends him. 3 Farewell forever in our God, Jesus Christ. I wish that in him you continue in the unity of God under his oversight. I greet Alce, a name very dear to me. Farewell in the Lord.

---

[29]Eph. 5:25, 29.
[30]Cf. 2 Tim. 2:4.
[31]Cf. Eph. 6:11-17.

CHAPTER SIX

Polycarp

"Polycarp is more interesting as a man and as a martyr than he is as a writer" (Tugwell, 129). In this honest sentence, Tugwell has actually captured much about Polycarp and his writing. Yet while many modern authors have stressed the rather banal nature of this "Letter to the Philippians," perhaps they have been a bit too harsh on him, in this writer's opinion.

POLYCARP THE MAN

As observed in the drama of Ignatius of Antioch on the way to his martyrdom, one of his letters was addressed to Polycarp, spiritual overseer of the church in Smyrna, the modern Izmir in Turkey. Eusebius records that Irenaeus of Lyons in a letter that he wrote around 190 CE (*EH* 5.20.6–7) recalls his own childhood spent in Smyrna at the school of this very Polycarp. Irenaeus tells us that he heard from him about John the Apostle and others of the Lord's disciples, whom Polycarp had known personally. In his own surviving work (*Haer.* 3.3.4) Irenaeus relates that Polycarp was ordained by the apostles as the overseer of the church in Smyrna, the same "congregation" that earlier was a recipient of one of the famous Seven Letters of the Apocalypse. This same writer also recorded that Polycarp became a martyr at a very advanced age, and we will see how that event was recorded by others in the *Martyrdom of Polycarp*. Through Eusebius again Irenaeus relates how Polycarp went to Rome during the time of Anicetus (*c.* 154) to discuss the vexed question about when to observe the resurrection (*Pascha*), although that visit did not resolve the issue (*EH* 4.14.1; 5.24.16). The question revolved around whether or not to observe the resurrection in conjunction with the Jewish observance of Passover on Nisan 14, which was the custom of the earliest Christian communities. The Roman leadership desired to follow their own custom of celebrating it on a Sunday and thus on a varying date each year. Although they did not agree, Polycarp remained in communion with the Roman bishop, which is possibly an example of how Rome's authority was viewed at the time. It was an attitude of respect without submission to absolute authority. This Roman practice finally prevailed around the end of the second century, and the whole debate came to be referred to as the Quartodeciman ("14th") Controversy.

Even limiting ourselves to the corpus of the AF, it is significant that we are better informed about Polycarp than any other Christian in the first half of the second century. There is one text written *to* him by Ignatius; one text written *by* him to the Philippians; and one text written *about* him, the *Martyrdom of Polycarp*, which took place also in Smyrna in the middle of the century and will be discussed in the next chapter.

THE FORM OF THE LETTER

Nine manuscripts preserve one letter of Polycarp, and there must have been others due to the respect with which he was held. The letter is addressed to the Church in Philippi, the same congregation that earlier had been blessed to receive a more well-known epistle from Paul. In each of the above manuscripts, the letter is followed by the so-called *Letter of Barnabas* and each of the manuscripts contains a gap between *Phil.* 9.2 and *Barn.* 5.7. This feature certainly indicates that each of these copies descended from a commonly damaged original. The earlier part of *Barnabas* was contained in the Bryennios manuscript discovered in Constantinople in the 1870s, but Polycarp's letter was not in that codex. Eusebius helps to restore chapters 9 and 13 through his citations (*EH* 3.36.13–15). The rest of the letter has come down to us through an early Latin translation. This mixed Greek-Latin text of Polycarp's letter was published in Cotelier's edition in 1672 and has continued to be viewed as one of the works of the AF ever since.

The well-known Ignatius addressed his letter to his esteemed younger colleague, Polycarp, around 110 CE. Our mention of Ignatius is to point out a problem in Polycarp's letter that has intrigued scholars for centuries. In 9.2 Ignatius is mentioned as already dead, but in 13.2 he appears to still be alive. The translation of the Latin is:

> The letters of Ignatius sent to us by him and all the others we have here we send to you, as you requested. These accompany this letter, and from them you will greatly benefit, for they deal with faith and endurance and all the edification that is suitable in our Lord. And let us know whatever you learn about Ignatius himself and those who are with him.

P.N. Harrison (1936) proposed the following explanation for the discrepancy. Chapters 13–14 comprise a brief letter written immediately after Ignatius' departure from Smyrna, and it was meant to accompany his letters to Philippi. Chapters 1–12 are actually a different letter that was written years later, perhaps around 135. Harrison's proposal has met with wide acceptance and is a creative solution to the problem. If we accept his suggestion, the note must have been written soon after Ignatius' departure from Smyrna for the time required for him to pass through Philippi and for Polycarp then to receive a letter from the church. As mentioned, the main section of the second letter that has come down to us must be dated around 135. If we maintain the original unity of the letter, then it must have been written after Polycarp received news of the martyrdom of Ignatius, thus a few months after his brief stop in Smyrna. Whatever be the specific explanation for what appears to be a contradiction, all seem to agree that the fourteen chapters that we read all came from the hand of Polycarp.

THE MESSAGE OF THE LETTER

Polycarp opens his letter by congratulating the Smyrna church for recently hosting Ignatius and the other prisoners on their fateful journey to Rome (1). It has always been fascinating to think about the entourage accompanied by those soldiers who evidently allowed the older man to have the time to visit these assemblies and the leisure to write to so many of them. He then exhorts his hearers/readers in Philippi to continue in the truth and in their faith in the risen Christ (2). He confesses that he is not on the same spiritual level as the Apostle Paul, who also had sent a letter to the same congregation that had helped them to advance in their faith (3). In chapters 4–5 Polycarp offers his version of a "household code" that would be familiar to readers of the earlier writings of Paul, at least in those letters attributed to him like Ephesians and Colossians. He counsels against greed and expounds on the duties of wives, widows, deacons, the presbyters, and the younger people. In a concise chapter, he exhorts them to both fear God and seek forgiveness from one another in light of the judgment tribunal of Jesus Christ (6). A negative note enters with a warning about false brothers who do not confess that Jesus has come in the flesh, then followed by a positive exhortation to be devoted both to the tradition and to Christ (7–8). With these exhortations in mind, the Philippians should persevere to the end in their patience. Examples of martyrs who did just that such as Ignatius and the otherwise unknown Zosimus and Rufus, plus the well-known Paul and the other apostles are presented as examples to follow (9). One wonders if Polycarp was knowingly preparing himself to eventually face what he would experience in the following decades.

Then follows a fervent exhortation to love one another and to behave blamelessly not only before the Lord but before their pagan neighbors (10). Polycarp then takes up the sad case of Valens, who had served as a presbyter but had departed, not primarily through a denial of faith, but through his greed (11). Polycarp pleaded not to be harsh with him and his wife, and then he follows with a fervent exhortation about patience and forbearance as well as prayer, even for the authorities who are persecuting the Christians (12). An interchurch issue is then mentioned, since Ignatius had asked him to thank his church in Antioch and to congratulate the congregation on the restoration of peace there. Polycarp promises that he will include a letter from the Philippians with his messenger. At the same time, he asks about the fate of Ignatius and his companions (13). See above for a possible explanation of this apparent timing contradiction. Polycarp finally commends to the church both Crescens, the bearer of this letter and his sister (14).

The sad mention of the case of Valens and his wife points up a connection that can be easily overlooked in Polycarp's letter, the theme of redemptive almsgiving. 2 Clement earlier stated this on the subject: "Charitable giving is therefore as good as repentance from sin" (16.4). Polycarp echoes this idea in 10.2: "When you can do good, do not put it off, for charitable giving frees from death." The Greek word ἐλεημοσύνη in Clement is the cognate *eleomosyna* in this surviving Latin section of Polycarp (chs. 10–12). What charitable giving does is to free one from that "love of money" which is severely condemned by Polycarp earlier in 2.2; 4.1, 3; and 6.1. The Greek word here is *philarguria*. Putting all this together means that in the chapter following the commendation of charitable giving, the pre-eminent sin of Valens appears to be his "avarice" (the Latin *avaritia*) or "love of money" (cf. 11.1 and 11.2). This love of money corrupted Valens and is a stark contrast with the charitable giving so stressed in the previous chapter. While it is not clear, one may wonder if the presbyter Valens had been guilty of siphoning off some of the funds that had been donated for almsgiving/charitable giving. Polycarp argues that charitable giving will keep one from "avarice" or the "love of money" and helps to avoid a tragedy like that of Valens and his wife. While this concept of redemptive giving may be difficult to trace in the New Testament, it also appears in *Didache* 4:5-8 and in the much earlier book of *Tobit* 12:8-9.

The combination of both personal and intensely spiritual matters in this letter recalls some examples in the Pauline correspondence in the NT. Since ancient papyri letters that survive are very rarely of this length, modern readers are reminded that the letters of the NT and from these early Christians often take on the nature of a tract utilizing the format of a letter. The fact that the letter is addressed to a congregation and not to an individual may also help to explain their length. One is reminded of the brief "private" letters from the "Elder" to the "chosen lady" and to "Gaius" which we call Second and Third John.

POLYCARP AND THE SCRIPTURES

A number of writers on Polycarp refer to his letter critically as primarily a pastiche of quotations and allusions to the early Christian literature that would become known as the New Testament. His extensive use of these sacred texts is actually of great value to the historian. Although the letter is quite short compared to other AF, he probably alludes to the NT books of Matthew, Luke, Romans, the Corinthian letters, Galatians, Ephesians, Philippians, both Timothy letters, 1 Peter and 1 John. John's Gospel is strikingly absent, although allusions to John 5:21 and 6:44 may be found in *Pol.* 5.2.

This is not the case, however, with his knowledge of and reference to the sacred writings that we call the Old Testament. Polycarp himself even admits that such familiarity was not his to possess when he compliments the Philippians: "I am convinced that you are well-trained in the sacred scriptures, and that nothing is hidden from you, but this has not been granted to me" (*Pol.* 12.1). The scripture he then cites was originally found in Ps. 4:4, but he cites its form in Eph. 4:26: "Be angry and do not sin," and "do not allow the sun to go down upon your anger." While he is familiar with the apostolic traditions, he had not succeeded in becoming familiar with the traditional scriptures, either in their Hebrew originals or in their Greek translation, the LXX. This may be due to his lack of any Jewish background, a heritage he shared with his fellow correspondent, Ignatius. In the following translation, we have limited the footnotes to fairly clear citations or allusions. A perusal of those reveals no references to OT books, although 10.2 may contain a reference to the Apocryphal book, Tobit.

On the other hand, it is probable that Polycarp thought Paul was the author of the disputed Pastoral Epistles above because he refers to these two letters in the context of other references to Paul's writings. In 3.2 he reminds the Philippians that when Paul was among them he taught them faithfully and when he was absent he wrote "letters" (*epistolas*) to them. This can be taken as meaning that he wrote more letters to them than the one we know as the *Letter to the Philippians*.

The issue of the "reception" of canonical scripture in Polycarp as well as in other AF must be balanced by the way in which the authors have referred to these texts. It is rare to find what we would call in modern terms a "quotation." This characteristic may simply be due to Polycarp and others referring to these texts in a general way that lacks the precision of an academic paper. A modern parallel may be like a modern preacher mentioning the idea in a biblical text without the rigor of a formal citation. Perhaps we should allow him some interpretive freedom instead of forcing him to fit into our own academic standards for citations.

THE "THEOLOGY" OF POLYCARP

If readers expect much speculative and dogmatic reflection in the letter, they will be disappointed. There are, however, some "theological" features that are worthy of notice. God is called "God and Father of our Lord Jesus Christ" as Jesus is said to be the "Son of God" and "eternal High Priest" (12.2). This concept of the priesthood of Christ is also found in Ignatius and in Clement. This may show familiarity with one of the fundamental ideas in the NT Letter to the Hebrews. Jesus Christ is described as descending even to death for our sins (1.2). Readers are exhorted to believe in this risen one to whom God has given a throne at His right hand, and to whom all are to submit in heaven and on earth. God will demand an account from those who do not believe in him (2.1). He will also raise us from the dead if we observe the commandments of His Christ (2.2). As in his contemporary Ignatius, the error later called Docetism is denounced as an imminent danger. "For everyone who does not confess that Jesus Christ has come in the flesh is an antichrist" (7.1). The perversion of Christian morality by false teachers is also associated with the Devil. "Whoever distorts the sayings of the Lord for his own sinful desires and claims that there is neither resurrection nor judgment, that one is the first-born of Satan" (7.1). All should avoid anyone who "distorts the sayings of the Lord for his own sinful desires and claims that there is neither resurrection nor judgment; that one is the first-born of Satan" (6.3).

The Father and Son are honored, but the absence of any clear reference to the Holy Spirit is surprising. There is a reference to the *pneuma* in 5.3, although readers might simply view this as a reference to the human spirit. Also surprising is that the Greek word *arrabon* ("guarantee" or "pledge"), used in Eph. 1:14 of the Holy Spirit, is applied to Jesus! "Let us persevere, therefore, without ceasing in our hope and in the *pledge* of our righteousness, who is Christ Jesus ..." (8.1).

Polycarp exhibits what might be called an applied theology. "The contents of the letter are more paraenetic than doctrinal" (Hartog, Cambridge, 234). Faith with hope and love should lead the way both toward God and one's neighbor (3.3). Believers should then reject the folly of the majority (i.e., pagans) as well as false teaching and return to the teaching which has been given us from the beginning, the teaching of the apostles and of the gospel. This apostolic tradition is the standard for Christian truth (7.2). His readers also should have their eyes fixed constantly on their hope and the promise of righteousness, Jesus Christ, who has endured all things, that they might live through Him. Finally, they should pray for all the saints, for the magistrates and princes, for our persecutors, and even for the enemies of the cross (12.3).

The larger or "catholic" church is not mentioned, but Polycarp does say: "May he also give you a share and a place among his saints, and to us with you, as well as to all under heaven who will believe in our Lord and God Jesus Christ and in his Father who raised him from the dead" (12.2). Prayer does not take place without fasting (7.2), and the recommended prayer is the Lord's Prayer (6.2; 7.2). The author's eschatology is confined to the resurrection of the dead (2.2; 5.2; 7.1), and to the judgment of both the living and the dead by Christ who comes to reward the righteous in heaven (2.1; 5.2; 9.2).

Later in the century, Irenaeus will refer to Polycarp as a sort of guarantor of orthodoxy. He refers in this regard to the confrontation between the Smyrnaean bishop and the heretic Marcion (*Haer.* 3.3.4). Perhaps Irenaeus was referring to the tradition about Polycarp rather than to his writing that survives. In this letter to the Philippians there is no real anti-heretical polemic. The letter rather offers an ecclesiological rather than a theological perspective of the early second century.

FURTHER READING ON POLYCARP

Barnard, L. W. "The Problem of St. Polycarp's Epistle to the Philippians" in *Studies in the Apostolic Fathers and Their Background*, 31–9. New York. Schocken, 1966.

Harrison, P. N. *Polycarp's Two Epistles to the Philippians*. Cambridge. Cambridge University Press, 1936.

Hartog, Paul. *Polycarp's Epistle to the Philippians and the Martyrdom of Polycarp. Introduction, Text, and Commentary*. Oxford Apostolic Fathers. Oxford. Oxford University Press, 2013.

———. "Polycarp's Epistle to the Philippians" in *The Cambridge Companion to the Apostolic Fathers*, ed. Michael Bird and Scott Harrower, 226–34. Cambridge. Cambridge University Press, 2021.

Hill, Charles E. *From the Lost Teaching of Polycarp. Identifying Irenaeus' Apostolic Presbyter and the Author of* Ad Diognetum. WUNT 2.186. Tübingen. Mohr Siebeck, 2006.

Holmes, Michael. "Polycarp of Smyrna. Epistle to the Philippians" in *The Writings of the Apostolic Fathers*, ed. Paul Foster, 108–25. London and New York. T&T Clark, 2007.

Lightfoot, Joseph Barber. *The Apostolic Fathers, Part II. S. Ignatius. S. Polycarp.* 2nd ed., vol. 3. London. Macmillan, 1889. Repr. Grand Rapids. Baker, 1981.

Maier, Harry O. "Purity and Danger in Polycarp's Epistle to the Philippians. The Sin of Valens in Social Perspective." *Journal of Early Christian Studies* 1 (1993). 229–47.

Schoedel, W. R. *Polycarp, Martyrdom of Polycarp, Fragments of Papias*. The Apostolic Fathers, vol. 5. Camden, NJ. Nelson, 1967.

THE LETTER OF POLYCARP TO THE PHILIPPIANS

Polycarp and the presbyters with him to the church of God sojourning at Philippi. May mercy and peace be richly increased in you from God Almighty and Jesus Christ our Savior.

Chapter One

I greatly rejoice with you in our Lord Jesus Christ that you have followed the pattern of genuine love and for having accompanied, as far as you could, those who were confined in chains appropriate for saints. They are the diadems for those who have been truly chosen by God and our Lord. 2 And I rejoice because the secure root of your faith, famous from ancient times, still flourishes and bears fruit for our Lord Jesus Christ, who for our sins endured to face even death. "Whom God raised up, having broken the labor pains of Hades."[1] 3 In him, "although you see him not, you believe with inexpressible and glorious joy,"[2] to which joy many desire to experience, knowing that "by grace you have been saved, not by works,"[3] but by the will of God through Jesus Christ.

Chapter Two

Therefore, binding up your loose robes, serve God in reverential fear and in truth, forsaking empty reasoning and the error of the many, and believing in him who raised our Lord Jesus Christ from the dead and gave him glory and a throne at his right hand. To him all things in heaven and on earth are subject; every breathing creature serves him and he will come as "the judge of the living and of the dead"[4] and God will hold accountable for his blood those who disobey him. 2 Now he who raised him from the dead will also raise us up, if we do his will and follow his commandments and love the things he loved, by avoiding all injustice, greed, love of money, slander, false witness, "not repaying evil for evil, nor insult for insult,"[5] nor blow for blow, nor curse for curse. 3 Instead remember what the Lord said when he taught, "Judge not, that you may not be judged.

---

[1] Acts 2:24.
[2] 1 Pet. 1:8.
[3] Eph. 2:5, 8-9.
[4] Acts 10:42.
[5] 1 Pet. 3:9.

Forgive, and you will be forgiven. Be merciful so that you may be shown mercy. With the measure you measure, it will be measured to you in return."[6] And again, "Blessed are the poor and those who are persecuted for righteousness' sake, for the kingdom of God belongs to them."[7]

Chapter Three

Brothers, I am writing you these things about righteousness, not on my own decision, but because you first invited me. 2 For neither I nor anyone like me can rival the wisdom of the blessed and glorious Paul, who when living among you carefully and accurately taught the word of truth in the face of his contemporaries and wrote you letters when he was absent. By the careful study of his letters you will be able to strengthen yourselves in the faith given to you, 3 "which is the mother of us all,"[8] with hope following and love leading the way toward God and Christ and our neighbor. For if a person is occupied with these matters, he has fulfilled the commandment of righteousness, for whoever has love is far removed from all sin.

Chapter Four

Now the beginning of all troubles is the love of money.[9] Since we know then that "we have brought nothing into this world and can take nothing out of it"[10] either, let us arm ourselves with the weapons of righteousness and learn first to follow the commandment of the Lord. 2 Then let us teach our wives to walk in the faith taught to them with love and purity, cherishing their husbands in all faithfulness, loving all others equally in all self-control, and to teach their children in the fear of God. 3 Teach the widows to be sensible in the faith of the Lord, and to intercede unceasingly for everyone, to keep far from all slander, evil speech, false witness, love of money and every kind of evil, knowing that they are an altar of God, and that he carefully inspects all things, and that not one of their reasonings or thoughts or hidden things of the heart escapes him.[11]

Chapter Five

Knowing, therefore, that "God is not mocked,"[12] we ought to walk in a manner worthy of his commandment and glory. 2 Likewise, deacons should be blameless[13] in the presence of his righteousness, as servants of God and Christ and not of people, not slanderers, not double-tongued, not lovers of money, but self-controlled in all things, compassionate, careful, walking according to the truth of the Lord, who became a servant of all. If we are pleasing to him in the present age, we will receive the future one in accordance with his promises to raise us up from the dead, and if we act in a manner worthy of him, "we will also reign with Him,"[14] if indeed we continue to believe. 3 The younger men must likewise be blameless in all things, being concerned above everything else about

---

[6] Matt. 7:1-2; 1 *Clem.* 13:2.
[7] Luke 6:20; Matt. 5:10.
[8] Gal. 4:26.
[9] Cf. 1 Tim. 6:10.
[10] Cf. 1 Tim. 6:7.
[11] 1 Cor. 14:25.
[12] Gal. 6:7.
[13] Cf. 1 Tim. 3:8-13.
[14] 2 Tim. 2:12.

purity and restraining themselves from every evil. For it is good to be cut off from the sinful passions in the world, because "every sinful passion wars against the Spirit,"[15] and "neither the sexually immoral nor the effeminate nor male prostitutes will inherit the kingdom of God,"[16] nor those who do such perverse things. Therefore, it is necessary to refrain from all these things and to be obedient to the presbyters and deacons as to God and Christ. The virgins must also walk in a blameless and pure conscience.

Chapter Six
And the presbyters must also be compassionate, merciful to all, turning back those who have gone astray, caring for all the sick, neglecting neither widow nor orphan nor the poor, but always aiming at what is good before God and people.[17] They must avoid all anger, partiality, unfair judgment, and keep away from all love of money; do not quickly believe anything against any man, nor be harsh in judgment, knowing that we are all under the debt of sin. 2 If we ask the Lord to forgive us, we ought also to forgive, for we all are before the eyes of the Lord God, and we "must all stand before the judgment seat of Christ," and "each must give an account of himself."[18] 3 Let us so serve Him with fear and all reverence, as he has commanded and as did the apostles who proclaimed the gospel to us, and the prophets who prophesied the coming of our Lord. We should be eager for what is good, refraining from tempting others and from false brothers, and from those who bear the name of the Lord hypocritically, and who lead foolish people astray.

Chapter Seven
"For everyone who does not confess that Jesus Christ has come in the flesh is an antichrist"[19]; and whoever does not confess the testimony of the cross is from the devil; and whoever distorts the sayings of the Lord for his own sinful desires and claims that there is neither resurrection nor judgment, this one is the first-born of Satan. 2 Therefore, let us abandon the speculations of the crowds and their false teachings and let us return to the word delivered to us from the beginning. Let us be watchful in prayers and persistent in fasting, beseeching in petitions the all-seeing God not to lead us into temptation, as the Lord said. "The spirit indeed is willing, but the flesh is weak."[20]

Chapter Eight
Let us persevere, therefore, without ceasing in our hope and in the pledge of our righteousness, who is Christ Jesus, who "bore our sins in his own body on the tree, who committed no sin, nor was deceit found in His mouth."[21] Instead for our sake he endured all things that we might live in him. 2 Let us, therefore, become imitators of his endurance, and if we should suffer for his name, let us glorify him. For he gave us this example through himself, and we have believed this.

---

[15] 1 Pet. 2:11.
[16] 1 Cor. 6:9.
[17] Prov. 3:4.
[18] Rom. 14:10, 12; 2 Cor. 5:10.
[19] 1 John 4:2-3.
[20] Matt. 6:13; 26:41.
[21] 1 Pet. 2:22, 24.

Chapter Nine

I exhort you all, therefore, to obey the word about righteousness and to practice all endurance like you saw with your own eyes in the blessed Ignatius and Zosimus and Rufus. This you saw also in others among you and in Paul himself and the rest of the apostles. 2 Be assured that all these did not run in vain, but in faith and in righteousness, and that they are with the Lord in the place they deserved, with whom they also suffered. For they "did not love the present age,"[22] but him who died for them and who was raised by God for us.

Chapter Ten

Stand fast, therefore, in these things, secure and immovable in your faith, and follow the example of the Lord, loving the brotherhood, caring for each other, united in the truth, helping one other with the gentleness of the Lord, despising no one. 2 When you can do good, do not put it off, for charitable giving frees from death.[23] You must all be subject to one another and keep your conduct free from reproach among the Gentiles, so that from your good deeds you may receive praise and that the Lord may not be blasphemed because of you. 3 But woe to the one through whom the name of the Lord is blasphemed. Teach self-control to all and also practice it yourselves.

Chapter Eleven

I have been deeply saddened for Valens, who was once a presbyter among you, that he so misunderstands the office given to him. I urge you, therefore, to abstain from love of money and to be pure and truthful. Keep away from every kind of evil. 2 If any man cannot control himself in these things, how can he preach it to others? If a man does not abstain from love of money, he will be defiled by idolatry, and will be judged as among the Gentiles, who do not know about the judgment of the Lord. Or do we forget "that the saints will judge the world,"[24] as Paul teaches? 3 However, I have not found nor heard anything like this among you, among whom the blessed Paul labored, who were found in the beginning of his epistle. For he boasts about you in all the congregations, which alone knew God at that time when we had not yet known him. 4 I am very sad, therefore, for that man and his wife. May the Lord grant them a true repentance. Therefore, you yourselves be sober in this regard, and do not consider such people as enemies, but call them back as frail and erring members, that you may heal your entire body. When you do this you edify one another.

Chapter Twelve

I am convinced that you are well trained in the sacred scriptures, and that nothing is hidden from you, but this has not been granted to me. Now, as it is said in those scriptures, "Be angry and do not sin," and "do not allow the sun to go down upon your anger."[25] Blessed is the one who remembers this, and I believe that this is so with you. 2 May the God and Father of our Lord Jesus Christ and the eternal High Priest himself, Jesus Christ, build

---

[22] 2 Tim. 4:10.
[23] Tob 4:10.
[24] 1 Cor. 6:2.
[25] Eph. 4:26; Ps. 4:5.

you up in faith and truth and in all gentleness, in freedom from anger, in patience, in long-suffering, in endurance and purity. May he also give you a share and a place among his saints, and to us with you, as well as to all under heaven who will believe in our Lord and God Jesus Christ and in his Father who raised him from the dead. 3 Pray for all the saints. Pray also for kings and authorities and rulers and for those who persecute and hate you and for the enemies of the cross, that the fruit of your effort may be clear to all, and that you may be made perfect in him.

Chapter Thirteen
Both you and Ignatius wrote to me that if anyone was going to Syria, he should also carry letters from you. I will do this if I get a suitable opportunity, either myself or the person whom I will send as a messenger for you also. 2 The letters of Ignatius sent to us by him and all the others we have here we forward to you, as you requested. These accompany this letter, and from them you will greatly benefit, for they deal with faith and endurance and all the edification that is suitable in our Lord. And let us know whatever you learn about Ignatius himself and those who are with him.

Chapter Fourteen
I am writing these things to you through Crescens, whom I recently commended to you and now commend again, for his conduct among us has been blameless, and I believe that it will be the same with you. And you will consider his sister as commended when she comes to you. Farewell in the Lord Jesus Christ in grace, with all those who are with you. Amen.

CHAPTER SEVEN

The Martyrdom of Polycarp

INTRODUCTION

Many authors have considered Polycarp the most important Christian leader of the first half of the second century. Certainly his influence went beyond his congregation in Smyrna. His association with Ignatius and his visit to Rome also are evidence of a measure of "fame." But what endeared him in the collective memory of early Christians was not so much his *Letter to the Philippians* but his martyrdom at an extremely advanced age in his "80s." The reader can and should be moved by reading the work that follows.

Christian readers should not forget that martyrdom did not have its origin in the early Christian period. Jewish martyrs who died for their monotheistic faith were being honored and celebrated long before the second century CE. 1 and 2 Maccabees both recount a number of martyrdoms suffered by Jews resisting forced Hellenization under the Seleucids in the second century BCE. These faithful Jews were executed for observing the Sabbath, circumcising their children, or refusing to eat pork or meat sacrificed to foreign gods. During the Maccabean Revolt from 167 to 160 BCE, thousands of Jews died in battle or were killed as martyrs, including some of the original extended Hasmonean family. Some of the best-known Jewish martyrs of this period are commemorated in the stories of Eleazar (2 Macc 6) as well as the mother with seven sons (2 Macc 7). The Jewish holiday of Hanukkah recounts and celebrates the miracle of the triumph of these Jews against the ancient Greeks and of Judaism and Torah over against Greek culture.

These Jewish martyrs are described in the NT "faith" chapter among other ancients who "witnessed" to their faith by their deaths (Heb. 11:35-38). Even Isaiah may be described in 11:37 as the one who was "sawn in two" (see the *Ascension of Isaiah*). The Jewish martyrs served as examples to the early Christians when they also were suffering. Other examples of martyrs are the deaths of Stephen (Acts 7) and of Antipas in Pergamum (Rev. 2:13), who may have been the first one to be called by the technical term "martyr" (*martus*), although most think that the emphasis is on his being generally "a faithful witness." Other exhortations like "be faithful unto death and I will give you the crown of life" (Rev. 2:10) allude to the martyrdom of Christian believers in the first century.

We have already examined how Ignatius, the overseer of the church in Antioch, wrote to various congregations about his almost certain impending death in Rome as food for the lions. Ignatius, however, does not use the noun *martus* in the technical sense of "martyr." While it is assumed that he met the fate that he was certain awaited him, no record or description of that event has survived. Polycarp requested in his letter to the *Philippians* to inform him of Ignatius' fate when they heard about it: "And let us know whatever you learn about Ignatius himself and those who are with him" (13.2). Again we must observe that the word *martus* does not appear in his letter either.

POLYCARP'S DEATH IN *MARTYRDOM*

The date of Polycarp's death and the eleven who accompanied him (19.1) is debated. From the text itself and from a statement by Eusebius that it took place under Marcus Aurelius, some scholars choose 167 but the name of the consul Philip the Asiarch may point to 156. Soon after his martyrdom, at the most a year, the story was written up about his betrayal, trial, and execution by the local church and then circulated widely. The *Martyrdom* is the first surviving document that uses the Greek word *martus* in its technical meaning of "martyr" (2.2; 14.2; 15.2; 17.3). It also uses the verb *martureo* in this same sense: "martyred" (1.1; 19.1; 21). Its purpose was not only for the readers to admire the martyr's courage and faith, but to illustrate what was a "a martyrdom which is in accord with the gospel" (*Mart*. 1). No doubt there were known occurrences of some believers who willingly handed themselves over to authorities in order to be martyred, only to lose their nerve and then recant. The account describes this as follows: "We do not approve those who hand themselves over because the Gospel does not teach this" (*Mart*. 4).

As the earliest example of hagiography, and one of the most moving at that, the book functioned to help form the social identity and communal character of early Christians. The moving account depicts Polycarp as worthy of imitation in his submission to the Divine will, his patient endurance, and his concern for others. The account of the passion of Polycarp has some striking literary resemblances to the passion of Christ. For example, he is betrayed by a traitor; the officer who arrests him is named Herod; the martyr resembling bread baked in an oven is perhaps a reference to the Eucharist; and the sweet fragrance emanating from him as he dies may allude to Paul's description of the sacrifice of Christ as "a fragrant aroma" (Eph. 5:2). While moderns may wonder at some of the supernatural events that are recorded (the reader can note these in the account), no one in the second century seemed to doubt that these events actually transpired as recorded by the eyewitnesses. More importantly, the account with all of these details served to edify the saints and to fortify many of them for the destiny that soon awaited them.

MARTYRDOM IN THE *MARTYRDOM*

The contribution of the *Martyrdom of Polycarp* to what has been called the "cult of martyrdom" was obviously enormous. Some writers have called attention to what 18.3 mentions, namely "the birthday of his martyrdom" (*marturion*). Was martyrdom considered a sort of process toward a new existence? While Ignatius had previously "processed" through Turkey and Greece to his martyrdom, Polycarp did also through the lanes of Smyrna (chs. 7 and 8). The reader will also note that Polycarp experienced a transformation (12.1; 15.2); was imbued with supernatural powers (13.2; 18.1–3); was described in the language of sacrifice (14.1–2); and as we have noted, was portrayed as the imitation of Christ (1.1–2; 19.1). While the sanctity of Polycarp's body, both before and after his death, is mentioned (13.2; 17.1; 18.2) and his remains were carefully interred (17–18), the text is clear that only the Son of God was to be worshipped: "For we worship this one as the Son of God and we love the martyrs as disciples and imitators of the Lord, for their unsurpassable affection for their own king and teacher" (17.3).

On the other hand, some scholars have raised serious doubts about the historicity of *Martyrdom* and the accuracy of the entire narrative concerning martyrdom that arose in the second and third centuries. Candida Moss has argued that the story of Polycarp's death was a third-century invention (*Myth of Persecution*, 94–104). This is because of the many elements in the account that appear to be recalling the Gospel accounts of Jesus' death. Then the miraculous events such as the heavenly voice heard when he enters the stadium in Smyrna and the smell of his burning flesh like baking bread or the odor of frankincense (15.2) indicate that the entire account is a fabrication. The reference to the relics of Polycarp's body (18.2–3) is also supposedly anachronistic since worship of relics did not arise until the third-century church. Finally, the account assumes that martyrdom existed as a developed concept, so it must imply that the account was written well after the events it describes as being set in the middle of the second century.

Moss is not the first writer to criticize some of the details of *Martyrdom*. Gibbon's *Decline and Fall* famously raised some of the same issues. Even if the parallels to Christ's suffering may be a bit contrived, this does not demand that we reject the entire account as inauthentic. Moss seems to imply that if any editorial flourishes were used, the whole account must be doubted. Even if the account contains such features, this does not necessitate that Polycarp was not martyred in Smyrna in the 150s. Even if Polycarp's burning flesh was *like* the smell of baking bread, it is a comparison not intended to be taken literally. The author is probably indicating that his death was well-pleasing to God like the Christian life is to be a sweet-smelling aroma to God (Eph. 5:2). As for the reference to his relics, this could be the initial act that eventually led to the later major emphasis on the cult of relics. Furthermore, the suggestion that *Martyrdom* was the first document to develop a so-called "theology of martyrdom" ignores the evidence of earlier references such as the mention of the martyrdom of Antipas (Rev. 2:13) and the rather developed view of his own martyrdom, without using that term, by Ignatius in his letters written early in the second century.

Moss' other comments about the development of the "cult of martyrdom" deserve a more detailed treatment that is outside the scope of this introduction. However, her view that the *Martyrdom* is a fiction simply attempts to prove too much. Even the presence of literary embellishments does not necessitate the rejection of the work as a fundamentally accurate account derived from the eyewitnesses whom it so carefully names.

JEWS IN THE *MARTYRDOM*

Readers familiar with another AF, namely *Barnabas*, will also recognize in Martyrdom some echoes of its rather strong statements about Jews. While one would expect the Gentile rulers and soldiers to take a harsh stance against Polycarp, the Jews in Smyrna also play an adversarial role in his "trial" and execution. This role appears three times (12.2; 13.1; 17.2–18.1). They join with the pagans in saying: "This is the teacher of impiety, the father of the Christians, the destroyer of our own gods, the one who teaches many not to sacrifice nor to worship the gods" (12.2). Such a statement like "destroyer of our own gods" seems a strange comment from Jews, although the author's including pagans in this charge may reveal an oversight on his part and an uninformed conflation in the charges. Furthermore, the Jews are charged with helping to gather the wood for the execution pyre (13.1), and also are strangely portrayed as insisting that the corpse be guarded, lest the Christians worship Polycarp and abandon Jesus (17.2). The phrase "as was their custom" (18.1) also adapts some rather harsh stereotyping. "This social construction owes as much to 'theological schema' as to historical accuracy" (Hartog, "The Martyrdom of Polycarp," 241).

INTERTEXTUALITY IN THE *MARTYRDOM*

Since it is a historical account, the *Martyrdom* should not be expected to utilize scripture quotations to the extent of the other works in this collection. In the account of the events leading up to and including Polycarp's death (chs. 11–22) no scriptures are clearly cited at all. Earlier possible citations are as follows. The narrator refers to Phil. 2:4 in 1.2 and 1 Cor. 2:9 in 2.3. The martyr himself apparently echoes Paul's statement "the will of the Lord be done" from Acts 21:14 in 7.1. Finally, Polycarp himself paraphrases Rom. 13:1 and 1 Peter 2:13 in 10.2.

Rather than engaging in a search for quotations of scripture in the book, a better approach is to trace the obvious analogies with Jesus' suffering and death as recorded in the Gospels. The author says as much when he writes: "by becoming a partner with Christ, he might fulfill his destiny and his betrayers might suffer the punishment of Judas" (6.2). The author continues by describing Polycarp as betrayed by a companion, as was Jesus (6.2). The official participating in his condemnation, as with Jesus, was named "Herod" (6.2). Jesus prayed to the Father in Gethsemane that his will should be done; so Polycarp affirmed, "May the will of God be done" (7.1). In the same passage officials came to arrest Polycarp as if they were seizing a criminal (7.1). Compare Jesus' statement to his apprehenders: "Have you come out with swords and clubs to arrest me as a robber?" (Matt. 26:55). While Polycarp, like Jesus, was served a final meal, he actually served those who arrested him (7.2). Both entered the town of their death on a donkey (8.1). Both were pierced by their executioners (16.1). A difference does arise when Polycarp, unlike his Lord, was not nailed but bound to a stake (13.3). Without casting doubt on the history of either of these parallels, their similarities are a far more effective exercise in intertextuality than mentioning simple quotations.

THE CHURCH IN THE *MARTYRDOM*

Martyrdom uses the phrase "catholic church" to apply to the universal church (title and 8.1; 19.2) as Ignatius also did (*Smyrneans* 8.2). The *Martyrdom*, however, also refers to "the catholic church in Smyrna" (16.2), evidently not in a geographical but in a doctrinal sense, probably to distinguish the "catholic church" from heretical groups. While some may prefer the translation "universal" as the word is defined in the lexicons (BDAG, 493), we use the transliteration "catholic" in lower case and in quotation marks.

The members of this "church" are described with familiar Christian terminology. These church members are "temporarily residing" (inscr.) in Smyrna and Philomelium, while some translations, including my own, use the verb "sojourning" (Lightfoot). This idea of course reflects a NT figure ("to those temporarily residing abroad," 1 Pet. 1:1). Believers are also called "the God-loving and God-fearing race of Christians" (3.2), as well as "the race of the righteous" (14.1). Other familiar terms for believers echo the NT as well: "the chosen ones" (16.1; 20.1) as well as the "servants" and the "saints" (20.1–2). There are no apocalyptic schema or metaphors like the "tower" or the "mountain" in the *Shepherd*. Any anti-heretical groups outside of the "church" are measured by the familiar expression "in accord with the gospel" (1.1; 2.1). Polycarp's role as a guardian of the church's orthodoxy, although not as expressive as found in Ignatius, is still assumed. "Polycarp certainly was one of the elect, an apostolic and prophetic teacher in our time and overseer of the 'catholic' church in Smyrna" (16.2).

The *Martyrdom of Polycarp* continues to initiate scholarly investigation about its dating and historical accuracy. In the subsequent two centuries it helped to form the social identity of its Christian readers and inspire multitudes to face bravely what the empire could have in store for them. Polycarp's faithful and prayerful submission to God's will, his concern for others, and his unswerving endurance set a truly remarkable example for both his immediate followers and others yet to suffer for their own faith. It also undoubtedly served as a "witness" to the unbelieving Gentiles as well.

FURTHER READING ON *THE MARTYRDOM OF POLYCARP*

Buschman, Gerd. "The Martyrdom of Polycarp" in *The Apostolic Fathers: An Introduction*, ed. Wilhelm Pratscher, 135–58. Waco, TX. Baylor University Press, 2010.

Frend, William H. C. *Martyrdom and Persecution in the Early Church. A Study of a Conflict from the Maccabees to Donatus.* Oxford. Blackwell, 1965.

Hartog, Paul. *Polycarp's Epistle to the Philippians and the Martyrdom of Polycarp. Introduction, Text, and Commentary.* Oxford Apostolic Fathers. Oxford. Oxford University Press, 2013.

_____. "The Martyrdom of Polycarp" in *The Cambridge Companion to the Apostolic Fathers*, ed. Michael Bird and Scott Harrower, 234–47. Cambridge. Cambridge University Press, 2021.

Moss, Candida R. *The Myth of Persecution: How Early Christians Invented a Story of Martyrdom.* New York. HarperCollins, 2013, 94–104.

Parvis, Sara. "The Martyrdom of Polycarp" in *The Writings of the Apostolic Fathers*, ed. Paul Foster, 126–46. London and New York. T&T Clark, 2007.

Schoedel, W. R. *Polycarp, Martyrdom of Polycarp, Fragments of Papias.* The Apostolic Fathers, vol. 5. Camden, NJ. Nelson, 1967.

THE MARTYRDOM OF POLYCARP

The church of God sojourning in Smyrna to the church of God sojourning in Philomelium and to all the congregations of the holy and "catholic" church in every place. May the mercy, peace, and love of God the Father and of our Lord Jesus Christ be multiplied.

Chapter One
We are writing to you, brothers, about those who were martyred, especially the blessed Polycarp, who ended the persecution by setting his seal upon it by his own martyrdom. Nearly all the events happened so that the Lord might show us once again a martyrdom which is in accord with the gospel. 2 He waited to be betrayed, just as the Lord did, in order that we too might imitate him, "not looking only to that which concerns ourselves, but also to that which concerns others."[1] For it is the mark of true and steadfast love to desire not only that we be saved, but all the brothers as well.

Chapter Two
Blessed and noble, therefore, are all the martyrdoms that have taken place in accord with the will of God (for we reverently assign to God the power over all things). 2 For who could not admire their nobility and patient endurance and loyalty to the Master? For even when they were so beaten with whips that the internal section of their flesh was visible as the inner veins and arteries, they endured so patiently that even those standing around

---

[1] Phil. 2:4.

had pity and were crying. They themselves reached such a level of courage that none of them uttered a cry or a moan, thus showing to us all that at the very time they were being tortured the martyrs of Christ were absent from the flesh, or that the Lord was standing by and speaking with them. 3 Turning their thoughts to the grace of Christ they despised the tortures of this world, purchasing with the cost of one hour a release from eternal punishment. The fire of their cruel tormenters felt cold to them, for they kept before their eyes the escape from that eternal fire which is never quenched, while with the eyes of their heart they looked upon the good things reserved for those who patiently endure. These are the things "which neither ear has heard nor eye has seen, nor has it entered into the heart of man,"[2] but were shown to them by the Lord, for they were no longer men but were already angels. 4 In a similar way those who were condemned to wild beasts endured those horrible punishments. They were forced to lie on sharp shells and were afflicted with various forms of torture that he might, if possible, by means of the continuous punishment compel them to deny their faith, for the devil attempted many things against them.

Chapter Three
The devil devised many torments for them, but thanks to God he did not overcome any of them. For the most noble Germanicus encouraged them, fearful though they were, by his own endurance, and he fought with the wild beasts in an outstanding manner. For when the proconsul wished to dissuade him and asked him to consider his youth, he willingly dragged the wild beast toward himself, desiring to be released without delay from this unjust and lawless life. 2 After this all the multitude, marveling at the bravery of the God-loving and God-fearing race of Christians, began shouting, "Away with the atheists! Find Polycarp!"

Chapter Four
But one named Quintus, a Phrygian recently come from Phrygia, upon seeing the beasts became a coward. He was the one who forced himself and some others to come forward voluntarily. The Proconsul persuaded him with many pleas to take the oath and to offer sacrifice. For this reason, therefore, brothers, we do not approve those who hand themselves over because the Gospel does not teach this.

Chapter Five
Now when the most remarkable Polycarp first heard of this, he was not disturbed, but wanted to remain in the city. However, the majority persuaded him to quietly leave, so he departed secretly to a farm not far from the city and remaining with a few friends, he did nothing but pray night and day for everyone and for all the congregations throughout the world, as was always his custom. 2 As he was praying, he had a vision three days before he was arrested and he saw his pillow burning with fire. Turning to those who were with him he said, "I must be burned alive."

Chapter Six
As they continued searching for him, he went to another little farm where the searchers immediately came after him. Not finding him, they seized two slave boys, one of whom made a confession after being tortured. 2 It was not possible for him to remain hidden, since those who betrayed him were members of his own household. Then the police chief called by the name of Herod hastened to bring him into the stadium so that by becoming a partner with Christ, he might fulfill his destiny and his betrayers might suffer the punishment of Judas.

---

[2] 1 Cor. 2:9.

Chapter Seven

So they brought the little boy along and on Preparation Day[3] around the dinner hour, the security officers and horsemen with their weapons came out as if against a bandit. And in the evening they converged on Polycarp and found him lying down in an upper room. Although he was still able to escape to another locality, he did not wish to, saying, "May the will of God be done."[4] 2 So when he heard they were there, he went down and talked with them. Those present marveled at his age and his composure and wondered why there was such an effort to arrest an old man. Immediately he arranged at that hour for them to eat and drink as much as they wished, while he requested that they give him an hour to pray without interruption. 3 When they agreed he stood and prayed, so filled with God's grace that for two hours he could not be silent. Those who heard him were amazed and many even regretted that they had come against such a godly old man.

Chapter Eight

When he finally concluded his prayer, after remembering all who had at any time come his way, both small and great, distinguished and undistinguished, and the whole "catholic" church throughout the world, the time came for him to leave. So they placed him on a donkey and brought him into the city on a great Sabbath.[5] 2 The chief of police, Herod, with his father Nicetas met him, and took him into their own carriage and seated at his side, tried to persuade him, saying, "So what harm is there in saying, 'Caesar is Lord,' and in offering incense and so forth, to be saved?" At first he did not answer, but when they persisted, he said, "I will not do what you advise me." 3 Having failed to convince him, they threatened him and made him descend so quickly that he scraped his shin as he came down from the carriage. Without even turning around, as though he had suffered nothing, he continued on eagerly and with haste and so was led into the stadium. The noise in the stadium was so great that no one could be heard at all.

Chapter Nine

When he entered the stadium there came a voice from heaven, "Be strong, Polycarp, and be a man."[6] No one saw who had spoken, but our people who were present there heard the voice. 2 Finally, when he was brought forward, the proconsul asked if he was Polycarp. When he said he was, he began trying to persuade him to deny the faith, saying, "Have respect for your age," and other such things as they usually say. "Swear by the Fortune of Caesar; repent and say, 'Away with the atheists!'" But Polycarp looked with a serious face at the entire crowd of lawless Gentiles in the stadium, motioning with his hand toward them, he sighed and looked up to heaven and said, "Away with the atheists!" 3 As the Proconsul urged him and said, "Swear the oath and I will release you; reproach the Christ." But Polycarp said, "Eighty-six years I have served him, and he has done me no wrong. How can I blaspheme my king who saved me?"

Chapter Ten

When he persisted and said, "Swear by the Fortune of Caesar," Polycarp answered. "If you foolishly suppose that I will swear by the Fortune of Caesar, as you request, and pretend not to know who I am, listen closely. I am a Christian. Now if you desire to learn

---

[3] Matt. 26:55. This was Friday.
[4] Acts 21:14; Matt. 6:10.
[5] Cf. John 19:31.
[6] Josh. 1:6.

the teaching of Christianity, appoint a day and listen." 2 The Proconsul replied, "Persuade the people." Polycarp replied, "I consider you worthy of an explanation, for we are taught to give proper honor to rulers and authorities appointed by God[7], as long as it does not harm us. But I do not consider these people worthy to make a defense before them."

Chapter Eleven

The Proconsul said, "I have wild beasts, and I will throw you to them unless you repent." But he said, "Call them, for it impossible for us to repent from better to worse, but it is good to change from what is wicked to what is right." 2 Again he said to him, "If you despise the wild beasts, I will have you consumed by fire, unless you repent." But Polycarp said, "You threaten with a fire that burns for an hour and in a short while is extinguished; for you do not know about the fire of the coming judgment and eternal torment, reserved for the ungodly. But why are you delaying? Bring on what you wish."

Chapter Twelve

While saying these and many other words, he was filled with courage and joy. His face was filled with grace, so that not only did he not collapse in fear at the things addressed to him, but on the contrary the Proconsul was amazed and sent his own herald into the center of the stadium to announce three times, "Polycarp has confessed that he is a Christian." 2 After the herald said this, the entire crowd of both Gentiles and Jews living in Smyrna cried out with uncontrollable rage and with a great voice, "This is the teacher of impiety, the father of the Christians, the destroyer of our own gods, the one who teaches many not to sacrifice nor to worship the gods." With these cries and shouts they began asking that Philip the Asiarch release a lion on Polycarp. However, he said that this was not legal since he had already concluded the animal hunts. 3 Then they decided to shout out in unison to burn Polycarp alive, because the vision revealed to him about the pillow he saw burning as he prayed had to be fulfilled. And he turned and spoke prophetically to the faithful who were with him, "I must be burnt alive."

Chapter Thirteen

These things then happened with incredible speed, quicker than it was spoken. The crowds immediately gathered and collected wood and kindling from the workshops and baths, the Jews especially lending eager assistance, as is their custom. 2 When the pyre was prepared, Polycarp took off his upper garments and loosened his belt, and he was trying to also remove his sandals, something he did not do in the past, since each of the faithful was always eager to be the first to touch his skin. He had been treated with such respect because of his holy way of life even before his martyrdom. 3 Then the materials prepared for the fire were placed around him. When they were about to fix him with nails, he said, "Leave me as I am, for he who enables me to endure the fire will also enable me to remain in the pyre without moving, even without the security of your nails."

Chapter Fourteen

So they did not nail him but they tied him. Then he put his hands behind his back and was bound like a ram from a great flock for sacrifice, prepared as a burnt offering acceptable to God. As he looked up to heaven, he said,

---

[7] Rom. 13:1; 1 Pet. 2:13.

Lord God Almighty, Father of your beloved and blessed child Jesus Christ, through whom we have received your knowledge, the God of angels and powers, and of all creation and of every race of the righteous who live before you. I bless you because you considered me worthy of this day and hour. 2 I bless you because I now may along with the martyrs have a share in the cup of your Christ, unto the resurrection of eternal life both of soul and body in the immortality of the Holy Spirit. May I be received among those before you today as a rich and acceptable sacrifice, as you the true God who does not lie prepared and foretold and fulfilled. 3 For this reason and for all things I praise you, I bless you, I glorify you, through the eternal and heavenly high priest, Jesus Christ, your beloved child, through whom be glory to you with him and the Holy Spirit, both now and for the coming ages. Amen.

Chapter Fifteen
When he had offered the amen and finished the prayer, the men appointed lit the fire. As a great flame blazed up, we saw a miracle, we to whom it was granted to see it and were preserved to report the events to the rest. 2 For the fire took the shape of an arch, like a boat's sail filled with the wind, and formed a wall around the martyr's body. He was there in the center, not like burning flesh but like bread baking or like gold and silver being refined in a furnace. We also noticed an especially sweet aroma like the smell of incense or the smell of some other fragrant spices.

Chapter Sixteen
When the lawless men saw that his body could not be consumed by the fire, they ordered an executioner to go up and stab him with a dagger. When he had done so, there came out a dove and much blood, so that the fire was extinguished, and the whole crowd was amazed that there was so great a difference between the unbelievers and the elect. 2 For the most glorious Polycarp certainly was one of the elect, an apostolic and prophetic teacher in our time and overseer of the "catholic" church in Smyrna. Every word that came forth from his mouth was fulfilled and will be fulfilled.

Chapter Seventeen
But the jealous and envious evil one, the adversary of the race of the righteous, when he saw the greatness of his martyrdom and his irreproachable life from the beginning, he saw also that he was crowned with the crown of immortality and had won an incontestable prize. So he made certain that his poor body should not be taken away by us, although many desired to do this and to touch his holy flesh. 2 So he incited Nicetas the father of Herod, and the brother of Alce, to request the magistrate not to surrender his body, "Lest," it was said, "they abandon the crucified one and begin to worship this man." They said this at the suggestion and instigation of the Jews who also watched as we were going to take the body from the fire. For they did not realize that we could never abandon the Christ who suffered on behalf of sinners for the salvation of those in this world who are being saved, and we are not able to worship any other. 3 For we worship this one as the Son of God and we love the martyrs as disciples and imitators of the Lord, for their matchless affection for their own king and teacher. With them may we also become partners and fellow disciples.

Chapter Eighteen
On seeing the quarrel stirred up by the Jews, the centurion set the body in the middle and burned it, as was their custom. 2 And so, afterwards, we took up his bones, more valuable

than precious stones and finer than gold, and put them in a suitable place. 3 There, as far as we were able, the Lord will permit us to meet together in happiness and joy and to celebrate the birthday of his martyrdom, both in memory of those who have engaged in the struggle and as a training and preparation for those about to do so.

Chapter Nineteen
These are the matters concerning the blessed Polycarp, who suffered martyrdom in Smyrna, and together with the others from Philadelphia was the twelfth martyr in Smyrna. But he alone is especially commemorated by everyone, and he is spoken of in every place, even by the Gentiles. For he proved himself not only as an exceptional teacher, but also as a notable martyr, whose martyrdom all desire to imitate, since it was in accord with the gospel of Christ. 2 Having overcome the unjust ruler by his endurance and thus having received the crown of immortality, he rejoices with the apostles and all the upright and he is glorifying God, the Father Almighty, and blessing our Lord Jesus Christ, the savior of our souls and helmsman of our bodies, the shepherd of the "catholic" Church throughout the world.

Chapter Twenty
You requested that these details should be explained to you at length, but for the present we have set down a summary through our brother Marcianus. So when you have this information, send the letter to the brothers further on, that they may also glorify the Lord, who selects his chosen ones from his own servants. 2 Now to him who is able to lead us all by his grace and gift to his eternal kingdom, through his only-begotten child, Jesus Christ, be glory, honor, power and greatness forever. Greet all the saints. They who are with us greet you plus Evarestus who wrote the letter and his whole house.

Chapter Twenty-One
The blessed Polycarp was martyred on the second day of the first part of the month Xanthicus, the seventh day before the calends of March, on a great Sabbath, at the eighth hour. He was arrested by Herod, when Philip of Tralles was high priest and Statius Quadratus proconsul. But Jesus Christ rules forever. To Him be the glory, honor, majesty, eternal dominion, from generation to generation. Amen.

Chapter Twenty-Two
We wish you farewell, brothers, who conduct yourselves in the word according to the gospel of Jesus Christ. To Him be glory to God and the Holy Spirit for the salvation of his holy elect. Even as the blessed Polycarp suffered martyrdom, may it be permitted for us to be found in his footsteps in the kingdom of Jesus Christ. 2 Gaius copied this from the account of Irenaeus, a disciple of Polycarp, and he lived with Irenaeus. 3 And I, Socrates, wrote it out in Corinth from the copies of Gaius. Grace be to you all. 4 And I, Pionius, searched for these things and wrote it out again from the former copies, because the blessed Polycarp showed it to me in a vision, as I will explain in what follows. I have collected it now when it is almost worn out by age, that the Lord Jesus Christ may gather me also with his elect into his heavenly kingdom. To him be the glory with the Father and the Holy Spirit forever and ever. Amen.

CHAPTER EIGHT

Epistle of Barnabas

THE AUTHOR OF "BARNABAS"

"Little can be said with certainty about the author of the *Letter of Barnabas* except that he liked blackberries (7.8)" (Tugwell, 21). One cannot improve on Simon Tugwell's clever but also accurate observation that opens his treatment of this document. In simplest terms, the epistle is anonymous. A long-standing tradition, however, has assigned it to Barnabas the co-worker of Paul who was known preeminently as an "encourager," following the example of his own name, "son of encouragement" (Acts 4:36). Clement of Alexandria quoted it as the work of "the apostolic Barnabas, who was one of the seventy and a fellow-worker of Paul" (*Strom.* 2.20). Origen speaks of "the catholic Epistle of Barnabas" (*Contra Cels.* 1.63). Eusebius calls it "the Epistle of Barnabas the Apostle" (*EH* 6.14). It was held in high esteem in Alexandria and since it was found in Codex Sinaiticus beginning on the leaf where the Revelation ends, one may conclude that it was once read in congregations, perhaps as authoritative scripture. In the West it never was regarded as canonical. Eusebius had objected to it and finally its connection with the NT was severed entirely. But its inclusion in that great uncial manuscript in the mid-fourth century testifies to the high esteem in which it was once held.

While the external evidence is actually in favor of an apostolic authorship, this testimony cannot outweigh the weighty issues drawn from internal evidence which make it problematic to ascribe it to that admirable companion of Paul. The apostolic Barnabas took a view of the Mosaic Law quite different from that reflected in this document. The "Son of Encouragement" belonged to the earliest stage of the Jewish Christian movement. He was ready to give the Gentiles liberty, but not soon ready to say that the Jews should abandon the Torah altogether (Gal. 2:13). In that text it appears that he was eager to obey the Jewish dietary laws, but the author of this letter allegorizes these laws in *Barn.* 10 (see the following translation). It is, of course, quite possible that after the incident of Gal. 2, Barnabas could have come to acknowledge the entire freedom of Jews as well, but even this would not bring him into the atmosphere of the letter under consideration. Here there is no question whether a believing Jew may or may not abandon the Law. For one of its main concerns is that no Jew, believing or unbelieving, ought ever to have observed the Law at any time, even before the Messiah came! It is difficult to think that any Jew who was nurtured in the observance of the Jewish traditions could come to have so little enthusiasm for these traditions that he could sweep it all away as things which never ought to have been. Whatever be those tendencies, a Jewish Christian writer simply could not express the following. "Before we believed in God, the dwelling place of our heart was corrupt and weak, since it was really a temple built by hand, for it was full of idolatry and was a house of demons because we did everything that was opposed to God" (16.7).

The author then was most probably a Gentile spiritual leader who was distinguished with a "gift" of teaching (1.8; 4.9). Though he disclaims any intention of writing professionally, he was conscious of having an ability to make himself understood to his readers. Two theories have been offered to account for the ascription of the *Epistle of Barnabas*. It was either the work of a namesake of Paul's companion, or because it emerged from Alexandria, it was then ascribed to Barnabas as one who was probably prominent in the early history of that Church. Readers also need to be reminded of the obvious that is often overlooked, namely, that the work emerged as a letter that was anonymous!

THE TEXT OF BARNABAS

Until the protracted discovery and eventual publication of the famous Codex Sinaiticus in the 1850s and 1860s, this work was known only in a Latin translation and in eight partial Greek manuscripts. The Latin version is found in a manuscript of the eighth century, but the translation was made from a text possibly earlier than the text in Sinaiticus, and does not contain the last four chapters. The other Greek copies all lacked exactly the same portion of the work, namely the first five and a half chapters, and joined the remainder of *Barnabas* on to the end of the *Epistle of Polycarp* as though it were all one letter. Being thus descended from a common source, they are not independent witnesses for the text. With the publication of Codex Aleph (Sinaiticus) by Tischendorf, a complete Greek text appeared for the first time. In this huge manuscript this letter follows Revelation, and then is followed by the incomplete *Shepherd of Hermas*. Another complete Greek copy was discovered in Constantinople by Bryennios in 1875 (along with the Clements and the Didache).

THE THRUST OF THE LETTER

Just as the apostle Paul loved the moral triad of faith, hope, and love (1 Cor. 13:13; 1 Thess. 1:2-3), so Barnabas early on states that there are three basic doctrines: hope, righteousness, and love (1.6). One might expect that he would follow this up by expounding on these virtues. Although he does mention "hope" again (4.8; 6.3, 9; 16.1–2), he never engages in any real development of this word. Furthermore, he never again mentions "righteousness" and rarely mentions "love" and never with an effort to explain and apply it.

The chief goal of the author lay elsewhere than in a description of the virtues that should mark the life of a Christian. His concern was to impart to his readers a knowledge of what pertains to salvation that they might be saved in the day to come (4.1, 9). The two lessons he wants to impress on his readers are: (1) that the literal observance of the Mosaic Law is absolutely useless for any hope of salvation, and (2) that there is a necessity and duty to live a moral life. Even with its sometimes harsh vocabulary, this is the letter of a true Christian pastor written with moral and spiritual sincerity. Whether he is "Barnabas" or "Mr. Anonymous," he is deeply concerned for the salvation of his readers and also deeply desirous to communicate to them the best advice that he has to offer.

The author's moral and spiritual aims need to be recognized because a large amount of what he says, especially those parts consisting of allegorical interpretations of the Mosaic

Law, will appear to modern readers as strangely unreal and even bizarre at times. But if his message abounds at times in allegorical fantasy, it is only because he is deeply impressed with the idea that if the Law is literally observed, it will destroy rather than enable our salvation (3.6). His sincere advice is "Let us flee from all that is futile and let us hate completely the deeds of the evil way" (4.10). In chapters 19–21 he finally abandons his allegorical method entirely and devotes himself to a setting forth of "the two ways," namely, the way of light and the way of darkness. The duties of loving, fearing, praising, and obeying God are named first. Then follows a series of commands, some negative and some positive, concerning our relations to others. A man's neighbor must be loved more than his own soul. The way of the "Black One" is set forth in the form of a catalogue of vices and evil deeds. Only two commandments are quoted from the original Decalogue, the third and the seventh. Surprisingly, there is no distinct appeal either to the teaching or to the example of Jesus the Lord.

ATTITUDE TOWARD JUDAISM

The main interest which the letter has for most readers today lies in the light (or darkness!) it sheds on the relations between Jewish people and the church. This new yet claiming to be old faith did not come into the world in a religious vacuum. It was founded by one who claimed to be the Anointed One (the Messiah) of a definite identifiable religion which had existed for many centuries. He and his apostles actually believed in the Jewish religion as the only true faith, utilized the Jewish Scriptures as the very word of God, and observed its national forms of worship as the divinely appointed way to serve the one true God. How then did His followers ever come to abandon the Law? There was no serious break or sudden "parting of the ways" but rather a reorganization of sorts. The followers of Jesus believed that as the promised Messiah, Jesus had authority from God to institute a new covenant between God and his people Israel, and he actually did so when he offered himself on the cross as a sacrifice for sin and then returned from that death! The logical consequences of this belief may not have been perceived all at once but were certain to come to light as the passage of time allowed the faith to develop.

What were the steps followed in a Gospel that first included and then excluded the Jewish people? If the death of Jesus was sufficient to obtain salvation, then the observance of the Law (i.e., the Torah) simply could not be demanded any longer. Although believing Jews could continue to observe the Law if they wished to do so, there was simply no sufficient ground for compelling Gentiles who turn to God and who believe on Jesus to do so also. This recognition of a Torah-free message for Gentiles is the first step in the process, and is the position reached at the so-called Council of Jerusalem (Acts 15). In other words, for the Gentiles to be "saved" they did not have to first become Jews (i.e., through circumcision). The next step was to admit that it was not necessary for believing Jews to observe the Law, when such observance caused them to separate from their Gentile brothers. This step was being taken during the ministry of Paul (Gal. 2:14ff; 1 Cor. 9:21). The last step was (sadly) to condemn all observance of the Law, whether by Jewish or by Gentile believers.

It is that last step that is reflected in the pages of the Letter of Barnabas, although it makes the rest of that process something that is not very attractive. There is, however, a peculiarity about its position since the mainstream of Christian thought, among both

Jewish and Gentile believers, was that the Mosaic Law had been originally given by God to ancient Israel and was to be literally fulfilled. Our author, however, does not even affirm that the Law was ever intended to be taken literally! He declares that it was announced in a spiritual sense but the Jews did not recognize that (10.9). This error in the Jewish misperception was the work of an evil angel (9.4). The true spiritual interpretation of the Torah story is known to Christians because God circumcised their ears (9.4). This spiritual interpretation of the Law is nothing more or less to "Barnabas" than a series of allegories. The "scapegoat" of the Day of Atonement is the type of Jesus who was to suffer (ch. 7). The prescription that certain animals must not be eaten is explained as meaning that one must have no dealings with certain kinds of evil persons (ch. 10). Abraham was said to have circumcised 318 men, but the real meaning of that account is about Jesus and the Cross. "The number eighteen is an Iota (10) and an Eta (8). So you have Jesus (IH). And because the cross in the letter Tau (T) was to convey grace, so it says 'and three hundred' (T). He thus indicates the name Jesus in the two letters and the cross in the other one" (9.8; cf. also his treatment of the Red Heifer of Numbers 19 in ch. 8). If modern readers are a bit taken aback by this hermeneutical maneuver, "Barnabas" stated that he was quite delighted by his own effort. Evidently he thought that God was also delighted in it because he states that "no one has ever learned from me a more excellent lesson, but I know that you are worthy" (9.9). Tugwell has a more sober evaluation. "It is worth noting that this particular gem only works in Greek, as the Hebrew numerals (in Genesis 14) would suggest neither Jesus nor the cross" (22).

The above conclusion about the futility of Judaism is also supported by citing the prophets' condemnation of the notion that sacrifice and ritual can be made a substitute for a moral life (chs. 2 and 3). In dealing with circumcision, the author then cites those passages which speak about a circumcision of the heart (Jer. 4:4 Deut. 10:16), and argues that Jewish circumcision "is abolished, for he has said that circumcision is not of the flesh" (9.4). The six days of creation in reality represent 6,000 years, so the true Sabbath cannot really be observed until the coming of the Son of God (ch. 15). In the same way the building of a physical Temple was a mistake. The true Temple is a spiritual one that is inside the hearts of those with whom God dwells (ch. 16). All that is outwardly distinctive about the Jewish religion is interpreted in a spiritual sense, such as the distinctions between clean and unclean animals, circumcision, the Sabbath, and the Temple.

Most Bible readers will recognize that Jesus followers believed that he came in fulfilment of promises made by God to the Jewish fathers. Thus, a Christian believer would regard the ancient Jewish Scriptures as the record of a unique revelation and treat them as the very word of God. Barnabas, however, regarded the literal observance of the Law as having been a fatal mistake from the very beginning. At the same time all his proofs for this are drawn from the OT itself and from what he believes to be its true exegesis. The words of Scripture he constantly quotes as words spoken from the mouth of God (2.4, 5, 7, 3.1, 4.8, 5.5, 12). Moreover, he uses the Scriptures to explain the mystery of the sufferings of the Son of God. "How did He endure to suffer at the hand of men? Understand that the prophets receiving grace from him, prophesied about him" (see 5.5, 6, 13, 14; cf. 6. 6, 7, 10, 11). The OT was his only source of authority in religion. He does not appeal to any Christian writing, or even to the words of Jesus, but he feels that he has fully proved his point if he can show that his teaching is grounded in the Jewish Scriptures.

If Jesus was the Messiah, he was clothed with full authority according to the will of God. Those who refused to believe and obey him refused to obey and believe God, and by their disobedience cut themselves off from the covenant and the resulting mercies of God. Those who did believe God and were obedient to his Messiah became the true people of God, the New Israel, the possessors of all the privileges and blessings that once belonged to the Jewish people. If the purpose of God in creating the world and in calling Abraham had been fulfilled in Jesus, then it was not for the sake of the unbelieving Jews but for the sake of the believers in the Messiah that the world had been created and Abraham eventually called as father of the promised seed. Barnabas, therefore, denied to the Jewish people any share whatever in the glorious heritage of their own Jewish nation, and claimed it entirely for Christian believers. Today we would call this effort the most virulent form of "replacement theology."

"Barnabas" is certain that the patriarchs from Abraham to Moses stood in a special relation to God and received special promises from him (5.7; 14.1). While Paul would say that the physical descendants of Abraham were not cut off from this special relationship until they cut themselves off by refusing to believe in Jesus (Romans 11), our author thinks that they were cut off long before this, as long ago as the day of Aaron's promotion of the worship directed toward the golden calf. A covenant was thus given to Moses to deliver to the Jews, but it was never really received. "He did give it (the covenant), but they were not worthy to receive it because of their sins" (14.1). When Moses saw their idolatry, he threw away the two tablets which he had received on Mount Sinai, and they were broken in pieces (14.1–4). The writings of Paul and the Letter to the Hebrews know of two covenants, an old one and a new one. The old was in force until the coming of the Messiah (Rom. 7:2ff., Gal. 3:24f.; 4:24, Heb. 8:13). The *Epistle of Barnabas*, however, says that only one covenant was ever in force, namely the covenant of Jesus.

One of the many severe critical analyses of Barnabas' attitude toward Judaism contrasts its spirit with another work in the Apostolic Fathers. "In contrast to the Didache, which presents keeping the Sabbath as still a communal reality and freely opts for the Lord's Day, Barnabas 15 holds Sabbath-keeping to be incompatible with Christianity. According to Barnabas, the church and Judaism are mutually exclusive" (Prostmeier, 43). A simple perusal of the book by a modern reader makes it hard to disagree with that blunt observation.

Despite these harsh judgments, our author does not completely divorce Christianity from any connection at all with its Jewish past. On the contrary, he denies a place of privilege to the Jews after Mount Sinai, in order to show that such a privileged place really belonged to the Christians. He reasons as follows. There are two peoples, the Jews and the Christians. The elder Jews are in the position of Esau and of Manasseh, who although the first-born of their respective fathers did not inherit the blessings which were received by their brothers. Christians, like the younger Jacob and Ephraim, have become the recipients of the promise (ch. 13). Therefore, Christians have now come into what was always their own and had never ever belonged to the people of Israel! "Do not then say, 'Our covenant remains to them also'." Ours it is, but they have lost it in this way forever when Moses had just received it" (4.6). The Christians are "the new people" of God (5.7, 7.5), a holy people (14.6), who have been cleansed and forgiven (6.11), whose hearts have been redeemed out of darkness (14.5), and "created again from the beginning" (16.8). "Thus he leads us into the incorruptible temple. For he who desires to be saved looks not to a person but to him who dwells and speaks in him and is amazed at him. For he has never heard such words from his mouth, nor has he ever desired to hear them. This is a spiritual temple being built for the Lord" (16.9, 10).

Remember that "Barnabas" accepted the Jewish Scriptures, the patriarchs, the promises, Moses, and the Law, but only in its correct spiritual understanding. His dislike was for the stiff-necked and hard-hearted Jews, not for the Jewish religion as such. Not simply from the time of Jesus, but even beginning at Sinai onwards, these stubborn Jews have stood outside that religion. Its privileges were in reality always the peculiar property of the Christians, held in reserve for them until the coming of the Messiah.

This extended, at times tedious, explanation of the thought process of "Barnabas" relative to the Jewish people is essential to understand his animus toward the Jews. Unlike modern examples of "antisemitism," which often attack this ancient people because of some supposed racial inferiority, that is *not* what is motivating this writer. It is a religious "disease" that blinds them, not a racial one. This explanation is not intended to ameliorate this warped approach, only to understand its religious roots, as strange and perverted as they are. Later forms of anti-Judaism which plagued the medieval church were actually mild compared to the scriptural perversions that marked this type of thinking.

BARNABAS AND THE BIBLE

Many authors have discerned the following approach to the Bible by the *Letter of Barnabas*. The book is essentially a treatise on the use of the Old Testament by Christians. With a strong Jewish animus, the author believed that the Old Testament could not be fully understood by Jews, because its significance could be understood only by those who read it and searched for types, or prefigurations, of Jesus. While needing further nuance, this brief statement is actually a fair summary of the intertextuality of "Barnabas." Regarding the scriptural record of God's covenant with Israel, the author claims that Israel forfeited the covenant because of idolatry (4.8) and disobedience to those same scriptures (8.7; 9.4). The Jews, not only in his day but also their forbears, were ignorant because they read the Law literally rather than "spiritually," as it was supposedly intended by the lawgiver (10.2, 9).

Barnabas arrives at this reading of the Old Testament law and prophets through what we call today "allegorical exegesis." This is a tradition of interpretation of literature even followed by some ancient Greek writers. The allegorical method claims to uncover the hidden meaning, or the "spiritual" meaning, of a text which can be quite foreign from the apparent meaning on its surface. The first-century Alexandrian Jewish writer, Philo, was probably the most articulate pre-Christian exponent of this method, and it permeates his handling of his Jewish texts. Our author offers a spiritual interpretation of the texts that would shock even Jewish allegorists because Jesus is supposedly uncovered in a way that seems obvious to Barnabas but would be quite surprising and even shocking to most Jewish readers. Mention has already been made of his infamous teaching in 9.7–8 about "the three letters." In that passage he engages in *gematria* or number symbolism to show that Jesus and the cross are embedded in the story of the 318 servants accompanying Abraham's hostage rescue! Actually, even though his allegorism seems extreme, he is an early Christian example of a method exemplified later by Origen and many medieval Christian interpreters with their "four-fold levels of interpretation" that should be applied to every Scriptural text!

CHRISTOLOGY OF BARNABAS

The facts of the earthly life of Jesus had little interest and find little expression in the *Letter of Barnabas*. From incidental notices one can discern that Jesus had performed wonders and miracles (5.8). He had chosen twelve apostles to preach His gospel (5.9) and he was crucified, rejected and spit upon (7.9), and given vinegar and gall to drink (7.3). Perhaps the writer did not think that his readers stood in need of instruction in the details of the life of Jesus. It is rather sad that he replaced these positive facts with a rather strident effort at reinterpreting the accounts of the Hebrew scriptures.

Also surprising is that he makes no extended effort to expound a doctrine of Jesus' person and work. When one does gather from the different parts of his work the passages which refer to Jesus, his teaching appears to be in line with what came to be called the "Catholic Church." Jesus is "the beloved one" of God (3.6, 4.3, 8). He "revealed himself as the Son of God" (5.9, 11; 7. 9). He was pre-existent and actually present and taking an active part in Creation (5.5, 10; 6.12). He appeared among men in the flesh (5.6, 10, 11; 6.7, 9, 14; 12.10). He should not be called simply Son of David but Son of God, for David himself called him not son, but Lord (12.10, 11). In line also with the later Apostles and Nicene Creeds, Jesus will come again to judge both the living and the dead (5.7; 7. 2; 21.3).

To Barnabas the "orthodox" view of the atonement belongs to this same early period of Christian teaching. He knows that Jesus suffered for us (5.5) and as a sacrifice for our sins (7.3, 5), in order that we might be forgiven, sanctified (5.1), and saved (5.10). We will reign with Him in the future when we have been made perfect (6.18, 19). He will abolish death and lead forth the resurrection (5.6) and give us everlasting life (7.2; 12.5). He has no further theory of the atonement and is content to show that according to the scriptures Christ died for our sins and that we thereby can be saved.

Such hermeneutical meanderings deserve an honest and blunt response. The writer's personal response to all the above is that it is sad to see such strong orthodox theology wedded to a view of the Jews that has to invent events in ancient history to convey such a biased view of an ancient and noble people.

PLACE AND DATE OF THE LETTER

There is a general agreement that Alexandria is the probable scene of its composition. The general style and the use of the allegorical method are thoroughly Alexandrian. Furthermore, in Alexandria the Jews were particularly strong and in constant conflict with the Christians as well. Thus, he may have been influenced in that city toward his bitter opposition to the Jews as a people. Anyone with a basic understanding of the Old Testament and the history of the Jewish people can see that he commits serious blunders about Jewish rites and customs. Perhaps, therefore, he betrays an actual unfamiliarity with real Jews and Judaism. One may be accurate in responding that his views could very well have developed because of a severe *lack* of contact with religious Jews!

There is less agreement on the question of the date of the letter. It is plainly later than the destruction of Jerusalem in 70 CE, for it alludes to that event. "Moreover, he says again, 'Behold, they who have torn down this temple will build it up again'" (16.3). The author then follows up with a fascinating remark. "It is happening now (present tense *ginetai*). For because they went to war, it was destroyed by their enemies. Now the servants of the enemies will themselves rebuild it" (16.4). The latter statement may refer to a Roman Temple of Jupiter. But the date is probably earlier than the second destruction of Jerusalem under Hadrian in 132–135 CE. If it was later, it would seem that the author would have delighted in referring to that humiliating defeat. The best window, therefore, would be between 70 and 130, although most scholars opt for the latter date of 130 CE.

STRUCTURE OF BARNABAS

Twice the author writes that he desires to impart "knowledge" to his readers, the first time near the beginning (1.5) and the second time toward the end (18.1). Hvalvik refers to these as "primary markers" for the two main sections. This conclusion seems to be accurate since in 18:1 Barnabas desires to "turn now to another kind of knowledge." He then suggests the following "rough structure."

1. Greeting and Introduction
2. –16. First main section. Knowledge from the Scriptures
17. Transition
18. –20. Second main section. Knowledge from the Two Ways Teaching
21. Closing (Hvalvik, 2021).

The lasting value of *Barnabas* is not simply that it preserves a rather virulent form of theological antisemitism. His examples of allegorical interpretation also prepare the way for such writers as Origen to do the same thing, but without the accompanying animus toward the Jewish people.

FURTHER READING ON THE LETTER OF BARNABAS

Barnard, L. W. "The 'Epistle of Barnabas' and Its Contemporary Setting" in *ANRW* 2.27.1, 159–207. Berlin/New York. De Gruyter, 1993.

Carleton Paget, J. *The Epistle of Barnabas*. Outlook and Background. WUNT 2.64. Tübingen. Mohr Siebeck, 1994.

_____. "The Epistle of Barnabas" in *The Writings of the Apostolic Fathers*, ed. Paul Foster, 72–80. London and New York. T&T Clark, 2007.

Draper, Jonathan A. "Barnabas and the Riddle of the Didache Revisited." *Journal for the Study of the New Testament* 58 (1995). 89–113.

Gunther, John J. "The Epistle of Barnabas and the Final Rebuilding of the Temple." *Journal for the Study of Judaism* 7 (1976). 143–51.

Hvalvik, Reidar. *The Struggle for Scripture and Covenant. The Purpose of the* Epistle of Barnabas *and Jewish-Christian Competition in the Second Century*. Tübingen. Mohr Siebeck, 1995.

_____. "The Epistle of Barnabas" in *The Cambridge Companion to the Apostolic Fathers*, ed. Michael F. Bird and Scott D. Harrower, 268–89. Cambridge. Cambridge University Press, 2021.

Kraft, Robert A. *Barnabas and the Didache*. The Apostolic Fathers, vol. 3. New York. Nelson, 1965.

Lookadoo, Jonathon. *The Epistle of Barnabas*. Eugene, OR. Cascade Books, 2022.

Lowy, S. "The Confutation of Judaism in the Epistle of Barnabas." *Journal of Jewish Studies* 11 (1960). 1–33.

Prostmeier, Ferdinand R. "The Epistle of Barnabas" in *The Apostolic Fathers: An Introduction*, ed. Wilhelm Pratscher, 27–46. Waco, TX. Baylor University Press, 2010.

THE LETTER OF BARNABAS

Chapter One
Greetings, sons and daughters, in the name of the Lord who loves us, in peace. 2 Since God's righteous ordinances for you are great and abundant, I rejoice greatly and beyond measure at your blessed and glorious spirits, for you have received such a deeply engrafted spiritual gift. 3 For this, therefore, I congratulate myself in the hope of salvation, because I truly see the Spirit poured out upon you from the abundance of the Lord's fountain. So greatly on your account has the long-desired sight of you amazed me. 4 With this conviction, then, and the realization that, while speaking much among you, I understand the Lord was my fellow traveler on the road of righteousness, I am completely bound to this: to love you more than my life, because great faith and love dwell in you because of the hope of his life. 5 Considering this, that if I care enough to share something with you of what I have received, it will be a reward for having ministered to such spirits. Thus I hasten to send you a brief message in order that you may have perfect knowledge along with your faith. 6 Therefore, there are three basic doctrines of the Lord of life: **hope**, the beginning and end of our faith; **righteousness**, the beginning and end of judgment; and **love**, a witness to the joy and gladness in the works of a righteous life. 7 For the Lord by His prophets made known to us things past and things present and gives us a foretaste of things to come. And as we see each of these things coming to pass as he spoke, we should make a more generous and higher offering in fear of him. 8 Not as a teacher, but as one of your own, I will show you a few things by which you will be gladdened in your present circumstances.

Chapter Two
Since the times are evil and the worker of evil himself has authority, we must commit ourselves to search out the righteous commandments of the Lord. 2 The helpers of our faith are fear and endurance, and our allies are patience and self-control. 3 While these remain in their purity in matters relating to the Lord, wisdom, understanding, perception, and knowledge rejoice with them. 4 For he has shown us through all the prophets that he does not need burnt offerings or regular offerings, saying in one place, 5 "What is the multitude of your sacrifices to me? says the Lord. I am full of burnt offerings and I desire neither the fat of lambs nor the blood of bulls and goats, not even if you come to appear before me. For who has sought these things from your hands? You will no longer trample my court. If you bring flour, it is futile; incense is an abomination to me; I cannot stand your new moons and sabbaths."[1] 6 These things he therefore nullified, so that the new law of our Lord Jesus Christ may be without the yoke of compulsion and without an offering made by humans. 7 Again he says to them, "Did I command your fathers when they came out from the land of Egypt to offer to me burnt offerings and sacrifices? 8 Rather I did command this: Let none of you bear a grudge in your heart against your neighbor, and do not love a false oath."[2] 9 We ought therefore to understand, if we are not ignorant, the good intention of our Father, for he speaks to us, desiring us not to be deceived like them, but to seek how to make our offering to him. 10 To us he speaks, "A contrite heart is a sacrifice to the Lord; a sweet fragrance to the Lord is a heart which glorifies the one who formed it."[3] We ought, therefore, to learn clearly about our salvation, brothers, lest the Evil One, having caused error to creep in among us, hurl us away from our life.

---

[1] Isa. 1:11-13.
[2] Jer. 7:22; Zech. 8:17.
[3] Ps. 51:17.

Chapter Three
So again he says to them about these things, "Why do you fast for me, says the Lord, when your voice is heard crying out today? I have not chosen this fast, says the Lord, not a person humbling his soul. 2 Not if you bend your neck into a circle, and put on sackcloth, and make your bed of ashes, not even so should you call this an acceptable fast."[4] 3 But to us he says, "Behold this is the fast I have chosen, says the Lord. Give up every attachment to wickedness, unravel the chains of forced agreements, send away the downtrodden with forgiveness, and tear up every unfair contract. Break your bread for the hungry and provide clothing if you see a naked person; bring the homeless into your house; if you see a humble man do not despise him nor should any of your house or of your family. 4 Then will your light break forth at dawn, and your healing will rise quickly, and your righteousness will go before you, and the glory of God will clothe you. 5 Then you will cry and God will hear you. While you are still speaking he will say, 'Behold, I am here.' If you remove bondage from you and the threatening gesture and give the hungry your bread from your heart, you will show mercy to the humbled soul."[5]

6 For this reason, brothers, the one who is patient foresaw that the people whom he prepared in his beloved would believe with innocence. So he revealed beforehand all things, that we should not be wrecked like newcomers to their law.

Chapter Four
Therefore, carefully looking into the present things, and seeking what is able to save us, let us flee completely from all works of iniquity, lest the deeds of iniquity overtake us. Let us hate the error of the present time, that we may be loved in the time to come. 2 Let us give no rest to our soul and so enable it to associate with sinners and evil men, lest we become like them. 3 The final stumbling block is at hand, about which it is written, as Enoch says. For this purpose the Lord has shortened the seasons and the days, that his beloved may hurry and arrive at his inheritance. 4 And the prophet also speaks thus, "Ten kingdoms will reign on the earth, and after them will arise a little king, who will humble three of the kings under one."[6] 5 Likewise, Daniel speaks of the same thing, "And I saw the fourth beast, evil and powerful and fiercer than all the beasts of the earth, and how ten horns rose up from it, and from them a small horn like an offshoot and it humbled three of the great horns under one."[7] 6 You ought then to understand, and yet I beg this of you as one of your own, one who loves you all individually more than my own life. Pay attention now to yourselves and do not be like some. Do not add to your sins and say that the covenant is both theirs and ours. But they lost it forever when Moses had only just received it. 7 For the Scripture says, "And Moses was on the mountain fasting for forty days and forty nights, and he received the covenant from the Lord, stone tablets written by the finger of the Lord's hand."[8] 8 But they turned away to idols and lost it. For the Lord speaks thus, "Moses, Moses, go down quickly, for your people whom you brought out of the land of Egypt have broken the law."[9] And Moses understood and threw the two tablets out of his hands and their covenant was broken in order that the covenant of

---
[4] Isa. 58:3-5.
[5] Isa. 58:6-10.
[6] Dan. 7:24.
[7] Dan. 7:7-8.
[8] Exod. 31:18; 34:28.
[9] Exod. 32:7.

EPISTLE OF BARNABAS

the beloved Jesus might be sealed in our hearts by the hope inspired by faith in him. 9 Although desiring to write much to you, not as a teacher, but as one who loves you and as your most humble servant, I hasten to write without omitting anything we possess. So let us be watchful in the last days, for the whole time in which we believe will profit us nothing, unless in this present lawless period of stumbling blocks yet to come, we resist as it becomes God's children. Thus the Black One may not sneak in. 10 Let us flee from all that is futile and let us hate completely the deeds of the evil way. Do not withdraw and live apart by yourselves, as if you were already justified, but come together to seek the common good. 11 For the Scripture says, "Woe to those who are wise in their own eyes and are knowledgeable in their own opinions."[10] Let us be spiritual and become a perfect sanctuary for God. As it is in our power, let us exercise ourselves in the fear of God, and let us strive to keep His commandments so that we may rejoice in his righteous ordinances. 12 The Lord will judge the world without partiality. Each person will receive as he has done. If he be good, his righteousness will lead him; if he is evil, the reward of iniquity will be before him. 13 Because we are called, let us never fall asleep in our sins, allowing the prince of evil to gain authority over us and force us out of the kingdom of the Lord. 14 And remember this also, my brothers, when you see that after such great signs and wonders were done in Israel, they were finally cast off. Let us be careful that, as it is written, lest we should be found as "many are called but few are chosen."[11]

Chapter Five
For this reason the Lord endured the deliverance of his flesh to corruption, that we might be cleansed through the forgiveness of sin, that is, by his sprinkled blood. 2 For the Scripture about him refers partly to Israel and partly to us and speaks thus, "He was wounded for our transgressions and was afflicted for our iniquities, and by his wounds we were healed. He was led as a sheep to slaughter, and like a lamb silent before his shearer."[12] 3 We ought therefore to be very thankful to the Lord that he has revealed to us the past and has made us wise in the present, and for the future events we are not ignorant. 4 The scripture says, "Not unjustly are the nets spread out for the birds."[13] This means that a person deserves to perish who, although he has knowledge of the way of righteousness, ensnares himself in the way of darkness. 5 Furthermore, my brothers, if the Lord endured suffering for our soul although he is the Lord of the whole world, to whom God said at the foundation of the world, "Let us make man in our image and likeness,"[14] how then did he allow himself to suffer at the hand of men? 6 The prophets with his grace prophesied about him, and to destroy death and demonstrate the resurrection from the dead, allowed himself to suffer because he must be manifest in the flesh. 7 It was also to redeem the promise given to the fathers, and prepare for himself the new people. It was also to show that while still on earth, having brought about the resurrection, he himself will judge. 8 Beyond this he taught Israel and preached by performing such great signs and wonders and loved them deeply. 9 When he chose as his special apostles to preach his gospel men who were lawless above all others and showed that "he came not to call the righteous but sinners," then he revealed that he was God's son. 10 For if he had not

---
[10] Isa. 5:21.
[11] Matt. 22:14.
[12] Isa. 53:5, 7.
[13] Prov. 1:17.
[14] Gen. 1:26.

come in the flesh, there is no way in which men could be saved by beholding him, since when they look at the sun, which will perish and is a work of his hands, they cannot look directly at its rays. 11 For this purpose the Son of God came in the flesh, that he might total up the sins of those who persecuted his prophets to death. 12 For this purpose he allowed himself to suffer, for God says that the wound of his flesh came from them. "When they strike their shepherd, then the sheep of the flock will be destroyed."[15] 13 It was his will to suffer this way, for it was necessary that he should suffer on a tree, for the prophet says about him, "Spare my soul from the sword" and "Nail my flesh because an assembly of evildoers has risen up against me."[16] 14 Again he says, "Behold I have given my back to whips and my cheeks to blows, and I have set my face like a hard rock."[17]

Chapter Six
Therefore, when he gave the commandment, what did he say? "Who is the one who condemns me? Let him oppose me! Or who justifies himself before me? Let him approach the servant of the Lord. 2 Woe to you, for you will all become old as a garment and the moth will devour you."[18] And again, bring assigned as a strong stone for crushing, the prophet says, "Behold, I will place as the foundations of Zion a precious stone, specially chosen, a cornerstone." 3 Then what does He say? "The one who trusts in him will live forever."[19] Is our hope therefore built on a stone? May it never be! He means that the Lord set his flesh up in strength. For he says, "He set me as a hard rock."[20] 4 And again the prophet says, "The stone the builders rejected has become the head of the corner." And again he says, "This is the great and wonderful day that the Lord made."[21] 5 I write to you simply that you may understand. I am the devoted servant of your love. 6 What, then, does the prophet say again? "The congregation of those who do evil has surrounded me; they encircled me as bees around a honeycomb"[22]; and "they cast lots for my clothing."[23] 7 Since he was to be revealed in the flesh and to suffer in the flesh, his suffering was revealed in advance. For the prophet says about Israel, "Woe to their soul, for they have plotted an evil plan against themselves, saying, 'Let us bind the righteous one, for he is irritating to us'."[24] 8 What does the other prophet, Moses, say to them? "Behold, thus says the Lord God, enter the good land which the Lord swore to give to Abraham, Isaac, and Jacob, and inherit it, a land flowing with milk and honey."[25] 9 But what does knowledge say? Learn! "Hope in Jesus, the one who will be revealed to you in the flesh." For man is earth suffering, for Adam was formed from the face of the earth. 10 What, then, does this mean, "into the good land flowing with milk and honey?" Blessed is our Lord, brothers, who has put within us wisdom and understanding of his secrets. The prophet is speaking a parable of the Lord. Who will understand except the wise and the learned who loves his Lord? 11 Because he renewed us through the forgiveness of our sins, he made us a

---

[15] Zech. 13:7; Matt. 26:31.
[16] Ps. 22:20, 16.
[17] Isa. 50:6-7.
[18] Isa. 50:8-9.
[19] Isa. 28:16.
[20] Isa. 50:7.
[21] Ps. 118:22, 24.
[22] Ps. 22:16; 118:12.
[23] Ps. 22:18.
[24] Isa. 3:9-10.
[25] Exod. 33:1, 3.

different type of person, and we have the soul of children, as if he were creating us again. 12 For the scripture says of us as he says to the Son, "Let us make the man according to our image and likeness and let them rule over the beasts of the earth, and the birds of the heaven, and the fish of the sea."[26] On seeing the beauty of our creation, the Lord said, "Increase and multiply and fill the earth."[27] These things he addressed to the Son. 13 Again I will show you how he refers to us. He made a second creation in the last days. And the Lord says, "Behold, I make the last things as the first."[28] The prophet referred to this when he preached, "Enter a land flowing with milk and honey, and rule over it."[29] 14 See that we have been formed anew as again he says through another prophet, "Behold says the Lord, I will take out from them (from those whom the Spirit of the Lord foresaw) their hearts of stone and will put in them hearts of flesh."[30] This is because he was going to be revealed in the flesh and dwell among us. 15 For, my brothers, the dwelling place of our hearts is a holy sanctuary to the Lord. 16 For the Lord says again, "And how will I appear before the Lord my God and be glorified?"[31] He says, "I will confess to you in the assembly of my brothers, and I will sing to you in the midst of the assembly of saints."[32] Then we are the ones whom he brought into the good land. 17 Then what is the milk and the honey? Because the child is made to live first with honey and then with milk. We also are nourished in the faith in the promise and by the word will live and rule over the earth. 18 As we said above, "Let them increase and multiply and rule over the fish."[33] Who is it that is able now to rule over wild beasts or fish or birds of the sky? For we ought to realize that to rule is a sign of authority, and that one who gives commands is the one who rules. 19 Therefore, if this is not happening now, he told us when it will happen—when we ourselves have also been made perfect to become heirs of the Lord's covenant.

Chapter Seven
Understand, therefore, children of gladness, that our good Lord revealed everything to us ahead of time, so that we might know to whom we should give thanks and praise for all things. 2 If, therefore, the Son of God, who is Lord and will judge the living and the dead, suffered so that that his wounds might give us life, let us believe that this Son of God could not suffer except for us. 3 But he also was given vinegar and gall to drink when he was crucified. Listen to how the priests of the temple revealed something about this. When the command that "whoever does not keep the fast will surely die"[34] was written, the Lord commanded it because he was planning to offer the vessel of his spirit as a sacrifice for our sins, in order that the type represented by Isaac, who was offered upon the altar, might be fulfilled. 4 What, therefore, does he say in the prophet? "Let them eat some of the goat that is offered for all their sins during the fast"—pay careful attention!—"and let all but only the priests eat the unwashed intestines with vinegar."[35] 5 Why? "Since you are going to give me gall with vinegar to drink, you alone must eat while

---

[26] Gen. 1:26.
[27] Gen. 1:28.
[28] Unknown; cf. Isa. 44:6.
[29] Exod. 33:3.
[30] Ezek. 11:19.
[31] Ps. 42:4.
[32] Ps. 22:22, 25.
[33] Gen. 1:28.
[34] Lev. 23:29.
[35] Source unknown. Cf. Lev. 16.

the people fast and lament in sackcloth and ashes, when I am about to offer my flesh for the sins of my new people." This was to show that he must suffer through their hands. 6 Pay attention to what he commanded. "Take two excellent and well-suited goats, and offer them, and allow the priest to take one for a whole burnt offering for sins."[36] 7 But what will they do with the other one? "The other one," he says, "is cursed."[37] Notice how the type of Jesus is unveiled! 8 "And all of you will spit on it and pierce it, and tie scarlet wool around its head, then let it be led out into the wilderness."[38] And when these things have taken place, the man in charge of the goat leads it into the wilderness, then he removes the wool and places it upon the bush commonly called the blackberry (the buds of which we are accustomed to eat when we find them in the countryside; only the fruit of the blackberry is sweet). 9 What is the meaning of this? Note it well. "The one is for the altar, and the other is cursed," and note that the one that is cursed is crowned. For they will see him on that day, wearing a long red robe about his body, and they will say, "Is this not the one whom we once crucified and ridiculed by spitting upon him? Surely this was the man who then said that he was the Son of God!" 10 But how is he like that goat? "The goats are similar, fine and well-suited," for this reason: in order that when they see him coming, they may be amazed at the likeness to the goat. Observe, therefore, the type of Jesus who was intended to suffer. 11 And what does it mean when they place the wool in the middle of the thorns? It is a type of Jesus, and is set forth for the church, because whoever wishes to take away the scarlet wool must suffer greatly because the thorns are so horrible and can only possess it through pain. In the same way, he says, "those who wish to see me and receive my kingdom must receive me through affliction and suffering."

Chapter Eight
What type do you think was intended when he commanded Israel that those full of sins should offer a heifer and slaughter and burn it? Then the children should take the ashes and place them in containers and tie the scarlet wool around a tree (notice again the type of the cross and the scarlet wool), and the hyssop, and then the children should sprinkle the people one by one, in order that they may be purified from their sins. 2 Understand how clearly he is speaking to you. The calf is Jesus; the sinful men who offer it are those who brought him to the slaughter. Then the men are no more, so no longer is the glory of sinners. 3 The children who sprinkle are those who preached to us the good news about forgiveness of sins and purification of the heart, those to whom he gave the authority to proclaim the gospel. There were twelve of those as a witness to the tribes, because there are twelve tribes of Israel. 4 And why are there three children who sprinkle? As a witness to Abraham, Isaac, and Jacob, because these men were great in God's sight. 5 And then there is the matter of the wool on the tree, which signifies that the kingdom of Jesus is on a tree, and that those who hope in him will live forever. 6 But why are the wool and the hyssop together? Because in his kingdom there will be dark and evil days, in which we will be saved, because the one who suffers in body is healed by means of the foul juice of the hyssop. 7 These things happened for this reason and are obvious to us, but to them they are obscure, because they have not heard the voice of the Lord.

---

[36]Lev. 16:7, 9.
[37]Lev. 16:8.
[38]Lev. 16:10, 20-22.

Chapter Nine

He speaks again about the ears, how he has circumcised our heart. The Lord says through the prophet, "With the hearing of the ear they obeyed."[39] Again he says, "Those who are far off will hear with their ears, and they will know what I have done."[40] And "Be circumcised in your hearts," says the Lord.[41] 2 Again he says, "Hear, O Israel, thus says the Lord your God. ..."[42] And again the Spirit of the Lord prophesies, "Who is the one who wishes to live forever? Let him hear carefully the voice of my servant."[43] 3 Again He says, "Hear, O heaven, and give ear, O earth, for the Lord has spoken these things as a witness."[44] Again he says, "Hear the word of the Lord, you rulers of this people."[45] And again, "Hear, children, the voice of one crying in the wilderness."[46] 4 Thus he circumcised our ears so that when we hear the word we may believe. But even the circumcision in which they trusted has been abolished, because he said that circumcision is not of the flesh. They disobeyed because an evil angel was tricking them. 5 He says to them, "This is what the Lord your God says" (here I find a commandment), "Do not sow among thorns; be circumcised to your Lord."[47] And what does He say? "Circumcise the hardness of your heart, and do not stiffen your neck."[48] Or this again, "Behold, says the Lord, all the Gentiles are uncircumcised in their foreskin, but this people has an uncircumcised heart."[49] 6 But you will say, "The people surely has been circumcised as a seal." But every Syrian and Arab and all idol priests are also circumcised. Are they also part of their covenant? Even the Egyptians practice circumcision. 7 Learn fully, therefore, beloved children. Abraham, who first instituted circumcision, was looking forward in the Spirit to Jesus. He received the doctrines of the three letters. 8 For it says, "And Abraham circumcised from his household three hundred and eighteen men."[50] What, then, was the special knowledge that was given him? Observe that he first mentions eighteen, and after an interval, three hundred. The number eighteen is an Iota (10) and an Eta (8). So you have Jesus (IH).[51] And because the cross in the letter Tau (T) was to convey grace, so he says "and three hundred" (T).[52] He thus indicates the name Jesus in the two letters and the cross in the other one. 9 He who placed the implanted gift of His covenant in us understands. No one has ever learned from me a more excellent lesson, but I know that you are worthy.

Chapter Ten

When Moses said, "You will not eat a pig, nor an eagle, nor a hawk, nor a crow, nor any fish without scales,"[53] he received three doctrines in his understanding. 2 Furthermore, he says to them in Deuteronomy, "And I will set forth My righteous requirements as

---

[39] Ps. 18:44.
[40] Isa. 33:13.
[41] Isa. 33:13; Jer. 4:4.
[42] Jer. 7:2-3; Ps. 34:12-13.
[43] Isa. 50:10; Exod. 15:26.
[44] Isa. 1:2.
[45] Isa. 1:10; 28:14.
[46] Isa. 40:3.
[47] Jer. 4:3-4.
[48] Deut. 10:16.
[49] Jer. 9:26.
[50] Gen. 14:14; 17:23.
[51] The number eighteen in Greek is Iota Eta, an abbreviation for the name "Jesus."
[52] The numerical value of a Tau (T) is eighteen. The appearance of the letter T resembles a cross.
[53] Lev. 11:7-15; Deut. 14:8-14.

a covenant with this people."⁵⁴ Therefore, it is not a commandment of God not to eat these creatures, but Moses spoke spiritually. 3 Accordingly, he mentioned the pig for this reason. You will not associate with men who are like pigs. This means that when they prosper they forget the Lord, but when they are in need, they acknowledge the Lord. Like the pig ignores its owner when it eats, but when it is hungry it squeals, and after receiving food is again silent. 4 "Neither should you eat the eagle, nor the hawk, nor the kite, nor the crow."⁵⁵ He means that you will not live with nor resemble such people who do not know how to provide for themselves food by labor and sweat, but lawlessly take other people's property. They lie in wait for it, with the appearance of innocence, and carefully look around to find someone to rob in their greed, just as these birds alone provide no food for themselves, but sit idly and seek how to eat the flesh of others, being diseased in their wickedness. 5 "You will not eat," he says, "eel nor octopus nor cuttlefish."⁵⁶ He means that you should not resemble people who are utterly wicked and are already condemned to death, just as these fish alone are wicked and swim in the depths, and do not swim like the others, but live in the mud beneath the depths. 6 Furthermore, "You will not eat the rabbit either."⁵⁷ Why? Do not become, he means, a corrupter of boys, nor will you become like such people. For the rabbit grows an opening in the body each year, and every year it lives, it has that many openings. 7 "You will not eat the hyena."⁵⁸ Do not become, he means, an adulterer nor a seducer, nor become like such people. Why? Because this animal changes its nature every year, and becomes now a male, then a female. 8 Moreover, he hates the weasel, and with good reason. Do not become, he means, like those who, as we are told, work iniquity with their mouth in their uncleanness nor associate with immoral women who work iniquity with their mouth. For this animal conceives through its mouth. 9 Moses thus received three precepts concerning foods, and spoke of them in a spiritual sense, but they understood them as referring to actual food in their desires of the flesh. 10 David also received knowledge about the same doctrines and says, "Blessed is the man who has not walked in the advice of the ungodly," as the fish go about in darkness in the deep waters; "and who has not stood in the way of sinners" (like those who, appearing to fear the Lord, sin like pigs) "and does not sit in the company of diseased people," (like the birds who sit waiting for their prey).⁵⁹ Now you have perfectly the teaching about food. 11 Moses says again, "Eat every animal that has a divided hoof and chews the cud."⁶⁰ What does he mean? That whoever receives food recognizes the one who feeds him and relying upon him, appears to be glad. He spoke well with regard to the commandment. What then does he mean? Associate with those who fear the Lord, with those who meditate in their heart on the meaning of the word they have received; with those who proclaim and obey the righteous requirements of the Lord; with those who know that meditation is a labor of joy and who ponder the word of the Lord. But what does "that divides the hoof" mean? It means that a righteous person both walks in the world and waits for the coming holy age. Observe how well Moses wrote the law! 12 But how could those people understand or comprehend these things? We, however,

---

⁵⁴Deut. 4:10, 13.
⁵⁵Lev. 11:13-16.
⁵⁶Source unknown.
⁵⁷Lev. 11:6.
⁵⁸Source unknown.
⁵⁹Ps. 1:1.
⁶⁰Lev. 11:3; Deut. 14:6.

because we rightly understand them, explain the commandments as the Lord intended. Because of this he circumcised our ears and hearts that we might understand these things.

Chapter Eleven

Let us inquire if the Lord desired to foreshadow about the water and the cross. Concerning the water, it is written about Israel that they would never receive the baptism that brings forgiveness of sins but would build something for themselves. 2 For the prophet says, "Be astonished, O heaven, and shudder greatly at this, O earth! Because this people has done two evil things: they have abandoned me, the fountain of life, and they have dug for themselves a pit of death. 3 Is Sinai my holy mountain a desert rock? For you will be as young birds, fluttering about when they are taken away from the nest."[61] 4 Again the prophet says, "I will go before you and I will level mountains and will break brass gates and will shatter iron bars, and I will give you dark treasures that are secret and unseen, that they may know that I am the Lord God."[62] 5 "You will live in a lofty cave of a strong rock." "His water is sure; you will see the King with glory, and your soul will meditate on the fear of the Lord."[63] 6 And he says again in another prophet, "And he who does these things will be like a tree planted near springs of waters, which will bring forth its fruit in its season. His leaf will not fall off, and whatever he does will prosper. 7 Not so the ungodly, not so; but they are like the dust which the wind drives from the face of the earth. Therefore, the wicked will not rise up in judgment, nor sinners in the counsel of the righteous. For the Lord knows the way of the righteous, but the way of the wicked will perish."[64] 8 Notice how he described the water and the cross together. He means this. Blessed are they who have put their hope in the cross and descended into the water. For he speaks of their reward "in its season." At that time, he says, "I will repay." But now, when he says, "Their leaves will not fall off," he means that every word which will come from your mouth in faith and love will profit many for conversion and hope. 9 And again another prophet says, "And the land of Jacob was praised above every land." He means this: that he glorifies the vessel of his Spirit. 10 What does he say next? "And there was a river flowing on the right hand, and beautiful trees grew out of it, and whoever eats from them will live forever."[65] 11 This means that we go down into the water full of sins and dirt, but we come up bearing fruit in our hearts, fear and hope in Jesus by the Spirit. "And whoever will eat from these will live forever." This means that whoever hears these things spoken and believes will live forever.

Chapter Twelve

In a similar way, he again describes the cross with precision in another prophet who says, "And when will these things be accomplished? says the Lord. When a tree will fall and rise again, and when blood will drip from a tree."[66] You again have a reference to the cross and to him who would be crucified. 2 And again he speaks in Moses, when Israel was attacked by foreigners, to remind those who were attacked that they were delivered to death because of their sins. The Spirit speaks to the heart of Moses that he should

---

[61] Jer. 2:12-13; cf. Isa. 16:1-2.
[62] Isa. 45:2-3.
[63] Isa. 33:16-18.
[64] Ps. 1:3-6.
[65] Ezek. 47:1-12.
[66] 4 Ezra 4:33; 5:5.

make a type of the cross, and of him who would suffer, because he says that unless they put their hope in him, they will be warred upon forever. Moses, therefore, piled up arms on arms in the midst of the struggle, and stood high above them all and stretched out his hands. Israel then began to win. But when he lowered them, they began to be killed.[67] 3 Why? That they might know that they could not be saved unless they trust in him. 4 And again he says in another prophet, "I have spread forth my hands all day long to an unbelieving people, who walk in a way that opposes my righteous way."[68] 5 Again Moses makes a symbol of Jesus. He must suffer and he himself will give life, although they will think that he has died by the sign given when Israel was falling. For the Lord made every serpent bite them, and they were dying. Because the transgression took place through Eve by the serpent, in order to convince them that they would be delivered to the tribulation of death because of their transgression. 6 Moreover, after Moses commanded them, "You will have neither a carved nor a molded statue for your God,"[69] he still makes one himself to show a symbol of Jesus. Moses, therefore, made a carved serpent, set it up publicly, and assembled the people with a proclamation. 7 They came together and were begging Moses to offer a prayer for their recovery. But Moses said to them, "Whenever one of you is bitten, let him come to the serpent that is placed on the wood, and let him hope and believe that, although he is dead, the serpent is able to give life, and he will immediately be saved."[70] And so they were doing. By this again you have the glory of Jesus in these things because all things are through him and for him. 8 Again, what does Moses say to Joshua, the son of Nun, when as a prophet he gave him this name that all the people should listen to him alone? It was because the Father revealed everything about his Son Jesus. 9 Moses says to Joshua, the son of Nun, after he gave him this name, when he sent him to explore the land. "Take a scroll in your hands, and write what the Lord says, that the Son of God will in the last days chop down the whole house of Amalek at the roots."[71] 10 See again that Jesus, not as a son of man, but as the Son of God, was revealed by a symbol in the flesh. So since they will say that Christ is David's son, David himself prophesies, fearing and recognizing the error of the sinners. "The Lord said to my Lord: 'Sit at my right hand until I make your enemies your footstool'."[72] 11 Isaiah also speaks thus. "The Lord said to Messiah my Lord, whose right hand I am holding, that the nations should obey in his presence, and I will break the strength of kings."[73] See how David calls him Lord and does not say son.

Chapter Thirteen

Let us see whether this people inherits or the former people and if the covenant is for us or for them. 2 Therefore, hear what the Scripture says concerning the people. "Isaac prayed for Rebecca his wife because she was barren and she conceived. Then Rebecca went to inquire from the Lord, and the Lord said to her, 'Two nations are in your womb, and two peoples in your belly, and one people will dominate the other, and the older will

---

[67] Cf. Exod. 17:8-13.
[68] Isa. 65:2.
[69] Lev. 26:1; Deut. 27:15.
[70] Num. 21:4-8.
[71] Exod. 17:14.
[72] Ps. 110:1.
[73] Isa. 45:1.

EPISTLE OF BARNABAS

serve the younger'."[74] 3 You must understand who is Isaac and who is Rebecca, and to whom he has shown that this new people is greater than that one. 4 In another prophecy Jacob speaks more clearly to Joseph his son, saying, "Behold, the Lord has not deprived me of your presence. Bring me your sons that I may bless them."[75] 5 And he brought Ephraim and Manasseh, desiring that Manasseh be blessed because he was the older one so Joseph brought him to the right hand of his father Jacob. But Jacob saw in the spirit a type of the people to come. So what does he say? "And Jacob crossed his hands and placed his right hand on the head of Ephraim, the second and younger son, and blessed him. So Joseph said to Jacob, 'Change your right hand to the head of Manasseh, for he is my first born son.' And Jacob said to Joseph, 'I know, child, I know, but the elder will serve the younger, and this one will be blessed'."[76] 6 Observe about whom he decided that this people is the first and the heir of the covenant. 7 Therefore, if this people is remembered also in the case of Abraham, then we reach the perfection of our knowledge. What, then, does he say to Abraham when he alone believed and was appointed for righteousness? "Behold, Abraham, I have appointed you as father of the Gentiles who believe in God while uncircumcised."[77]

Chapter Fourteen

Yes but let us see if he has really given the covenant which he swore to the fathers that he would give to the people. He did give it, but they were not worthy to receive it because of their sins. 2 For the prophet says, "And Moses was fasting on Mount Sinai forty days and forty nights to receive the covenant of the Lord for the people. And Moses received from the Lord the two tablets, written by the Spirit by the finger of the Lord's hand."[78] And Moses took them and was carrying them down to give to the people. 3 And the Lord said to Moses, "Moses, Moses, go down quickly, for your people whom you brought out of the land of Egypt have broken the law." And Moses realized that they had once more made cast images for themselves, and he threw the tablets out of his hands, and the tablets of the covenant of the Lord were broken in pieces. 4 Moses received the covenant but they were not worthy. Learn how we received it. Moses received it as a servant, but the Lord himself gave it to us, the people of the inheritance, by suffering for us. 5 Now he was made manifest both that they should be filled with their sins and that we should receive the covenant through Jesus the Lord who inherited it. For he was prepared for this purpose, that having appeared in person, he might redeem from darkness our hearts already handed over to death and delivered to the iniquity of error and might by his word make a covenant with us. 6 For it is written how the Father commands him to redeem us from darkness and prepare a holy people for himself. 7 So the prophet says, "I the Lord your God have called you in righteousness and taken you by the hand and preserved you. And I have given you as a covenant of the people, for a light of the Gentiles, that you may open the eyes of the blind, and free prisoners from their bonds and from their dungeon those who sit in darkness."[79] We realize then from what we have been redeemed. 8 Again

---

[74] Gen. 25:21-23.
[75] Gen. 48:11, 9.
[76] Gen. 48:14, 19.
[77] Gen. 15:6; 17:4.
[78] Exod. 24:18; 31:18.
[79] Isa. 42:6-7.

the prophet says, "Behold, I have given you as a light to the Gentiles, that you may be my salvation to the end of the earth. Thus says the Lord the God who redeemed you."[80] 9 And again the prophet says, "The Spirit of the Lord is upon me, because he anointed me to preach the gospel to the humble, he sent me to heal those who are crushed in heart, to proclaim release to the captives, and recovery of sight to the blind, to announce the acceptable year of the Lord, and a day of repaying, to comfort all who mourn."[81]

Chapter Fifteen
Furthermore, it is also written concerning the Sabbath in the ten commandments in which he spoke to Moses on Mount Sinai face to face. "Sanctify also the Lord's Sabbath with pure hands and a pure heart."[82] 2 In another place he says, "If my sons keep the Sabbath, then I will bestow my mercy on them."[83] 3 Concerning the Sabbath he speaks at the beginning of creation, "God made in six days the works of his hands, and on the seventh day he finished and rested on it and sanctified it."[84] 4 Pay attention, children, what "he finished in six days" means. It says this: that the Lord will make an end of all things in six thousand years for a day with him represents a thousand years. And he himself is my witness, saying, "Behold, the day of the Lord will be as a thousand years."[85] So in six days, that is in six thousand years, everything will be finished. 5 "And he rested on the seventh day." This means that when his Son comes he will abolish the time of the lawless one, judge the godless, and change the sun and the moon and the stars. Then he will indeed rest on the seventh day. 6 Furthermore, he says, "You will sanctify it with pure hands and a pure heart." If anyone is able to sanctify the day which God sanctified, by being pure in heart, we are deceived. 7 You see that we will indeed sanctify it when we enjoy a good rest, when we will be able to do so because we ourselves will have been made upright and will have received the promise, when there is no more lawlessness, but all things have been made new by the Lord. Then we will be able to sanctify it, after we ourselves have been sanctified first. 8 Finally, he says to them, "I cannot stand your new moons and your sabbaths."[86] See what he means. The present Sabbaths are not acceptable to me, but what I have made, in which giving rest to all things, I will make a beginning of an eighth day, the beginning of another world. 9 Therefore, we also celebrate the eighth day with gladness, on which Jesus also rose from the dead and when appearing again he ascended into the heavens.

Chapter Sixteen
I will now speak to you also about the temple, since those wretches erroneously put their hope not on their God who made them, but in the building, as if it was the house of God. 2 For they consecrated him within the temple almost like the Gentiles. But learn what the Lord says to abolish that. "Who has measured the sky with his span or the earth with his hand? Have not I says the Lord? Heaven is my throne and the earth is the footstool for my feet. What kind of house will you build for me or what is the place of my rest?"[87] You

---
[80] Isa. 49:6-7.
[81] Isa. 61:1-2.
[82] Exod. 20:8; Deut. 5:12.
[83] Jer. 17:24-25.
[84] Gen. 2:2-3.
[85] Ps. 90:4; 2 Pet. 3:8.
[86] Isa. 1:13.
[87] Isa. 40:12; 66:1.

realize that their hope was in vain. 3 He says again, "Behold, those who destroyed this temple will themselves build it."[88] 4 It is happening now. For because they went to war, it was destroyed by their enemies. Now the servants of the enemies themselves will rebuild it. 5 Again it was revealed that the city and the temple and the people of Israel would be handed over. For the scripture says, "And it will be in the last days that the Lord will hand over to destruction the sheep of his pasture and the sheepfold and their tower."[89] And it took place just as the Lord said. 6 But let us inquire if there is any temple of God. Yes there is, where he says he is making and completing it. For it is written, "And it will come to pass when the week is ended that a temple of God will be gloriously built in the name of the Lord."[90] 7 I find, therefore, that there is a temple. Learn then how it will be built in the name of the Lord. Before we believed in God, the dwelling place of our heart was corrupt and weak, since it was really a temple built by hands, for it was full of idolatry and was a house of demons because we did everything that was opposed to God. 8 "But it will be built in the name of the Lord." Now, pay attention that the temple of the Lord will be gloriously built. How is this? When we received forgiveness of sins and placed our hope in the name, we became new, created again from the beginning. Therefore, God truly resides in us as his dwelling. 9 How? His word of faith, his call of promise, the wisdom of his righteous ordinances, the commandments of the teaching, he himself prophesying in us and dwelling in us who were enslaved to death, opening to us the door of the temple which is the mouth, granting us repentance. Thus he leads us into the incorruptible temple. 10 For he who desires to be saved looks not to a person but to him who dwells and speaks in him and is amazed at him. For he has never heard such words from his mouth, nor has he ever desired to hear them. This is a spiritual temple being built for the Lord.

Chapter Seventeen
As far as it is possible to set forth a simple explanation, my soul hopes to have fulfilled my desire that nothing pertaining salvation has been omitted. 2 For if I write to you concerning things present or future, you would not understand because they are set forth in parables. So these things will be sufficient.

Chapter Eighteen
Let us turn now to another area of knowledge and teaching. There are two ways of teaching and of authority, that of light and that of darkness, and there is a great difference between the two ways. Over the one are stationed light-bearing angels of God, but over the other, angels of Satan. 2 And the one is Lord from eternity to eternity, but the other is the ruler of the present time of lawlessness.

Chapter Nineteen
The way of light, therefore, is as follows. If anyone wants to follow the path to the appointed goal, let him be zealous in his works. This is the knowledge given to us to walk in such a path. 2 You will love the one who made you. You will fear the one who formed you. You will glorify the one who redeemed you from death. You will be sincere in heart and rich in spirit. You will not join with those who walk in the way of death. You will

---

[88] Isa. 49:17.
[89] 1 Enoch 89:56.
[90] Dan. 9:24; 1 Enoch 91:13.

hate everything that is not pleasing to God. You will not abandon the command of the Lord. 3 You will not exalt yourself but be humble in all things; you will not take glory for yourself. You will not receive evil counsel against your neighbor; you will not allow arrogance into your soul. 4 You will not commit sexual immorality; you will not commit adultery; you will not corrupt children. The word of God will not go out from you among the impure. You will not show partiality in rebuking anyone for transgression. You will be gentle; you will be quiet; you will tremble at the words which you have heard. You will not bear a grudge against your brother. 5 You will not be double-minded whether a thing will be or not. You will not take the name of the Lord in vain. You will love your neighbor more than your own soul. You will not murder a child in an abortion nor kill it after birth. You will not remove your hand from your son or from your daughter but will teach them the fear of God from their youth. 6 You will not covet your neighbor's things nor show greed. You will not be joined in soul with the haughty but associate with the humble and the righteous. You will receive the trials that befall you as good, knowing that nothing happens apart from God. 7 You will not be double-minded nor double-tongued. You will obey your master as a pattern of God in modesty and fear; do not bitterly command your servant or maid who hope in the same God, lest perhaps they cease to fear the God who is above you both. For he came not to call people with partiality, but those whom the Spirit prepared. 8 You will not be quick to speak because the mouth is a snare of death. So far as you can, you will be pure for the sake of your soul. 9 Be not one who holds out his hands to receive but shuts them when giving. You will love as the apple of your eye everyone who speaks to you the word of the Lord. 10 Remember the day of judgment night and day, and seek each day the company of the saints, either laboring by speech and going out to exhort or striving to save souls by the word, or working with your hands for the ransom of your sins. 11 Do not hesitate to give and when you give do not grumble, but you should know who is the good paymaster of the reward. Keep the teachings which you have received, adding nothing and subtracting nothing. Hate thoroughly the evil one. Judge righteously. 12 Do not cause divisions but bring together and reconcile those who quarrel. Confess your sins and do not go to prayer with an evil conscience. This is the way of Light.

Chapter Twenty
But the way of the Black One is crooked and full of cursing. For it is a way of eternal death with punishment, and in it are the things that destroy their soul: idolatry, audacity, arrogance of power, hypocrisy, double-heartedness, adultery, murder, robbery, pride, transgression, fraud, malice, stubbornness, sorcery, magic arts, covetousness, and lack of the fear of God. 2 They are persecutors of good people, haters of the truth, lovers of lying, who do not know the reward of righteousness, not cleaving to the good nor to righteous judgment, who pay no attention to a widow and an orphan. They are not vigilant for the fear of God but for the pursuit of vice. Gentleness and patience are far from them, loving vanity and seeking rewards; without pity for the poor; doing nothing for the oppressed. They are eager to speak evil, ignore their maker, are murderers of children, and are corrupters of God's creation. They turn away the needy and oppress the afflicted, they are advocates of the rich, they are lawless judges of the poor, altogether sinful.

Chapter Twenty-One
Therefore, it is good that for a man who has learned all the righteous commandments of the Lord written here to walk in them. For he who does these things will be glorified in the kingdom of God. He who prefers those other things will perish along with his deeds.

For this reason there is a resurrection and this is why there is a retribution. 2 I ask those of you in high positions if you will accept advice that comes from my good counsel, to keep those among you to whom you may do good. Do not fail to do this. 3 The day is near when all things will perish with the wicked one. The Lord is near as is his reward.[91] 4 I beg you again and again to be good lawgivers to another, continue to be faithful advisors to one another and to remove all hypocrisy from yourselves. 5 And may God who rules over all the world give you wisdom, understanding, perception, knowledge of his commandments, and patience. 6 Become those who are taught by God, searching out what the Lord seeks from you, and do it that you will be found worthy in the day of judgment. 7 If there is any remembrance of what is good, remember me when you think on these things, that both my desire and my vigilance may lead to a good result. I ask this of you and request it as a favor. 8 While the good vessel is still with you, do not fail in any of these things, but seek them fervently, and fulfill every commandment, for they are worthy. 9 Therefore, I have been all the more eager to write what I could to make you glad. Farewell, children of love and peace. May the Lord of glory and all grace be with your spirit.

---

[91]Cf. Isa. 40:10; Rev. 22:12.

CHAPTER NINE

Letter to Diognetus

"No text and no context!" With that starkly negative and exclamatory sentence Paul Foster begins a chapter on "The Epistle of Diognetus" (Foster, 147). These two absences (of a text and of a context) confront every modern reader of this document. So what does it mean for an ancient work to exist today without a text or a context?

THE DISCOVERY OF DIOGNETUS

One lovely day in Constantinople around the year 1436 CE, before the Turkish conquest of that Byzantine capital, a young cleric named Thomas d'Arezzo turned into a fishmonger's shop. Such a common and mundane event as this eventually led to the including of this chapter in a book about the Apostolic Fathers! Thomas noticed among a pile of materials that the shop owner was using to wrap his fish what appeared to be the leaves of a parchment codex! He rescued the manuscript and subsequent events, some of which are difficult to piece together, led eventually to its destruction in a fire in 1870 CE during one of those never-ending European wars! That destruction is what is meant by the two words, "no text," as they are applied to the *Letter to Diognetus*. Unlike the other works in this collection (except for *Papias*), no manuscript copy from the Middle Ages exists today that contains the *Letter to Diognetus*!

The bumpy career of this text, however, is not as pessimistic as it may initially appear. While the facts are a bit murky, we know that the manuscript found its way into the possession of a Roman Catholic Cardinal and after his passing it was held by the Dominicans and Carthusians in Basel. The great Renaissance humanist, Johannes Reuchlin, secured it in the early 1500s, and it was he who added a note in the margin of the manuscript describing its previous owners. From there its subsequent itinerary included a stop in a monastery in Alsace around 1560 until it finally arrived in Strasbourg, France around 1795. There in 1870 it perished as a casualty of war when the building in which it was housed was bombed! Fortunately, during its pilgrimage through Western Europe, at least three copies were made and one of those was by the Parisian scholar Henri Estienne (Stephanus, better known for his work on the Greek NT). Stephanus published the *editio princeps* of the work in 1592, based on a transcription he had made in 1586. One of the other two copies was unknown until it was rediscovered in 1880, ten years after the fiery destruction of the original! The manuscript in which it was found, along with a few other works by Justin Martyr, was known as *Codex Argentoratensis Graeca* after the Latin name of Strasbourg, *Argentoratentum*.

But what of that second negative expression mentioned by Foster? What is meant by it having "no context"? This characteristic can be explained briefly. To the great surprise of many of its modern readers, the work has left no trace or citation from any writers of the early centuries of the Church's history. No one refers to it; no one quotes it; if it was known, no mention of it has survived. While we will see that the original writings of some other ancient Christians have not survived in any copies (such as the writings of Papias to be considered in the next chapter), many fragments of those writings survive in citations and quotations in numerous other ancient writers. Another example is the *Didache*, well known among the ancients but without any manuscript evidence until its rediscovery in Constantinople in 1873. It was found in a codex copied in 1054 alongside some other known works such as those contained in this volume! But Diognetus was never quoted nor even mentioned by any ancient or medieval writer, at least in any of the surviving Christian literature.

As has been mentioned, Diognetus usually is included among the Apostolic Fathers, but occasionally it will be absent. Whatever its date, it is the only work among the Apostolic Fathers that may be classified as an "apology," or a defense of the Christian faith. In other words, while the other works in this collection are addressed to those who followed Jesus, Diognetus addresses an initial reader and subsequent readers *outside* the Christian fold. That is why some scholars prefer that the work *not* be included in the Apostolic Fathers but rather with the Apologists. The fourteenth-century manuscript in which it was found contained some works of the apologist Justin Martyr; hence the original readers of this codex read it among a collection of apologetic works. Its value had been recognized as early as 1765 when it, along with the Papias fragments, appeared in a collection of the Apostolic Fathers by A. Gallandi. Since then Diognetus usually is included in books like the one before you, although more out of tradition rather than out of certainty about its dating close to the Apostles.

THE NATURE OF DIOGNETUS

A brief work of only twelve chapters, *Diognetus* illustrates the serious concerns of Christian authors probably in the middle to latter part of the second century, including writers such as Justin Martyr, Melito of Sardis, and Athenagoras of Athens. The author offers a strong argument for the existence of the church in the midst of both opposing pagan and Jewish claims to superiority.

As has been noted, we know little about the background of the literary work, including if it was actually addressed as a letter to an individual named Diognetus. The opening line of the work indicates that initially it was directed to someone by that name, accompanied by the same adjective *kratiste* that accompanied the Theophilus addressed in Luke 1:3. Some scholars have suggested that this was the Alexandrian procurator Claudius Diogenes, who ruled at the end of the second century. But was this work originally an actual letter that was sent to a reader named Diognetus? The "letter" seems to function more as a literary epistle rather than as a personal letter. Perhaps its intended role was similar to that of "To the Hebrews" in the New Testament. One would not think that they were reading a letter if they read the first twelve chapters of Hebrews, since it looks like a letter only in the last chapter. Perhaps the author and sender of Hebrews took one of his "sermons" (cf. 13:22, "a word of exhortation") and sent it as a literary letter with more personal matters located in chapter 13. Something like that may be going on with what is called in Latin the *Epistula ad Diognetum*.

Others have suggested that *Diognetus* is actually the lost *Apology of Quadratus* that was addressed to the emperor Hadrian early in the second century, a letter whose existence we know from Eusebius of Caesarea. This suggestion, however, is based upon a measure of speculation. Because the destroyed codex included some writings of Justin Martyr, a few researchers have favored Justin as the author. Most scholars, however, reject this option, and prefer alternative writers like Melito of Sardis, Hippolytus of Rome, or Theophilus of Antioch. The most autobiographical statement in the book is 11.1, "I am not preaching strange things, nor asking irrational questions, but as a disciple of the apostles, I am now becoming a teacher of Gentiles." From this statement some have even tried to provide a name for the otherwise anonymous author, that is, *Mathetes*, the Greek word translated "disciple." However, on the basis of this verse, we could just as quickly give him the name *Didaskalos*, the Greek word for "teacher." In a well-argued volume, Charles Hill proposed that the author of Diognetus was the better-known Polycarp, whose valuable letter to the Philippians was discussed earlier, as well as the work describing his martyrdom. Few scholars, however, have felt the force of his case for Polycarp as the author (Hill, *From the Lost Teaching of Polycarp*). In the end, we must conclude that both the author and the date must remain uncertain. A safe approach is to attribute it to an unknown Christian writer who penned it in the latter half of the second century.

The twelve chapters of Diognetus may possibly be a compilation of two originally different works. The "epistle" itself, which seeks to defend the validity of the Christian faith in the midst of its religious competition, seems to extend from the beginning of the text through chapter 10, which ends abruptly in mid-sentence. The authorial treatment of the Father in chapter 10 supposes a corresponding treatment of the Son, which is not given in the text that survives. The rest of Diognetus' material (chs. 11–12) appears to be more of a homily expounding the theme of "The Word of God" or the *Logos*. Other features point to some differences between the sections. The "you" singular of the pagan addressed in the first part is then replaced by the "you" plural of a community addressed. The final two chapters seem to presuppose a familiarity with Christian vocabulary rather than the apologetic appeal to unbelievers without such knowledge in the first part. The argument of the second part is based on a reading of Gen. 2–3 while there is no appeal to the Old Testament in the first part. The transition from one section to the next was marked in our manuscript tradition by an empty space, perhaps suggesting the end of one text and the beginning of another. Thus both the theme and literary style of the writing change as *Diognetus* comes to a conclusion in its final two chapters. Some have suggested, however, because of some actual similarities in style, that both sections may be from the same author, who spliced them together himself (Barnard, 170-1). The above "Logos doctrine," along with additional evidences of "Johannine theology," plus the similar usages of the important word "faith" comprise common themes that are shared between the two sections of 1–10 and 11–12. I personally think that this last argument for unity is the best approach to this issue.

Like the other apologies that are known from early Christian literature, *Diognetus* follows the impassioned concerns of a well-informed author who is attempting to convince his audience of the truth of Christianity as the much better alternative to both paganism and Judaism. While it is possible that the work was addressed to an actual person named Diognetus, it could be that our author intended the work for anyone who might be inquiring about the validity of this new movement that had recently appeared on the world scene. In any case, *Diognetus* is written in a literary Koine Greek that has earned the admiration of many readers for its rhetorical style. Its high register of Greek is probably an indication of a literary education, and the eloquence of its style is certainly the "best" to be found in the other Apostolic Fathers and even among the Apologists. Many authors have cited J.B. Lightfoot's accolade that it is "the noblest and most impressive of early Christian apologies in style and treatment" (Lightfoot, 488). Other tributes come from Neander, "among the finest remains of Christian antiquity"; and Norden, "one of the most brilliant things ever written by Christians in the Greek language" (Barnard, 172). More recently, Bird and Mackerass conclude, "This *Diognetus* is something of a sublime crescendo in early Christian literature" (Bird and Harrower, 310).

A SURVEY OF DIOGNETUS

The opening chapters of *Diognetus* are concerned with what the writer considers as the foolishness of both Jewish and pagan religious ideas and practices. The author is also aware that the "newness" of Christianity requires an explanation. He is aware that Romans deeply valued age and tradition in their religious life and he is certainly cognizant that Judaism went back well over a millennium. In this writer's opinion, he does not directly address that "problem" but launches into a rather pointed attack on the Roman gods in chapter 2 and the religious practices of the Jews in chapters 3 and 4. If modern readers are looking for a polite "ecumenical" dialogue, they will not find it here. To put it bluntly, Diognetus asserts that pagans worship dead idols that are created by human beings, not deities who observe humans from afar and occasionally push into their affairs! Furthermore, even though Jews could be viewed as more spiritually related to Christians, our author declares that they now participate in empty customs and rituals. It appears that the late arrival of Christianity is intended to replace the failed efforts of paganism and Judaism.

Christians are distinctly better, however, and chapters 5 and following explain how they are both different and better, because they inhabit this world as the soul resides in the body. His description of the distinguishing traits of Christians is better appreciated by a simple reading of this effort at eloquence of the author, rather than a description of it. "Christians are not distinguished from the rest of humanity by country nor language nor customs. They do not dwell in cities of their own, nor do they use a special language, nor practice a peculiar way of life" (5.1–2). On he goes offering surprising characteristics that opponents would not expect. Ancient readers are to know that Christians are not threat to the empire and in many ways are quite ordinary. They are not subversive but are obedient to the laws (5.10). Despite their innocence of any diabolical crimes, they are still mistreated, although their opponents do not really know why they hate this new breed of humans (5.17). While non-Christians are being addressed, early Christian readers, assuming there were any, were helped in framing their own social and spiritual identity by these rhetorical efforts.

In an oft-quoted section in chapter 6, the author describes in a rhetorically effective manner the character of Christians as they live out that role of the world's "soul." "Briefly, what the soul is in the body Christians are in the world" (6.1). The soul is different but still somehow joined with the body. The expression often heard that believers "are in the world but not of the world" is not far different from the analogy of Diognetus. They are rejected for their beliefs and actions but remain true to their God and their calling which is reflected in their different but consistent lifestyles. "Such is the position to which God has appointed them, and it would not be right to abandon it" (6.10). Christians are people on earth like everyone else, but because they belong to Christ, they are even at this moment citizens of heaven. Therefore, they surpass the other citizens of the world in both their existence and their conduct, even as the soul surpasses the body in which it temporarily dwells.

Chapters 7 and 8 consist of concise instruction regarding the divine origin of the Christian faith which was revealed through the Son of God and that he is commending to Diognetus. God the Father sent to mankind "the very craftsman and maker of all things, by whom he created the heavens, by whom he enclosed the sea inside its boundaries, whose mysteries all the elements of creation guard carefully … Him he sent to them" (7.2). There is a break in the manuscript at 7.6–7, which is even noted by the scribe who must have known that the break was there in his exemplar. The question, "Do you not see …" is inserted at the beginning of 7.7, following the example that begins the next verse. Chapter 8 continues to expound on the one sent from God. God manifested his divinity through this one called His "beloved *child*" (8.9–11). While *Did.* 9.2; 10.2 and *Barn.* 9.2 use the Greek noun *pais* in the Isaianic/Septuagintal nuance of "servant," we cannot assume that *Diognetus* used it in that more "Hebraic" sense (see also its meaning of "servant" in Acts 3–4). The God of the Christians is also omnipotent, the Creator of all, as well as being invisible and good. By this admittedly powerful rhetoric, he critiques the various Greek philosophical conceptions of God and substantiates the faith and life of Christians. These are incredibly lofty thoughts but to the sincere author, this is not just rhetoric, it is the truth!

In regard to the question he asked in chapter 1 about why Christianity should appear so late in time, the author has a simple answer. The kingdom appeared late because God desired to show mankind its helplessness and its need of redemption (9.1, the longest verse in the book, nearly 100 words!). Our author is more than a dramatic preacher who must have been able to hold an audience's attention; he was also an excellent theologian. The eloquence and power of the writer's words are put to good use in what is the most soteriological passage in the book. If his readers and hearers were not converted through this message, they must have been stirred by the following words.

> Oh, how great are God's love and kindness! Instead of hating and rejecting us and bearing a grudge for our sins, he was compassionate and forbearing and took upon himself our sins. He gave his own son as a ransom for us who were sinful; he gave up the holy one; for the wicked the innocent one; the just one for the unjust ones; the incorruptible one for the corruptible; and the immortal one for the mortal. For what else could have covered our sins but his righteousness? In whom else except in the son of God alone could we lawless and sinful be justified? O the sweet exchange! O the incomprehensible creation! O the unexpected blessings, that in the just one the sin of many should be hidden, that the righteousness of one should justify many sinners.
> (9.2–5)

These powerful words, however, reflect more than just a lofty rhetorical style. They also provide evidence for a second-century view of justification that speaks to modern debates about such ideas as imputed or incorporated righteousness. Such ideas were not invented by sixteenth-century theologians but are possibly reflected in this second-century writer! The distinct echoes here of Pauline passages such as Rom. 5:18-19 have led one scholar to this conclusion. "Given the Pauline resonances in *Diogn.* 9, the author's focus on the Son's righteousness may be an example of an early Christian interpretation of Rom. 5" (Crowe, 109).

In his conclusion, at least to this part of the book, our author fervently exhorts Diognetus directly, in what ancient rhetoricians termed a *peroratio*, to accept the Christian faith and its Savior (ch. 10). When Diognetus "gains this knowledge" (10.3), it will be manifested in joy and love. Some writers have observed the influence of Gnosticism in his use of word "knowledge." The *gnosis* here, however, is not secret nor attained through any of the Gnostic emanations but manifests itself in concrete love of one's neighbor in this world but with an eye always on heavenly truths. The eloquence of the author is again on display in this appeal.

> And with what joy do you think you will be filled when you come to know these things? And how you will love him who first loved you? And when you love him, you will be an imitator of his kindness. Do not marvel that a person may become an imitator of God. He is able if he desires it. You know that there is no real happiness in ruling over your neighbors, or in desiring to have more than the weak, or in being rich and able to order those in need. It is not in such ways that a person can imitate God, for these things are not part of his greatness. Rather anyone can be an imitator of God if he takes up the burden of his neighbors, if he chooses to use his own abundance to help someone who is in need, if he takes what he has received from God and gives to those who are in need. For such a person becomes God to those who are helped. When you have faith you will see that God is ruling in heaven even though you are on earth, and then you will begin to speak about the mysteries of God. You will love and admire those who suffer because they refuse to deny God. You will condemn the deception and error of the world when you recognize the true life of heaven, and despise the apparent death in this world, and fear the real death reserved for those who are condemned to the eternal fire which will torment to the end those who are given over to it.
>
> (10.3–7)

In other words, "(Christians) do not seek to lord it over others (10.5), but to become a god—in the sense of benefaction and beneficence—to their neighbors (10.6)" (Bird and Mackerass, 325).

In chapters 11–12 the author turns from addressing an individual to exhorting a group of hearers, possibly reflecting another text or a sermon that he appended to his personal appeal in chapters 1–10. He expounds on Christ as the living witness of God's concern for humanity. Earlier in the second century, 2 Clement preserves what is probably the earliest reference to both the testaments together in 14.2: "the scrolls and the apostles" (*ta biblia kai hoi apostoloi*). In this final section Diognetus also contains a reference to the contents of both testaments in the following elegant description. "And so the fear of the Law is sung, and the grace of the prophets is known, and the faith of the Gospels is established, and the tradition of the Apostles is guarded, and the joy of the Church leaps" (11.6). He thus refers first to the Law and the Prophets (i.e., the Old Testament), and then to the Gospels and the (writings of) the Apostles (i.e., the New Testament).

The so-called "Logos doctrine" is prominent in these two chapters. The Logos is eternal, from the beginning, and yet ever young so as to be born in the saints. As the Son the Logos enriches the saints by revealing and increasing grace among them. The incarnate Logos speaks to those whom he wills and he is always the teacher of the saints (12.9). Therefore, both the historic incarnation and the continual spiritual presence of the Logos are linked together.

Diognetus concludes his more "sermonic" section with a vivid comparison. Just as Christ was sent to deliver mankind from sin and death, so God also has planted a "love garden" where all believers can now partake of the fruit of salvation.

Let your heart be knowledge and your life be the true Logos, fully understood. Bearing the tree of this truth and picking its fruit, you will always harvest that which God desires and **which the serpent cannot touch. Eve is not corrupted but a virgin is trusted. Salvation is made known and the Apostles are instructed, and the Lord's Passover goes forward, and the seasons are gathered together and all things arranged in order. By teaching the saints the Logos rejoices. Through Him the Father is glorified.** To Him be the glory forever. Amen.

(12.7–9)

I have quoted the above passage instead of just referring the reader to the entire translated text below for the following reason. The rhetorical flourish concluding the book demonstrates a concluding rhyme called *homoioteleuton*. Verses 8b and 9a consist of no less than eleven consecutive clauses, each with a verb ending in *-tai* (-ται). These clauses have been bolded but the reader of Greek can also appreciate the following layout:

ὄφις οὐχ **ἅπτεται**
οὐδὲ πλάνη **συγχρωτίζεται**
οὐδὲ Εὕα **φθείρεται**
ἀλλὰ παρθένος **πιστεύεται**
καὶ σωτήριον **δείκνυται**
καὶ ἀπόστολοι **συνετίζονται**
καὶ τὸ κυρίου πάσχα **προέρχεται**
καὶ καιροὶ **συνάγονται**
καὶ μετὰ κόσμου **ἁρμόζονται**
καὶ διδάσκων ἁγίους ὁ λόγος **εὐφραίνεται**
δι' οὗ πατὴρ **δοξάζεται**.

This rhetorical flourish ending the book exemplifies the ways that Diognetus qualifies as the most literary of the Apostolic Fathers.

INTERTEXTUALITY OF DIOGNETUS

Treatments of a religious text usually include a section on its "intertextuality" or its "reception of other sacred texts." With Diognetus, this section will be short. The Old Testament is not explicitly cited, and there are few passages that could be influenced by OT concepts. Humans are made in the image of God (10.2/Gen. 1:26-27). The "paradise of delight" (12.1–3) may be influenced by Gen. 2:8-9. The New Testament is clearly cited only once (1 Cor. 8:1 in 2.5), but numerous hints of Pauline and Johannine themes appear in chapters 5–12. Diognetus 8.5 states that no one has seen God (cf. John 1:18). The numerous references to the "Logos" in chapters 11–12 definitely could be influenced by the appearance of the word in John 1. Pauline thought may be echoed in the revelation of mysteries in chapters 7–8. The salvation of sinners through God's love and kindness in the gift of His Son (ch. 9) certainly echoes similar Pauline affirmations, although these are *loci communes* found often in Christian thought!

The conclusion of the most recent commentator on this book offers a fair summary of this important issue.

The text of *Diognetus* is chiefly dependent on Pauline texts and themes and on a Logos Christology that is likewise evident within Johannine literature. The author is aware of a broad variety of literature that now appears in the NT but places no particular emphasis on anything beyond these two traditions. So too, the work reveals knowledge of numerous OT passages and themes, but once again makes no effort to incorporate any of these as the basis of reflection with the single exception of the "fall narrative" of Genesis 3 that appears in the final chapter.

(Jefford, *Diognetus*, 126)

THE RECIPIENT, DIOGNETUS

As is the case with other second-century apologetic works, an individual is addressed as the initial recipient. The name Diognetus is addressed accompanied by the epithet "most excellent" (*kratiste*). This name was not unknown in Greek literature and means "born of Zeus." This elevated title has led some to conclude that he was a high-ranking official and/or member of some Roman administration. It has often been suggested that he was the tutor of Marcus Aurelius who was mentioned by that emperor in his *Meditations* 1, 6. As mentioned earlier, another possible candidate was a procurator of Alexandria around 200 CE mentioned in some papyri of the period. Many have preferred the idea that Diognetus was simply a "literary name," a pagan who was invented for the purpose of the apology. This is also possibly the function of "Theophilus" in the New Testament volumes (Acts 1:1; with same title in Luke 1:3). The value of the work as an apologetic treatise is not really affected by the reality of any specific person with the name, Diognetus.

VALUE OF DIOGNETUS

What can be concluded with certainty about this evidently ancient document that almost seems predestined to be ignored, lost, and destroyed? More than one modern commentator has observed that in only a few well-constructed chapters the anonymous author has addressed many of the basic issues covered in the typical early Christian apologies. These are such vital subjects as (1) the folly of false religions, (2) the preeminence of Christianity, (3) the need for repentance, and (4) the hope of eternal salvation through Christ and the love of God. This document deserves its rank among the most brilliant and most eloquent works of Christian literature that survives in the Greek language. The author's rhetorical style and sentence structure are full of balance and charm. His words sparkle with vitality that expresses a wide knowledge and a vital faith. It is sad that it seems not to have left a trail among its readers.

Despite its many deserved accolades, there are some shortcomings in this significant work. Because his Greek is so good and his rhetoric so powerful, it is easy to overlook what, in my opinion, is the biggest flaw in the work. I mention his lack of any substantive engagement with the Old Testament writings. One author suggested that his "negative judgment of Judaism" as the cause (Lona, 200). That, however, is not an adequate explanation since the *Letter of Barnabas*, whose low view of Judaism is even more infamous, constantly draws on the OT even when he is using it to castigate the Jews! In defense of Diognetus, someone else may point to its purpose being apologetic and not expository. The contemporary apologist Justin Martyr, however, constantly appeals to Old Testament prophecy and fulfillment in his *First and Second Apologies*, to say nothing of his *Dialogue with Trypho*! I must conclude, therefore, that the author's lack of attention to the writings in that Older Testament is a flaw in his otherwise powerful argument for the superiority of the Christian way. Could this lack also be a possible contributing factor to why the work left no trail in the church until its recovery in the fifteenth century?

So we are still left with the description of Diognetus with which we began. It is a work without both a "text" that survives intact and a work that left no "context" among its possible contemporaries and readers. What circumstances that preserved this work through the centuries are unknown and rather puzzling, to say the least. What it does testify to, however, is the appeal of a gifted rhetorician presenting rationally the superior role of the Christian faith to both the Gentile and Jewish worlds. In the end he presents a rigorous faith worthy of some serious consideration by all ancient and modern readers.

FURTHER READING ON DIOGNETUS AND QUADRATUS

Andriessen, Paul. "The Authorship of the *Epistula ad Diognetum*." Vigiliae Christianae 1 (1947). 129–36.

Barnard, L. W. "The Enigma of the Epistle to Diognetus" in *Studies in the Apostolic Fathers and Their Background*, 165–73. New York. Schocken Books, 1966.

Bird, Michael F. and Kirsten H. Mackerass. "The Epistle to Diognetus and the Fragment of Quadratus" in *The Cambridge Companion to the Apostolic Fathers*, ed. Michael Bird and Scott Harrower, 309–31. Cambridge. Cambridge University Press, 2021.

Crowe, Brandon D. "O Sweet Exchange! The Soteriological Significance of the Incarnation in the Epistle to Diognetus." *Zeitschrift für die neutestamentliche Wissenschaft und die Kunde der älteren Kirche* 102, no. 1 (2011). 96–109.

Foster, Paul. "The Apology of Quadratus" and "The Epistle to Diognetus" in *The Writings of the Apostolic Fathers*, ed. Paul Foster, 147–56. London and New York. T&T Clark, 2007.

Grant, R. M. *Greek Apologists of the Second Century*. Philadelphia. Westminster, 1988.

Hill, Charles E. *From the Lost Teaching of Polycarp. Identifying Irenaeus' Apostolic Presbyter and the Author of* Ad Diognetum. WUNT 2.186. Tübingen. Mohr Siebeck, 2006.

Jefford, Clayton. *The Epistle to Diognetus (with the Fragment of Quadratus). Introduction, Text, and Commentary*. Oxford Apostolic Fathers. Oxford. Oxford University Press, 2013.

Lightfoot, J.B. *The Apostolic Fathers*, ed. J. R. Harmer. New York. Macmillan and Co., 1893.

Lona, Horacio E. "Diognetus" in *The Apostolic Fathers*, ed. Wilhelm Pratscher, 197–213. Waco, TX. Baylor University Press, 2010.

Meecham, Henry G. *The Epistle to Diognetus. The Greek Text with Introduction, Translation and Notes*. Manchester. University of Manchester Press, 1949.

DIOGNETUS

The more elegant style of Diognetus' Greek requires at times a functional equivalent rather than a formal equivalent style of translation. Many of the complex sentences are broken down into shorter ones.

Chapter One
Most excellent Diognetus, I see that you are very eager to learn about the religion of the Christians. Your inquiries in regard to them are composed with great clarity and concern. You ask a number of questions. In what God do they believe? How does their worship of him help all of them to disregard the world and to despise death? Why do they neither recognize the gods considered so by the Greeks nor observe the observances of the Jews?

What is the character of the love that they have for one another? And why is it that this new race or way of living has now come into existence in our time and not before? 2 I welcome this eagerness of yours, and I pray to God who enables us both to speak and to hear so that I may be enabled to speak so you may profit from listening, and that you may listen so that, after I have spoken, I may have no regrets.

Chapter Two
Come then and purge yourself from all the prejudices that clutter your mind and leave behind any habit of thought that is leading you into error. You must begin by being, as it were, a new person, as you yourself admit, ready to hear a new message. You must take a look not only with your eyes, but with your intellect, at what you call and regard as gods, and ask: What substance or form do they really have? 2 Is not this one made of stone, like that under our feet, and another of bronze, no better than the utensils forged for our use? Is not another made of wood and already rotting away, and another of silver and in need of a guard lest it be stolen? Is not another made of iron corroded by rust, and still another of clay no more attractive than what is made for the lowliest service? 3 Are not all of them made of destructible matter, or forged with iron and fire? Was not this one made by either a sculptor, or a coppersmith, or a silversmith, or a potter? Could any of them not have been changed into any other shape before it was given its form by one or another of these craftsmen? And given the right artisans, could not any of these utensils be turned into gods from the same material just like these? 4 And could not any of these gods worshipped by you be once more formed by human hands into utensils similar to the rest? Are they not all deaf and blind and lifeless and unable to perceive and to move? Are they not all rotting and decaying? 5 You call these things gods; you serve these things; you bow down before these things; and in the end you become like they are. 6 Is this the reason why you hate the Christians, because they refuse to consider these objects as gods? 7 But do you who now esteem and worship them despise them much more than the Christians do? You leave the gods of stone and clay which you worship unguarded, while at night you lock up the gods of silver and gold and set guards over them by day lest they be stolen. Do you then not ridicule and insult them much more than the Christians do? 8 And so with the honors you imagine that you pay them. If they are aware of them, you insult them; if they are insensible, you convict them, while you are worshipping them with the blood and fat of your sacrifices. 9 Imagine one of you submitting to this or allowing anything of this sort to happen to him! There is no one who would endure such punishment willingly, for the simple reason that he can feel and think. But a stone endures it because it feels nothing. And so you prove that it cannot perceive. 10 I could say many other things about Christians not being enslaved to such gods as these, but if anyone finds what I have said insufficient, I think it is useless to say more.

Chapter Three
The next issue I think you are anxious to hear is about why Christians do not worship in the same way as the Jews. 2 The Jews indeed, so far as they abstain from the worship I just mentioned, are right in claiming to worship one God and Master over all; but as they worship God in ways like those just mentioned, they go astray. 3 If the Greeks give evidence of their foolishness by making offerings to images that can neither see nor hear, so the Jews, in making the same offerings to God as though he needed them, should think this foolishness rather than reverence. 4 For he who made heaven and earth and

all that is in them[1] and provides us all with what we need, could not himself need the very things which he gives to those who think they are giving to him. 5 As for those who think they can offer him sacrifices with blood and fat and burnt offerings, and by such honors are honoring him, they differ in nothing, it seems to me, from those who show the same respect to deaf images. The latter think they can give to beings unable to receive the honor; the former desire to give to one who needs nothing.

Chapter Four
Now I doubt that you need any instructions from me about certain superstitions that call for no discussion, such as their scruples in regard to meat, their observance of the Sabbath days, their pride about circumcision, and the postured observance of their fasting and new moons. 2 For how can it be other than irreligious to receive some of the things which God has created for men's use and to reject others, as though some were created for good purposes and others were useless and superfluous? 3 And how can it be other than impious to lie against God, pretending that he has forbidden us to do a good deed on the Sabbath day? 4 And is it not ridiculous to be proud about mutilation of the flesh as a sign of election, as if they were particularly loved by God? 5 Consider again their constant watching of the stars and the moon in order to mark the observance of months and days, and to commemorate the seasons ordained by God and the changes of the seasons according to their own inclinations, making some into feasts and others into times of mourning. Who would look on all this as evidence of religion and not much more as foolishness? 6 So then I think I have said enough to show you how right the Christians are in abstaining from the general silliness and deception and fussiness and pride of the Jews. But as to the mystery of their (the Christians) own way of worship, you must not expect to learn from any human.

Chapter Five
Christians are not distinguished from the rest of humanity by country nor language nor customs. 2 They do not dwell in cities of their own, nor do they use a special language, nor practice a peculiar way of life. 3 Their teaching has not been discovered by the wisdom or reflection of inquisitive people, nor are they outstanding in human learning as are some. 4 Whether living in a Greek or a barbarian city, they follow local customs in clothing, in diet, and in the rest of life; yet the character of the citizenship they demonstrate is wonderful and admittedly unusual. 5 They live in their own countries, but as strangers there. They participate in all duties like citizens and suffer all hardships like foreigners. Every foreign country is theirs and every country is a foreign land. 6 They marry like everyone and have children, but they do not expose their offspring. 7 They share a table, but not a common bed. 8 They happen to be in the flesh, but they do not live according to the flesh. 9 They live on earth, but their citizenship is in heaven. 10 They obey the appointed laws, but in their private lives they surpass the laws. 11 They love all people but are persecuted by all people. 12 They are unknown, but yet they are condemned. They are put to death yet they are brought to life. 13 They are poor, but they make many rich. They are in need of everything, and yet in everything they abound. 14 They are dishonored, yet they are glorified in their dishonor. They are slandered, yet they are vindicated. 15 They are cursed, and yet they bless. They are insulted, yet they offer respect. 16 When they do

---

[1] Psa. 146:6; cf. Acts 14:15.

good, they are punished as evildoers. When they are punished, they rejoice as receiving life. 17 They are attacked by the Jews as foreigners and they are persecuted by the Greeks, yet those who hate them cannot state a reason for their hostility.

Chapter Six
Briefly, what the soul is in the body Christians are in the world. 2 The soul is spread through all the members of the body, and Christians are spread through all the cities of the world. 3 The soul dwells in the body, and yet it is not of the body. So Christians dwell in the world, but are not of the world. 4 The soul which is confined in the visible body is invisible. In the same way, Christians are known as being in the world, but their religion remains invisible. 5 The flesh hates the soul and wages war on it, because it is hindered from indulging in its pleasures. The world also hates Christians, not that they have done it wrong, but because they oppose its pleasures. 6 The soul loves the flesh that hates it and its members, and Christians love those who hate them. 7 The soul has been locked up in the body, but it holds the body together. So Christians are confined in the world as in a prison, yet in fact they sustain the world. 8 The immortal soul dwells in a mortal tent, so Christians sojourn amid perishable things, but they wait for the imperishable things in heaven. 9 When the soul is mistreated in food and drink, it becomes all the better. So, when Christians are mistreated daily, they increase even more. 10 Such is the position to which God has appointed them, and it would not be right to abandon it.

Chapter Seven
For it was no earthly discovery that was given to them, nor is it a mortal thought that they feel bound to guard so jealously, nor have they been entrusted with the administration of human mysteries. 2 But the all-powerful Creator of all things, the invisible God himself, from heaven placed among them the seed of truth and of holy thought which cannot be comprehended by humans, and he firmly established it in their hearts. He did not send a servant or a ruler or principality, whether of those that direct the affairs of earth or of those entrusted with heavenly affairs, but he sent the very craftsman and maker of all things, by whom he created the heavens, by whom he enclosed the sea in its proper boundaries, he whose mysterious laws all the elements faithfully guard, and by whom the measures of the length of days were given to the sun to guard, he whom the moon obeys when he commands it to shine by night and whom the stars obey by following the course of the moon, he by whom all things are set in order and given their boundaries and told to obey—the heavens and the things in heaven, the earth and the things in the earth, the sea and the things in the sea, fire and air and abyss, the things in the heights and in the depths and those that are in between. Him he sent to them. 3 Do you really think, as might be humanly possible, that he sent him to impose his tyranny with fear and terror? 4 Certainly not. He came in gentleness and humility. He sent him as a king would send a son and king. He sent him as God for the sake of men. 5 In sending him, he acted as a Savior, appealing to persuasion and not to power, for God does not use force. He acted as one inviting, not as one pursuing; to show his love, not to judge. 6 Later he will send him as a judge, and then who will be able to withstand His coming? ... 7 [Do you not see][2] them thrown to wild beasts to make them deny their Lord, and yet they are

---

[2]There is a break in the manuscript at this point, which was even noted by the copyist. The question, "Do you not see ..." is inserted, following the example that begins the next verse.

not overcome? 8 Do you not see that the more of them who are punished, the more they grow in number? 9 Such things do not look like the works of men; these things are the power of God; these things are the proofs of his coming.

Chapter Eight
Was there one among all mankind who understood what God was like before he came? 2 Perhaps you prefer to accept the empty and silly professions of those pretentious philosophers! One group of them said that God was fire. What they call God is the place to which they are likely to go! Another group said God was water; a third one of the other elements created by God. And yet if any one of these arguments is acceptable, there is no reason why any one of the other created things should not also have an equal claim to be God. 4 The fact is that all these ideas are an illusion and deceit of impostors. 5 Not one of them has seen or known him but God revealed himself to them. 6 He revealed himself by means of faith, for by this alone it is possible to see God. 7 For God, the Master and Creator of all who made all things and set them in order, was not merely benevolent, but also patient. 8 He always was and is and will be kind and good and free from anger and true and he alone is good. 9 The great and inexpressible idea which he conceived, he communicated to his child alone. 10 For a time he did keep the plan of his wisdom to himself and guarded it as a mystery, appearing to have no concern and thought for us. 11 But through his beloved child he removed the veil and revealed what he had prepared from the beginning. He then gave us all at once to see and to understand his kindly acts. Who among us would have ever expected these things?

Chapter Nine
By himself and with his child, his providence planned everything. If, for a time before he came, he permitted us to be carried along by our own impulses being led astray by pleasures and lusts, it was not because he took any delight in our sins, but he merely permitted them. He did not approve of that former period of our iniquity, but he was preparing the present season of righteousness. He wanted us who, by our own former sins, were convicted of being unworthy, to now become worthy of life by the goodness of God. He wanted us who proved that on our own we could be able, by the power of God, to enter into the kingdom of God. 2 Once our unrighteousness was full and overflowing, and it was clear that nothing but punishment and death as the wages of sin were to be expected, the time came which God had decided. Finally he revealed His goodness and power. Oh, how great are God's love and kindness! Instead of hating and rejecting us and bearing a grudge for our sins, he was compassionate and forbearing and took upon himself our sins. He gave his own son as a ransom for us who were sinful; he gave up the holy one; for the wicked the innocent one; the just one for the unjust ones; the incorruptible one for the corruptible; and the immortal one for the mortal. 3 For what else could have covered our sins but his righteousness? 4 In whom else except in the son of God alone could we lawless and sinful ones be justified? 5 O the sweet exchange! O the incomprehensible creation! O the unexpected blessings, that in the just one the sin of many should be hidden, that the righteousness of one should justify many sinners. In the former time he proved the inability of our nature to attain life and having now revealed a savior powerful to save the powerless. For both these reasons he wanted us to believe in his goodness and to regard Him as guardian, father, teacher, counselor, physician, mind, light, honor, glory, strength, life, and to not worry about clothing and food.

Chapter Ten

If only you desire this faith, you can have it if you first acquire the full knowledge of the Father. 2 For God loved human beings and for their sake made the world and all things on earth subject to them. He gave them their reason and their mind and they alone he permitted to look up to him. He formed them in his own image and to them he sent his only son. To them he promised a kingdom in heaven and he will give it to those who love him. 3 And with what joy do you think you will be filled when you come to know these things? And how you will love him who first loved you? 4 And when you love him, you will be an imitator of his kindness. Do not marvel that a person may become an imitator of God. He is able if he desires it. 5 You know that there is no real happiness in ruling over your neighbors, or in desiring to have more than the weak, or in being rich and able to order those in need. It is not in such ways that a person can imitate God, for these things are not part of his greatness. 6 Rather anyone can be an imitator of God if he takes up the burden of his neighbors, if he chooses to use his own abundance to help someone who is in need, if he takes what he has received from God and gives to those who are in need. For such a person becomes God to those who are helped. 7 When you have faith you will see that God is ruling in heaven even though you are on earth, and then you will begin to speak about the mysteries of God. You will love and admire those who suffer because they refuse to deny God. You will condemn the deception and error of the world when you recognize the true life of heaven, and despise the apparent death in this world, and fear the real death reserved for those who are condemned to the eternal fire which will torment to the end those who are given over to it. 8 When you have faith you will admire those who for the sake of righteousness endure the temporal fire, and you will consider them blessed when you know that other fire. ...[3]

Chapter Eleven

I am not preaching strange things, nor asking irrational questions, but as a disciple of the apostles, I am now becoming a teacher of Gentiles. To those who are becoming disciples of the truth I am trying to be a worthy minister of the teachings that have been handed down. 2 Is there anyone who has been rightly taught and become a friend of the Logos, who is not anxious to learn as clearly as he can the lessons openly taught by the Logos to the disciples? The Logos appeared and revealed the truth, although not understood by unbelievers, but speaking at length to the disciples about his mysteries. Furthermore, those who were regarded by him to be faithful learned the mysteries of the Father. 3 For this reason he sent the Logos, that he might appear to the world. Dishonored by the people, he was preached by apostles and believed by Gentiles. 4 This is the one who was from the beginning, who appeared as new but proved to be old and always young as he is born in the hearts of saints. 5 This is the Eternal One, who today is considered a son, through whom the church is enriched, and among the saints and unfolding grace is multiplied. This grace provides understanding, reveals mysteries, announces seasons, rejoices over the faithful, is given to those who seek, to those by whom pledges of faith are not broken and the boundaries of the fathers are not transgressed. 6 And so the fear of the law is sung, and the grace of the prophets is known, and the faith of the gospels is established, and the tradition of the apostles is guarded, and the grace of the church

---

[3] A gap is indicated in the manuscript at this point.

leaps for joy. 7 If you do not grieve at this grace, you will understand what the Logos says through whomever he chooses and when he wishes. 8 We have been prompted to express with difficulty whatever was the will of the commanding Logos, through the love of the things revealed to us we are becoming partners with you.

Chapter Twelve
Now that you know and have listened eagerly to these truths, you will learn what God grants to those who love him properly. You have become a paradise of delight, a flourishing tree bearing every fruit, growing up and adorned with various fruits. 2 For in this field were planted a tree of knowledge and a tree of life, but it is not the tree of knowledge but disobedience that kills. 3 For the scriptures record how God from the beginning planted "a tree of knowledge and a tree of life in the middle of Paradise,"[4] revealing that life is through knowledge. Those who did not use it purely in the beginning became naked through the deceit of the snake. 4 For life is not apart from knowledge nor sound knowledge apart from true life. For this reason each tree was planted next to the other. 5 When the apostle saw the power of this, blaming the knowledge exercised without the truth of the command that leads to life, he says, "Knowledge puffs up, but love builds up."[5] 6 For the one who claims to know something apart from the true knowledge attested by life, knows nothing. He is deceived by the snake because he has not loved life. But the one who has knowledge with reverence and seeks after life plants in hope and expects fruit. 7 Let your heart be knowledge and your life be the true and fully understood Logos. 8 If you bear this tree and pick its fruit, you will always harvest what God desires and which the serpent cannot touch. Eve is not corrupted but a virgin is trusted. 9 Salvation is made known and the apostles are instructed, and the Lord's Passover goes forward, and the seasons are gathered together and all things are arranged in order. By teaching the saints the Logos rejoices. Through him the Father is glorified. To Him be the glory forever. Amen.

QUADRATUS

Reference was made in the discussion of *Diognetus* to the more well-known *Apology of Quadratus*. The only section of that second-century apologetic tract that survives is in a quotation by Eusebius. That fourth-century historian considered Quadratus as a "man of understanding and of Apostolic faith." He has been reputed as the first Christian to write an *apology* or a reasoned defense of the Christian faith, and Eusebius asserts that he addressed that appeal to the Emperor Hadrian (117–35 CE). Jerome preserves a later tradition that he was the bishop of Athens, but he may have confused him with the Quadratus who was bishop in that city in the late second century. Some scholars also have suggested that his work was part of the above *Letter to Diognetus*, and that the brief quotation, along with other material, was originally in that missing section of Diognetus mentioned previously, between 10.6 and 7 (Andriessen, 136). While falling short of any measure of certainty, Andriessen's suggestion is probably the best proposal about authorship that has been offered.

---

[4] Gen. 2:17; 3:24.
[5] 1 Cor. 8:1.

As was mentioned, Quadratus' book, titled *Apology for the Christian Religion*, only survives in citations by later writers. The largest of these quotations is from Eusebius and reads as follows.

> The works of our Savior were always present for they were true. Both those who were healed of their diseases and those who rose from the dead were not only seen when they were healed and raised up, but they were constantly present. Nor did they remain only during the life of the Savior, but also a long time after his departure. Some of them have survived even down to our own times.
>
> (*EH* iv, 3)

This reference to those who experienced the healing miracles of Jesus may have been intended to indicate the superiority of Jesus' healings to some other miracle worker. The fact that this specific type of argument was not later used by other Christian apologists may also work against the effort to identity *Quadratus* with *Diognetus*. Finally, it would involve another set of miracles altogether to imagine that those healed by Jesus around 30 CE would still be alive in 120 CE! "Quadratus' main concern is to defend the veracity and efficacy of Jesus' miracles" (Bird and Mackerass, 329). This theme will be picked up by the later apologists, Justin Martyr and Irenaeus, who apply the argument from lasting miracles to various contexts (see Foster, 58–9).

What can be said about the value of a such a small surviving fragment of a larger work? It was hard for the religious leaders of Jesus' day to deny his "miraculous" healings, so they provided another explanation (Matt. 10:22-24). "In the case of Quadratus, though very brief, it attests to belief in the miraculous works of Jesus and to tradents who were eyewitnesses to Jesus' mighty deeds" (Bird and Mackerass, 331).

CHAPTER TEN

Fragments of Papias

Occasionally antiquarians wonder about and sometimes wish for what will be the next great manuscript discovery. They may long for another huge cache of Jewish literature to be found in the Judean Wilderness (like the Dead Sea Scrolls), or perhaps a jar containing Coptic manuscripts will be unearthed in Egypt (like the Nag Hammadi Papyri). I offer my wish that the long lost five books of Papias' *Exposition of the Sayings of the Lord* (or *the Dominical Oracles*) will emerge from the dusty shelves of some Orthodox monastery in Greece or the Middle East. Photius, the ninth-century patriarch of Constantinople, refers to the writings of Papias as do some other early medieval authors, although we are not certain that these later authors actually had a copy in front of them. Possibly a copy of Papias' "lost" work survived the pillages of the Crusaders and the Turks and will emerge into the light someday. Well, at least I can hope!

PAPIAS THE MAN AND MINISTRY

Papias, like his younger contemporary Polycarp, was believed to have been a disciple of the apostle John. He was the spiritual leader of the Christian congregation in Hierapolis (western Asia Minor) during the early decades of the second century CE. His lifespan, however, reached well back to the last decades of the first century, possibly as early as the destruction of Jerusalem and the Temple in 70 CE, a fact not to be overlooked in the following discussion. For centuries his writing was assigned by many writers to a later date (*c.* 135?), but recently scholars are opting for the writing of the *Exposition* during the first decade of the second century. As argued effectively by Yarborough, Eusebius' *Chronicon* places in order the Apostle John, Papias, Polycarp, along with Ignatius and then assigns the equivalence of the date we know as 100 CE (Yarborough, 186–90). Irenaeus, who wrote around 180, describes Papias as "an ancient man" and as "a hearer of the Apostle John" (*Haer.* 5.33.4; Eusebius, *EH* 3.39, 1, 13). Efforts to place Papias decades later are based on a statement by Philip of Side (*c.* 430), associating him with Hadrian's rule, but there are very good reasons to conclude that he garbled information that he received from Eusebius, confusing a Quadratus the prophet with the earlier Quadratus the apologist. Yarborough argues this point convincingly (182–6) and concludes that Papias wrote *c.* 101–8. He is followed in this regard also by Gundry (*Mark*, 1027–9) and increasingly numerous scholars (see Carlson, *Papias* and "Fragments").

The location of Papias' ministry in Hierapolis suggests his key role as a tradent of Jesus' deeds and *logia*. Hierapolis, only briefly mentioned in Col. 4:13, was at a crucial crossroads between Laodicea and Colossae. Lightfoot and Bartlett concur that the location of the city in that central Roman province of "Asia" placed him at what could be called the "centre of gravity in the Church" for a century after the death of Paul (Bartlet, 15). While Eusebius called him a "bishop," this may be an anachronistic usage of *episkopos*.

What we know about his *Exposition*, however, certainly implies that he was an informed spiritual leader in the West Asian city of Hierapolis.

The writings of Papias are known to us only in fragments and *testimonia* quoted and mentioned by later Church Fathers. The number of the actual "fragments of Papias" ranges in the editions from a half dozen to over two dozen, some of which are probably based on oral traditions themselves! Holmes mentions twenty-eight of them, but a few are doubtful, and others repeat information that is found in other fragments (Holmes, 732–67). Ehrman limits the number of exact quotations to sixteen (Ehrman, II, 93–119). In the citing of possible fragments in the rest of this chapter, we will follow Holmes' numbering of them. It is useful, however, to distinguish between actual quotations of Papias, which can be called "fragments," and comments by later writers about Papias which could be called "testimonies." Carlson has carefully argued that only a handful of the ninety-eight so-called Papian sources are genuine "fragment" quotations of the *Exposition* (Carlson, *Papias of Hierapolis*, 3–15).

Eusebius initially accepted the claim that Papias was a hearer and eyewitness of the apostles, but later disputed it due to an interpretation of one of Papias' own statements. He attributes to Papias a work consisting of five treatises and entitled "Exposition of the Sayings of the Lord." Some prefer the last expression as "Dominical Oracles" (e.g., Carlson). In this work, which has not survived intact in its march through history, Papias claims to draw his information from "the presbyters" about what things Jesus' disciples had said or were reported to be said by actual auditors. For Eusebius "presbyters" and "apostles" were used interchangeably. One surprising fact is that Papias never is actually quoted as using the word "apostles." Eusebius tried to draw a distinction between the two, especially when he mentions John the apostle and argues that the later John the elder/presbyter is named as a contemporary of Papias. Not all modern readers have automatically concluded that two different Johns are mentioned although both times the name occurs it refers to a "disciple of the Lord," and both times it is found in close association with the word "presbyter."

Eusebius described Papias as a "man of very little intelligence" (*EH* 3.39.13). This verdict is perhaps a bit unfair based on such limited data, and it was probably motivated because Eusebius did not like Papias' rather fulsome depictions of eschatological millennial plenty. It is true that Papias seems to have been fascinated by eschatological themes, especially when they involved extravagant projections of certain features of the present life into the future. This rather harsh judgment on Papias by Eusebius was certainly not deserved. If he was known as a distinguished contemporary of Ignatius and if he was a spiritual overseer and if he could write a five-volume commentary and earn a name worthy to be associated with Polycarp, he was probably not a man of very little intelligence!

TITLE AND GENRE OF PAPIAS' WORK

As mentioned, Eusebius attributes to Papias a work that evidently consisted of five treatises and was entitled "Exposition of Dominical Oracles." The document probably did not take the form of an interpretation of Jesus' sayings but was possibly a narrative about Jesus with a prelude on creation and a postlude on apostolic stories following the resurrection. Papias considered himself as a historian, particularly emphasizing the importance of eyewitnesses whom he interviewed or those who heard the apostles. Many writers conclude that the work was not a commentary on or exposition of written Gospels, but itself was something like a Gospel account of the deeds and words of Jesus arranged in the form of a historical narrative. The meaning of Papias's title has also been understood to convey a commentary on Matthew, or a commentary on a sayings source, or even a commentary on Revelation.

On the other hand, Stephen Carlson has argued that the overwhelming usage of λογία in both testaments and in the early Fathers was in reference to the Divine oracles in what Christians later called the "Old Testament." Thus, these oracles collected by Papias were more likely Messianic oracles fulfilled by Jesus. Carlson cites J.B. Gregory who argued that Papias's work was a commentary on Messianic promises and prophecies from the Old Testament (*Papias of Hierapolis*, 34–40). These Messianic oracles were then supplemented "with additional material from oral traditions" (Carlson, *Papias of Hierapolis*, 39). If Carlson is correct, Papias' *Exposition of Dominical Oracles* would be joined in his Christological methodology later by the *Epistle of Barnabas*, as well as by Justin Martyr's *Dialogue with Trypho*, Melito's *Peri Pascha*, and Eusebius' *Preparation for the Gospel*. In response to Carlson, however, it is possible that Papias was simply building on these "Old Testament" divine "oracles" (*logia*) by applying the term to what he viewed as divine oracles coming from Jesus.

While Carlson has offered an interesting proposal, there should still be caution against dogmatism on the specific genre of *Exposition*. As we shall see, there are just too few undoubted "fragments" on which to base a firm decision about its genre. There was simply too much material in Papias' *Exposition* that we are unable to evaluate.

PAPIAS IN IRENAEUS (1)

The longest and probably the most reliable descriptions of the Papias fragments come from Irenaeus and Eusebius. Perhaps we should allow Papias to describe his own views, or at least at first through the quotations about him from the late second-century Church Father, **Irenaeus.**

"This blessing that was predicted belongs without question to the times of the kingdom, when the righteous will rise from the dead and rule, when the renewed creation is set free and will bring forth an abundance of food of all kinds from the dew of heaven and from the fertility of the soil. The presbyters who saw John, the disciple of the Lord, remembered hearing him say how the Lord used to teach about those times, saying.

> Days are coming when vines will bud, each having ten thousand boughs, and on a single bough will be ten thousand branches. On a single branch will be ten thousand shoots, and on every shoot ten thousand clusters, and in every cluster will be ten thousand grapes, and every grape when pressed will yield twenty-five measures of wine. And when any saint grabs hold of a cluster, another will cry out, "I am better, take me; bless the Lord through me." So also a grain of wheat will produce ten thousand heads, and every head will have ten thousand grains, and every grain will yield ten pounds of pure and exceptionally fine flour. So too the remaining fruits and seeds and vegetation will produce in similar proportions. And all the animals who eat this food drawn from the earth will live in peace and harmony with one another in complete submission to humans.

"Papias, an ancient man who heard John and was a companion of Polycarp, witnesses in writing about these things in the fourth of his books, for he wrote five books. And he also says. "These things can be believed by those who believe." He also says that "the betrayer

Judas did not believe but asked, 'How, then, can such growth be brought forth by the Lord?' The Lord replied, 'Those who come into those times will see'." (Irenaeus of Lyons, *Haer.* 5.33.3–4, written c. 180–5).

The Dominical oracles cited by Irenaeus appear to be from Matt. 26:27–29 (the "fruit of the vine"). The comments are dependent on Jewish apocalyptic ideas, perhaps from texts like 2 Baruch 29.5–6 and 1 Enoch 10.19. The number "ten thousand" may be drawn from Gen. 27:28 and the Messianic oracle in Gen. 49:12. The peace among animals recalls apocalyptic texts like Isa. 11:6-9. If Eusebius' remark about Papias being a person of little intelligence was made because of Papias' extravagant millennial eschatology, we have a passage here that illustrates some of that millennial plenty! The Lord's quoted response to Judas was an encouragement to him to believe. If he does, then faith will help him to believe what appears to be unbelievable.

Irenaeus describes Papias as "an ancient man" when he wrote around 180 CE. The adjective that Irenaeus used to describe Papias, *archaios*, means "ancient" or "of the early period." It is the same word that Luke applies to Mnason as an "early disciple" or "disciple of long standing" in Acts 21:16 (BDAG, 137). As Mnason was from the earliest period of the Jesus movement in Jerusalem, so Papias was from the earliest days of the Jesus movement in Phrygia of Asia Minor.

PAPIAS IN EUSEBIUS (2–3)

The following collection of sayings about and by Papias are preserved by **Eusebius**. "There are five books written by Papias in circulation, entitled *Exposition of Dominical Oracles*. Irenaeus remembers these as the only works written by him, saying somewhere (here he cites Irenaeus' quotation as above). Thus says Irenaeus. Yet Papias himself, in the preface to his "oracles," makes it clear that he was neither a hearer nor an eyewitness of the holy apostles. Instead, he declares by the language he uses that he received the matters of faith from those who had known them. As he says.

> I also will not hesitate to draw up for you, along with these expositions, an orderly account of everything I carefully learned and recalled from the presbyters, certifying their truth. For unlike most people, I took no pleasure in hearing those who had a lot to say, but only the ones who taught the truth. Nor did I enjoy those who recalled commandments from strangers, but only those who recalled the commandments given faithfully by the Lord and which proceed from the truth itself. But whenever someone arrived who had been a companion of the presbyters, I would carefully inquire about their words, what Andrew or Peter said, or Philip or Thomas or James or John or Matthew or any other disciples of the Lord, and whatever Aristion and the presbyter John, disciples of the Lord, are saying. For I did not suppose that what came from books would benefit me as much as that which came from a living and abiding voice."

In this genuine "fragment" of Papias he mentions twice the name John. In the first list he includes this John along with Peter, James, Matthew, and other disciples, clearly referring, therefore, to John the brother of James. In the second short list, he mentions a "John" in the group of those who are not among the original "twelve" disciples, along with an otherwise unknown Aristion preceding him, and clearly calls him "the Presbyter." He continues:

FRAGMENTS OF PAPIAS

> This Papias, whom we have just been discussing, acknowledges that he received the words of the apostles from those who had been their followers, but he says that he himself was a hearer of Aristion and John the Presbyter. And so he often recalls them by name and as well includes their traditions in his writings. These comments of ours have not been mentioned uselessly.

Although not cited by Ehrman, Eusebius also mentioned that there were two persons of the same name in Asia, as well as two tombs in Ephesus where each one was referred to as belonging to "John." In his opinion, the second "John" was the person who saw the Apocalypse.

Before continuing with the Eusebian quotation, it will be helpful to summarize the points he made in actually quoting Papias (a "fragment") and also what he has said about Papias (a "testimony"). Papias states that he was not an actual hearer of the apostles but depended on hearing those who heard the apostles. He preferred the reports of eyewitnesses to written reports about Jesus. He lists seven of the apostles whom he calls "presbyters." These include the brothers James and John, but he then adds that he inquired about some others of the Lord's disciples. He seems to distinguish between what these presbyters "said" (aorist tense) and what two additional ones, Aristion and Presbyter John, "are saying" (present tense). While he does not actually say that he heard Aristion and Presbyter John, Eusebius interprets him as meaning that he did. It is obvious to most readers that he did distinguish between what the Apostle John "said" and what the Presbyter John "is (later) saying." Finally, while Papias does not actually say it, Eusebius states that the Presbyter John was the one who saw the NT Apocalypse. The subsequent interpretations of Papias' and Eusebius' words have fueled discussions that can fill volumes. The ascription of the Gospel and the Apocalypse to John the Apostle is supported by an ancient and long tradition. The second one named "John the Presbyter" may very well be the author of the second and third Epistles of "John" who only styles himself as "the Presbyter" in those small books.

Returning now to Eusebius' passage:

> It will be worthwhile to supplement these remarks of Papias given above some other of his words, in which he recounts some miracles and other things which came to him from the tradition. We have already seen that Philip the Apostle lived in Hierapolis with his daughters; now I should point out that their contemporary Papias recalls an amazing story he learned from Philip's daughters. He indicates that in his own time a man rose from the dead. He then relates another miracle about Justus who was also called Barsabbas, who drank deadly poison and yet by the grace of the Lord suffered no ill effects because he was sustained by the Lord's grace. The same writer recorded other matters that came down to him from oral tradition, some bizarre parables of the Savior and his teachings and other legendary accounts. He says that after the resurrection of the dead there will be a period of a thousand years when Christ's kingdom will be physically set up on this very earth.
>
> (EH 3.39)

Eusebius continues to explain that Papias got these ideas through misunderstanding the apostolic accounts by not knowing that these things were spoken in figurative language. It is then that he uttered his famous conclusion about Papias that he was "a man of very little intelligence" and that many church fathers held the same views because they knew that he was "an ancient man." This also reflects that he knew that Irenaeus also held these same views.

The above "fragments" of Papias and "testimonies" about Papias deal mainly with events associated with Jesus and the Apostles that an elder told him, one who had heard about them from the eyewitnesses to those events. We learn also about the eschatological views of Papias and how strongly Eusebius disagreed with those views. His demeaning comment about Papias' intelligence was most probably motivated by his strong disagreement with his eschatological views that reflected an early chiliasm.

The following fragments and testimonies, also preserved by Eusebius, deal with issues related to the eyewitness accounts. We also learn some interesting traditions concerning the origins of the Gospels Matthew, Mark, as well as writings of John and Peter.

"In his writing he passes along other accounts of the sayings of the Lord from Aristion, whom we have already mentioned, and the traditions of John the Presbyter, to which we refer those who are interested. For our present purpose we must add to his already quoted statements a tradition he gives about Mark, who wrote the Gospel. These are his words.

> And the Presbyter used to say this. "Mark became Peter's interpreter, and he wrote down accurately everything that he recalled of the Lord's words and deeds, although not in order. For he neither heard the Lord nor accompanied him, but later accompanied Peter. He adapted his teachings for the needs at hand, but he had no intention of arranging an orderly account of the Lord's sayings. So Mark did nothing wrong by writing down some of the matters as he remembered them. For he made it his one purpose to leave out nothing that he heard nor to include any falsehood among them."
>
> This then is what Papias related about Mark. But concerning Matthew he said these things.
>
> So Matthew then arranged the sayings in the Hebrew language and each one interpreted (translated?) them as he was able.

"The same writer also made use of testimonies from the first letter of John and likewise from that (letter) of Peter. And he set forth another account about a woman falsely accused of many sins before the Lord,[1] which is also found in the Gospel according to the Hebrews" (*EH*, 3.39).

Regarding Papias' description of Mark and Matthew, we summarize his points and briefly interpret them. Papias did not know Mark and Matthew and Peter but cites the "Presbyter" or "Elder John" rather than passing on general tradition. The "Elder John" ascribes a Gospel to the Apostle Matthew and another Gospel to Peter as the source of Mark's material. Mark "wrote" down what Peter said in his gospel, while Matthew "arranged" the sayings of the Lord into his gospel. The contrast between Mark and Matthew has to do with style and not the language form. While the expression "Hebrew language" may also be Aramaic, a good case can be made that the expression refers to a Hebraic style or dialect into which Matthew crafted the Jesus *logia*. Mark was an "interpreter" of Peter in that he explained Peter's preaching. Matthew was an "interpreter" of the Jesus *logia* by providing a structure for them that Mark lacked. Thus

---

[1] Cf. John 7:53–8:11.

we should view Matthew's effort as an explanation rather than a translation. The obscure young man known as Mark would be an unlikely character to falsely credit with a Gospel. Furthermore, the apostle Matthew would probably not be the first choice of anyone to assign authorship of a possibly apocryphal work. We should conclude that Papias and his "Elder" source should be heeded more than they have been. Just as Papias' words about the disciples and the elder John have been discussed thoroughly by scholars, his comments about Mark and Matthew have continued to provide scholars with material to ponder and debate. We will suggest our own view about the lasting value of Papias' observations later in the chapter.

PAPIAS IN APOLLINARIS (4)

While Irenaeus and Eusebius are our primary sources for the Papias' sayings, a few more isolated traditions traced to him are preserved in later fathers, some even bordering on the bizarre. Acts 1:18 contains a rather gory description of the end of Judas, but Papias' elaboration preserved by **Apollinaris** of Laodicea is one in which we could be spared the details: "Papias, the disciple of John, recounts this clearly in the fourth book of *Exposition of the Dominical Oracles*, as follows.

> Judas was a terrible, walking model of impiety in this world. His flesh became so bloated that he could not pass through a place that was wide enough for a wagon to easily pass; not even his swollen head could fit! They say that his eyelids were so swelled that he could not see the light at all, and his eyes could not be seen even by a doctor using an optical device, so far had they sunk into the surrounding flesh. His genitals became more disgusting and larger than anyone's, and when relieving himself he emitted pus and worms from his body, much to his shame. After suffering numerous torments and punishments, he finally died and because of the stench that land is desolate and uninhabited until now. Indeed even to this day no one can pass by the place without holding his nose. This was how great was the discharge from his flesh as it spread over the ground."
>
> **Apollinaris** of Laodicea (fourth c., *EH* 4.27.1)

PAPIAS IN VICTORINUS

Because ancient writers were not always concerned about attribution in the way that moderns do in our academic citations, we should not be surprised that there may exist in the tradition some "anonymous" but genuine uses of Papias. For example, the third-century **Victorinus** of Pettau wrote a commentary on the Revelation in which he had the following to say about Rev. 4:4. "Mark, Peter's interpreter who remembered what he taught in his role and wrote them down, but not in order, began with the word of prophecy announced by Isaiah …" The expression "but not in order" about how Mark wrote Peter's words is paralleled in Eusebius' quotation from Papias mentioned earlier. Since Victorinus predated Eusebius, this is probably evidence that he used Papias (Carlson, "Fragments of Papias," 349). This also raises the possibility that Victorinus may have utilized Papias elsewhere since we know of the latter's fondness for the teachings found in the "Apocalypse." Because of examples like this, we may also reflect on how many other unattributed fragments, or "testimonies" as they should be called, may have survived in the first millennium of Christian writers.

PAPIAS IN ANDREW (8–9) AND ANASTASIUS (10–11)

Although our primary concern has been to discover how Papias related matters concerning Jesus and the canonical Gospels, a few of the "fragments" actually convey his views on some Old Testament matters. Fragments 8 and 9, preserved by **Andrew of Caesarea** (sixth century), for example, relate the story about the fall of the angels to whom God entrusted the governing of the world.[2] Furthermore, **Anastasius** of Sinai (seventh century) relates how Papias interpreted Genesis 1 as referring to Christ and the church, and the account of Paradise in Genesis 2–3 as referring to the church of Christ (fragments 10 and 11). It is unclear if these fragments, especially from Anastasius, are also from *Exposition of the Sayings of the Lord*, or from another unknown volume or simply passed down as "Sayings of Papias"!

PAPIAS' FRAGMENTS AND TESTIMONIES

We have mentioned that there are numerous authors who reference Papias through the early Middle Ages. In the most thorough treatment ever of the possible reception of Papias, Carlson cites and translates around ninety-eight of these "fragments" and "testimonia" (Carlson, *Papias of Hierapolis*, 8–15). We are doubtful that the later writers actually had a copy of his *Exposition* in their possession, but maybe are simply citing what Eusebius had previously written about him. As we look back, authors like Irenaeus, Eusebius, Apollinaris, Andrew, and possibly Victorinus provide the most reliable of the "fragments" of Papias on which we can rely for information on what he originally wrote (Carlson, "Fragments of Papias," 337–49).

THE VALUE OF PAPIAS

What can we say about the value of the scattered remains of this ancient "Apostolic Father"? Of particular interest is the high regard that Papias placed on eyewitnesses who saw and heard Jesus. Past scholarship has not always held Papias in great esteem, and Eusebius' comment about his intellectual ability ("a man of very little intelligence") may have contributed to some pessimism about the value of his reports. It should be kept in mind, however, that Eusebius' comments reflected his dislike of Papias' millenarianism or chiliasm. Apart from his eschatological beliefs, we should look also at what he said about the "eyewitnesses" in evaluating the value of the fragments that have come down to us. What he wrote about the origins of the Gospels of Matthew and Mark also can have great value. It is in these last areas that Papias can have the most value for us today.

Richard Bauckham has made a significant effort to rehabilitate the reputation of Papias for modern scholarship. What follows draws on his significant analysis of the surviving fragments of this bishop of Hierapolis. Papias' work is important because he speaks about the time he was gathering information about Jesus' words and actions. He states that his inquiries were focused on the actual statements of Jesus and the early eyewitnesses. It is important to recognize that the "presbyters" and many of Jesus' disciples were still living at the time when Papias was a young man and making inquiries. While most of the apostles had died, at least "Aristion and John the Presbyter" were still teaching. While

---

[2]Cf. Gen. 6:1-4.

Aristion cannot be identified, Papias considered him a personal disciple of Jesus. If Papias was born between 50 and 70 and wrote his work around 110, he would have been able to hear from many of the eyewitnesses of the Apostles even while they were still alive. This fact provides a fascinating alternative to some attitudes of higher critical scholarship since the Gospels were being written about the same time that Papias was gathering his information.

Papias states that he preferred a "living and surviving voice" rather than information in books. It should be noted that he had nothing against books since he was writing one! In ancient times consulting oral sources was considered as the best way of gathering authoritative information. The emphasis in Papias is not on the chain of transmission of an idea but on the reliability of the witnesses who convey the ideas. The "living voice" which Papias sought was not the voice of a lengthy oral tradition, but the literal voice of a living eyewitness, reporting information at first hand. Papias gathered his information from disciples of living presbyters who had known the first-generation disciples. But he also gathered information from disciples of some of the still living first-generation disciples. Much of the reason for receiving reports from secondary sources was due to Papias' location in Hierapolis, not in the same location as the primary sources. It is also easy to forget that the prologue of Luke's Gospel (1:1-4) refers to the same priority of eyewitness testimony. Interview with an eyewitness was recognized as the best way to obtain reliable information to be passed down.

We can learn from Papias that although he did not know the apostles, he heard from these "presbyters" by way of those who heard them. But he did know Aristion and the Presbyter John, although it is not certain that this is the Apostle John (Bauckham thinks so). Papias connects us with two generations of Christians about whom far too little is known today. The impression left is that Papias can vouch for what was being said about Jesus since he heard from those who had heard their voices. The presence of the eyewitnesses was both a guarantee of the reliability of Jesus' sayings and deeds and an authentication of those who were writing things about Jesus (Bauckham, 30).

The contributions of Papias remind us that the written Gospels represent only a part of the material from Jesus that was circulating at the turn of the first century. It is good to remind ourselves of the statement by the author of the Gospel of John that Jesus did and said much more than he has recorded (John 20:30; 21:25). Furthermore, after the composition of our canonical Gospels, oral traditions continued to circulate and even influence the written text. These oral traditions were highly valued in a socio-cultural setting that highly valued memory more than is customary today. Papias' preference for the "living voice" should not be viewed as his privileging of orality over writing. He claims to distinguish between "those who teach the truth" and "those who say a lot." It is only the sources that Papias already considers authoritative because of their connection to Jesus that he treasures for their orality (Walls, 137–40). This close connection to Jesus enables them to provide a more accurate picture of Jesus' teaching than what books can provide. The isolation of these sources is one of Papias' most valuable contributions toward a reconstruction of the Gospel narratives.

Finally, Papias is a witness to a period of time in an important region of the early Christian movement in which the literature that would someday be called the "New Testament" was viewed as authoritative sources for life and doctrine. He was thus an early Christian leader who provides evidence for the recognition of several books later included in an authoritative canon. "The information he passes on from 'the elder' about Gospel origins has a permanent place among the *instrumenta studiorum* of both Church and academy" (Hill, 51). "What is clear is that Papias is an invaluable witness to Christian views about eschatology and the origin of the Gospels—especially that of Mark—in the decades immediately following the composition of the Gospels" (Carlson, "Fragments of Papias," 350).

I now return to the opening comment in this chapter about my personal "wish" that someday Papias' five volumes of *Exposition of Dominical Oracles* would be found and published so we can see all that he originally wrote. Even if my wish is not granted, the fragments of Papias that have been recovered from later writers have certainly enhanced our understanding of the earliest days of the Christian movement. This also results in a better understanding of the Founder's teaching that launched that movement.

NOTE. Because the work of Papias does not survive as a document, no primary texts of *Exposition of Dominical Oracles* are added. The reader is encouraged to read the "fragments" of Papias in the above chapter, especially the excerpts in Irenaeus and Eusebius.

FURTHER READING ON PAPIAS

Bartlet, Vernon. "Papias's 'Exposition'. Its Date and Contents" in *Amicitiae Corolla. A Volume of Essays Presented to James Rendel Harris*, ed. H. G. Wood. London. University of London Press, 1933.

Bauckham, Richard. "Papias on the Eyewitnesses" in *Jesus and the Eyewitnesses. The Gospels as Eyewitness Testimony*, 2nd ed., 12–38. Grand Rapids. Wm. B. Eerdmans, 2017.

Carlson, Stephen C. *Papias of Hierapolis Exposition of Dominical Oracles. The Fragments, Testimonia, and Reception of a Second-Century Christian Commentator*. Oxford Early Christian Texts. Oxford. Oxford University Press, 2021.

_____. "The Fragments of Papias" in *The Cambridge Companion to the Apostolic Fathers*, ed. Michael Bird and Scott Harrower, 332–50. Cambridge. Cambridge University Press, 2021.

Gundry, Robert H. *Mark: A Commentary on His Apology for the Cross*. Eerdmans, 1993.

Hill, Charles. "Papias of Hierapolis" in *The Writings of the Apostolic Fathers*, ed. Paul Foster, 42–51. London and New York. T&T Clark, 2007.

Kortner, Ulrich H. J. "The Papias Fragments" in *The Apostolic Fathers: An Introduction*, ed. Wilhelm Pratscher, 159–79. Waco, TX. Baylor University Press, 2010.

Schoedel, W. R. *Polycarp. Martyrdom of Polycarp, Fragments of Papias*. The Apostolic Fathers, vol. 5. Camden, NJ. Nelson, 1967.

_____. "Papias" in *Anchor Bible Dictionary*, ed. David Noel Freedman et al. vol. 5, 140–2. New York. Doubleday, 1992.

Varner, William. "The Fragments of Papias" in *The Apostolic Fathers*, ed. Paul Foster, ALNTS, vol. 4. Grand Rapids. Zondervan, 2023.

Walls, A. F. "Papias and Oral Tradition." *Vigiliae Christianae* 21 (1967). 137–40.

Note. Translations of the *Fragments of Papias* are by the author but their numbering is from Ehrman, Bart D., *The Apostolic Fathers*, vol. II. Loeb Classical Library 25. Cambridge, MA. Harvard University Press, 2003, 92–118. See also Holmes, Michael, *The Apostolic Fathers: Greek Texts and English Translations*, 3rd ed. Grand Rapids, MI. Baker Books, 2007, 732–67.

CHAPTER ELEVEN

The Apostolic Fathers in the Twenty-First Century

Thus far we have witnessed the value of these writings for a better understanding of the New Testament and the formative years of the "Jesus Movement" that came to be called Christianity.

These writings can be helpful to help us measure our own understanding of that early phase of church history. In other words, is our own perspective different from the way in which the second generation interpreted the meaning of the events that gave birth to the faith which they possessed? The reading of the AF can also prove to be profitable for the concrete questions and issues that Christians face today.

Clayton Jefford offers a balanced perspective on the value of the AF to the modern reader.

> In the final analysis it would be a gross overstatement to claim that the Apostolic Fathers offer an answer to all of our modern questions about the development of the church after the New Testament period. At the same time, however, it is certainly fair to say that our helpful knowledge of these materials enables us to better understand how the views of the biblical authors came to fruition in the subsequent years of Christianity's historical evolution.
>
> (*The Apostolic Fathers: An Essential Guide*, 129)

It is always helpful to look back at the sources of a movement to see if its subsequent and current history has followed the earlier exemplars. This approach is not intended to "canonize" those earlier documents, but to force us to ask if we understand the issues the way that the early generations of Christians understood them and responded to them. Despite the vast social and economic differences from the second to the twenty-first century, the same religious and social issues in our complex world resemble that ancient context far more than we recognize at first. Actually historians can witness to the fact that the second century was almost as pluriform a world as exists today. The Roman Empire comprised a kaleidoscope of different religions and philosophies that can challenge the mind of students attempting to comprehend them all. These ancients faced similar fundamental problems, but under the different conditions of their time. Ask yourself if you ever really responded to the prescriptions of these writers by responding, "Oh that will certainly not work in today's world!" Maybe you have thought that, but I have not. There are important issues that emerge from their reading, such as the vital subjects of identity formation; conflict with a syncretistic environment; a theology that is relevant and not other-worldly; and how to respond to a culture that views committed Christians as strange aliens. These are just a few of the parallels between these centuries so far apart in time and historical context.

Finally, we should not exalt these writings as containing the long-lost solutions to our modern problems. The AF themselves would resist such an elevated evaluation of the things that they were often simply sharing from their hearts and minds. This corpus of writings is not simply a treasure house for specialists whose interests are historical theology and arcane religious practices. These people were attempting to live their lives as Christians do today, and to find a way through the same dense forests that we also encounter. These writers merit a careful reading if for no other reason than that they are not always uniform in their modes of expression, as a church manual is not the same type of document as an allegory! But a careful review of them can still return us to the center of their world which should also be ours, namely that of a first-century Nazarene whose teachings and actions, both in his earthly life and in his death and afterlife, had transformed their lives and can still do so today for those who have ears to hear.

SCRIPTURE INDEX

Old Testament

Genesis 1	232	Exodus 17:8-14	202
Genesis 1:26	195, 197	Exodus 20:8	204
Genesis 1:26-28	105, 215	Exodus 20:13-17	15
Genesis 1:27	123, 134	Exodus 20:16	16
Genesis 2–3	211, 232	Exodus 24:18	203
Genesis 2:2-3	204	Exodus 31:18	194, 203
Genesis 2:8-9	215	Exodus 31–32	112
Genesis 2:17	223	Exodus 32:7	194
Genesis 2:23	95	Exodus 32:7-10	112
Genesis 3	216	Exodus 33:3	197
Genesis 3:24	223	Exodus 33:1-3	196
Genesis 4:3-8	94	Exodus 34:28	194
Genesis 5:24	96		
Genesis 6:1-4	232	Leviticus 11:3	200
Genesis 6:8	96	Leviticus 11:6	200
Genesis 7	95	Leviticus 11:7-15	199
Genesis 12:1-3	96	Leviticus 11:13-16	200
Genesis 12:22	28, 104	Leviticus 16	197
Genesis 13:14-16	96	Leviticus 16:7, 9	198
Genesis 14	104	Leviticus 16:8	198
Genesis 14:14	199	Leviticus 16:10	198
Genesis 15:5	104	Leviticus 16:20-22	198
Genesis 15:5-6	96, 203	Leviticus 19:18	15
Genesis 17:4	203	Leviticus 23:29	197
Genesis 17:23	199	Leviticus 26:1	202
Genesis 18:27	99		
Genesis 19	97	Numbers 12	94
Genesis 22	96	Numbers 12:7	17, 99, 107
Genesis 22:17	104	Numbers 16:1	94
Genesis 25:21-23	203	Numbers 16:33	133
Genesis 26:4	104	Numbers 19	188
Genesis 27	94	Numbers 21:4-8	202
Genesis 27:28	228		
Genesis 37	94	Deuteronomy 4:2	17
Genesis 48:11, 9	203	Deuteronomy 4:10	13, 200
Genesis 48:14, 19	203	Deuteronomy 4:34	104
Genesis 49:12	228	Deuteronomy 5:12	204
		Deuteronomy 6:5	15
		Deuteronomy 9:12-14	112
Exodus 2	94	Deuteronomy 10:16	188, 199
Exodus 3:11	99	Deuteronomy 12:32	17
Exodus 4:10	99	Deuteronomy 14:2	104
Exodus 14:23	111	Deuteronomy 14:6	200
Exodus 15:26	199	Deuteronomy 14:8-14	199

SCRIPTURE INDEX

Deuteronomy 14:10	200	Psalm 51:1-17	100, 112, 193
Deuteronomy 27:15	202	Psalm 62:4	98
Deuteronomy 32:8-9	202	Psalm 69:30-32	112
Deuteronomy 32:15	93	Psalm 71:5	17, 123
		Psalm 78:36-37	98
Joshua 1:6	181	Psalm 90:4	204
Joshua 2	97	Psalm 110:1	106, 202
Joshua 2:18	89	Psalm 115:3a	127
		Psalm 116:12-14	127
1 Samuel 13:14	100	Psalm 118:12	196
1 Samuel 18	94	Psalm 118:19-20	110
		Psalm 118:22-24	196
Esther 4–7	113	Psalm 139:7-8	103
		Psalm 141:5	113
Job 1:1	99	Psalm 146:6	219
Job 4:16-18	106		
Job 4:19–5:3	106	Proverbs 1:17	195
Job 5:17-26	113	Proverbs 1:23-33	114
Job 11:2-3	104	Proverbs 2:21-22	98
Job 14:4-5	99	Proverbs 3:4	172
Job 15:15	106	Proverbs 3:12	113
Job 19:26	103	Proverbs 3:34	104, 145
Job 38:11	101	Proverbs 7:3	93
		Proverbs 10:12	135
Psalm 1:1	200	Proverbs 18:17	150
Psalm 1:3-6	106	Proverbs 20:27	101
Psalm 3:5	103		
Psalm 4:4	168	Isaiah 1:2	199
Psalm 4:5	173	Isaiah 1:10	199
Psalm 12:4-6	98	Isaiah 1:11-13	193, 204
Psalm 18:25-26	110	Isaiah 1:16-20	95
Psalm 18:44	199	Isaiah 3:9-10	196
Psalm 19:1-3	103	Isaiah 5:21	195
Psalm 22:6-8	99	Isaiah 6:3	105
Psalm 22:16	196	Isaiah 9:23-24	97
Psalm 22:18	196	Isaiah 11:6-9	205
Psalm 22:20	196	Isaiah 12:4	204
Psalm 22:22, 25	197	Isaiah 13:33	102
Psalm 24:1	112	Isaiah 16:1-2	201
Psalm 28:7	103	Isaiah 19:13	123
Psalm 31:18	98	Isaiah 26:60	111
Psalm 32:10	102	Isaiah 28:14	199
Psalm 33:9	147	Isaiah 28:16	196
Psalm 34:11-17	101	Isaiah 29:13	98
Psalm 36:1-2	111	Isaiah 33:13	199
Psalm 37:9	98	Isaiah 33:16-18	201
Psalm 37:11	16	Isaiah 34:4	123, 135
Psalm 37:35-37	98	Isaiah 34:41	35
Psalm 42:4	197	Isaiah 40:3	199
Psalm 49:14	111	Isaiah 40:10	105, 207
Psalm 50:14-15	112	Isaiah 40:12	204

SCRIPTURE INDEX

Isaiah 41:8	96	Jonah 3	95
Isaiah 42:6-7	203		
Isaiah 44:6	197	Zechariah 8:17	193
Isaiah 45:1	202	Zechariah 13:7	196
Isaiah 45:2-3	201	Zechariah 14:5	21
Isaiah 49:6-7	204		
Isaiah 49:17	205	Malachi 1:11 & 14	20
Isaiah 50:6-7, 8-9	196	Malachi 1:13	20
Isaiah 50:10	199	Malachi 3:1	102
Isaiah 52:5	123, 132, 152	Malachi 3:19	123
Isaiah 52:53	114	**New Testament**	
Isaiah 53	88	Matthew 3:15	159
Isaiah 53:1-12	99	Matthew 5:5	16
Isaiah 53:5, 7	195	Matthew 5:7	97
Isaiah 54:1	123, 130	Matthew 5:10	171
Isaiah 58:3-5	194	Matthew 5:26	15
Isaiah 58:6-10	194	Matthew 5:44-47	15, 123
Isaiah 58:9	123, 135	Matthew 5:48	15
Isaiah 60:17	107	Matthew 6:9-13	13, 18
Isaiah 61:1-2	204	Matthew 6:10	181
Isaiah 64:4	124	Matthew 6:13	172
Isaiah 65:2	202	Matthew 6:14-15	97, 127
Isaiah 66:1	204	Matthew 6:16	18
Isaiah 66:2	97	Matthew 6:24	123, 131
Isaiah 66:18	123, 135, 136, 139, 150	Matthew 7:1-2	97, 171
		Matthew 7:6	13, 18
Isaiah 66:24	123, 132, 136	Matthew 7:12	15, 97
		Matthew 7:21	123, 131
Jeremiah 2:12-13	201	Matthew 9:13	123, 130
Jeremiah 4:4	188, 199	Matthew 10:10	13, 20
Jeremiah 7:2-3	199	Matthew 10:16	131, 162
Jeremiah 7:11	123, 134	Matthew 10:22-24	224
Jeremiah 7:22	193	Matthew 10:28	131
Jeremiah 9:26	199	Matthew 10:32	123, 130
Jeremiah 17:23	199	Matthew 11:7	13
Jeremiah 17:24-25	204	Matthew 12:31	13, 19
		Matthew 12:33	146
Ezekiel 3:12	111	Matthew 12:42	20
Ezekiel 11:19	197	Matthew 12:50	123, 133
Ezekiel 14:14	132	Matthew 15:3	98
Ezekiel 14:14-20	123	Matthew 15:8	131
Ezekiel 33:11, 33	95	Matthew 16:26	123, 131
Ezekiel 47:1-12	201	Matthew 16:41	172
		Matthew 19:12	160
Daniel 2 & 6	108	Matthew 21:13	134
Daniel 7:7-8	194	Matthew 22:11-14	127, 195
Daniel 7:10	105	Matthew 22:37-39	15
Daniel 7:24	194	Matthew 24:10-13	21
Daniel 9:24	205	Matthew 24:30	21
		Matthew 25:41	131

SCRIPTURE INDEX

Matthew 26:7	147
Matthew 26:27-29	228
Matthew 26:31	196
Matthew 26:55	178, 181
Matthew 26:64	110
Matthew 28:19	17
Mark 2:17	123, 130
Mark 3:35	133
Mark 4:3	102
Mark 8:35-36	123
Mark 8:36	131
Mark 9:44, 46, 48	132
Mark 12:30	131
Mark 14:3	147
Luke 1:1-4	233
Luke 1:3	210, 216
Luke 5:32	123, 130
Luke 6:20	171
Luke 6:28	15
Luke 6:30	15
Luke 6:32, 35	134
Luke 8:21	123, 133
Luke 9:25	131
Luke 10:3	131
Luke 10:27	15
Luke 12:8	123, 130
Luke 16:10-12	124, 132
Luke 16:13	123, 131
Luke 17:2	110
Luke 24:4	139
Luke 24:39	159
Luke 24:40	139
John 1:14	139
John 1:18	215
John 3:8	158
John 4:10	14, 155
John 5:19	139
John 5:21	168
John 6:33	139
John 6:44	168
John 7:53-8, 11	230
John 10:7, 9	158
John 16:28	149
John 19:31	181
John 20:29	139
John 20:30	233
John 21:25	233
Acts 1:1	216
Acts 2:24	170
Acts 3 & 4	13
Acts 3:15	121
Acts 4:36	185
Acts 7	175
Acts 10:42	130, 170
Acts 14:15	219
Acts 15	187
Acts 20:35	93
Acts 21:14	181
Acts 21:16	228
Romans 1:27	127
Romans 2:6-10	128
Romans 4:9-11	124
Romans 5	213
Romans 5:18-19	213
Romans 7:2	189
Romans 8:5, 8	145
Romans 13:1	182
Romans 14:10	172
Romans 15:27	127
1 Corinthians 1:12	110
1 Corinthians 1:20, 23	147
1 Corinthians 2:9	105, 124, 133, 178, 180
1 Corinthians 2:10	158
1 Corinthians 3:1-2	152
1 Corinthians 3:16	147
1 Corinthians 4:4	155
1 Corinthians 6:2	173
1 Corinthians 6:9-10	147, 157, 172
1 Corinthians 7:1	12
1 Corinthians 7:25	12
1 Corinthians 8:1	12, 215, 223
1 Corinthians 9:21	187
1 Corinthians 9:24-27	124, 153
1 Corinthians 12:1	12
1 Corinthians 12:21	106
1 Corinthians 13:4-7	111
1 Corinthians 13:13	186
1 Corinthians 14:25	171
1 Corinthians 15:8-9	156
1 Corinthians 15:12	88
1 Corinthians 15:20	102
1 Corinthians 16:1	12
1 Corinthians 16:12	12
1 Corinthians 16:22	19
2 Corinthians 2:1	30
2 Corinthians 3	30
2 Corinthians 5:10	172

SCRIPTURE INDEX

2 Corinthians 6:13	127	2 Timothy 2:4	163
2 Corinthians 9:7	30	2 Timothy 2:12	171
2 Corinthians 7:10	30	2 Timothy 4:10	173
2 Corinthians 9:7	30		
		Titus 3:1	93
Galatians 2:13	3, 185	Titus 3:8	128
Galatians 2:14	187		
Galatians 3	124	Hebrews 1–12	121
Galatians 3:24	189	Hebrews 1:3-13	90, 105
Galatians 4:24	189	Hebrews 2:18	105
Galatians 4:26	171	Hebrews 3:1	105
Galatians 4:27	130	Hebrews 3:2	99
Galatians 5:6	25, 128	Hebrews 3:5	107
Galatians 5:25	128	Hebrews 8:13	189
Galatians 6:7	171	Hebrews 10:23	133
Galatians 6:14	155	Hebrews 11	89
		Hebrews 11:35-38	175
Ephesians 1:14	169	Hebrews 11:37	99
Ephesians 2:5	170	Hebrews 12:1-2	110
Ephesians 2:8-9	170	Hebrews 12:6	113
Ephesians 2:10	128		
Ephesians 4:18	136	James 2:23	94
Ephesians 4:26	168, 173	James 3–4	30
Ephesians 5:2	176, 177	James 4:6	104, 145
Ephesians 5:4-6	110	James 5:20	135
Ephesians 5:25, 29	163		
Ephesians 6:1	138	1 Peter 1:1	178
Ephesians 6:11-17	163	1 Peter 1:8	170
		1 Peter 2:11	172
Philippians 1:11	128	1 Peter 2:13	178, 182
Philippians 2:4	178, 179	1 Peter 2:22, 24	172
Philippians 3:15	161	1 Peter 3:9	170
Philippians 4:3	85, 89	1 Peter 4:5	130
		1 Peter 4:8	111, 135
Colossians 1:10	128	1 Peter 5:5	104, 145
Colossians 1:16	152	2 Peter 3:8	204
1 Thessalonians 1:2-3	186	1 John 3:4-6	142
1 Thessalonians 2:12	128	1 John 3:16	127
1 Thessalonians 4:9	12	1 John 4:2-3	172
1 Thessalonians 5:1	12		
2 Thessalonians 2:4	154	Revelation 2:10, 13	175, 177
		Revelation 4:4	231
1 Timothy 1:17	136	Revelation 5:1	27
1 Timothy 3:8-13	171	Revelation 20:11-15	27
1 Timothy 6:7	171	Revelation 22:12	105, 207
1 Timothy 6:10	171		

INDEX OF AUTHORS

Ancient
Anacletus 85
Apollinaris 231
Aristion 228, 229, 230, 232, 233
Athanasius 2, 10, 12, 23
Athenagoras of Athens 210
Augustine 23, 92

Clement of Alexandria 1, 2, 9, 23, 85, 91, 185
Chrysostom, John 7, 9
Cyril Lucaris 115

Didymus the Blind 10, 12
Dionysius the Areopagite 1

Eldad and Modat 30, 35, 123
Eusebius 1, 2, 10, 85, 90, 118, 137, 138, 139, 165, 176, 185, 210, 223, 224, 225, 226, 227, 228, 229, 230, 231, 232

Gregory of Nyssa 89, 92

Hegessipus 85
Hippolytus 211

Irenaeus 1, 2, 23, 24, 85, 90, 91, 119, 165, 169, 227, 228, 230

Jerome 23, 139, 223
Justin Martyr 1, 124, 209, 210, 211, 216, 224, 227

Leon the Scribe 9, 86, 118
Linus of Rome 85

Maria of Cassoboloi 9
Melito of Sardis 210, 211, 224, 227
Mnason 228

Nicephorus 10, 11

Origen 2, 9, 10, 23, 24, 85, 89, 118, 185, 190, 191

Philo 190
Photius 119, 225
Pius of Rome 24

Severus of Antioch 119
Simon Magus 85

Tertullian 2, 23, 85, 91
Theophilus of Antioch 210, 211

Victorinus 231, 232

Modern
Andriessen, Paul 217, 223

Barnard, L.W. 3, 15, 192, 211, 212, 217
Bartlet, J.V. 225, 234
Batovici, Dan 28, 31, 91, 92
Bauckham, Richard 232, 233, 234
Baur, Ferdinand 91
Bird, Michael 3, 4, 31, 92, 129, 170, 179, 192, 212, 214, 217, 224, 234
Brannan, Rick 3, 30
Bryennios, Philotheos 1, 6, 7, 8, 9, 86, 117, 166, 186
Brent, Allen 142, 143
Bunyan, John 25

Carlson, Stephen 225, 226, 227, 231, 232, 234
Clarke, W. K. L. 92
Cotelier, J.B. 1, 117, 166
Crowe, Brandon 213, 217

D'Arezzo, Thomas 209
Donfried, Karl 118, 120, 121, 122, 124
Draper, Jonathan 13, 14, 192

Ehrman, Bart 4, 23, 30, 117, 226, 229, 234
Estienne, Henri 209

Foster, Paul 4, 14, 32, 92, 129, 143, 170, 179, 192, 209, 217, 224, 234

INDEX OF AUTHORS

Gallandi, Andreas 1, 210
Gibbon, Henry 177
Grant, R.M. 3, 4, 31, 42, 92, 129, 143, 217
Gregory, Andrew 4, 92
Gregory, J.B. 227
Grosvenor, Edwin 7, 8
Gundry, Robert 234, 235

Hagner, Donald 90, 92
Harnack, Adolph 8, 14, 86, 91, 92
Harris, Rendel 9, 234
Harrison, P.N. 166, 169
Hartog, Paul 169, 170, 177, 179
Hellholm, David 24, 31
Herron, Thomas 90, 91, 92
Hill, Charles 170, 211, 217, 234
Holmes, Michael 4, 30, 170, 226, 234
Hvalvik, Reidar 192

Ittig, Thomas 1

Jefford, Clayton 4, 13, 14, 216, 217, 235

Kelhoffer, James A. 118, 122, 127, 129
Kortner, Ulrich 234

Le Clerc, Jean 1
Lightfoot, J.B. 14, 92, 118, 119, 122, 127, 178, 211, 212, 225
Lona, Horacio 216, 217
Lookadoo, Jonathon 31, 192

Mackerass, Kirsten 212, 214, 217, 224
Meecham, Henry 217
Milavec, Aaron 13, 14

Moss, Candida 177, 179
Muratori, Lodovico 24

Neander, August 212
Niederwimmer, Kurt 13, 14
Norden, E. 212

Osiek, Carolyn 29, 31

Paget, Carlton 192
Pernveden, Lage 31
Prostmeier, Ferdinand 189, 192

Quasten, Johannes 4, 27, 31, 90, 92, 127, 129

Reuchlin, Johannes 209

Tischendorf, Constantine 186
Torrance, T.F. 127
Tuckett, Christopher 4, 117, 121, 122, 128, 129
Tugwell, Simon 8, 14, 24, 91, 92, 121, 122, 137, 143, 166, 185, 188

Ussher, James 1

Varner, William 14, 127, 129, 234

Wake, William 1
Walls, A.F. 233, 234
Whittaker, Molly 25, 32
Wilhite, Shawn 13, 14

Yarborough, R.W. 225, 234

CPSIA information can be obtained
at www.ICGtesting.com
Printed in the USA
LVHW061549050523
746220LV00005B/591